MOTHERHOOD ON ICE

ANTHROPOLOGIES OF AMERICAN MEDICINE: CULTURE, POWER, AND PRACTICE

General Editors: Paul Brodwin, Michele Rivkin-Fish, and Susan Shaw

Motherhood on Ice

The Mating Gap and Why Women Freeze Their Eggs

Marcia C. Inhorn

NEW YORK UNIVERSITY PRESS

New York

NEW YORK UNIVERSITY PRESS
New York
www.nyupress.org

© 2023 by New York University
All rights reserved

Library of Congress Cataloging-in-Publication Data
Names: Inhorn, Marcia C., 1957– author.
Title: Motherhood on ice : the mating gap and why women freeze their eggs / Marcia C.
Inhorn.
Description: New York : New York University Press, [2023] | Series: Anthropologies of
American medicine: culture, power, and practice | Includes bibliographical references
and index.
Identifiers: LCCN 2022027630 | ISBN 9781479813049 (hardback) | ISBN 9781479813032
(ebook) | ISBN 9781479813063 (ebook other)
Subjects: LCSH: Motherhood—United States. | Reproductive technology—United States. |
Infertility—United States—Prevention.
Classification: LCC HQ759 .I493 2023 | DDC 306.874/30973—dc23/eng/20220816
LC record available at https://lccn.loc.gov/2022027630

New York University Press books are printed on acid-free paper, and their binding materials
are chosen for strength and durability. We strive to use environmentally responsible suppli-
ers and materials to the greatest extent possible in publishing our books.

Manufactured in the United States of America

10 9 8 7 6 5 4 3 2 1

Also available as an ebook

To all the thirty-something single women still hoping for partnership, pregnancy, and parenthood

CONTENTS

TABLES

ABBREVIATIONS

AMH anti-Müllerian hormone

ART assisted reproductive technology

ASRM American Society for Reproductive Medicine

CoQ10 Coenzyme Q10

DHEA dehydroepiandrosterone

ESHRE European Society of Human Reproduction and Embryology

FSH follicle-stimulating hormone

HESC human embryonic stem cells

GP general practitioner

GPI Gender Parity Index

ICSI intracytoplasmic sperm injection

IFFS International Federation of Fertility Societies

IT information technology

IV intravenous

IVF in vitro fertilization

LH luteinizing hormone

OB/GYN obstetrician and gynecologist

OHSS ovarian hyperstimulation syndrome

PCOS polycystic ovary syndrome

PGD preimplantation genetic diagnosis

POA premature ovarian aging

POF premature ovarian failure

POI premature ovarian insufficiency

SART Society for Assisted Reproductive Technology

SBNR spiritual but nonreligious

SMC single mother by choice

STD sexually transmitted disease

PROLOGUE

Kayla's Egg Freezing and Partnership Predicaments

This book tells the story of American women who have frozen their eggs, mainly because they cannot find a reproductive partner. To write this book, I interviewed a rather remarkable group of 150 women, who shared their egg freezing stories with me in an outpouring of research generosity. These women were candid and courageous in describing their intimate lives and the paths that led them to egg freezing. They also revealed the heavy physical, financial, and emotional toll of egg freezing, an expensive new reproductive technology that is never guaranteed to produce a baby.

I hope that after reading this book, any woman who has frozen her eggs or who has ever considered doing so or perhaps who is starting to think about it now will feel less alone in realizing the shared nature of her experience. The women who volunteered for my study wanted this book to be written for exactly this reason. I have changed these women's names and identifying details to protect their anonymity, but their stories are real and, I hope, well presented. This is especially true for the eloquent women whose stories open each chapter.

Kayla's Egg Freezing

I begin this book by telling Kayla's story, because in many ways, it encapsulates what egg freezing is all about. Raised amid a brood of athletic brothers in a "very strict" Irish American family, Kayla graduated from a Catholic university with dual science and engineering degrees, eventually earning her master of business administration (MBA) from an Ivy League business school. "We all did well," Kayla said of her family. "We all have master's degrees. We're all successful. There's no black sheep."

After working in New York City, then taking several overseas job postings, Kayla moved to the San Francisco Bay Area to venture into a new tech start-up. With her friendly and outgoing demeanor, Kayla found it easy to make good "guy friends," but none of these friendships evolved into serious romantic relationships. "You're already under stress that you're a highly accomplished female," Kayla emphasized. "That threatens a lot of men, unintentionally. And I'm not a threatening personality. But I certainly probably made more money than most of my guy friends, and I think the curse of smart women is you want to marry smart men, versus men who sometimes do the opposite. So I think it does make it twice as hard for women who are accomplished."

As Kayla entered her thirties without a partner, her parents began to relentlessly question her: "Why aren't you married yet?" Becoming tearful as she spoke, Kayla described how this negatively affected her relationship with her family, as well as her own sense of self.

> We never talked about it my entire life, and then suddenly at age thirty, it's like, "Well, next step. You graduated from [named] business school. You have this great job. When are you getting married?" And I had to do an intervention with them to say, "You know, I could have married my boyfriend from my twenties, but I wasn't in love with him. It's not another thing on my to-do list. It's not another accomplishment. Like, I've already done so much, and yet it's still not good enough for you, because I'm not married yet." I think that weighed on me more than I probably realized at the time. And it went on for like five years. It wasn't until I was thirty-five, when I finally said, "I'm not coming home anymore. I'm not—until you stop pressuring me. Like, it's not fully in my control. It's not like I'm sitting home every night. I'm out all the time." But to have that in the back of your head I don't think is a great step forward in the dating world either. In your early thirties, that's like your time to be out and about and having a great time. And instead I was walking around and probably unconsciously giving off this energy of "What's wrong with me?" Because my family kept being like, "Why are you not married?" Because all my brothers had been married at that time. I still think I'm harboring some resentment around that.

At the same time, Kayla started watching the struggles of some of her married friends to get pregnant. One of these women, Beth, "spent her whole life trying to find the right guy," according to Kayla. But when Beth finally married at age forty, she faced age-related infertility that four rounds of in vitro fertilization (IVF) could not overcome. This was a wake-up call for Kayla. "Holy shit! I'm thirty-five. If I want to have a kid, I should have been married yesterday."

Slightly "freaked out," Kayla consulted her gynecologist, who falsely reassured her, "You're fine. Don't worry about it." Eventually, at age thirty-eight, Kayla found her way to an IVF clinic, where she underwent actual tests to assess her reproductive hormone levels and her ovarian reserve (i.e., the capacity of her ovaries to produce eggs). "I'm not going to scare you," the woman physician told Kayla, "but you should do this [egg freezing] as soon as possible."

The results of Kayla's first egg freezing cycle were not hopeful. After a month of daily hormone injections, work disruptions, lifestyle restrictions, and $13,000 spent out of pocket, Kayla's ovaries produced only three eggs, far below the eight eggs initially seen on ultrasound scans. Feeling both shocked and conflicted about what to do next, Kayla consulted with her mother. "I was nervous," Kayla admitted. "I didn't want my family to know, because I'm sure the Catholic Church doesn't agree with it."[1] Much to Kayla's surprise, her mother, a devout Catholic, not only was supportive but secretly wrote a $13,000 check for the second egg freezing cycle in order to avoid any confrontation with Kayla's strict Catholic father. Kayla supplemented her second cycle with multiple vitamin prescriptions, several acupuncture sessions, and a relaxing Valium on the day of egg retrieval. The results were much better, and Kayla banked a total of eleven eggs.

As Kayla reflected on her experience two years later, she expressed deep satisfaction with her decision, telling me how she had become "a voice for egg freezing" in her friend group. Working in the tech industry with other thirty-something women, Kayla saw a definite need for egg freezing in her professional circles—not to "lean in" to work but to give women in tech more time to find their soul mates.

I'm not doing it because I want to spend more time on my career. Like, I'm pretty sick of my career [laughs]! I've worked really hard, and now I want the next phase of my life. So I'm doing it because I want to make sure I'm with the right guy and that I have the option [to have children]. When you're in your twenties, you're thinking, "Of course I'm going to meet the guy I'm going to marry" and "Of course I'll have kids by forty." You're not thinking, "I'm going to freeze my eggs so I can put my career first." And all this talk on the radio right now about Facebook and Apple reimbursing egg freezing, that's not really how women think. They think like, "I really like what I do. I want to contribute to society. I want to support myself. And I believe that along the way, I'm going to meet some great guy, and we're going to get married and have kids." It's not, "Oh, I'm going to egg freeze and put off dating so I can climb the ladder." That's not how women think, at least not in my circle. I've never heard that kind of discussion before. It's so misrepresentative! And I also don't believe that if a company paid for my egg freezing that I'd think I'd have to do it or else I wouldn't get promoted. I don't even believe that either.

Kayla's comments succinctly summarized the media coverage and feminist debates over egg freezing, which have always assumed that egg freezing is about career building, even though most women's experiences are distinctly different. In Kayla's case, her egg freezing was clearly motivated by her inability to find a male partner who was also committed to marriage and children. In the Bay Area, Kayla explained to me, women in her circles were constantly lamenting the "Peter Pans"—men who never grow up and do not want to start a family. "They have all the money that they want. They can buy all the toys, and women are somewhat disposable to them," Kayla opined. "So they just wine and dine you."

Kayla described her last partner, Matt, as fitting this profile to some extent. "He was a really successful, handsome boyfriend," Kayla told me. "We used to go out to favorite restaurants. We used to go fly places." But it was clear to Kayla that Matt's main passions were surfing and skiing and that he had no desire to settle down. When Kayla finally decided to freeze her eggs, Matt was supportive but silent about his own intentions. It was then that Kayla realized the truth about Matt: "a trust-fund kid who was never going to commit." Kayla broke it off after a year and a half spent together.

When I asked Kayla if egg freezing had somehow taken the pressure off finding another partner, she told me emphatically, "It's the best decision I ever made!"

Like, turning forty was hard enough, but knowing that I had frozen my eggs was this huge relief off my shoulders, because I want kids. And I've told guys I've dated, 'cause they'll say, "Oh, you're forty. Do you want to have kids?" And you can see they're looking at you with this like, "Oh shit! If you say yes, that means you want to get married next month, and I'm out of here." But if you say, "Yeah, I want to have kids. I froze my eggs," they're a little bit shocked that you talk about it. But I'll be like, "Yeah, I do want to have kids, and I froze my eggs a couple years ago."

Eventually, through online dating, Kayla met her current boyfriend, Will. Will was not the "Irish-Catholic finance guy" that Kayla had always imagined she might marry, and he was also divorced—a huge demerit in the eyes of the Catholic Church. Still, Kayla found Will to be "handsome, fun, and flirty," and she was very impressed by Will's insistence on their first date, "I want to get married and have kids."

Yet, on their second date, Will asked Kayla why she had never been married, telling her, "Look, I'm really attracted to you. I think you're incredibly smart, clearly well traveled, and you're really good at witty banter, which guys love and most girls suck at. So what's wrong with you? Why are you still single?" Apparently, Will's friends were asking him the same question, which put Kayla immediately on the defensive. She explained that she had wasted valuable time on her last relationship with Matt, a "Type B surfer dude."

Now four months into her relationship with Will, Kayla was feeling insecure and anxious. Will admitted to Kayla that he had cheated on his ex-wife, leading to marital acrimony, a drawn-out divorce, and alimony payments that included egg freezing. Kayla was beginning to wonder whether she could trust Will. "My concern right now is that he likes to tease by saying he's a narcissist, and I don't really want to be with a narcissist. . . . And right now he's being chased by this thirty-year-old Russian girl, and it's driving me bonkers! He's pinning me as the 'jealous girlfriend'; and it's pissing me off, 'cause I was like, 'I think you're being really disrespectful to me, 'cause why can't you set boundaries with her?'" Kayla went on to describe another recent conversation she had had with Will and his friends about what they were looking for in a woman:

I mean, they can be just really critical, like, "I don't like her nose" or "I don't like her this or that." They can be very focused on the physical, for sure. And their younger friend, he wants a really professional woman who's a pro skier, who's traveled the world. I was like, "I know a ton of those women, and they're still single. So you say that you want that, but why won't you date that? Is it because they're also not a Victoria's Secret model on top of it all? Like, what's the unicorn that you're chasing? Because you're not perfect either."

Kayla was also disconcerted by the way that Will and his friends talked about women's aging and the "risk" of partnering with an older woman. Trying to appear nonjudgmental, Will had told his friends, "Yeah, but Kayla's totally derisked. Like, she's forty, she's gorgeous, and I know what I'm going to get. It's not like I'm dating this thirty-year-old who's going to turn into this gnome when she's fifty." Kayla had never heard the "derisked" term before, but she wondered whether her frozen eggs were part of Will's risk assessment.

Will had recently told Kayla that he loved her, but as she confided to me, "I can't really say it back until I feel more secure." She continued, "I think right now, the influence of the thirty-year-old, hot Russian girl chasing him, you know—men, they do get pulled in [other] directions. . . . You know, it's like, the last week he's been doing more behaviors of a thirty-year-old. So I want to say, "I love you back, but I'm not feeling secure right now because of your behavior."

Over two hours and a box of Kleenex, Kayla spilled out her story, inciting my own disquiet and dismay. On the surface, Kayla was a bright, friendly, attractive, highly educated, professional woman, who felt that she had done "everything right, yet things just seemed to be getting worse and worse." While professional success had come easily to Kayla, stable romantic relationships continued to elude her. With her best reproductive years well behind her, Kayla had frozen her eggs at age thirty-eight at a staggering cost—more than $25,000, an amount totaling more than one-third of the average US household income in 2020. This investment served to relieve Kayla's reproductive stress and boost her dating confidence. But those frozen eggs were cold comfort amid the larger gender and relationship issues that she still faced.

Partnership Predicaments

Over a multiyear study, I met dozens and dozens and dozens of highly educated professional women like Kayla from diverse racial, religious, and regional backgrounds. Although the details of their stories varied, they were overwhelmingly freezing their eggs for one reason: heterosexual relationship troubles. This would be a disturbing finding for any gender scholar. But for me, my discomfort ran deep for several reasons.

First, I could not help but compare what I was hearing from American women to what I already knew about gender relations in the Middle

East—the region of the world where I have conducted research for more than thirty-five years. In fact, I have written six books on gender, reproduction, and family life in the Middle East, arguing that gender relations have changed for the better over time.[2] In my most well-known book on this subject, *The New Arab Man*, I provide multiple examples of what I call "emergent masculinities," or the ways in which new-generation Arab men are challenging patriarchy, changing norms of manhood, and practicing more egalitarian gender relations.

To take but one example, Arab men today now strive for what I call "conjugal connectivity"—the intense sharing of romantic love, sexual intimacy, everyday companionship, and a firm sense of committed, long-term partnership within marriage. Overall, Arab men are very marriage oriented, making the Middle East the "most married" region of the world, with more than 90 percent of all adults marrying at least once in their lifetimes. Arab men see marriage as a fundamental aspect of their masculine identities, and they strive to achieve this important marker of masculine success, even amid the "waithood," or marriage delay, caused by serious economic obstacles.[3] Indeed, in uncertain political and economic circumstances, marrying an educated woman with a career path is seen by most men as a tremendous asset.[4]

Moreover, once married, both Middle Eastern men and women generally want children, considering them to be the greatest joy and reward in life. Middle Eastern men generally cherish their fatherhood roles, taking great pride in being loving *babas*, or daddies, to their children. For example, on any Middle Eastern airplane flight, men can be seen carrying and cuddling their babies, walking with their toddlers up and down the aisles, going to the restroom to change diapers, finding food and entertainment for their older children, and generally sharing the mundane tasks of parenthood with their wives. They also lavish this attention on other people's children, a kind of affection rare to behold in the West. (Just think of long-haul flights where children are considered a nuisance and their crying an affront.)

In short, over more than three decades, I have enjoyed watching and documenting this increasingly gender-egalitarian Arab world, where good marriages and happy families are many men's passionate commitment. Thus, returning to my own country and hearing countless stories like Kayla's came as something of a shock. What was happening to gender relations in my own country? Why were educated women having so much trouble finding men? Was this the "tragedy of heterosexuality" described by the queer theorist Jane Ward, who has argued powerfully that being straight benefits men but not always women?[5] Indeed, women in the West are often portrayed as the greatest beneficiaries of feminism, freedom, reproductive rights, and gender equality, making their lives seem the best and most fulfilled. Yet many women I interviewed had confronted patriarchy, misogyny, ego fragility, and sexism—male attributes that are assumed to exist in other places like the Middle East but may, in fact, govern heterosexual women's lives and relationships in the US and perhaps in other Western countries.

In story after story, American women told me about men's feelings of intimidation, with women's higher earnings invoking particular feelings of emasculation. I learned a great deal about men's ageism and particularly the rejection of women in their late thirties, who were seen as "over the hill" and "desperate" for marriage. I heard about men's objectification of women's bodies and their critique of women's appearances, both online and in person. I listened to women's stories of men's bad behavior, from the casual ghosting in online dating to the actual cheating in sexual relationships. And I heard about Peter Pans and many other types of men—from alpha males to beta males and so on—who were simply unready or unwilling to commit to women. Although these women fit all the markers of success in the US and all the characteristics deemed worthy of marriage, the men they met were far from their fantasies. Thus, the vast majority of women I interviewed found themselves in their late thirties without partners. Egg freezing was not about their careers. It was about being single or in very unstable relationships with men who were unwilling to commit to them.

This situation also caused me to ask, Why have things not changed since my generation? These kinds of stories felt achingly familiar to me, spurring me to reflect back on my younger self. Growing up in a beer-drinking, sports-loving, midwestern college town, I found myself always out of place. Nicknamed "Inhorn the Egghead" and voted "Most Likely to Succeed" in high school, I entered college on a full-tuition cello scholarship and spent more time in concert halls and on the university arts newspaper than attending football games and drinking beer with the guys. Heading straight to New York City after graduation to work as a journalist, I still did not find my soul mate, settling instead for some very unequal and unsatisfactory romantic relationships. Eventually, I moved across country for graduate school, where most of my classmates were women entering their early thirties and in the same situation. Although they obtained their PhDs, many of my friends never went on to marry or "settled" for suboptimal relationships that subsequently ended. I was in the latter category, painfully extricating myself from a dysfunctional relationship with a much older man, including a brief and disastrous marriage.

Following my divorce, I contemplated using donor insemination to become a single mother. Children were the one thing I knew I wanted, even if I never partnered again. But I eventually met the man who was to become the father of my children. He had yet to finish college, but he was intelligent and kind and not opposed to moving for my job or having children. Over the next several years, my new husband returned to college, eventually obtaining his master's degree. I, meanwhile, struggled to bear our children amid the ticking of both my biological and tenure clocks.

Our first pregnancy ended with malpractice. The physician who performed an amniocentesis for me as I turned thirty-five failed to detect my twin pregnancy—even though, with my distended belly, I had asked him about this possibility and he callously brushed me off in a dismal display of poor bedside manner. At the beginning of my third trimester, my second twin was finally detected on ultrasound. But by then, my pregnancy was in serious trouble due to a complication of the identical twins' shared placenta. Sadly, I delivered our baby daughters stillborn, at twenty-six weeks' gestation. This was followed by an early miscarriage. Finally, our son was born when I was thirty-seven, our daughter at age forty, the same year I received tenure. Frankly, if egg freezing had been available at the end of the twentieth century, I would have strongly considered it, simply to relieve the reproductive pressure and to give myself some kind of backup.

Having gone through my own reproductive losses and heartache, I feel great compassion for any woman whose reproductive desires go unrequited, whatever the obstacles might be. I also know how much partnership and parenting mean to me and why these desires are so strongly felt by many other women. As this book on egg freezing will clearly show, women like Kayla are doing the best they can, under less-than-ideal circumstances, to give themselves a hard-fought reproductive chance. Thus, in reflecting back on Kayla's story, the question should not be, "What's wrong with Kayla?" but rather, "What societal factors are causing women like Kayla to freeze their eggs?" Decades on from my own struggle, why is it still so difficult for educated professional women—from every race, religion, and region of the country—to achieve stable partnerships and to mother the children of their dreams? Why has a substantial shift in gender relations *not* occurred since my baby boom generation? Given the disheartening reality of these ongoing gender troubles, what can egg freezing achieve for modern women like Kayla? What kind of cold comfort do their frozen eggs provide? These are the questions to be taken up in this book, which may be about a woman like you or about someone you know and love.

* * *

And what about Kayla? She contacted me five years after our first meeting, and this is what she had to say: "I'm still in the camp of 'where is my partner?!' Which is never how I expected my life to pan out. I'm incredibly grateful that I froze my eggs but I'm also so sad that I'm turning 45 this year and still do not have a partner and family. I never expected this to be my life. I'm moving to [a different state] and hope that a fresh start and a focus on making time to actively date will result in a much better love life than in SF and NYC. I'm determined to stay positive and hopeful." Ultimately, egg freezing technology could do nothing to solve Kayla's ongoing partnership predicament. But with frozen eggs in the bank, at least Kayla could hold out hope of achieving her motherhood dream.

Introduction

The Rise of Egg Freezing

Egg Freezing: A Brief History

To begin the story of egg freezing—and why women like Kayla are now staking their reproductive futures on it—we must take a brief journey backward in time to the beginnings of IVF. On July 25, 1978, Louise Brown, the world's first "test-tube baby," was born in Oldham, England. For Lesley and John Brown, the working-class parents of baby Louise, IVF was their "hope technology," allowing them to overcome nine years of heartbreaking involuntary childlessness.[1] Although both feminists and religious leaders were quick to condemn IVF on various grounds, the first generation of infertile couples to use IVF were full of enthusiasm and admiration, describing this new reproductive technology as a "miracle," a "good fortune," and a sign of "scientific progress."[2]

Fast-forward four decades to 2018. Louise Brown, now a mother of two young sons, has turned forty with great media fanfare. Her memoir, *Louise Brown: My Life as the World's First Test-Tube Baby* (2015), is promoted as part of IVF's fortieth anniversary celebration. The European Society of Human Reproduction and Embryology (ESHRE), one of the two main IVF professional organizations in the world, announces that more than eight million IVF babies have been born, including at least 4 percent of all children in Western societies.[3]

But IVF has birthed more than babies. IVF has been called the "platform technology" for all that has followed, including a multitude of second-generation assisted reproductive technologies (ARTs).[4] These range from intracytoplasmic sperm injection (ICSI) to overcome male infertility, to preimplantation genetic diagnosis (PGD) to detect chromosomal abnormalities and the sex of IVF embryos, to human embryonic stem cells (hESC) for therapeutic use in regenerative medicine.

1

Egg freezing is one of these IVF offspring. Techniques to freeze human sperm were already mastered by the 1970s, and human embryo freezing followed within the first few years of IVF's existence. But the freezing of human eggs proved technologically difficult. The human egg is the largest cell in the human body, with a high water content, and therefore prone to lethal ice crystal formation during the freezing process. Slow freezing techniques being used in the 1980s and 1990s were unreliable. Eggs that survived freezing and rewarming often demonstrated chromosomal damage, leading to poor embryo development and ultimately low overall birth rates. So, although the first reported frozen egg baby was born in 1986, only eight years after Louise Brown's birth, egg freezing was not considered safe or effective by the end of the twentieth century.[5]

Not until 2005 was a new method of flash-freezing called "oocyte vitrification" successfully developed by a research embryologist in Japan and eventually introduced into clinical trials in the US and other countries.[6] Vitrification is a process by which human eggs are first treated with cryoprotective substances and then submerged into liquid nitrogen. The cells cool so rapidly to −320 degrees Fahrenheit that they become "vitrified," or glass-like in their structure. Unlike older slow freezing methods, which took hours to complete, the vitrification process takes minutes. Furthermore, egg survival post-rewarming can be as high as 90 percent with vitrification, with good evidence that fertilization and pregnancy rates are similar between "fresh" and frozen eggs.[7] Safety data are also reassuring, with no apparent increased rates of birth defects or developmental deficits in the children born from frozen eggs.[8] Thus, the birth of vitrification technology at the turn of the twenty-first century has proven to be a game changer. It has simplified the egg freezing procedure, increased its efficiency, and improved overall birth outcomes.

Initial demand for this new egg freezing technology was found in the world of clinical oncology. Female cancer patients of reproductive age—generally, young women in their teens, twenties, or early thirties—are at risk of infertility, because many forms of oncological treatment, including both radiation and chemotherapy, destroy or diminish a woman's ovarian function. If patients' eggs can be retrieved from their ovaries, then frozen and stored prior to cancer treatment, female cancer survivors can be given the chance to use their frozen eggs at a future date to conceive biogenetically related offspring. (This opportunity was already available to young male cancer survivors through sperm freezing.) Egg freezing clinical trials thus began with cancer patients, but they soon opened up to women with other fertility-threatening medical conditions. These include severe endometriosis, benign ovarian tumors, autoimmune disorders, and a variety of genetic profiles, such as BRCA1 and 2, Turner syndrome, and fragile X syndrome.[9]

However, the major expansion of egg freezing clinical trials occurred when otherwise-healthy single women in their mid- to late thirties began volunteering for egg vitrification studies, most of which were being conducted in academic IVF clinics. Healthy women's concerns revolved around reproductive aging—the fact that a woman's "ovarian reserve," or the number and quality of her eggs, diminishes over time, beginning around age thirty-two and accelerating rapidly around age thirty-seven.[10] If a woman freezes her eggs at age thirty-five, she can potentially use those thirty-five-year-old eggs in her forties and beyond, because as a woman ages, her frozen eggs do not. Furthermore, egg age, not womb age, appears to be the most critical variable in a woman's ability to carry a pregnancy to term (as had already been demonstrated through the successful use of younger donor eggs to help older women become mothers). Thus, even a postmenopausal woman can carry and give birth to a frozen egg baby with the support of hormone therapy and an IVF cycle. In other words, egg freezing by vitrification has made possible the extension of a woman's reproductive life span, forestalling the inevitability of age-related infertility, which, for most women, occurs by the time they reach their early forties.

The clinical trials undertaken throughout the early 2000s thus helped to confirm two main categories of egg freezing. One became known as "medical" egg freezing and was being offered mainly to young cancer patients within an emerging field of "oncofertility."[11] The other was called by a number of names, including "nonmedical," "social," or "elective" egg freezing, but was being directed at otherwise-healthy women who were concerned about age-related fertility decline. Even though medical and nonmedical egg freezing were categorized separately, it is important to point out that both were ultimately directed at the prevention of future infertility, a condition that affects approximately 10 percent of all reproductive-aged women worldwide.[12]

Egg freezing by vitrification remained experimental in the US, as elsewhere, until the beginning of the 2010s. Israel, a country always on the cutting edge of assisted reproductive technology development, was the first to move egg freezing by vitrification into clinical practice, in January 2011.[13] The United States soon followed. On October 19, 2012, the American Society for Reproductive Medicine (ASRM), the world's other main IVF professional organization, lifted the "experimental" label, allowing egg freezing to be used for both medical and nonmedical purposes.[14] (ASRM's European counterpart, ESHRE, agreed with this decision the same year.)[15] Still, ASRM urged caution, stopping short of recommending egg freezing as a way to actually postpone childbearing. As it pointed out, there were insufficient data on safety, success rates, cost effectiveness, and physical and emotional risks to women, who might be lulled into a false sense of security through egg freezing. Furthermore, reliable data on the ultimate success of egg freezing were not readily available, as so few women in the experimental phase had yet returned to use their frozen eggs. In other words, according to ASRM, the viability of egg freezing and what it would ultimately mean for women and their future children remained highly uncertain.

Having said this, as soon as the experimental restrictions were lifted in late 2012, IVF clinics across the US began providing egg freezing cycles to women, and some clinics also began creating their own frozen egg banks. The response on the part of American women was also immediate. Approximately five thousand egg freezing cycles were undertaken in the US in 2013, the first full year of clinical approval. By 2018, five years later, that number had more than doubled to nearly eleven thousand cycles, according to the Society for Assisted Reproductive Technology (SART), which is charged with keeping track of such cycles in the US. By the end of the decade, more than thirty-six thousand American women had frozen their eggs, with that number expected to increase exponentially.[16]

Today, most US IVF clinics now offer both medical and nonmedical egg freezing as a routine service, and several commercial stand-alone egg freezing clinics, such as Extend Fertility and Kindbody, have opened up in major cities such as New York and San Francisco. It is important to note that although many US IVF clinics temporarily closed due to the onset of COVID-19, their reopening in the summer of 2020 led to a surge in egg freezing requests, reflecting pent-up demand for services among American women.[17] For example, in Manhattan, New York University's Langone Prelude Fertility Center recorded a 41 percent increase in egg freezing cycles during the period from June to September 2020.[18]

Portraying Egg Freezing

So, why are American women clamoring for egg freezing? What new opportunities does egg freezing afford? From the very beginning, much has been said about what egg freezing can do for women. For example, egg freezing has been called a "reproductive backstop," a form of "fertility insurance," a means to create an "egg savings account," and a way for thirty-something women to "rewind the biological clock."[19] With egg freezing, younger women in their twenties can potentially "put their fertility on hold," "defer childbearing," and "postpone motherhood" until they are ready.[20] The ability to "freeze fertility in time"—putting off childbearing until a later date—has been heralded as a "reproductive revolution," equivalent to the introduction of the birth control pill in the 1960s.[21]

Prominent IVF physicians have contributed to these optimistic portrayals, including in a series of review articles on egg freezing's potential.[22] Egg freezing, they have argued, is not only a way to forestall age-related infertility; it can also be used by women in an intentional, forward-looking manner to "delay," "defer," or "postpone" their fertility, especially for educational and career purposes. Such fertility postponement, in turn, can help women to achieve "reproductive autonomy" and also "level the playing field" with men, given that men have no equivalent reproductive time pressure.

ASRM, too, has weighed in on egg freezing's potential. In an important 2018 ASRM Ethics Committee statement titled "Planned Oocyte Cryopreservation for Women Seeking to Preserve Reproductive Potential," ASRM called egg freezing an "emerging but ethically permissible procedure that may help women avoid future infertility."[23] The most notable aspect of this ASRM statement was the use of the word "planned" as the most appropriate descriptor for nonmedical egg freezing, a rhetorical move with several important implications.

First, ASRM's advocacy of the term "planned" as the proper adjective for nonmedical egg freezing suggested that the older term "social" be supplanted.[24] For many women, this represented a welcome step forward, given their critique of the ways in which the term "social" trivialized their experiences, even suggesting that egg freezing might be "fun."[25] Second, ASRM's use of the term "planned" solidified the distinction between medical and nonmedical egg freezing. Medical egg freezing can rarely be planned in advance, as it most often occurs on an urgent basis immediately following a cancer diagnosis and prior to chemotherapy. Thus, adding the term "planned" for nonmedical egg freezing acknowledged the distinction between urgent versus nonurgent fertility care. Third, calling nonmedical egg freezing "planned" suggested that this technology could be used for intentional planning purposes, for example, to forestall fertility during the period of graduate education. Furthermore, by invoking issues of planning, ASRM placed this technology squarely within the realm of "family planning," as another reproductive "choice" women could make to shape their reproductive destinies.

Yet, whereas most modern family planning methods are more than 90 percent effective, egg freezing is not. As we will see, the existence of frozen eggs cannot guarantee the birth of a future frozen-egg baby. Perhaps recognizing the danger of creating false hopes and expectations, the ASRM Ethics Committee added an important caveat to its 2018 statement, arguing that "because egg freezing is new and evolving, it is essential that women who are considering using it be informed about the uncertainties regarding its efficacy and long-term effects."[26]

ASRM's somewhat ambivalent stance—namely, technological optimism tinged with uncertainty—was echoed in the media portrayals of egg freezing over the same time period. As soon as egg freezing's experimental label was lifted in 2012, hundreds of news stories and opinion pieces began to be published, often emanating in the US media, then circulating rapidly around the globe. In this regard, the New York Times was at the forefront of egg freezing coverage. Fully six months before egg freezing's experimental label was lifted, the New York Times published its first cover story, one that focused on the potential benefits of egg freezing for would-be grandparents, who might "nudge" their thirty-something daughters by paying for egg freezing, thereby increasing their own chances for future grandchildren.[27] The second New York Times piece, published five days after egg freezing's experimental label was lifted, was an editorial written by the health and science journalist Sarah Elizabeth Richards. An early advocate of egg freezing, Richards told women readers, "We need to talk about our eggs."[28] The following year, she published a book called Motherhood, Rescheduled: The New Frontier of Egg Freezing and the Women Who Tried It (2013), based on her own and three other women's experiences of egg freezing undertaken during the experimental period.

A decade on, the tone of the *New York Times*' media coverage had shifted. Stories increasingly focused on the problems of egg freezing, including unequal access to this costly procedure, uncertainties in egg survival rates following freezing and rewarming processes, lack of success among those who had attempted to use their frozen eggs, and the thousands of frozen eggs still remaining in storage, given that most women did not return to use them.[29] The *New York Times* also began to question the promotion and financing of egg freezing. Stories focused on the "aggressive" marketing strategies directed toward younger millennial and Gen Z women by clinics that "really, really, really want to freeze your eggs," luring them in through ethically questionable, champagne-soaked egg freezing "parties" and incessant social media advertising.[30] They also covered how egg freezing "benefits" from companies such as Facebook (now Meta) and Apple were actually conveying a "dark message" to women workers about the need for mandatory fertility postponement.[31] Five out of six editorials on egg freezing published in the *New York Times* between 2016 and 2020 were either negative or ambivalent in nature. Most were written by women who had undergone egg freezing with various painful and untoward outcomes.[32]

One of the most powerful *New York Times* editorials published during this period pointed to egg freezing's discriminatory potential as an expensive technology for "White women only."[33] Indeed, stereotypical images of the kind of women who might turn to egg freezing were beginning to form in the media. First, these women were presumed to be White and economically privileged. Second, they were often referred to as "career women," a term that has no masculine equivalent and is sometimes used in a pejorative sense to criticize women with professional ambitions. The implication was that freezing their eggs, either by choice or necessity, was presumably a way for these career-driven women to climb the corporate ladder.

But was this true? In a prescient article titled "Portrayals of Healthy Women Seeking Oocyte Cryopreservation," the bioethicist Heidi Mertes questioned whether this image of the egg freezing woman was, in fact, correct or whether it oversimplified women's egg freezing motivations and experiences.[34] Mertes pointed to three distinct ways in which egg freezing women were being cast: first, as "selfish career-pursuing women"; second, as "victims of a male-oriented society that makes it difficult for women

to combine motherhood with a good education or professional responsibilities"; and third, as "wise, proactive women who will not have to de-
pend on oocyte donors should they suffer from age-related infertility."[35]
Instead, Mertes asked, Might the absence of a male partner be the most
common reason why otherwise-healthy women are freezing their eggs?

Reconceiving Egg Freezing

In this book, I aim to answer Heidi Mertes's important question. In
doing so, I hope to shift the dominant portrayals of egg freezing women
and their motivations. Through in-depth interviews with 150 American
women, I have learned, definitively, that egg freezing is really *not* about
career planning. Most women who freeze their eggs *are* successful professionals, ones who can afford this expensive technology. But the notion that
women are egg freezing to "lean in" to their careers, per Sheryl Sandberg's
advice, is simply inaccurate.[36] By extension, ASRM's advocacy of the term
"planned" is probably misdirected, given that it too closely associates egg
freezing with career planning, thereby overemphasizing women's inten-
tionality in this regard.

Notions of egg freezing and the women who do it need to be recon-
ceived, as the stories in this book will show. Most women do *not* con-
form to the dominant stereotypes, which circulate in the media and
some brands of feminist scholarship. To wit, women who freeze their
eggs are *not*

- *twenty-somethings*, planning for their future careers, while also taking time
  to date, party, and have fun;
- *thirty-somethings*, climbing the corporate ladder so hard that they "forget
  to have children";
- *docile employees*, paid by firms to freeze their eggs and put off childbearing
  indefinitely;
- *gullible victims*, lured into egg freezing by employers and a profit-oriented
  fertility industry; or
- *ardent feminists*, fighting for reproductive equality with men through egg
  freezing.

Women who freeze their eggs are almost always gainfully employed
in careers they enjoy, but by the time they undertake egg freezing, their

careers are already well established. Thus, egg freezing is rarely about *planned fertility postponement*, in the sense of women actively "deferring," "delaying," or "postponing" their fertility for the sake of their professions. Rather, as we shall see, egg freezing is about *unplanned fertility preservation* among a group of American women who are hoping to retain and extend their remaining reproductive potential. Women who freeze their eggs are trying to give themselves a decent chance of biologically connected motherhood. They freeze their eggs not to delay parenthood but rather to enable it at a time when they have met the right partner with whom to become pregnant and have children. Egg freezing, I argue, is their *new hope technology*, allowing women to imagine what life would be like with the *three p's of partnership, pregnancy, and parenthood.*

Women's turn to egg freezing has not arisen out of nowhere. Egg freezing is women's technological concession to a US gender problem—namely, the challenges women face in their attempts to form meaningful and lasting heterosexual relationships. Most American women who freeze their eggs wish that they could have children *now* in a committed relationship with a man they love. But in the absence of a partner, women are using egg freezing as a potentially powerful new tool to preserve and extend their fertility, thereby taking some of the pressure off finding a partner, while buying time toward the end of their reproductive life spans.

Undertaking egg freezing is not an easy choice for most women. As the stories in this book will reveal, egg freezing can be logistically complicated, physically taxing, financially demanding, emotionally draining, and uncertain in its effects. Furthermore, because the vast majority of women who freeze their eggs are single, "going solo" to a crowded IVF clinic can be extremely isolating. In this book, women's stories include reflections on their various clinical encounters and stress the need for better fertility education, improvements in patient-centered care and support, and increased access to egg freezing services for single women of all backgrounds.

This book also attempts to examine outcomes, asking what becomes of women and their frozen eggs. Although most frozen eggs remain in cold storage—not only for the women I spoke with but for women around the world—frozen eggs represent "future unborn children" for many women, bespeaking the immense hopes and investments placed in this still relatively novel fertility preservation strategy. This book explores this futurity, asking what is at stake and what kind of cold comfort frozen eggs can provide for women who are still searching for those three *p*'s of partnership, pregnancy, and parenthood.

Egg Freezing Stories

This book is full of women's stories. It is only through such stories that we can come to understand what motivates women to freeze their eggs and what the experience is like. As a medical anthropologist and gender scholar, I have been privileged to gather such egg freezing stories from 150 American women across the country. I met these women through four US IVF clinics, two academic and two private, located along the East Coast corridor and in the heart of Silicon Valley. All of these IVF clinics had active egg freezing programs, some having participated in early clinical trials. They allowed me to circulate a flier seeking volunteers for an interview-based study of those who had already undertaken the procedure.

Many of the women who volunteered were from my home state of Connecticut, especially from the cities of New Haven and Hartford, the state capital. However, over time, most of the women who joined the study came from other major US cities, including New York City, Baltimore, Maryland, Washington, DC (and its suburbs in Maryland and Virginia), and the San Francisco Bay Area, including Silicon Valley.[37] Reflecting the high degree of professional mobility in the US, many women had moved for their jobs. Thus, I also spoke with women living in Austin, Texas; Boston, Massachusetts; Chicago, Illinois; Denver, Colorado; Los Angeles, California; Savannah, Georgia; Seattle, Washington; St. Louis, Missouri; and the North Carolina "Research Triangle" cities of Raleigh, Durham, and Chapel Hill. Four women had relocated overseas for jobs in Europe, the Middle East, and Asia; thus, we spoke across many time zones.[38]

Given the potential sensitivity of this subject matter and the profound importance of research ethics, all of the women who volunteered to speak with me were given an informed consent form to read and sign before agreeing to a confidential, audio-recorded interview in a private setting of their own choosing. No one refused to sign, and most women seemed eager to share their stories. Our conversations unfolded in a variety of quiet spaces, including my office, women's homes and offices, libraries, cafés, restaurants, and, in some cases, private rooms in an IVF clinic.

When I could not meet a woman because of distance, we spoke by phone or video calls.[39]

I always began our conversations with a few basic demographic questions, asking each woman about her age, place of birth, residential history, education, employment, and relationship status and how she would describe her ethnicity and religion. I also asked a few key questions about reproductive history, including the age of first menstruation, contraceptive usage, and any reproductive problems experienced.

I then asked each woman to tell me her egg freezing story, in her own words. Women were eloquent and often loquacious storytellers, describing their life circumstances at the time of egg freezing, the details of their decision-making process, and how their egg freezing procedures had unfolded. Their stories were lengthy, often ranging from one to two hours, and tinged with emotions, ranging from happiness, enthusiasm, and relief to sadness, disappointment, and despair. Some women laughed or filled their stories with ironic humor, while others struggled to hold back tears. Many women were angry, primarily at men but also at doctors. I came to realize through these egg freezing stories that much was at stake for these women who had put their bodies on the line to preserve their fertility. For them, egg freezing was much more than a medical procedure.

Because these conversations were "person centered," allowing women to express their thoughts, feelings, ideas, opinions, and subjective experiences, I came to realize that egg freezing serves as a kind of *repro-lens* into many other aspects of American women's lives.[40] Women often dwelled on their love lives and breakups, their feelings about the places where they lived, their relationships with family members, the support they received from friend groups, what they liked about their jobs, their experiences with online dating, their perceptions of men, and their opinions about reproductive health care in the US. Women also highlighted dimensions of their lives that are rarely covered in egg freezing discussions, such as religion and the morality of egg freezing, feelings about their reproductive bodies and sexuality, and how egg freezing might serve a healing function after illness, heartbreak, or trauma.

Of the 150 egg freezing stories I collected from those who had completed at least one cycle, 114 women had undergone nonmedical egg freezing, 33 had undergone medical egg freezing (mostly because of cancer diagnoses), 2 had frozen their eggs because of their husbands' sterility, and 1 transgender individual had undergone egg freezing prior to his male gender-affirming transition. I also interviewed twelve women who had not yet completed egg freezing but had consulted with a physician, started the procedure, started but canceled the procedure, or, in one case, decided not to move forward. Some of these women were referred to me by their friends who had already participated in my study, or they found out about my study and volunteered on their own. Overall, fourteen women I interviewed were either friend or self-referrals. The rest of the women contacted me through fliers circulated by email and hard copy in the four participating IVF clinics.

I also interviewed eight male and three female IVF physicians. Their clinics were located in diverse regions of the country, including the East Coast (Washington, DC), the Southeast (Florida and Georgia), the Midwest (Michigan and Missouri), the Mountain region (Colorado), and the Northwest (Oregon), as well as Southern California and Hawaii. Through these interviews, I was able to get a sense of how egg freezing was unfolding across the country, and I include excerpts of these interviews at various points in this book. I also interviewed two individuals with in-depth knowledge of demographic disparities in infertility care and education in the US. The discussion of educational disparities is critical to the arguments that will unfold.

All in all, I conducted audio-recorded interviews with 176 individuals, including 166 women, 150 of whom had completed at least one cycle of egg freezing. This is the largest ethnographic exploration of egg freezing ever undertaken, not only in the US but anywhere in the world. At the core of this book are women's egg freezing stories, gathered over two years, hundreds of hours of interviewing, and thousands of hours of verbatim transcription.[41]

In this book, I aim to carefully "preserve" women's egg freezing stories in their own words, while also signaling points of laughter, exclamation, exasperation, and tears. All of the names used are pseudonyms. Particular details of women's lives are also covered by more general terms (e.g., "academic physician" rather than "oncologist at such-and-such university") so as to protect their anonymity. But women's stories with their verbatim quotes are real.

This book is centered on the stories of the more than one hundred women who had completed at least one cycle of nonmedical egg freezing. Although women undertaking medical egg freezing are vitally important and will be introduced to readers later in the book, women undertaking nonmedical egg freezing constitute the majority of new users of this technology, not only in the US but elsewhere around the world. Who are these women? As we will see in the next section, they compose a particular *egg freezing demographic* of highly educated professional women, like Kayla, who are now turning to egg freezing by the thousands.

The Egg Freezing Demographic

How can we characterize American women who freeze their eggs? As my study clearly reveals, egg freezing women are part of a particular US demographic defined by eight key features. Women who compose the egg freezing demographic are (1) racially and ethnically diverse, (2) secular, (3) late thirty-something, (4) high earning, (5) highly educated, (6) professionally successful, (7) heterosexual but single, and/or (8) facing ongoing partnership problems. All eight features do not apply to every single woman, but these characteristics are widely shared across this group, having major relevance for the ways in which women's egg freezing experiences unfold. A brief synopsis will paint a clearer picture of this egg freezing demographic, which, in turn, will help to inform all of the stories that follow.

Racially and Ethnically Diverse

Women who freeze their eggs come from a variety of racial and ethnic backgrounds—backgrounds that are reflective of the cosmopolitan urban areas in which professional women tend to live and where IVF clinics are also located. In this study, slightly more than two-thirds of the women (69 percent) self-identified as White, but nearly one-third (31 percent) self-identified as non-White. Among these, Asian American women of East, Southeast, and South Asian heritage backgrounds constituted the single largest minority group, at 18 percent overall. Black, Latina, and mixed-race women were also represented, making up about 3 to 4 percent each of the study population. Women of Middle Eastern heritage, both Arab and Persian, also volunteered for the study, at 2 percent of the total.

Sixteen women (14 percent) had been born in other countries, specifically Canada, Chile, China, Colombia, Ethiopia, Ghana, Guatemala, India, Japan, Pakistan, Poland, Taiwan, and the United Kingdom, as well as Puerto Rico (the Caribbean island still designated as a US territory). Two had retained their birth citizenships. However, most of these women had been raised in the US or had come for schooling, eventually obtaining US citizenship. Minority women's specific concerns regarding egg freezing will be taken up later in this book. But suffice it to say here that egg freezing in the US is *not* limited to White women only, as diverse women's stories, including immigrant women's stories, showcased throughout this book will show.

Secular

Women of many religious backgrounds are also freezing their eggs, often with the explicit support of religious authorities.[42] More than half of the women in this study (58 percent) had been raised in Christian households, both Protestant (26 percent) and Catholic (32 percent), with Catholic women representing the single largest group in the study. As seen in Kayla's story, Catholic women may have particular moral concerns regarding egg freezing, because the Catholic Church is singularly restrictive, disallowing all forms of reproductive technology.

In contrast, Jewish religious authorities have been exceptionally supportive of egg freezing. Not surprisingly, then, Jewish women were significantly overrepresented in the study, at 18 percent of the total, even though Jews make up only 2.2 percent of the US population. Hindu and Muslim women, mostly from South Asian immigrant families, each made up 3 to 4 percent of the overall group, while women who identified as Buddhists made up 2 percent of the total. Nearly 16 percent of women had no religious background, especially women from East Asian immigrant families, who often identified themselves as agnostic, atheist, or secular.

No matter their religious upbringing, 90 percent of egg freezing women said that they no longer practiced any kind of religion and considered themselves to be secular. Many women identified themselves as "spiritual but nonreligious" (SBNR), a category that is growing among younger-generation Americans.[43] Having said this, 10 percent of women in the study considered themselves to be practicing Christians, Jews, or Muslims. For these religious women, egg freezing had consequences for notions of virginity, marriage, and motherhood, issues that will be explored further.

Late Thirty-Something

As studies around the world consistently show, women who freeze their eggs are most frequently in their late thirties, generally between the ages of thirty-six and thirty-eight.[44] This proved to be true in my study as well, where the average age at first egg freezing was 36.6. In fact, nearly three-quarters (73 percent) of women in the study were in their late thirties (ages thirty-five to thirty-nine) by the time they pursued egg freezing, and 10 percent were in their forties (ages forty to forty-three).[45] With more than four-fifths of women age thirty-five and above, only 17 percent of women froze their eggs in their early thirties (ages thirty to thirty-four), indicating the degree to which egg freezing is a *late*-thirty-something endeavor.

Only one woman was younger than thirty when she froze her eggs. But she was a special case because her father was a retiring IVF physician who encouraged her to freeze her eggs before he left his practice. The stark absence of "twenty-somethings" in this and other egg freezing studies suggests that younger women have not yet been convinced to try this costly and invasive technology, including as a tool for career planning. Furthermore, cost-benefit analyses suggest that egg freezing does not really make sense for fertile twenty-somethings, many of whom will eventually partner and conceive without any technological assistance.[46] Instead, egg freezing is most applicable to the lives of thirty-something women, who, as we will see throughout this book, are weighing the benefits of this technology against its high costs.

High Earning

Indeed, egg freezing is expensive, averaging between $10,000 to $15,000 per cycle but costing anywhere from $7,500 to $18,000 per cycle, depending on the IVF clinic and the amount and cost of accompanying medications. Women must also pay annual storage fees, which average between $500 to $1,000 but can range from $300 to $1,500, depending on the clinic and its egg bank. If women return to use their frozen eggs, then they must pay for the second half of an IVF cycle, which includes rewarming the frozen eggs, fertilizing them through ICSI techniques, and transferring the best quality embryo(s) to the uterus—a process that can cost an additional $6,000 on average. Given these high costs, only women with substantial financial means can afford this technology, making it out of reach for the vast majority of American women.

In this study, most women were entirely self-supporting and able to pay for egg freezing on their own. Although well-to-do parents often volunteered to pay for egg freezing cycles, nearly 90 percent of the women were able to pay for their egg freezing cycles by themselves, relying on their salaries, savings accounts, family inheritances, or health insurance provided by their employers. More than half (57 percent) of the women had undertaken one egg freezing cycle, while one-third (31 percent) had undertaken two cycles and 12 percent had undertaken three or four cycles, effectively multiplying their expenses.

Although I did not routinely ask women about their salaries, a few reported high salaries in the six-figure range, for example, $120,000, $148,000, $175,000, $200,000, $275,000, $325,000, $500,000, and $600,000. Such salaries put these women significantly above the $82,535 annual salary made by the average US taxpayer. Most of these egg freezing women were in the top 10 percent of earners (who average $158,002 annually), and some were in the top 5 percent (who average $309,348).[47]

In short, most of these high-earning women could easily afford their egg freezing cycles. Still, their major recommendation was that the price be brought down to make the technology much more accessible and affordable to lower- and middle-income women, including some of their own friends and relatives. In my study, about 10 percent of women fell into this middle-income bracket. Even though most were well employed and self-supporting, they did not make such large salaries (for example, $70,000 as opposed to $170,000), and some were paying off substantial student loans. These women often struggled to put together the money for even one cycle, resorting to zero-interest credit cards, small loans, or depletion of their savings accounts. For example, a woman who worked as a federal regulator in a government agency in Washington, DC, had accumulated just enough money in her savings account to afford a $15,000 egg freezing cycle. But when only one egg was retrieved and frozen, she was bereft, considering her $15,000 expenditure to be a "sunk cost."

In contrast, an academic physician spent $35,000 from her savings on three cycles that produced fifty-five eggs, the highest number retrieved and frozen by any woman in this study. For her, egg freezing was inherently affordable, something that she compared to the cost of "another car." For most women, being able to afford these high-cost egg freezing cycles made the choice less difficult, and the egg freezing itself brought many women some measure of success and relief. Indeed, women in this study froze an average of eighteen eggs—a number close to twenty, which has been recommended for a woman in her late thirties to achieve at least one live birth.[48]

Highly Educated

Women's affluence was clearly tied to their high levels of education. Most women in this study had not only completed college; nearly 80 percent of them had earned advanced degrees, including master's degrees (45 percent), medical degrees (14 percent), doctoral degrees (10 percent), and law degrees (7 percent).[49] More than 10 percent of all women had earned dual advanced degrees, such as MD-PhDs, MD-MPHs, and PhD-MPPs.

Furthermore, among these highly educated American women, one-third (32 percent) had attended Ivy League institutions, and another one-quarter (26 percent) had attended highly ranked public (e.g., the University of California–Berkeley) or private (e.g., Massachusetts Institute of Technology) universities. In other words, well over half (58 percent) of these American women had attended so-called elite academic institutions. As a group, they were exceptionally well-educated high achievers, whose years of schooling had prepared them for diverse and rewarding careers.

Successful Professionals

Most women in this study were not only gainfully employed; they were successful professionals with impressive jobs skills and sometimes remarkable career trajectories. Although the women's job descriptions varied considerably, their careers tended to cluster in ten key areas. The largest single category consisted of (1) women in *health care*, including many physicians who had frozen their eggs, as well as nurses, nurse-practitioners, health-care management professionals, and women in the pharmaceutical sector. The health-care category was followed, in rank order, by (2) women in *government*, including many women who worked in federal agencies, in US scientific and medical organizations, on Capitol Hill, in the foreign service, or in the US military or intelligence; (3) women in *tech*, including women who had started or owned tech companies or worked as engineers, designers, programmers, and finance directors in the information technology (IT) industry; (4) women in *consultancies,* including women who worked as management consultants, political consultants, policy advisers, and lobbyists; (5) women in *communications,* including journalists, filmmakers, and marketing and communications directors; (6) women in *business,* including women who worked for major corporations, as well as small business owners and entrepreneurs; (7) women in *law,* including public and private attorneys and those working in the legal profession in a variety of capacities; (8) women in the *arts,* including musicians, performers, actors, artists, and architects; (9) women in *psychology,* including clinical psychologists, licensed clinical social workers, and other types of therapists; and (10) women in *academia,* including university professors, graduate students, and private school teachers.

Because these women were in their late thirties, the vast majority were already well established in their careers, with the exception of a few graduate students and physicians still in training. Most women stressed that their careers had kept them busy, sometimes impinging on their free time and energy for dating. But most women had always hoped to meet a partner along the way. Thus, they were not using egg freezing as a career planning strategy or as way to further postpone their fertility for the sake of their professions.

Only one woman in the entire study had explicitly undertaken egg freezing for career-advancement purposes. At age thirty, she was significantly younger than most of the other women interviewed, had attended two Ivy League universities on the way to an advanced degree, and was using egg freezing en route to becoming a tech entrepreneur in Silicon Valley. She was clear that she needed to delay childbearing for at least a decade to accomplish her professional goals. She was also one of only three women who identified as bisexual. Thus, her profile was significantly different from the rest of the women in the study. Another one of the younger women, age thirty-three, was less explicit about her intended fertility postponement. But she had just passed the difficult US Foreign Service exam and had frozen her eggs in order to pursue her new career in Latin America.

In fact, deployment overseas was one of the only career paths that directly impinged on women's lives in ways that led them to egg freezing; 10 percent of the women in this study worked in "deployable" positions in humanitarian organizations, US foreign aid agencies, US diplomatic security, the US Foreign Service, and the US military. As they explained, they often faced long-term deployments overseas, sometimes lasting up to three years, with movement from one foreign country to another. Although they were not freezing their eggs for career advancement, their careers involved substantial personal sacrifices and a high degree of mobility, which made relationship formation very difficult and egg freezing seem necessary. Not surprisingly, all of these women were single, with only one having ever been married.

Four of these women were high-ranking, active-duty military officers and intelligence analysts, who had been deployed multiple times to war zones or "other dodgy places," as one of them put it. These women were all single and lamented the difficulties of finding a partner, given the dangers of their jobs, the military's antifraternization policies, and the fact that most military men are already married. Freezing their eggs comforted these women and their families, lest their lives be lost in the line of duty. Recognizing the dangers and sacrifices that military women must make, the Department of Defense attempted in 2016 to forward a bill offering subsidized egg freezing services to all female soldiers prior to deployment in combat zones. But as of this writing, no Republicans in Congress have signed onto this legislation.[50]

Heterosexual but Single

As with all of the military women, 82 percent of all the women in the study were single, with no partner in sight. All but three of these single women were heterosexual, and even the three bisexual women declared an interest in partnering and parenting with men. Yet the lack of a partner was a shared feature of women's lives, as it has been in every single egg freezing study ever conducted.[51]

Single women in this study were of two types: the never married and currently unpartnered, and the previously partnered but broken up. Fully half of all women (51 percent) fell into the first category. Some of these women had had one or more serious relationships in the distant past, but those relationships had ended some time ago. Some women had never been in a serious relationship, for reasons that they could not quite understand. Many of these single women expressed regret and puzzlement over how they had "ended up" this way. But without a partner, these single women had turned to egg freezing to "buy time," while continuing to search for a partner with the hope of future marriage and motherhood.

The second group of single women, nearly one-third (31 percent) of the total, were turning to egg freezing in the aftermath of relationship break-ups. These included both divorces (17 percent) and breakups from long-term relationships and engagements (14 percent). Although these women's stories will be told in greater detail, suffice it to say here that these relationship traumas were often painful, leaving women quite bereft. In such cases, egg freezing provided a path to healing, as women attempted to repair their disrupted life courses.

Facing Ongoing Partnership Problems

Between the never-married singles and the women whose relationships had ended, fully four-fifths of women in this study (82 percent) were single. Being single—or what other studies describe as "lack of a partner"—was the main reason these women had frozen their eggs. But even women *with* partners faced ongoing partnership problems. In this study, about one-fifth (18 percent) of the women had a partner at the time of egg freezing, but half of these relationships were unstable. Several women had met "new boyfriends" around the time of egg freezing. But in these cases, it was very difficult for them to ascertain whether the relationship was going to last. In other cases, women found themselves in very unstable relationships with partners who were immature, unsupportive, unready to have children, or unfaithful. In these cases, it was very unclear whether the relationships would survive. In both cases, egg freezing was being undertaken as a kind of backup plan, to see whether a relationship would develop or fall apart.

Among the nearly 10 percent of women who were in stable relationships, women were undertaking egg freezing while waiting for their partners to be "ready" to have children. Men who were "unready" cited various reasons for their delay, for example, completion of advanced degrees or professional training, significant career moves, or in some cases, because they were significantly younger than their female partners. In other cases, men simply did not feel prepared to become fathers and were asking their female partners to wait.

The "Men as Partners" Problem

In summary, then, fully 91 percent of women in this study were either single (82 percent) or in a tenuous relationship (9 percent)—the relationship problems that underlie the egg freezing phenomenon. To wit, highly educated American professional women like Kayla are often trying their hardest to find compatible male partners, with whom they can build families. But Kayla's story exemplifies women's three major partnership challenges:

- Men who are reluctant to partner with high-achieving women, leaving these women single for many years
- Men who are unready for marriage and children, often leading to relationship demise
- Men who exhibit bad behavior, including infidelity and ageism, which often leads to relationship instability and rupture

Because of these heterosexual relationship problems, otherwise-accomplished American women are pursuing a stopgap measure—namely, egg freezing—in an effort to preserve a path to motherhood.

Although this may seem like an obvious point, reproduction is inherently relational. It requires both men and women, or at least their sperm and their eggs, to come together in procreation. Ideally, it also involves men's and women's emotional investments in one another and in their children. But what happens when these reproductive relations and investments are untethered and go missing? In international reproductive health circles, this issue has been called the "men as partners" problem: men in the Global South have been heavily criticized, sometimes fairly, sometimes not, for their negative influences on women's reproductive lives and well-being, including abandonment of their female partners and offspring.[52]

But I would argue that educated American women have a specific "men as partners" problem as well, one that needs to be recognized, called out, and confronted. In the stories to be told in this book, the lack of stable reproductive relationships is the bane of women's existence, with significant deleterious consequences for women's reproductive lives. Although this is a "First World professional women's problem," as one woman put it, it is nonetheless forcing them into a demoralizing state of reproductive suspension. Only by listening carefully to what educated American women have to say about this can we begin to understand the magnitude of this *American mating gap* and ultimately why American women are turning to egg freezing as a reproductive suspension bridge.

PART I

Motivations

1

The Mating Gap

Educated Women and Missing Men

The Eternal Mystery of Clarissa's Singleness

Washington, DC, is a city packed with dynamic professional women. Clarissa is one of them. Born to a South American mother and North American father, Clarissa grew up in the Washington, DC, suburbs, attending an elite university and eventually obtaining her master's degree in economics. Fluent in multiple languages, Clarissa began working as an international economist, a job that she still loved a decade later. Clarissa's work involved frequent interactions with the World Bank and International Monetary Fund, as well as occasional trips overseas. When I told Clarissa that her work sounded very exciting, she was enthusiastic in her response. "Oh yeah! It's a very neat job. My career has been a sort of very happy part of my life. So, no problem with that." But then she added, "The fact that it's been hard to get into a relationship is the eternal mystery to me. And you try to suss [it] out, sort of like, 'Is it me? Is it where I live? Is it because I have a career?'"

Like almost every other DC-based woman I met throughout my study, Clarissa had reached her late thirties without a steady partner. She had dated a number of European men, whom she had met through her work and travel. But as she reached her late thirties, she found herself inexplicably single.

I thought, you know, I probably will have children when I meet somebody. And then I'll want to have children with them presumably, you know. I'm going to feel so strongly about them. But the relationship thing never really panned out. It never really did. I have, like, pretty much had one serious relationship ever. I guess, you know, it's funny. When you are thirty-four, thirty-five, you start to have these really hard conversations with yourself and a lot of soul searching. It was very hard for me. I was involved with somebody at the age of thirty-five, and I really liked him. And very quickly it just didn't pan out. And it really, like, really shook me, because I thought it's starting to get harder when things don't work out [laughs]. It's starting to get much harder. Things become much more meaningful and frustrating [laughs].

Although Clarissa laughed as she told her story, the "Why me?" question clearly haunted her. She had begun to blame herself for being too choosy about men, but her friends had reassured her that she was the "nicest person" in their group—the one who was the most positive and least judgmental, including about the men they dated. However, their overall assessment of the DC dating scene was bleak.

I find that I have a lot of single female friends, and everybody has a very different opinion or a different view of what's wrong [laughs]! And because it's so different, I think it's so individual. I think it's really a case-by-case kind of thing. I think, you know, some women feel like there are just a lot of bad men out there. It's a problem with men, and it's a problem with the city. It could be the city—just that the numbers are skewed in favor of men versus women. So it's a very challenging question. But I think I find that . . . I'm also very picky. And I think that I have—I think my [role] models have given me very high standards. I have my father, and he's been a great, positive presence and just an admirable figure. And I think that it's just hard to find somebody that matches up.

Although Clarissa found it difficult to "settle" for a man who could not measure up to her father, she also explained how her educated Latina mother had influenced her priorities.

I think that my mother's generation, the baby boomer generation, is all about empowering women. You don't have to get married. You don't have to have children. You have your career, your self-worth. You can do whatever men can do. But then I told my mother—I think I must have been around thirty-four, thirty-five—I was saying, "I'm screwed! I'm not going to find anybody, and I'm not going to be able to have children." I think that her major concern, and my father's major concern, is that I would have gotten pregnant before I had all the opportunities to do what

I eventually ended up doing. That was a far, far bigger priority than the possibility of being infertile at the age of thirty-eight, thirty-nine.

When Clarissa shared her fertility concerns, her mother tried to calm her, telling Clarissa that she had "five good years" left in which to have a baby. But Clarissa was totally unsure of her fertility status. She blamed herself for being "such a poor science student," and she blamed her gynecologist for providing "no information whatsoever."

The turning point for Clarissa came when she read a *Bloomberg Businessweek* article about a high-powered corporate businesswoman, Brigitte Adams, who was still single and had frozen her eggs at the age of thirty-nine.[1] This was Clarissa's introduction to the topic of egg freezing, and she was excited. Even though her younger sister disapproved, citing the Catholic Church's argument that egg freezing is "unnatural," Clarissa's close friend with age-related infertility problems urged Clarissa to move quickly.

Clarissa had plenty of money in the bank, as she had received a $110,000 legal settlement after barely surviving a medication-induced blood clot. For Clarissa, this brush with death, followed by a legal win, felt like a "sign for egg freezing." So she forged ahead, spending $19,000 on two successful egg freezing cycles and banking a total of twenty-five eggs at age thirty-seven. Her frozen eggs felt to her like "insurance, available if needed." Overall, Clarissa found the egg freezing experience to be "very liberating," because, as she put it, "You know that you don't have to be in a rush and that being thirty-seven doesn't mean so much."

Egg freezing also gave Clarissa peace of mind to put herself "out there again" on the dating scene. Seven years of mostly fruitless online dating had been an "interesting odyssey," according to Clarissa. But she hoped that newer dating apps might give her an edge.

At first it was like torture [*laughs*]! It was like real torture. And I think that the dating market is very local; it feels very domestic. And so I haven't really kind of been enthused about anybody. Well, there have been isolated examples. But I think the most amazing thing is that the online dating scene has evolved so much, and it's become so much better, I think. Like, at first, I did eHarmony, which was very sort of structured, and you had to answer all of these questions, and you had to pay all this money. And it's just like, the sample was pretty—it was just awful. It was really poor—men that lived far away from DC, didn't have very interesting jobs, didn't really have a very interesting profile. And now it's just been getting better and better. You have Tinder, which, you know, people make fun of for being sort of the hookup app, [but] I find it wonderful! It's very representative of the population. You can tailor your profile. You can let people know right away who you are. They let you know very quickly who they are. It's easier to just meet up quickly. There's no sort of beating around the bush and questions, and you're not beholden to this website. It just really allows you to kind of like go on and develop a relationship outside of the platform. It's really just sort of a facilitator app. And then there's this other company called Hinge, and they're trying to get even better than Tinder. . . . They usually give you a batch of like twenty, and then you can't go anymore. So it's not like a time suck. So that's been more pleasant. But, long story short, the dating market is difficult [*laughs*]!

Still, Clarissa was hopeful that her luck had changed. Following months of back-and-forth messaging with "a really smart guy" who was also multilingual, Clarissa had finally arranged a lunch meeting. "So I guess I have a date!" she laughed. Still, she told me that the man in question "fell off the face of the Earth" twice for several weeks, which Clarissa found "really weird": "And now you're gone?" When he reemerged without an apology or explanation, Clarissa was skeptical, but she decided to give him a chance. "Yeah, that's what dating is like," Clarissa sighed. "It's *very* difficult."

Given the vagaries of the DC dating scene, Clarissa, now thirty-eight, took solace in her close circle of friends and the career she enjoyed. But she told me that she no longer harbored any false illusions about the inevitability of marriage or motherhood.

I don't want to feel obliged to get married, because if you do, you could end up in a bad, bad marriage, you know. Better to be alone than to be with the wrong person. Absolutely! I have had a number of friends who've had very unhappy, very unhappy outcomes in Washington, people who have, like, everything going for them. But, you know, the issue that I also see with my friends that are still single is that they just weren't willing to settle. They weren't willing to settle. And they are—it's almost like they have too much going for them, you know. They're in jobs, really fulfilling jobs. They're paid a lot. They travel. They have really interesting colleagues, including male colleagues. I mean, you're with a group of people you find so inspiring or, you know, interesting and fun to be around. And so it's hard to be in a relationship with people who are not in this sort of like bubble. I mean, we single girls don't have to worry about it too much because we enjoy what we do. We kind of get a kick out of all of it. We find that we get a lot of respect at work. We're valued. We get to do kind of awesome things. So, you know, you're getting your butt kicked in the dating market, but you're getting a lot of glory in your job, you know? And I had the experience with a couple of things not working out that were pretty upsetting in the last ten years, and I have to say that going into work was, like, very comforting actually. You know? . . . I think it was a good thing to have my job, because my hunch, my intuition tells me that it can't only be me or my demographic. It's got to be a much wider issue.

Women's Gender Laments

Clarissa was one of the more than fifty single, heterosexual women in the DC metro area who eagerly joined my study. Like Clarissa, these women were bright, interesting, articulate, and insightful and had deep bonds of friendship with women just like them. Yet all of them were missing partners. As one DC woman asked wistfully, "I'm a normal woman who's dateable, so why am I still single?"

The "Why me?" question wafted through my conversations as a leitmotif, including with Clarissa, who had exerted considerable effort in trying to discern the answer. Clarissa was an exceptional analyst, homing in on four key hypotheses.

- *Self-blame*: Is it me? Is it that I love my career too much? Is it that I consider online dating to be torture?
- *Women's higher expectations*: Am I too picky? Are my standards too high? Am I comparing all men to my father? Should I settle for something less?
- *Men's lower commitments*: Why have I only ever had one serious relationship? Why am I getting my "butt kicked" in the dating market? Why don't the men I date commit to me? Have I become too old to keep their interest? Why is it beginning to hurt so much?
- *Missing men*: Why are there so few interesting men on dating sites? Is it because I live in Washington, DC? Why do the numbers seem skewed in favor of men? Is this a wider issue?

Over time, these four lines of inquiry came to capture much of what I learned from other women, too, as they reflected on their singleness. Often with sadness in their voices, women expressed their disbelief that they had somehow "ended up" this way. Most women were frustrated, sometimes anguished, over their inability to find a male partner. They spent much time reflecting on the absence of men in their lives and in the lives of other women they knew.

I came to think of these women's haunting reflections as their *gender laments*. These highly educated American women could only speculate as to why stable relationships with American men today are so difficult to achieve. But without such partnerships, these women had all been thrust into a state of involuntary singleness. To reiterate an important point, 82 percent of the women in my study were single at the time of egg freezing. They were literally *missing men* in their lives, as lovers, husbands, coparents, soul mates, and lifelong companions. Egg freezing was thus being used by these women to *hold on* to their remaining reproductive potential while *holding out* hope that a loving partner might still come along.

Self-Blame and Self-Doubt

Women's gender laments came in many different forms. But the one that troubled me the most is when women blamed themselves for their singleness, having internalized negative judgments, often from men, to the point of self-doubt. For example, a year into my study, I met an impressive woman named Aziza, who nonetheless vacillated between moments of self-deprecation and sarcasm as she shared her painful relationship history with me. An academic physician at an elite East Coast medical school, Aziza was highly specialized in two separate fields of medicine. But she had reached her midthirties without a partner, because, as she explained to me, her one-and-only physician boyfriend had callously rejected her, clearly affecting her morale.

AZIZA: So I have a very limited relationship history. I've had one boyfriend, and I've dated very little.

MARCIA: Okay.

AZIZA: Very little. I mean, I think maybe I'm just really ugly or something. You know, I've always thought, like, I'm not a very pretty

person, you know. So that could be it. I don't know. So I haven't dated
very much.

MARCIA: Well, I have to tell you, after your last comment, . . . I have to
tell you, you are not ugly. You are pretty. You *are* pretty.

AZIZA: No need to build my confidence or anything. I'm fine.

MARCIA: No, I am not kidding. You are a very pretty woman. So
do not say that you are not pretty. That is not true. Really, I'm
saying that honestly to you. You look really good. So, at any rate,
something beyond your looks is, you know, getting in the way of
your having relationships, which, you know, I guess that's sort of
where we ended. You haven't had that many relationships. That's
right?

AZIZA: Just one boyfriend, and it was like—it was like my first week of
fellowship, and he was just like—he really liked me. And we started
going out. And then that was it.

MARCIA: So did that last for a while?

AZIZA: No, only a year.

MARCIA: Because you moved apart or something?

AZIZA: He told me I wasn't good enough for him and that he could do
better.

MARCIA: Oh, no! That's a terrible—that's terrible.

AZIZA: He could do better. He was like almost perfect, so, like, he
could do better.

MARCIA: Oh, but, no. That's not the right thing for him to say. Did he
go on and—

AZIZA: I actually don't have a problem with him saying it. It was
the truth. It was how he felt, and, I mean, that's the truth. There's
no blinder than the truth, you know? He could do better. He was
smarter than me, looked better than me. Like, everything was better
than me, so he felt like he could.

MARCIA: Oh my God! Did he go on to like meet and marry somebody
else?

AZIZA: Yeah, he married some blond nurse.

MARCIA: Oh God. But that's like such a cliché, right?

AZIZA: I mean, she—I don't know her, so—so, um, you know, I don't
know what else to say.

MARCIA: Yeah, yeah. Oh that's—that's heartbreaking.

Although I felt outrage that such a talented and attractive woman (with especially beautiful long black hair) could be treated this way, Aziza seemed to have accepted the cold realities of the dating world. She had not given up all hope, but neither was she optimistic about the future of finding a partner.

Like, you know, if you can't find someone, I mean, let's be honest: the only reason why I did this egg freezing is because I hadn't found someone, and so that's why I froze my eggs, you know? If I found a man, I'd move to Alaska! But most men don't want relationships. They just want to meet and date. And most women won't go out with the check-stand dude, but men will. So I think I have about a 0.9 percent chance of meeting someone. And meanwhile, I was feeling like, "OMG, my biological clock, it's ticking, it's ticking, it's ticking," you know? So, even though I'm 1,000 percent happy I did it [egg freezing], it felt somewhat like a defeat. I felt like I gave up, because I couldn't find a man.

Feelings of defeat and failure were shared by other women who had experienced various forms of male rejection. For example, Kimberly, who had recently moved from the East Coast to Chicago to take a major management position, admitted to long-term, deep-seated feelings of womanly inadequacy.

I've been successful in my life professionally, academically. I graduated the top of my class in high school, graduated the top of my class in college. I have done very well professionally. And this is one part of my life that has never gone—it's sort of like, What's wrong with me? And I've dealt with this sort of awkwardness, like there is something wrong with me. So I think that it wasn't about putting the professional part first; it was more, "Oh my God! My life is passing me by, and I haven't been fortunate enough to find a man that wants to bear—have children with me." I think for me it's more my sense of inadequacy—inadequacy, in the sense of being forty-five and never being married, that a man didn't—or I wasn't fortunate enough to have met someone who really wanted to grab me up. Yeah, like, sometimes if you're in a room and everyone's hooked up except for you—now I know that not everyone's in happy marriages, but it's still, if you look around and go, from a social perspective, What's wrong with me? Yeah, it's just been something that's haunted me since I was sixteen, when the boys didn't like me. It's just a life theme.

In other cases, women blamed themselves for their choices, for example, that they were attracted to the wrong "type" of man or that they had chosen a challenging career that had somehow detracted from their love lives. For example, Melissa, a youthful-looking, thirty-five-year-old founder of her own Silicon Valley tech start-up, admitted that she was most attracted to alpha-male "founder" types. But Melissa had had her heart broken twice, including by her last boyfriend, who left her the day after her egg retrieval. Melissa explained why alpha males often "bristle" at alpha females like her.

Founders are crazy people, who are very, like, "take on the world," similar values to me. Of course, not really great husband material . . . because they knew that their career was number one, and so therefore . . . they need someone not focused on their career. . . . And then also, they don't want to have someone who challenges them. It takes, I think, a special type of man who wants more out of a relationship, more out of a marriage, to want to be intellectually stimulated and have somebody who pushes back and enhances your life in that way. But I think they just want somebody who fits into their lives, and that's not me. And, well, I think it's hard to not think that there's something wrong with me, because it's hard at this age, because I want it so badly. I want marriage so badly. I want kids so badly. To think like it's not like work, where I tried so hard, I could make it happen. And if I tried so hard, like, why can't I make this person love me? So I think I have some self-esteem issues there. So yeah. I mean, it's not for lack of trying.

Almost without exception, women in this study were "trying hard" to find a loving partner, primarily through the online dating sites that have become a ubiquitous means of meeting and mating. For example, Clarissa had tried eHarmony, Tinder, and Hinge. But I also heard a great deal about OKCupid, Match, Bumble, JDate (for Jewish singles), The League (for Ivy League graduates), and LDS Planet (for Mormon singles). Women sometimes blamed themselves for not putting enough "energy" into online dating or for "giving up" because of the "crap that goes with it." Although a few women in this study had met nice men online, most had not, with one woman describing her online adventures as an "epic fail." Clarissa, for her part, described seven years of "real torture" in an online "odyssey" that had yet to produce any real results. Most women complained that online dating was a huge time sink, almost like interviewing for a "second job" that was "overwhelming," "exhausting," and "anything but fun." Some women had even hired online dating "consultants" to help them shape their profiles in such a way as to increase the number of "hits" and make the task seem less onerous.

Many women felt the need to alter aspects of themselves in their online profiles, for example, by deleting some of their educational credentials to make themselves seem less intimidating to men. But one aspect that was not alterable was age. Mei, a physician who had undertaken egg freezing at age thirty-seven, described the "online ageism" of men who tend to "screen out" women in their late thirties, leading to feelings of self-doubt and shame. "It's easy to start feeling a little humiliated sometimes, just because, you know, you don't want to be like so many of the portrayals of the 'cougars,' the desperateness. They're always high strung and kind of bossy and Type A. They're always running around trying to catch the man. You know? It's this neurotic kind of crazy person. And so, you know, it is scary initially, to feel like you might be typecast like that, like, 'What's wrong with me?'"

Like Mei, many women could not help but feel that they were somehow to blame for their situations. This negative discourse of self-blame has been called out and questioned by author Sarah Eckel in an insightful book called *It's Not You: 27 (Wrong) Reasons You're Single* (2014). Eckel argues that single women are expected to "pick apart their personalities," often with the encouragement of the people around them, to answer the question, "What's wrong with you?" But Eckel critiques the very question, as well as the twenty-seven answers often given to explain women's singleness (for example, "you're too intimidating," "you're too desperate," "you're too old"). Women in my study routinely wrestled with these kinds of self-doubts, feeling that they might somehow be responsible for their own singleness. But the question they asked most often of themselves is whether they might be "too picky," as if their own high expectations for relationship satisfaction were somehow to blame.

Women's Higher Expectations

Clarissa was one of these women who described herself as "very picky" and wondered whether her unrealistic expectations of men might be the reason why she was still single at the age of thirty-eight. Clarissa attributed her high standards to both her father and her mother—her father by virtue of his excellent role modeling and her mother by virtue of her feminist messaging. Like Clarissa, many women in this study had close relationships with their fathers, who, as we will see, were often their daughters' most stolid egg freezing supporters. But mothers were often women's major influences, instilling in their daughters high expectations for themselves, their careers, and their relationships.

These Gen X and millennial women often told me that they had been raised to believe in gender equality and egalitarian relationships at work and at home. Thus, they hoped to partner with a man who was their equal in every way—educated, professionally accomplished, and committed to similar interests and life goals, including getting married and having children. Searching for this egalitarian relationship with a male "soul mate" could take time and effort. But it was seen as important for achieving relationship fulfillment and ultimate happiness.

It is important to note that the women in this study were not necessarily looking for a "better" partner, one more accomplished or financially successful than themselves. These women had largely achieved the highest levels of education and career success. Thus, the chance of these women marrying "up" with even more successful men—a phenomenon known in anthropology as "hypergamy"—was highly unlikely. What these women wanted were "equal" partners, ones who "matched" them on both social and emotional levels. Gail, a Manhattan filmmaker who froze her eggs at age thirty-five, explained what an equal relationship meant to her.

I just recently came to realize, okay, now that I'm thirty-six, that I am now one of those people that I looked at in my twenties and wondered, "What's wrong with them? Why don't they have a partner?" And I'm now thinking that my perception of what's out there is so different. I just want to have a rich partnership with someone who's intellectually and personally and physically stimulating. And I don't meet them very often. I do meet plenty of options, but I mean, yeah, I have a very limited pool of what I'm looking for. I want someone who wants to have a family now, someone who's driven and successful and has their priorities together in terms of their career, but also someone who's not intimidated by the fact that I'm the same. And I don't blame them for feeling that way, because . . . we put out a very conflicting message, which is, "I am a strong woman. I can do everything for myself, and I don't need a partner." But I *do* want a partner, and I *do* want a fulfilling relationship and partnership that lasts and a family. I'm not super vulnerable, you know, on the surface, when it comes to connecting with men. So I don't think they know what to do with us [*laughs*]! I mean, I don't get hit on very often any more, and the funny thing is, it's only by not-so-bright men. But for men of the same educational-slash-professional level? Yeah, it's almost never.

Women were very clear that finding this equal partner became more and more difficult over time, especially as women reached their late thirties. Lindsay, a political consultant in Washington, DC, explained the problem in this way.

I think the more women take care of themselves and let themselves get better with who they are, the more picky they are about the type of men they're willing to accept, and we can't be as picky the older we get. But the problem is you become wiser and you love yourself more the older you get. And then it's kind of like an inverse relationship. So it's hard, right? You don't want to settle because you want the best person you can be with, because you're becoming a better person every year. And you want a better person, too, but the better people have been taken in that age group, so that's why it's hard.

Women's fears of "settling," or committing to the "wrong person," were ubiquitous. Women had observed other people's bad marriages, including those of friends, family members, and sometimes their own parents, and they did not want to repeat the same mistake. They also did not want to settle out of "desperation" to have children. Sydney, a tech entrepreneur, explained how easily this could happen: "Settling is when the biological clock really weighs on your relationship decisions. I was beginning to prefer men who looked like they might be good dads, but they were men who weren't challenging to me. My personal attraction preferences were being trumped by security."

For many women, settling also meant "dating down" to less educated or less successful men, a phenomenon in anthropology known as "hypogamy." Women characterized such hypogamous relationships as fraught with "intimidation" on the part of men, who were generally emasculated by a woman's superior professional status, living situation, or earnings. Indeed, feelings that men were inevitably intimidated by successful women ran deep among women in this study. For example, Aneela, a finance director at a major Silicon Valley firm, described how her perceptions of men's intimidation had taken a toll on her.

> I try to be optimistic with everything, but I do think when you are—if I call myself a sort of successful woman, and you know, finding that combination of intelligence and attraction . . . I hate to say that men are intimidated. It's interesting. I find myself downplaying myself a lot. I'm not going to lie, you know. And I struggle with that a little bit. . . . There are some men who love that there's a strong woman out there. I don't know. I think he would have to be someone who is just equally or more successful than I and who's confident in his own skin.

Aneela was not the only one who felt that she had to "downplay" her qualities in order to assuage men's threatened egos. Carmen, an economist for an international banking organization, was also encouraged by her friends to keep her PhD off her online profile so as not to discourage men from meeting up with her. "For years, I didn't put my education, because it looked pretentious. So I went on four dates or something. But then men just like jumped in their seats when they realized [I] have a PhD. And some of them were worse than others. One of them said, like, 'What do you mean? To start with, you are more intelligent than I am?' And I was like, 'Oh my God!'"

In general, tacit or unconscious societal expectations of women's hypergamy (marrying "up") and men's hypogamy (marrying "down") were not favoring these highly educated women. In most societies, including the US, one could argue, women are expected to marry up to men who are somewhat older, more educated, and more successful with regard to salary and social standing. But for these high-achieving, highly accomplished women already "at the top," marrying up meant hitting a glass ceiling. Marrying down was also fraught, given that most men appeared uncomfortable pairing up with more educated, successful, or intelligent women. Moreover, women noted that most men were very "ageist," preferring to marry down to younger women, rather than to women in their late thirties or early forties who might place immediate pressure on a partner to have children.

Ultimately, finding an equal man, one who was educated, ego secure, and wanting to marry and parent with a strong woman age-mate, was the primary goal of most of these women. But, as we will see, women complained that finding such an equal partner was extraordinarily difficult—the equivalent of searching for a "unicorn," or an imaginary being who does not exist.

Men's Lower Commitments

Establishing an egalitarian relationship with an equal partner was extremely challenging, women told me, because of men's lower commitments to the family building project. Although I did not interview men directly for this study—and thus must emphasize that I cannot fairly represent their side of the story—I did spend hundreds of hours listening to women's gender laments, including their perception that men of their own generation had become much less committed to marriage and parenthood. They sometimes used the expression "commitment phobia" or "attachment phobia" to describe men's unwillingness to settle down. This was especially true of men who had lived through their own parents' divorces. These "children of divorce" were afraid of being hurt or of hurting a woman, I was told, and thus tended to avoid close attachments at all costs.

Beyond these cases of commitment phobia, women were simply uncertain that American men of their generation shared the same desires and life goals. Women pointed out that men were not necessarily socialized by their parents or peers to want egalitarian relationships with highly educated professional women, with whom they could balance the burdens and responsibilities of family life. Furthermore, many women had observed that men no longer needed marriage or fatherhood to achieve feelings of masculine fulfillment. Men's primary commitments were often elsewhere—to work, business ventures, friendships, travel, recreation, and perhaps to their nieces and nephews rather than to children of their own. Eleanor, a Manhattan journalist who had frozen her eggs at age thirty-five, had much to say on this subject.

> Of the people lately that I've met, who *I've* wanted to be in a relationship with, they haven't wanted to be in a relationship with anybody. Like, they just want to not have that kind of obligation. So I think it's like they don't want to be emotionally responsible for another person. That's what I find to be the particular challenge—that there *are* men out there, you know,

but the ones who are single in my age group don't want a relationship. And there are ones who do, but the ones that I've met lately don't. It's really interesting. I mean, I was talking about this with some of my cousins recently, and all of us are thinking about our fathers and how there are so many things that are different today, like tons of things that are different today. But one of them is that for our fathers, being a father and having a family was huge, you know. And I don't think they imagined anything else. But I think that a lot of men today—and I can tell you, like, I've met *many* of them, and some of them are my friends, too, who are in their midthirties, late thirties, early forties—like, they just, they don't have that same sense that they need to be a father or they need to have a partner in order to fulfill whatever dreams they have or, you know, to be who they want to be.

Women on the West Coast complained about a particular version of this problem, which they called the "Peter Pan syndrome." According to them, Peter Pans are "man-children" who never grow up. They are often successful, well-to-do, venture capitalist types, who have lots of "toys" (such as cars, boats, and ski cabins) and want to delay marriage indefinitely, while "playing the field" with multiple women and never committing to any of them. They may be "polyamorous," having multiple "open" relationships with primary, secondary, and even tertiary female partners. According to Simone, a graduate student and one of the few stably partnered women in my study, these polyamorous Peter Pans were the bane of her single friends' existence in the Bay Area. "A lot of men here, they're not ones that I would introduce my single friends to! Because my friends, they all want to be in a monogamous relationship that will hopefully have children. They're not interested in dating someone who long term wants to have other relationships as well. And that's a real thing here, which is totally a choice. But my friends who want families are not really interested in those."

Indeed, women from California took the time to educate me about the different "types" of men that they regularly encountered in their social worlds. Not only did I hear a great deal about Peter Pans, but I was also told repeatedly by women in the male-dominated Silicon Valley tech world that "the odds are good, but the goods are odd." They explained that men in tech are often very socially awkward and low on "emotional intelligence." But these men may also try to compensate by acting "hip" and by asserting their polyamorous and bisexual preferences. One woman,

Whitney, a journalist who had tried hard to date many of these IT "nerds," joked with me, "I'm still hoping that the miracle worker, the spaceship will land, the bright guy will walk out. But I've been on so many goddamn date lists, I've met everyone in California!"

Single women in California also complained about the "beta males," or men lacking in ambition and unable to fulfill the roles normally assumed by adult men in society. Beta males came in many different forms. For example, some could be "surfer dudes," who preferred to "chill" and enjoy life rather than to commit to a woman or found a family. Others came from wealthy families and lacked ambition because they were living off their trust funds. On the other end of the spectrum, some of these beta males were barely getting by, as they were unwilling or unable to hold steady jobs and were living with friends or, in some cases, their parents, given the high cost of housing in California.

From domineering alpha males to underachieving beta males to over-stretched polyamorists to Peter Pans who never grow up, women described the many types of men to be assiduously avoided, as revealed in their rich lexicon of terms in table 1.1. These types of men were generally not interested in marriage and children. If they were, they would not necessarily choose to mate with an accomplished professional woman who might outearn or outperform them. Love, marriage, and parenthood, the traditional trifecta of heteronormative family life, were no longer seen as men's main ideals. Thus, women could hold out for a rare unicorn, but finding one was not guaranteed.

While women on the West Coast complained about the "arrested development" of the men they encountered, women on the East Coast complained about the dearth of men in the cities where they lived. They explained that men of their own backgrounds, namely, single, heterosexual, college-educated professionals with successful careers, were simply missing from the local population. This was especially true in New York City and Washington, DC, cities where, as one woman put it succinctly, "the caliber of women is just higher than the caliber of guys."

Martha, who had left a position in a federal agency in Washington, DC, to take a job in California, found the number of "dateable" men far superior on the West Coast. Before moving, she had learned through a news report that Washington, DC, and Baltimore, Maryland, "have the highest ratio of women to men in the country." Thus, she knew it was time to leave.

TABLE 1.1. Ten Types of Men: Women's Lexicon

Type	Definition	Sayings	Women's thoughts
1. Alpha males	Men with high ambition, who are workaholics, putting career over marriage; they marry younger, trophy wives, not career-oriented alpha females like themselves	"They want to be challenged by work, not by their partners."	"Those kinds of men don't want women like me. When I come home from a long day at work, they don't want to talk about work or other things that are equally, like, serious. They just want to hear about, like, you know, the yoga class that you took and just, 'I want it to be easy. I want to be, like, in control.' So, you know, I think a lot of men feel like they want somebody who's an equal, but in reality, they'd rather be the dominant partner."
2. Beta males	Men with low ambition, who are happy to be taken care of by a woman who is the dominant partner in the relationship	"They're just 'floating along' in life. They're portable."	"A beta male is one that's going to follow you around or who's got a portable career. I lose respect for that person if I feel like I can manipulate them. You know, and the other thing is, what I'm looking for in a relationship is not to take on more responsibility. I'm like a hyperresponsible person right now. I don't want to take on somebody else. I want somebody to help me with my responsibilities. And so, if it's somebody who's not a strong force, who cannot, like, help me in certain ways, you know, I don't need that. And I don't find that attractive."
3. Feminist men	Men who claim they are feminist but do not pitch in, pay, or help out, all in the name of gender equality	Men who say, "I'm not old-fashioned like that!"	"It's really convenient. You guys want to be feminist, and then you want us to pay for your dinner and open doors for you. But then they really don't end up doing anything. I think very few of them are on purpose doing it, but I think that they are convinced that that's the way it should be. And then in many ways, I think it also emasculates them, because they essentially are not contributing anything to the relationship."
4. Foreign Service men	Elite White men who are diplomats and who want a stay-at-home wife to raise their children; they don't want to marry a woman in the Foreign Service	"Yale, pale, and male"	"They have a stay-at-home spouse that supports them. I mean, the Foreign Service is still an institution that hasn't evolved with America. And so it is kind of like this old school. There's more diversity on Wall Street than I've seen in serious foreign policy decisions."

(*Continued*)

TABLE 1.1. (*cont.*)

Type	Definition	Sayings	Women's thoughts
5. Peter Pans	Men who are prolonging their adolescence, sometimes well into their forties and beyond, with no immediate plans for marriage	"Men who never want to grow up"	"So, when I meet a lot of older guys, particularly who have never been married, I realize it's because they have this sort of Peter Pan syndrome, where somehow to grow up has a negative connotation, to be grown up. The men are just like, 'I'm going to be young forever! Yay.'"
6. Polyamorous men	Men who want more than one relationship, claiming that their multiple attachments to women are all "committed"	"A fetish subculture, especially in the [San Francisco] Bay Area, where it's cool to say you're polyamorous"	"Like, you know, I'm not interested in that. And I think I'm pretty particular about selecting against things like that. So I have never been on a date with someone who's been like, 'Oh, by the way, I'm polyamorous.' I do get a sense that there's some implication that people who feel uncomfortable in, like, stable, one-on-one relationships would feel more comfortable sort of spreading themselves out."
7. Start-up men	Men, particularly in California, who wait to marry until their start-up succeeds	Men who say, "I have this idea that's going to change the world!"	"One nice thing about California is everyone's super idealistic, like, 'I'm going to pursue my dreams and start a company, blah blah blah.' And the truth is, obviously, 95 percent of them don't. So they expect the woman to make the bacon, come home, cook it, clean up, and you know."
8. Tech men	Men who are overrepresented in the tech industry but are not good to date or marry; they tend to be awkward men with low emotional intelligence	"The odds are good, but the goods are odd."	"The downside of the majority of men being tech workers [where I work] is that it sucks; [tech] certainly selects for . . . a certain type of emotional immaturity [which] tends to be overrepresented . . . like, people who are kind of socially awkward, have trouble communicating. So the emotional intelligence piece, also, I think, narrows the field."
9. Unicorns	Men who want age-appropriate, equal relationships with women and are interested in marriage and a family	"That pool doesn't exist."	"I wish I had a superpower so everyone could find one. I would like to help everyone find their soul mates, because if I was able to do that, then I'd bring about world peace, because everybody would be so happy to think about the amazing things they could do in the world, because they would no longer be focused on themselves, 'cause they were such happy people and fulfilled."

Type	Definition	Sayings	Women's thoughts
10. Younger men	Men who no longer believe in dating and don't know how to do it	"They only know how to meet on-line and hook up with women."	"Overall, younger people tend to be single, so I often end up dating guys who are younger, and they literally will say to me—one said dating is 'anachronistic.' Another said, 'I've never dated my entire life.' They actually are kind of interested in it when I say, 'I would like you to call me and ask me somewhere. You don't have to take me to France or to Paris but just invite me some-where and spend time with me.' I think people don't know how to do that anymore."

In DC, I got the sense that men kind of see women as disposable—like "easy come, easy go" or kind of "a dime a dozen"—and they have lots of options. So I got the impression that it was really hard to find men who really valued a woman as a partner, because they felt like they had so many options. And I think there's more of a patriarchal social attitude on the East Coast than on the West Coast, where it's more of an egalitarian approach to a relationship in general. And it's not just me. Many of the female friends in my age group have also moved to find mates elsewhere.

Women who were still living in Washington often suspected that the female-to-male gender ratio was "off," with many more highly educated women than men in the local population. Olivia, a scientist who worked for the federal government, described the imbalance.

You know, it's funny. I'm living in DC, and we joke about this in Washing-ton. It's like I know a lot of really brilliant, amazing women. The friends of mine who do have partners did not meet their partners here. They met them in graduate school, and they married them like right after grad school, and then they moved here. Because when you read the statistics on DC, there are, you know, like 60 percent women and 40 percent men and all this horrible stuff. And I know *lots* of amazing women scientists. Literally, [where I work] I can point out, like, all of our names are on the website. I mean we're all on there, right? And I can point out to you how many of them are single and amazing and are in their thirties, right, and are single and have probably been single for a long time, actually, or have dated for a while and then broken up or whatever. And that's just how DC is. It's not uncommon. Like, a very close friend of mine who got her PhD from Harvard and is doing something amazing here in DC, you know, she just had a kid on her own. And she just kind of, she just got a sperm donor and just did the whole thing and just had her kid last year. And that's actually, I think, something that I had thought about doing. But the egg freezing was a pathway that I was willing to go down, I'll say, because then I could continue to date and still hope that I find someone.

Like Olivia, many women living in Washington, DC, said that they found few single men of their own age who were eager to partner and have children. Men who were available were more often older, divorced, and, if they had children, reluctant to have any more. Or they were incompatible in other ways, often based on marked differences in educational background. In general, single, thirty-something women described Washington, DC, as a "hard dating town." Indeed, their overall appraisal was quite negative. They called Washington, DC, the "Hollywood for Ugly People," the "Hollywood for Nerds," where "a lot of women are catches," but the city is filled with "short men on ego trips who go into politics." Others said that the city is "miserable," a place "so hard to find a guy," where "every man turns rude and gross when they're forty." Although there are plenty of "really cool women," there are definitely "no cool guys" in DC, as women explained. So it's a "depressing place," one woman lamented, with "so many single women," who are "all a little negative."

This notion that educated and eligible men were missing from the overall population was shared by women in New York City as well. "The City," as it is often called, was described by women as a "really hard" place to date. Women described the single heterosexual men in their thirties as "not ready to have a family," "not mature enough to have a family," and "not wanting the responsibility." Men in their thirties and even early forties were described as still enjoying "that party life," "going out like teenagers," and "living like college frat bros." New York City was described as "full of amazing women in their thirties," who are "still single, beautiful, smart, and capable." But "guys feel like they've hit the jackpot—so why should they settle?"

Angela, a New York City–based architect who had "lived" this scenario for more than a decade, described her troubled dating life with both pathos and humor.

The last thing I want to do is, like, drop my work and go out to a bar and hope I meet somebody. You know, prioritizing meeting people feels so in-authentic when you're just going to a place because you hope maybe you're going to find your husband there. And when you get there and it's all girls, you're like, ugh! I don't like that experience. It feels like I'm not really pres-ent. Now I am scratching up the dregs, savoring them, while I wait for the divorces to release some decent men so I can have a turn. But the pick-ings are slim! I've gone on a couple dates recently, and you know, this guy smoked two packs of cigarettes a day for twenty years, quit a couple years ago, is now sober for eight years, and he's a rock-and-roll star or a rock-and-roll singer. And he sends me all these intense, heavy-metally tracks. Like, really? This is what I have? If I could teach a daughter one thing it would be, "Snatch up one of those uninjured, healthy, ambitious college boys! And save a couple hundred thousand dollars! Have babies pronto!"

The Mating Gap

Insightful women like Angela sense that something is "wrong" with the ratio of men to women in the cities where they live, although few of them can put their finger on the exact nature of the problem. But as seen in their narratives, these women are literally facing a *mating gap*, in which men characterized by *three e's—eligible, educated, and equal*—are literally missing as potential male partners. Where are all of these missing men, who should presumably want to mate with the United States' most edu-cated women? Should the mating gap be taken for granted as a "natural fact" of educated women's lives? These are haunting questions, ones that require answers and ideally some solutions.

To understand the magnitude of this American mating gap, it is impor-tant to emphasize that only about one-third (36 percent) of US adults age twenty-five or older are fully college educated with a bachelor's degree or higher, an increase from 29.9 percent a decade before.[2] With only about one-third of Americans having graduated from college, women who are highly educated, with bachelor's degrees and beyond, are facing what might best be described as an American *college education deficit*, in which two-thirds of American adults have missed out on opportunities to either start or complete a college education.

But beyond the overall deficit in highly educated Americans, a growing gender gap in college education has also emerged. In the prescient book,

Date-onomics: How Dating Became a Lopsided Number Game (2015), author Jon Birger analyzes US census data to describe the growing gender gap in college education. To wit, American women have been attending college at higher rates than men since the 1980s and at much higher rates since the 1990s. Thus, by 2012, the same year that egg freezing was introduced to the American population, 34 percent more women than men graduated from US four-year colleges, or four women for every three men. The number was even higher at the United States' private colleges and universities, where 50 percent more women graduated than men, or three women for every two men. Furthermore, for every thirteen women who graduated and went on to earn an advanced degree that year, only ten men did the same.

These skewed gender ratios translate into 5.5 million college-educated American women in their twenties (ages twenty-two to twenty-nine) for only 4.1 million college-educated American men. This is a ratio of 4:3. For those in their thirties (ages thirty to thirty-nine), there are 7.4 million college-educated American women for only 6.0 million college-educated American men. This is a ratio of 5:4. Adding the two groups together, there are nearly three million more college-educated American women than college-educated men between the ages of twenty-two and thirty-nine, the period that could best be described as women's prime childbearing years.

Birger himself calls this situation the "man deficit," one that involves a "massive undersupply" of college-educated men and a corresponding "oversupply" of non-college-educated men in the US population. This man deficit continues to grow from year to year as young women continue to matriculate and graduate from four-year colleges and universities at much higher rates than men. As of 2018, the year in which ASRM issued its supportive statement about planned egg freezing, the educational disparity in the US had grown to 27 percent more women in US higher education that year than men.[3]

Although these educated man deficits exist across the country, including in many parts of the rural US, Birger notes that they are most acute in major East Coast cities, including, from north to south, New York City and all of its surrounding suburbs (including in New Jersey); Philadelphia, Pennsylvania; Washington, DC; Charlotte, North Carolina, and the Research Triangle area (Raleigh–Durham–Chapel Hill); Atlanta, Georgia; and Miami, Florida. In these eastern cities, educated professional women now outnumber educated professional men by the thousands. For example, New York City alone has one hundred thousand more college-educated women than men under the age of thirty-five. Of educated women between the ages of thirty and thirty-nine in Manhattan, 50 percent have never been married. And with regard to the college-educated male population, 9 to 12 percent are gay. Among heterosexual New York men, 39 percent admit to cheating on their partners.[4]

According to Birger, such urban gender disparities lead to a "bad dating market for college-educated women."[5] Although urban professional women pour considerable time and energy into online dating, as we have seen, online dating sites have created a limitless marketplace of options for college-educated men, who, as Birger found, can "keep their options open" and "play the field." Indeed, Birger warns that "these lopsided gender ratios may add up to a sexual nirvana for heterosexual men, but for heterosexual women—especially those who put a high priority on getting married and having children in wedlock—they represent a demographic time bomb."[6]

Birger also notes that because educational "intermarriage" is less common today than at any point over the past half century, many educated women who have not married by their thirties will be unable to find educated partners. To overcome this mating gap, he offers three solutions: first, to get more young men back into college; second, to encourage women to move to "woman-friendly" western states, such as Colorado, Utah, or Alaska, where the male-to-female gender ratio is reversed; and third, to get women to accept what he calls "mixed-collar marriages." Indeed, Birger opines in *Date-onomics* that "if there were one investable idea to come out of this book, it would involve setting up a dating agency or online dating site that breaks through social barriers and matches college-educated women with appealing, non-college-educated men."[7] In his new book, *Make Your Move: The New Science of Dating and Why Women Are in Charge* (2021), Birger urges women to be bold in their dating lives and to initiate romances with men, including mixed-collar matches that might otherwise seem unlikely.

Mixed-Collar Mating

In my own study, there *were* a handful of women who had made these bold moves. Kimberly, whom we met earlier, was one of these women. She had already moved from the East Coast to the Midwest and had recently moved in with her fifty-something, ex-military, working-class, divorced boyfriend with two children. Kimberly could not say enough good things about her blue-collar partner, who had never gone to college. He was not intimidated by Kimberly, and he made her feel good about herself, telling her how crazy he was about her and how he could not believe his good fortune. Kimberly also described him as politically progressive, smart, athletic, kind, upbeat, and a fabulous cook. Having never dated a working-class man before, Kimberly thought that her partner might be "unusual." But she was immensely grateful to Match.com for leading her to him.

Although a few other women had made these kinds of mixed-collar matches, most were reluctant to take the plunge by dating "downward." As one woman stated bluntly, "I would never consider marrying someone who hasn't been to college. Like, never! Or even grad school, frankly. That's just not me [laughs]."

Jocelyn, who had spent years working in Congress for a Democratic senator, was less dogmatic, but she still felt quite ambivalent about mixed-collar mating.

I don't have like a visceral negative reaction. I would say, throughout my life, if I'm being honest, I've dated, you know, people who were probably—I don't know what the PC way to say this is—but of like lower economic whatever than myself and my family. When I am looking for a man and I'm going on dates, you know, whatever, I'm not looking at that. I mean, I know that I can take care of myself. I would like to have a partner in life. If it works out that I'm more of a breadwinner, as long as he is confident enough to deal with that. And that is a big "if." Like, you know, there are lots of guys who are uncomfortable with that. You know, like, "Sorry dude!" So I don't have a problem with it. It may, for me, be more a question of like, "Does he just have a four-year degree as opposed to like a graduate degree?" I'm not sure if at the end of the day it matters, [but] I'm just being honest. I'm just not sure I can interact with a lot of people who don't have any college, who, you know, haven't spent any time in college.

In this regard, Jocelyn was fairly typical. She was explicit that she was looking for a life partner, ideally one who was an equal. Jocelyn worried about dating down to a man who was less educated and less successful than herself. She feared that he would be uncomfortable looking up to her and her accomplishments and that she would have trouble interacting with him on equal terms. But Jocelyn also realized that the DC dating scene was wretched. She sighed, "DC is so super hard. It just makes me want to cry in my corner." Not wanting to become a single mother either—a move that Jocelyn admitted "also scares the shit" out of her—she did what other women in this study did. She froze her eggs, a grand total of thirty-five over two cycles, while hoping that the right man might still come along.

Bridging the Gap through Egg Freezing

In today's world, the mating gap is the underlying reason why so many highly educated American women are involuntarily single in their late thirties and why so many of these single, thirty-something women are unable to achieve the three *p*'s of partnership, pregnancy, and parenthood. Without committed reproductive partners, women in their late thirties find themselves facing a gap between their reproductive desires and their reproductive realities, for which egg freezing now serves as a kind of protective bridging technology.

Indeed, educated single women like Jocelyn are turning to egg freezing as a technological solution to the mating gap problem. This mating gap, I argue, is *the* major driver of egg freezing across the US. Egg freezing has become highly educated women's way to *bridge the gap*, helping them to preserve their fertility, and their dignity, too, while waiting for an eligible, educated, and equal partner to come along. Whether most educated American women will find these partners, the rare "unicorns" who are still available in the thirty-something population, remains an open question. As seen in Kimberly's story, mixed-collar mating with less educated men and relationships with divorced men, some of whom may already have children, may be the most viable path forward to partnership among single women in their late thirties.

Meanwhile, "to freeze or not to freeze" has become the leading question among some of the United States' most educated women.[8] The IVF clinicians I interviewed from around the country verified this, noting a perpetual increase in such egg freezing inquiries from highly educated professional women, the vast majority of whom had reached their late thirties without a desired partner. As one academic IVF physician based in the Los Angeles area explained it to me, "I actually ask all of my patients who come in, thinking of freezing their eggs, kind of whether it's professional goals or what, what the primary reason is. And almost all of them say that they haven't met the right guy yet. If they had met the right guy, you know, even if their profession is very time-consuming and demanding, they would still, you know, find time to have the kid. And they would still get pregnant, you know, if they had met the right guy."

In other words, American women are not turning to egg freezing because they are *waiting to have children*. Rather, they are *waiting to find a man with whom to have children* and are turning to egg freezing to hold onto that hope. As we have seen, skewed gender dynamics are taking a significant toll on the lives of these educated women, for whom marriage and motherhood are still high priorities. The sadness and incomprehensibility of this situation reverberates throughout women's egg freezing stories, where they lament the ways in which they are missing out on romantic love, companionship, sexual intimacy, and reproductive partnership. A manless world, where professional women find it difficult to meet educated men who are interested in them and willing to commit and, in turn, are themselves unwilling to commit to men who are not educated and do not seem to meet their priorities and expectations, is driving many women into egg freezing, less by choice than by necessity.

Instead of achieving motherhood, these exceptionally well-educated, thirty-something American women find themselves in a poignant position that author Melanie Notkin calls "otherhood"—namely, single and approaching the end of their fertility but without a loving partner in sight.[9] Although egg freezing holds out hope for these women, promising to make mothers out of "others" in a traditional, heterosexual, couples-oriented world, it is a technomedical solution to a much larger social problem involving a mating gap that is growing ever wider.

In the important book *The End of Men and the Rise of Women* (2012), author Hanna Rosin argues that we should be celebrating the amazing achievements of a new generation of highly educated women, while also feeling great concern over men's simultaneous educational decline. Clearly, we need to address why men are falling behind on their educational trajectories. But we also need to understand why many men who *have* completed college are now waiting to marry and become fathers or are opting out of these pathways altogether.

As we saw in Clarissa's opening story and in the stories of many other single women in this chapter, highly educated professional women in the US are facing an enormous mating gap problem, one that is sending them down the path to egg freezing. Egg freezing is, in fact, highly indicative of the difficult choices facing educated American women with regard to partnership and family formation. In chapter 2, we will see another manifestation of this "men as partners" problem, one where once-partnered women undertake egg freezing when their partnerships come undone.

2

The End of Romance

Relationship Trauma and Repair

Lily's Breakup

Lily, a successful art curator, invited me to her spacious office in Lower Manhattan. There, surrounded by colorful art books, we sat and talked for nearly two hours—or, rather, Lily poured out her story. To my listening ears, the relationship breakup that Lily described was quite tragic. But it was clear that she had made peace with her situation. Lily conveyed her story with a healthy dose of laughter and an occasional string of expletives.

Unlike the single women we met earlier, who bemoaned their inability to find a man, Lily had spent nearly a decade with the man whom she still considered to be her soul mate. They had met when she was thirty-one, after she had received her MBA from an Ivy League university and had started her own art business. Her partner, Jack, was a fledgling academic, just beginning his tenure-track assistant professorship in the humanities. Lily told me how much she admired him. "You know, he's like one of the smartest people I've met and funny and so grounded." But then she added, "And, you know, totally flaky and deeply indecisive, from a pathological standpoint."

What exactly "pathological indecisiveness" meant to Lily became clearer and clearer as she revealed her story. Over the first five years of their relationship, Lily occasionally mentioned to Jack that she wanted to have children. But Jack always replied that he was "not ready." Lily was deeply understanding of Jack's predicament.

> He was a professor and an academic, and I don't know if that has any-
> thing particularly to do with it, but I think he just couldn't commit. And I
> wanted to get married and have a kid, and he just couldn't get there in the
> same timeline, [while he] was getting tenure. But you know the life of an

academic: a lot of stress and pressure. . . . The reality is you always have a monkey on your back. . . . It becomes this invasive way of life that sort of permeates your whole existence. Anyway, but maybe that's particular to him.

When Lily turned thirty-six, she felt that it was time to get married, but Jack balked at the idea. He reluctantly agreed to their engagement, but when Lily raised the topic of children again, Jack told her that he was still unready. "He was like, 'I really want it. I see myself with kids, playing ball, and "JJ, get down from there!" In theory, when I close my eyes, it's in the picture, but in reality, I'm totally paralyzed with fear.'" Lily joked, "And so, you know, I was sort of sick of clubbing the baby seal over the head!"

When Lily turned thirty-eight, she and Jack headed to Europe for several months, where Lily made an important decision. "I traveled for like two or three weeks on my own, and during that two or three weeks apart, I went off the Pill, because it was hard for me to do it with him around. Because he was like, 'I'm not ready.' And, you know, I wanted it to be this participatory thing, where both of us decided to have a child together. I was just like, 'Okay, I'm going off the Pill myself.'" When Lily told Jack that she was no longer using contraception, "he wouldn't sleep with [her] for fourteen months." The sexual rejection along with the unwillingness to conceive a baby was especially painful for Lily. As she approached her fortieth birthday, she decided to leave. "So fourteen months, and then I was just over it. Whatever. I think I kissed someone else. It wasn't even about that guy. I realized I emotionally had moved on. There comes a point when you can only take so much, and I had just—not consciously— just realized that and just had to leave."

Contemplating next steps, Lily asked her father what to do. Her father was a physician, who had survived the Holocaust as a boy in Poland. Fiercely dedicated to his only child, he told Lily to freeze her eggs, after doing considerable research on the subject. "And I did, thank goodness," Lily emphasized.

With sixteen frozen eggs in the bank, Lily felt some temporary relief. But she also began dating with the hope of falling in love.

I think I was on Match or one of those for like a short period of time. I had a very strange interaction with one person who basically lied. And it seemed to me that he was in graduate school for architecture at Princeton, and then he was like, "No, I live in Princeton. I'm taking classes in engineering at the local school, and I'm out of work. I'm unemployed." I was like, "Huh? Sorry, I can't meet you today.'" And he left me a ranting message like, "I was clear with you, and I took the train all the way into the city." I was like, "Sorry!" I don't know. I'm on this Ivy League dating thing, but I'm not sure that everyone's really Ivy League. I really don't know. I'm not judgmental about it, but I don't know. I haven't really figured it out, this online dating thing.

By the time I met Lily in her quiet office, surrounded by her beautiful art books, it had been four years since her breakup with Jack, and she was still single at the age of forty-four. Admitting to me, "I feel like, okay, I have no choice," she had decided to pursue motherhood on her own, undergoing IVF with her own "fresh" eggs, donor sperm, and her father's financial help. "But now, you know, I'm forty-four, and this really is a fucking bitch—sorry for the French!" Lily exclaimed. "It's just that getting pregnant is a bitch."

After Lily had told me about her IVF trials and tribulations, I asked Lily if she had any regrets about staying with Jack for so long. Lily was impressively magnanimous toward Jack, even though she blamed him for "fucking up" her ability to have children. This is how our conversation went.

LILY: No, I wish it had worked, because, you know, as life goes on and we get older—this is personal experience, but I've had this discussion with some other smart people that I know, who feel the same way—there are fewer and fewer people in life that I like and want to be around and tolerate and trust. And he is one of those people. I mean, he—

MARCIA: And he still is?

LILY: Yeah, he still is. Totally. Like, I really miss him as like a sounding board and a friend and like laughter, and like he's great. I don't think I did anything wrong. I don't think I could have changed anything. I maybe regret not leaving when he wouldn't get engaged. That's probably what I regret. Because as soon as I left, he was like, "Wait, where are you going? I bought you a ring. Can we hang out?" And I was just like, "What do you mean, 'I bought you a ring. Can I give it to you?' Like, either show up and give it to me and propose and, like, do it, or . . .'" But I really didn't want it at that point. I felt so humiliated by him. I didn't trust that he was going to change. And he's not. Tomorrow he's turning forty-seven. And he's, I think, with this woman for like three or four years, who's under forty. She probably is like thirty-eight, thirty-nine. And my prediction—he was with someone for seven years before me—and my prediction is that he is going to have troubles, or she's going to break up with him, or they're going to start, like—I think they've already started rumbling. But they're going to break up when she's forty, you know, because the girl wants to get married and, like, is freaking out, right? So, I mean, how many times will this happen?

As I left Lily's office that day, feeling deeply unsettled, I could only wonder about the answer to her question. How many other women's reproductive lives would Jack put on hold? Although I never knew the answer, what I did know is how Jack's behavior had hurt Lily.

* * *

I later learned from Lily that she had tried thawing and using her sixteen frozen eggs. And much to my surprise, Jack had actually acceded to Lily's request to donate some of his sperm, perhaps out of his own sense of guilt. But Jack never committed to coparenting with Lily, and he was ultimately relieved of any future obligation when Lily failed to become pregnant. Lily's physicians cited her age as the limiting factor, given that she had frozen her eggs at the age of forty-three. But for her part, Lily considered her story to be a cautionary tale—not only about the "false sense of security" provided by egg freezing but also about "relationship trends in current society," particularly men's lack of commitment. Reflecting on her breakup with Jack, Lily concluded, "I'm telling you, these men over forty who have never been married, there is a reason why, and there is something wrong with them, if you look at it from this perspective of coupling. There is something wrong."

Egg Freezing at the End of Romance

The kind of situation faced by Lily is rarely represented in depictions of egg freezing.[1] As we have seen, egg freezing is most often cast in aspirational terms as a "new hope technology" for single women, so that they can imagine future motherhood while giving themselves time to find and fall in love with equal partners who will become the fathers of their children. Egg freezing in such depictions is about love and romance—a step toward "anticipating coupledom," with the "end goal of bundled marriage and childbearing."[2] Indeed, "the allure of egg freezing," according to some scholars, is that it upholds the possibility of a traditional heterosexual "love story."[3]

That single women are freezing their eggs while looking for love in a prospective, forward-looking manner is an extremely important part of the egg freezing story. But it is not the only one. Here, I want to focus on another major pathway to egg freezing that is decidedly less romantic and more retrospective in nature. Rather than turning to egg freezing in hopeful anticipation, once-partnered women like Lily are turning to this technology in moments of despair, while navigating their ways through the death throes of a failed or failing relationship. Instead of "freezing for love," many women, as we shall see, are undertaking *egg freezing at the end of romance.*

Relationship failure must be understood as one of the major causes of egg freezing. The breakdown of relationships underlies the singleness of many women who freeze their eggs. And it is also the main reason why some married and partnered women are freezing their eggs, often in the midst of significant relationship instability or uncertainty. Egg freezing at the end of romance may involve divorces, marital separations, broken engagements, and breakups from partners. Such relationship endings may be mutually negotiated, peaceful, and ultimately liberating. But more often than not, they are filled with anger and betrayal, trauma and tragedy, disappointment and despair.

Despair, or the loss and absence of hope, is a running theme in many women's egg freezing stories. As they turn to egg freezing at the end of romance, many women ask, "What else am I to do?" In such narratives, egg freezing is no longer cast as a technology of hope but rather as a *technology of despair.* The sense of loss, betrayal, hopelessness, even desperation may be particularly pronounced for women in their late thirties or early forties, who, like Lily, are running out of reproductive time. Losing a relationship at such a critical reproductive juncture represents a significant assault on one's very sense of self and hopes for the future. Speaking of such reproductive disruptions, the medical anthropologist Gay Becker has noted, "In all cultures, the life cycle is structured by expectations about each phase of life, and meaning is assigned to specific life events and the roles that accompany them. Particular emphasis is given to young and middle adulthood because a series of specific life events such as marriage and childrearing usually occur during this life phase and lay the groundwork for the remainder of the life cycle. When expectations about the life course are not met, however, people experience inner chaos and disruption to the fabric of their lives. Such disruptions represent loss of the future."[4]

In this chapter, we will hear the stories of women like Lily, who experienced relationship failure in their mid- to late thirties and early forties. In in-depth interviews, these women shared their "breakup stories," sometimes tearfully and often involving heartbreak, loss, and future uncertainty. Like Lily, women also shared their feelings about their former partners, many of whom were "equal" with regard to age and education but who ended up being the "wrong" partner in one or more crucial ways. Whether women left their partners or their partners left them, these forms of relationship dissolution were often preceded and followed by intense moments of angst and despair, in which women undertook egg freezing in the midst of heartache.

Yet many women were ultimately glad that they had made this life-changing decision to freeze their eggs at the end of romance. For women whose anticipated life-course trajectories had been disrupted or broken, egg freezing provided them with a temporary biological reprieve, allowing them to heal their relationship wounds, recalibrate their sense of identity, and attempt to restructure the future out of their disrupted life courses. Egg freezing also fueled some women's visions for different futures, in which partnership no longer became an end goal. In such cases, egg freezing served as a *technology of repair*, resetting women's biographical trajectories. Although egg freezing may occur at the end of romance, in its aftermath, some women may find new strengths and opportunities, as they reflect on egg freezing and its outcomes.

Relationship Trauma

Lily was among the first women to volunteer for my study. But in a dozen prior interviews, I had already heard about a seven-year relationship with a man who refused to have children; a marriage that ended because of a husband's repeated infidelity; a mentally unstable boyfriend who impregnated his girlfriend then cut off relations with her and the child once it was born; a long-term boyfriend who was unfaithful and impregnated someone else; and a brief marriage that ended because of controlling behavior on the part of the husband, who then sued his wife for spousal support. One after another, these sad and sometimes shocking stories were beginning to form a pattern, one that I had yet to name. But when I interviewed an IVF physician in the southern US, he described his egg freezing patient population in this way, referring to social "shocks" and "traumas" as significant factors in women's decisions.

> Okay, so right now, the profile is a woman age thirty-seven to almost forty, mainly thirties, who has either recently experienced some kind of social shock or trauma, like a divorce or a breakup, or some other kind of loss. Yeah, it's not always a breakup of a relationship. Sometimes these women are in stable relationships, but whatever the shock is, it has really diverted them away from the idea of making a baby. You know, thirty-seven or thirty-eight, they can't—they can't waste much time, and they are terrified of letting the cards fall as they may. They are mostly professional women, not all. . . . But they're coming for the same reason. There's been a trauma. Or there's been a little lightbulb going off in their head that basically says, "Oh my God, I'm not married" or "I haven't had kids yet, and I'm thirty-seven, thirty-eight. What am I going to do?"

Although this physician's focus on shock and trauma initially surprised me, his summary was, in fact, both precise and prescient. As my own study progressed, I came to realize that more than one-third of the women I was meeting were turning to egg freezing because of various kinds of relationship traumas. Nearly half were divorced or divorcing; one-third had broken up from long-term partners; and the rest were equally divided between marital separations and broken engagements. More than two-thirds of these women were single at the time of the interview.

It is important to note that in the US, nearly half of all marriages—44.6 percent, to be exact—end in divorce, although the percentage is significantly less for educated women.[5] But 60 percent of divorces in the US involve spouses between the ages of twenty-five and thirty-nine, during women's prime reproductive years. This problem of "divorce in one's prime" redounded throughout my study. Of the 17 percent of the women in my study who were divorced, their divorces had occurred in their mid- to late thirties, often causing panic over lost reproductive potential.

Indeed, every woman in this study who had experienced a relationship's ending was already in her mid- to late thirties, thereby bringing issues of future childbearing to the fore. Many had been in long-term relationships with their partners and thus were hurt and despairing when these relationships, in which they had invested so much time, energy, and emotion, ultimately fell apart. Some women cried when retelling their stories. Those who had loved their partners described themselves as "heartbroken," even "devastated." Some women admitted that it took them months, even years, to "recover" from their breakups.

Other women whose partners had betrayed them in one way or another were bitter, even livid. Many women used negative epithets to describe their ex-husbands and ex-partners, calling them "assholes," "big jerks," "narcissists," "crazy," even "psychopaths." Divorces themselves were often described as "very complicated," "vindictive," "acrimonious," "antagonistic," "contentious," "soap-opera-ish," and "passive aggressive." The verb "dragged" was often used to describe the ways in which women were pulled into divorce proceedings that were difficult, complicated, and often costly.

The women in this study had a variety of different stories to tell about their divorces, separations, broken engagements, and relationship breakups. Their stories involved men's infidelity, controlling behavior, career ambitions, and sexual rejection. However, the major reason for relationship endings was men's unreadiness for fatherhood, the problem that Jack experienced and expressed so directly to Lily. In some cases, men's unreadiness for fatherhood eventually morphed into outright refusals to have children, outcomes that were experienced by women as ultimate betrayals, especially when they had committed many years to a relationship (e.g., "most of my thirties"). Hearing women describe these causes of relationship dissolution reveals feelings of anger, disappointment, rejection, and despair.

Men's Infidelity

One genre of relationship dissolution that was particularly difficult for women involved a husband's infidelity, always accompanied by deceit and sometimes by emotional and substance abuse. In most of these cases, infidelity and its consequences ultimately led to divorce. Aneela, an IT director in Silicon Valley, who had married within the Indian American community in her early twenties, discovered that her husband had been cheating on her for over a decade of marriage.

> I think he had been unfaithful, frankly, throughout the whole marriage. . . . So we separated at thirty-one, but if you believe it, the divorce dragged on for like three and a half years. You know, I was very young when I was married, so I hadn't really dated that much. And to be honest with you, Marcia, I really wasn't really ready up until late last year. I really wasn't. For me it was a bit of a traumatic experience. . . . I was kind of a naive type of a girl. I was very protected. I had a very protective childhood. I went to private schools my entire life, and like, kind of always, luck had always worked out for me. But I see now the flip side, that you're not sort of prepared for something like that. . . . I think it took maybe about five or six years to really be, like, okay.

Another woman, Elsa, had already turned thirty when she married her husband. Together, they joined the US Foreign Service and headed overseas. But when Elsa became pregnant and miscarried at the age of thirty-six, her marriage began falling apart.

> He was apparently cheating for a while, and everybody knew except for me kind of thing [*laughs*]. My husband was unfaithful and had a bunch of other issues. But once I lost the pregnancy, he admitted to me that he didn't feel ready to be a father and that he was secretly relieved. And then once I realized that children were probably not going to happen with this man, it didn't seem like there was much point in staying in the relationship. And I didn't actually find out about the infidelity until I'd already moved out. So it took two years for the divorce to come through because he was overseas for much of it. And we had some disagreements about how we would split things up, and it was challenging. But it was during that window of time actually, before my divorce came through but after we were separated, that I made the decision to freeze my eggs.

Freezing eggs upon the discovery of infidelity was one of the most despairing moments for women, as it also involved crucial decisions about whether to reconcile or leave a relationship with an untrustworthy man. This was especially difficult for women who already had a child when they discovered that their husbands were cheating. Sadie, a business analyst living in the Baltimore suburbs, volunteered for my study because she thought her situation might be "different." She had been with her Irish-born husband for fourteen years and already had a young son when she discovered that her husband was living a "double life." Calling herself a "broken-hearted single mother," she explained,

> He was an alcoholic. He had been unfaithful. I didn't know this until after the separation, but I, you know, I suspected some things. But I just didn't think he was capable of these things. The irony being that he—he ended up getting someone pregnant by accident. So [*laughs*] it's just ironic. . . . It was during our separation, but it was sort of during a time I thought we were reconciling. But—and he remains very awful and antagonistic and dragged me through a four-year divorce. . . . And I don't know why, because he was the one that, you know, had created the situation. He was already with this person, with this other person with a child, and, you know, it's awful. He's just awful. . . . I've been trying to make peace with that, and I, you know, still struggle with, you know, a lot of the betrayal and the marriage and the divorce and how it continues, the antagonism continues. So there's a lot of things that I still am kind of not quite whole on.

One evening, when Sadie was viewing a video of her now seven-year-old son as a toddler, she was seized with longing for those happier days and perhaps for a future with another child. Having already turned forty, Sadie used all of her savings for one low-yielding cycle of egg freezing, which, as she explained to me, represented her effort to "invest in some part" of her future.

Perhaps an even more troubling story came from Penelope, an attorney who spoke to me by phone from her master bedroom walk-in closet, out of earshot of her husband, who was still living in their Washington, DC, townhouse. Mother to an eighteen-month-old daughter and stepmother to her husband's nine-year-old son from his previous marriage, Penelope had recently discovered that her pilot husband had accumulated more than forty paramours around the globe, some of them during the course of their marriage. Speaking in hushed tones, she told me about the adultery.

> He's kind of the typical, I guess, if you think of a man having an affair: like, super charming, says the right things, leading a complete double

life. . . . I don't know what to do. I mean, I've got a home now with him, which I have more money in it than he does. I've got an amazing eighteen-month-old daughter who I love more than life itself. I love being a mother more than anything in the world, and I want to have another family. But I'm forty years old, and I can't reproduce again with this [husband], you know. We're in therapy, but he continues to deny he's done anything wrong, you know, even though there's like, black-and-white, out-of-town adultery. I mean, that's better than in-town adultery. But I've got pictures of the naked [women] . . . and, I'm like, "What am I supposed to do?"

When Penelope told her husband that she wanted a divorce and custody of their daughter, her husband became violent. "We just had a huge blowup, a huge blowup . . . and he smashed my head into the bed and jumped on top of me. I called the police. Like, it was bad. And I couldn't fathom, like, ever staying in this relationship. But now I'm looking at trying to leave. I have no family around. I've got nothing. It's just like—he's going to make my life hell—hell when I leave." Still, all of Penelope's friends and family were encouraging her to "get the hell out," and she was taking steps in that direction. In addition, two of Penelope's friends who had frozen their eggs encouraged her to do so as well, a move that Penelope accepted so that she could "buy [her]self a little bit of time." Having undertaken two egg freezing cycles that produced eighteen frozen eggs, Penelope was starting her third cycle when we spoke, telling me, "I'm not ready to fore-close the opportunity of having more children at this point in my life, you know?" But, she concluded wistfully, from the inner sanctum of her walk-in closet, "I wish I was lesbian. I mean, I honestly do. I like women a lot better than men. I'm just not attracted to them [i.e., women]. But, mentally, I know so few good guys. I really do."

Men's Controlling Behavior

Penelope's relationship demise was particularly caustic and complicated because of custody concerns, but even brief marriages without children could involve quite contentious endings. Several women in my study made quick exits from marriages in which men's behavior changed from "charming" to "controlling." Kara, a biomedical engineer living in the DC suburbs, was hoping for an official annulment from the Catholic Church at the time of our interview. Her husband, whom she described as having "narcissistic personality disorder," was making it as difficult as possible, after drawing out their divorce proceedings with vengeance.

> Once we got married, you know, all of a sudden [he] became very controlling and dominating. . . . He had never been married before [in his forties], and yeah, that was a huge red flag. . . . You know, he kind of talked me [into marriage]. I mean, very manipulative, you know, very charming, very whatever, you know? So some of these guys are just really good at their craft, you know? And he manipulated everyone in his whole life. . . . Even my family, friends, like, they all thought he was amazing. You know, I thought he was amazing, too! . . . I had no choice but to get out, dealing with someone like that. . . . He knew that I wanted to have kids, but then he was mad that I was leaving him. So then he decided time was the most precious thing for me, and he was going to extend that as long as possible as like a passive aggressive tactic to get back at me for doing that. . . . I think coming out of such a short difficult marriage, obviously, I made a mistake, and I didn't want to be rushed to get into another relationship, just because I wanted to have kids again or rush to get married again, because of my biological clock. So it [egg freezing] was a decision to hopefully extend the clock a little bit. So I had a little bit more time to be able to recover from this . . . not rush to make another, essentially, bad decision.

In another case of a controlling husband, a British-born attorney, Cecilia, described herself as going through a "particularly acrimonious" divorce in California—one that she thought might be "slightly unusual," in the sense that she "actually had a husband who wanted children." Laughing, she added, "I just didn't want children with him!" Cecilia explained how she and her husband had met and how she quickly learned that he was not the man he pretended to be.

> He actually sold me my car, which should have been a warning sign that he was effectively a used car salesman [*laughs*]! It's a whole, "This isn't where I want to be. I'm a very focused, motivated individual. It's post-2008, the financial meltdown, and this is just kind of what I'm doing, but really I'm going to be in sales. And I'm going to be this, and I'm going to be that." And he came from a very nice, wealthy family and had been to a good school, but that wasn't really—he really is a second-hand car

salesman, to be fair, in a nutshell. He's neither financially nor intellectually my equal, I think is the most polite way to put it. And I was hoping that what he was saying was true, in terms of that wouldn't bother him and didn't factor into anything. But sadly, that wasn't correct. . . . He's emotionally and intellectually very immature-slash-stunted and has been enabled by his dysfunctional parents.

Describing her situation as "a great cautionary tale," Cecilia found herself, literally from her wedding night, in a controlling relationship with an "incredibly entitled" bully. Within months, she decided she must leave, as he "turned out to be an absolute psychopath." Still, Cecilia was grateful that she had continued to use contraception throughout the marriage. "Thank God! I did make the right decision, because if we'd have had a child now . . . The battle over money and assets has been nasty enough, with my husband dragging me back into court to argue about a few sticks of IKEA furniture. Shame on him! So, if we'd have had a child, I could have foreseen many custody battles, which would have just broken my heart. So I'm very glad I didn't. I am very grateful. That's the one thing that keeps me going." Now that she was almost out of the marriage, Cecilia was also grateful that she had decided to freeze her eggs, an experience that she found to be transformative.

> Oh, it's entirely empowering! And I think that's one of the things that I found so exciting through the process, that it made me feel empowered. Because it made me feel that I wasn't the victim anymore of having to stand there and have those awkward conversations when people say, "So why aren't you married yet?" And then you're always like, "Well, you know . . ." And then, "Why haven't you got kids?" Actually, people never ask that, because they always ask, "Why aren't you married?" And then it's assumed that of course you wouldn't have kids, because if you're single, you're definitely going to be barren. So I think, for me, I found it empowering, because it's just like, you know what? I had a crappy marriage, and I could have stayed in a crappy marriage and had a really unhappy family, or I could have made the hard choice, which is to extricate myself from an unhappy marriage.

At the time of our interview, Cecilia had just begun her third egg freezing cycle, but this time it was different. Having just chosen a sperm donor from the California Cryobank, Cecilia told me, "Now the time feels right to have a child on my own."

Men's Career Ambitions

Cecilia's decision to pursue single motherhood was not the most common trajectory among women in this study, for reasons that will be discussed later in this book. Instead, most women, including divorced women, were still looking for partners. Yasmeen, an academic physician in California, had a situation somewhat similar to Cecilia's but with a different outcome. Like Cecilia, Yasmeen had managed to extricate herself from a brief, unhappy marriage to a rigidly controlling fellow physician. "I didn't know him very well," Yasmeen admitted. "I think we married the idea of each other, which probably a lot of people do. . . . And yet he wanted to dictate everything I did, from the underwear I wore, to the people I talked to, to the toothpaste I used."

Although Yasmeen realized that she had made the wrong decision to get married, she thought she had made the right choice when she became engaged again. However, her fiancé effectively abandoned their relationship, breaking off their engagement before moving across country for an Ivy League law degree. As a physician nearing the age of forty, Yasmeen knew that her time was running out. So she undertook three egg freezing cycles in rapid succession, banking a record number of fifty-five eggs. Three years later, at the time of our interview, Yasmeen had just learned that her former fiancé was now engaged to someone else. "So it's kind of ironic that it ended because he wasn't ready to get married, but now he's finishing law school. A lot of life has to do with what stage we're in."

Yasmeen ended up being one of several women whose relationships ended when partners' career ambitions got in the way. Career moves to other parts of the country, or even abroad, were usually involved in these breakups. However, sometimes men were simply unwilling to make professional sacrifices when their partners began wanting a family. Naomi, a sustainability lobbyist in Washington, DC, was a casualty of such a career-related breakup, when her partner finally got his "dream job" in the US Foreign Service and left her in order to be deployed overseas.

He got in, and then we had to make the decision if I'm going to go with him or not. And it was this horrible, yearlong, back-and-forth on what we should do. And then finally we decided I'm not going to go, and so he left. He went, and I stayed. . . . Oh, it was so horrible! Because we were, probably as close to, you know, getting married and all that as anybody else I know. We would've been fine. But that's his dream, and he needed to live it. And it didn't make sense for me . . . to give up everything just for the relationship.

Naomi talked to her doctor because her stress levels were so high, and she ended up having a conversation about egg freezing. "So it was in the middle of all that . . . and it was hard, I mean, emotionally. . . . I was kind of like, 'What else am I going to do? This is the best option I have right now, so I'm not going to be upset about it. I'm going to feel good that at least I'm doing something.'"

Similarly, Laila, who had met her husband in her early twenties and had been with him for fourteen years, found herself alone at the age of thirty-eight, nearing thirty-nine. Her husband had a prominent career as an overseas human rights lawyer. But when Laila asked him to return to the States and start a family with her, he became what she described as "just very super weird," followed by "ghosting" her. Commenting on her subsequent divorce and egg freezing, Laila explained, "It's like I was divorcing myself. It's like there's no evidence of the relationship. . . . I think he feels a lot of guilt for many things—most, you know, like, essentially abandoning the relationship. . . . It's hard because you're plotting along, and you have to make decisions because you can't just bury your head in the sand at my age. Like, what are your choices going to be? In the end, after like ten months and many, many thousands of dollars, I have what I call 'my three golden eggs.'"

Men's Sexual Rejection

While Yasmeen, Naomi, and Laila were all left by partners who prioritized their careers, some women were the "leavers." Irreconcilable differences often played a role, the most irreconcilable one being men's sexual rejection. For example, Rebecca, a scientist working for the federal government in Washington, DC, had been together with her scientist husband, who was still her "best friend," for fourteen years. But she believed he was on the autistic spectrum and largely asexual, which had made her marriage increasingly untenable.

He is a very interesting person. I think he is definitely somewhere on the Asperger spectrum, and I was the only person he'd ever been with and maybe only person he ever will be with. He's very sweet, very loyal. . . . [But] one of the problems was that our relationship had become—he's become fairly asexual. And that was a big deal to me [*laughs*]. And I wanted to have an active sex life with my partner or even a sex life. So, you know, it was something that we went to counseling for and, you know, we worked on, as much as we could. And even when we, you know, went to a couple of therapists, who asked us the final time, you know, "I don't know if I've ever seen two people with so much mutual respect and care for each other, but you should still get divorced." . . . It makes me sad, I mean, because he still, for a long time, he was the person, the first person I go to for anything, you know, everything. . . . [On the night before egg retrieval] he had a four-wheel drive, so he drove me up, and we stayed in a hotel. And then he took me in, and it was—it was definitely emotionally difficult in a lot of ways because of that.

Similarly, Gretchen, a software financial director in the DC suburbs, had married her college boyfriend, whom she described as her best friend and first lover but who was never keen on having sex with her. The sexual rejection was emotionally painful and psychologically insidious, taking its toll on Gretchen's physical and mental well-being.

Like, I went through phases where I would lose a ton of weight to try and see, "Well, maybe I'm just not attractive to him?" you know. It became, like, very detrimental for me. But I think at the end of the day, I just kind of realized that the rejection was—it was very hurtful. Not that he ever intended it to be, but it was just hard. I mean, there were many, many years when he was just—he was not interested as well, so I think it was very hard. I didn't understand. He rejected me physically or, you know, sexually, a lot even early on in the marriage. But because he was my first and only, I really didn't know any better. But then as I was getting older, and then I started to talk to friends and my therapist about this. It was like, "Well, wait a minute. This isn't normal."

Over six and a half years of a mostly commuter marriage, Gretchen's sex life with her husband eventually dwindled to nothing. Through both therapy and a guilty but sexually affirming affair with another man, Gretchen eventually came to realize that her husband might be gay but closeted, having come from a conservative southern Christian background.

> We're still very close, but we were not supposed to be married. . . . And so, you know, as much as I love him and he probably still loves me, there was just something missing that—we tried to go to therapy together, and he went two sessions, and that was it. He wouldn't go again. . . . I couldn't see that someone would actually want to be with me, that I would ever be able to meet someone else, but it was just this part of me that was like, "I need an insurance policy. If I am going to have children, I don't know when that might be."

Gretchen ended her sexless marriage and also spent $30,000 of inheritance money from her grandparents on three egg freezing cycles that yielded twenty-four eggs. As with Rebecca, it was Gretchen's ex-husband, still her "best friend," who flew across the country to be with her at the final egg extraction.

Men's Unreadiness for Fatherhood

Although men's infidelity, controlling behavior, career ambitions, and sexual rejection brought many relationships to an end, men's unreadiness for marriage—the major theme of Lily's story—also emerged as the key factor in many relationship breakups. Reasons for men's unreadiness were varied and included financial instability, unpleasant prior divorce experiences, or already having children from a prior relationship and not wanting more. However, in most cases, the source of men's unreadiness for marriage and fatherhood was more elusive and difficult to pinpoint.

For example, Jenni, an actor, producer, and filmmaker in Los Angeles, had just broken up with a frustrating "beta male" partner, who was more interested in hanging out with his friends and smoking weed than in marrying her and having children. Calling herself the "queen of three-year relationships," Jenni opined,

> Men and women, from the day that they are born, are raised—are given this impression of marriage that is so different. Women, it's like, "I'm a princess. He's going to save me. We're going to live happily ever after." Men, it's, "This is my ball and chain." You know what I'm saying? From

the time that we are young, that is how we're brought up. And I think that conversation needs to change, because that's exactly what men think, no matter what age they are. They think they're going to be on lockdown, and they're not going to be able to live their life anymore.

Jody, a communications director in Washington, DC, was partnered with a somewhat different kind of beta male—a younger man who claimed that he wanted to marry her but who effectively paralyzed their relationship through his overall passivity. Jody explained why this kept their relationship from moving forward.

I sometimes felt like I was responsible for everything. Like, if we went on vacation, I was doing all the booking, I was doing all the planning. And I was wondering, "Wow, if we get married, is it going to be me handling everything?" And I've always made, like, a lot more money than him. And I'm fine with that. But just feeling like in every aspect of the relationship I was in charge—and, you know, I'm certainly a feminist, but there's something weird about feeling like I'm in charge of everything. Like, everything we do, I plan. Every time, I'm arranging it. Every interview he gets, I'm arranging it for him. I just felt like he's super passive in life, in general, and it just used to drive me crazy.

Feeling like she had become the "mom" to a "big kid," Jody finally broke up with her partner and immediately turned to egg freezing.

In a few years I'll be forty. I'm one of those women that everybody dreads being, kind of the single woman that everybody talks about . . . in this almost sorry-for-them kind of way. I hate the idea. I mean, everybody does, but [I] fucking hate the idea of somebody talking about me that way, which some people do. Like, "Oh, poor Jody. She just broke up." It's just ugh. The idea of being pitied is just the worst, right? I think for me it's really—I can't say enough [about egg freezing]. From my experience, it was kind of—it made me feel like, "You know what? I can have the type of life I want. That's a possibility for me. I'm not in the danger zone. I can kind of create life on my own terms." And that's for me what it's done.

Egg freezing also came as a major relief to Marianne, a New York City journalist who had spent three valuable years in her late thirties trying to make a life with a man who was commitment phobic. Although Marianne considered her partner to be her soul mate, she realized that her feelings were not shared.

> I really felt like we were meant to be together, even though he had put up plenty of signals that he wasn't—that he had real issues with kind of commitments—not in the way that he was some sort of player and he wanted to be with other people, just that he was really afraid of commitment, for whatever reason. And I still—no one can figure it out. But anyway, I felt we were great together, but it didn't work out. And then all of a sudden I was thirty-eight, about to turn thirty-nine. And I knew I was going to have a lot of time on my hands, because I was out of this relationship. I wasn't going to be ready to date for a while. So I did a triathlon. I got a book deal. And I was like, "Hey, I'm going to freeze my eggs." . . . I just felt like I wanted to take some control over my reproductive future. This new thing was available, and to me, it was a no-brainer. And, you know, it was just a no-brainer. "Why wouldn't I do this?" I had no idea what my future was going to unfold. I haven't had the best luck in relationships, and I just felt like I wanted to make sure that this might be an option for me down the road.

By the time I met Marianne, she was now forty-three with seventeen frozen eggs in the bank. For three years, she had been living with a new partner and was about to embark on a second IVF cycle with him. But as a father of four children from two previous relationships, her partner's desire to have children with Marianne was beginning to wane.

> We're now having other discussions. He has children. He's older than me. And he—this is more on the personal side—but he's kind of having a change of heart over whether he wants kids. You know, it's become a little bit of an issue lately. But, you know, we're moving forward with this cycle, and we'll see what happens. It's possible that if he really doesn't want—if it doesn't work out, and he doesn't want to move forward again, it's possible I would have to make a very big, really very hard decision. So we'll see. It's not easy.

Another New Yorker, Danielle, was engaged to a man whom her therapist called "the almost guy." Calling him a "straight-up narcissist," Danielle explained her fiancé's fear of commitment on multiple levels.

I was in couples' therapy with him, and the therapist is like, "This is the worst kind of man you could ever date. He's the almost guy. He will almost always commit. He will just keep you stringing along and almost do everything and keep shuffling things around to make it look like it's happening, but it's really not ever going to happen. . . . You need to leave. Log out now. . . . He loves you, but this is all he's capable of. He will never give you a child. He hasn't slept with you in a year. Like, read the writing on the wall. You need to leave. . . ." It was really painful. It was terrible.

Danielle finally left her fiancé and underwent one cycle of egg freezing. But it did not bring her the kind of relief that it had for Jody and Marianne. As a late-thirties single woman living in Manhattan, Danielle described to me how she now felt.

Yeah, I'm completely overwhelmed. . . . But who are you going to blame? You know what I mean? Like, you can't just victimize yourself . . . because I couldn't get this relationship to, for lack of a better way of explaining, to work out. So it was, like, really awful. Like, I tried everything. Therapy, just nothing, nothing, nothing. And then I said, "This is the only thing I can control." So what's a girl gonna do? I went into it [egg freezing] really upset. It was like not a positive experience, I guess. I don't know that it's positive for most people, but I went into it in just a very emotional space. . . . I cried for five straight days.

An even more tragic story involved Sasha, a California legal professional who thought that she had partnered with a genius of the tech industry. When Sasha experienced an unplanned pregnancy with her boyfriend, he remained noncommittal, ultimately abandoning Sasha and their newborn son shortly after birth. Sasha described his unreadiness to be a father.

It was shocking [laughs]. . . . We've now broken up, and no, it did not end up happily. He provides regular child support, but I otherwise don't have any contact with him. . . . He's really smart, but he has his own personal issues that were hard to deal with. And [now] I have sole legal and physical custody from a court order, and he only has supervised visitations. Again, he's a really smart guy. He had, like, a perfect SAT score. But it's just—it's just not working out for my son. I mean, I look back, my life was totally different. But I try not to dwell too much, because there's really, you know, there's really nothing I can do about it, at this point. . . . So at my age [thirty-nine] and with my son who's four, I have no idea when I'm going to get married or what's happening. [But with egg freezing] I wanted to still have the possibility of having another child.

Whereas Sasha's partner refused to marry her and act like a father to their child, men who were already married sometimes refused to have children after the fact. Such was the case for Ruth, a mental health researcher, who had only agreed to marry her fiancé on the condition that he would have children with her. Ruth had told him, "If you propose, this means you're having children. If you decide you don't want to have kids, then you need to break up with me." Thus, Ruth was convinced that he was sincere when "he proposed in an extremely grand way . . . on a glacier in a national park." Ruth and her fiancé married, bought a house, and then headed straight into a marital crisis when her husband changed his mind about becoming a father. "He doesn't really like children. He thinks they're loud and screamy. But I think the biggest thing is—well, the biggest thing is that he thinks he won't enjoy it, and then he'll be depressed. And he's fearful of, like, racing up his depression, and he works to, like, not be depressed. And that is a very big challenge as it is. So, like, bringing something so dramatic like a child in his life would take him into a lifelong depression." For her part, Ruth experienced her husband's postmarital refusal as a "huge betrayal," especially when he stopped having sex with her because she decided to go off her birth control. At the time we spoke, Ruth was debating whether to leave him. "I think I made a very bad choice," she said. "What the hell was I doing?" As a stopgap measure, Ruth undertook three cycles of egg freezing, ending up with twenty-five frozen eggs. But she asked herself, "Why the hell would you be freezing these eggs if you were married? Right? I mean, of course, it's like the weirdest situation." Ruth admitted to weeping on the ultrasound table, telling the technician, "I should be having sex with my husband, having a baby. And I'm here freezing my eggs."

Egg freezing for Ruth was neither empowering nor comforting. Instead, she described herself as being "super sad," "very stressed," with the process itself being "just a real slam." Now thirty-six, Ruth was contemplating whether she still had time to divorce, recover, find a new partner, remarry, and have children.

Another woman, Molly, had just turned thirty-eight when she finally fell "crazy in love." She hastily eloped, moved with her husband to a different city, and started a new graduate program. But the honeymoon phase soon ended. Her new husband began "pulling away" and manifesting some "really scary red flags." Although Molly became pregnant twice, including with twins, her husband insisted on abortions. By the time I spoke with Molly, she was in a state of deep regret. "I feel very, very alone, actually. He's not ready, not supportive whatsoever, and doesn't grasp how much it [motherhood] means to me." When I asked Molly why she wanted to be a mother, she told me,

> I realize that there is some tremendous spiritual beauty in having that connection with another human being that endures, you know. You know, that's beautiful; that gives life meaning. And my life does feel kind of empty. It's like, "What am I living for, you know?" [Laughs] I'm really just living for myself, and I'm really tired of that. So it's like these human connections give life so much depth, and I'm afraid I'm going to miss that. I'm like, "What's going to happen to me, ten to fifteen to twenty years from now, when I'm in my sixties? Am I going to want to be alone like this? Just living for myself, you know?" I don't think so . . . and I actually do have survival concerns here. I don't feel like I have a lot of money, and I am afraid of dying alone and in poverty. I really am. But that's not my prime motivator for having children. But, you know, it does—it is a fear of mine.

Now approaching the age of forty and not willing to give up on motherhood, Molly had decided to freeze her eggs, receiving a generous clinic discount because she was living on a graduate student's income. At the time of our interview, Molly was thinking of becoming a single mother within her marital home but "absolving him of his parental obligations" and "pretty much parenting and dealing with this child alone."

Egg Freezing beyond Romance

After hearing stories like Sasha's, Ruth's, and Molly's, one might ask, "What's wrong with today's men? How can they be so ambivalent, so inconsiderate, and so cold?" But it is important to emphasize here that not all men are callous jerks—as will be clearly shown in later chapters.

Even Lily, whose story began this chapter and who lost her opportunity to become a mother because of Jack's indecision, could not condemn him completely and remained friends with her ex-partner, now a tenured professor.

If there is one bit of good news to be told, it is that more than one-quarter of the women who shared their breakup stories with me had already moved onto their next relationships, and three of these women had become mothers. This included Jenni, "the queen of three-year relationships," who froze her eggs, made a documentary film about it, found a loving husband, and became the mother of an adorable son. More surprisingly, Ruth, whose husband had "betrayed" her by refusing to have children, went on to have a darling daughter after her husband reconsidered his oppositional stance. Rebecca and Gretchen, both of whom had been sexually rejected by their husbands, found new love and passion after their divorces. And Sasha, whose partner abandoned her and their son at birth, was being courted by a longtime male friend, who wanted them to move in together and become a family. In short, some women found love with men who could only be described as "good eggs." And some were able to bear the children of their dreams.

Furthermore, as all the stories in this chapter have shown, women going through traumatic relationship breakups were not helpless and hapless victims. In each case, they took proactive measures to protect themselves and their future fertility. Many women spoke of the "empowerment" and the "peace of mind" that they felt by having frozen their eggs—doing something "for themselves" and "for the future" at a difficult life juncture. Egg freezing provided some measure of "control" when women's relationships had spun out of control. Egg freezing felt restorative, a first step in a healing process to repair a major biographical wound.

In this reparative mode, some women received additional help. One of the trends I discovered through my research on egg freezing was its negotiation in divorce settlements. Three of the women in my study fought hard for egg freezing to be paid for by their difficult ex-husbands. All three won their egg freezing settlements, awarded by sympathetic male judges. To take one example, Pamela, an emergency-room physician, who was undergoing a contentious divorce, was accused of "lavish spending" by her husband's attorney. When she explained to the older male judge that she had been paying for an egg freezing cycle, he took her side, telling the ex-husband's attorney, "I don't think her wanting to be a mom and trying to do this is wasteful." Pamela was very grateful for the judge's support. "Thank you, judge, for standing up for me! I'm not throwing money away. And it's not fun. It's not like I'm putting myself on a cruise ship, you know? I'm sticking myself with needles and going to doctor's office appointments at six in the morning, when I've been up until three in the morning the night before, you know?" Egg freezing "took the pressure off" Pamela, so that she did not feel compelled to "repeat the same mistake" by rushing into another unstable relationship. In general, egg freezing provided divorced women with a perceived biological, emotional, and relational reprieve during a difficult time in which their futures needed rethinking and recalibration.

Yet, even beyond divorce settlements, the most interesting outcome might be described as *egg freezing beyond romance*. As we will see, several women in this study opted to make embryos out of their frozen eggs using donor sperm, and some of these women went on to become mothers, with or without male partners. Others were considering coparenting a child with their siblings or with a close male friend rather than a romantic partner. In other words, egg freezing afforded new possibilities and trajectories for women as they emerged from the major life disruption that relationship dissolution often entailed. Egg freezing in this sense served as a form of healing, relief, and inspiration, helping women to move on with their lives and to imagine novel pathways to motherhood.

3

The Minority Concerns

Race, Religion, and the Fertility Paradox

Tiffany's Frozen Egg Vow

When I began this study of egg freezing, I never imagined that I would meet so many women in senior management positions. Tiffany was one of these women. With both an engineering degree and an MBA, Tiffany had risen to the ranks of project manager in a Washington, DC–based engineering firm. Although Tiffany was surrounded by men at work, managing them did not mean dating them. When I asked Tiffany, "Are you single, partnered, divorced, married?" she laughed heartily, answering, "Single, single, single!"

As a self-identified African American woman in Washington, DC, Tiffany held out hope that she would meet the man of her dreams, given the presence of many Black men in the city.[1] But at the age of thirty-nine, Tiffany had been forced to assess the reasons why she was still alone.

So it's odd. I tell people I never have any problem finding a good guy. Like, people I've dated in my past have always been good to me. It's just that it's a numbers game. So I have never been "their person," you know what I mean? Something has always just happened, and I've just never been able to take it to that next level for one reason or another. And just being in DC, it's very difficult. The odds are stacked against me. There are more females here for men. I think another reason here is that people from big cities, they don't come to settle down. They come for education and college purposes. And then, also, I'm just older now. So I don't go out as much, and a lot of my girlfriends are either married or [have] moved away. So, for me, it's like the social scene, trying to figure out. Well, I can't go to a forty-year-old club. That's not going to work. And I really don't want to go like line dancing, because that's like for the older folks. So I do online stuff, and I've been successful with that the whole time. But that's work also. It's like a second job, and I have to do that every day in order to get results. . . . So I have to make time to find a partner.

Tiffany had grown up in a middle-class, Catholic family, where education, hard work, and marriage were expected for Tiffany and her sisters.

And that's the thing, you know? And I hate stereotyping people, but the way I grew up and the people I grew up around with, like—how do I say this?—you know, we didn't get pregnant in high school. You know, we didn't get pregnant out of, you know, wedlock. That just wasn't something that was like—I hate to say this—in our lives, in our situations, you know. We all came, me and my girlfriends, we all came from, you know, happily married moms and dads who got married and did it all the right way. You know, we don't have any half brothers, half sisters, you know what I mean?

Given her upbringing, Tiffany had been on hormonal contraceptives for many years with the firm understanding that "I can't have a baby before I get married." But now, nearing age forty, she began to worry about her fertility. "How do I know I *can* get pregnant, you know? Because I never purposely tried to get pregnant when I was younger, and so that's a little bit scary, too. Because it's like, well, do I have fertility issues? Like, finding out fertility issues at forty is a little bit late, as opposed to figuring out you had fertility issues when you were like, you know, twenty-six, twenty-seven, or so."

Tiffany scheduled an appointment with a Black female gynecologist, who proved helpful in this regard. On the very first visit, she told Tiffany, "You don't have to talk about it right now, but I just want to put this in your head. So you may want to consider doing egg freezing." Tiffany had read about egg freezing in newspapers and magazines, as well as on social media. But it was her favorite TV show, *Being Mary Jane*, in which the single, forty-year-old reporter played by Gabrielle Union decided to freeze her eggs, that clinched the idea in Tiffany's mind. She began researching different options, asking two close friends and her family what they thought.

My younger sister, she was encouraging. But my mom, she was confused because she didn't understand. You know, she's sixty-five. And she grew up in a time where she got married by twenty-three. And she had three kids by the time she was thirty-five, I want to say. So this was all foreign to her. Like, "Why are you doing this?" My dad is my dad. He just went along with it. He was like, "Okay, honey, if this is what you want to do, go ahead and do it." I have one girlfriend who is married, has two kids, and she was just like, "Yeah, go for it." And then I have another girlfriend who's single like me, and she was just kind of excited. Because she talked about it with me, about doing it, but I think she is resolved that she's just not going to do it. She's just going to let Mother Nature take her course. And so, if she's meant to have kids, she'll have kids. If she's not meant to have kids, you know, she won't have kids. But I *do* want to have kids. I've always thought I'd be married by now with two kids and all that other stuff. Obviously, that's not the case. But yes, I do want kids.

In deciding to move forward with egg freezing, Tiffany hoped that she could find an IVF clinic in the greater DC area with at least one Black female physician. "It's more relatable, that's all," Tiffany explained. "I mean, with my doctors, like my OB/GYN [obstetrician and gynecologist], like I prefer females anyway. It's just, I think it's weird to have a man looking down there at you! But I wanted a female and, on top of that, just African American—just more relatable and someone that looks like you."

Tiffany never managed to find such a physician, despite the large number of IVF clinics in the greater DC area. Still, she forged ahead, finding herself among mostly White patients in an IVF clinic headed by a White male physician. For Tiffany, the big surprise came when she bumped into another Black female colleague in the IVF clinic waiting area.

I was like, "Hey! What are *you* doing here?" And she was like, "Hey! What are *you* doing here?" And I was like doing the same thing [as her], and I had no idea. . . . So it was a shock to see her there. And she said, "Hey, I'm going through this process, too." But it was funny to me, because I was like, "Oh wow! She's African American and someone I knew." Because, you know, I didn't have anybody to go through this experience with. And it was like, you know, good to know that there was someone else who was literally going through the same thing I was going through, only she's doing a little bit extra.

In fact, Tiffany's colleague had already undertaken IVF with donor sperm from a male high school friend, who had also agreed to become a legal coparent. When I asked Tiffany if she would ever consider such an option, she had this to say:

> So that's funny you said that, because when I told my mom that, my mom was like, "I totally support you if you wanted to do that. I'd come down there and help with the baby." And I was like, "Really?" I was like, "I thought you wanted me to get married." And she was like, "If you're not married by now, then I don't know when you're going to get married. And I don't want you to wait around." So she's like, "Yeah, go for it!" So I told myself that if I don't have anybody by forty-two, I would just go ahead and do the single thing by choice. But I don't have a friend who I think I would want to coparent with. So I probably would just go to the sperm bank. Get on to the sperm bank! You flip through the book [*laughs*]!

Tiffany had already been asked by her IVF physician if she intended to use donor sperm to fertilize some of her eggs. Having been raised Catholic, Tiffany found the idea of embryo freezing "a little weird," and she was unsettled by the idea of having to dispose of any unused embryos. "Not that I've ever taken a stand on abortion, but that was just a little bit too uncomfortable for me," she explained. Throughout the complicated decision-making process, Tiffany yearned for greater support, wishing to find other Black women with whom to share her egg freezing journey. But her search came up empty.

> I just happened upon like a listserv for urban DC women who are doing egg freezing, who are just like posting questions and things like that. And I wish there was maybe like a listserv for African American females or just, you know—I hate to say African American, because we are all single females that are doing it, but just maybe people that I can relate to or go into the process who have been through it before. Because it would have been nice to be able to speak to someone who's been through this before, you know? Telling me what to expect and things like that.

Without such guidance, Tiffany ended up relying heavily on online tutorials. Learning how to self-inject hormonal medications was especially daunting. "I was like, 'Okay, I can do this!' And so, by the third day, I was like, 'All right, I got this! This is no big thing.' And then the trigger shot, it had to go in your behind. I was like, 'Oh my God! How am I going to do this?' But I did it, and I got through it. . . . If you don't like needles, boy oh boy, I was getting poked [*laughs*]! Looking like a drug addict [*laughs*]!"

Despite all of the hormonal injections, Tiffany's egg freezing results were not promising. Only two mature eggs were retrieved and frozen, and Tiffany was advised to undertake another egg freezing cycle immediately. This cycle, too, was disappointing. "As a result, it's not recommended that I do another cycle of egg freezing. So I only have two mature eggs that are frozen and a little less than two dozen immature frozen from my two cycles."[2] Understanding that her advancing age was partly to blame, Tiffany regretted that her path to egg freezing had not been swifter.

> I feel like had I known about this earlier, when I was younger, I probably would have done it. But then when you're young, you don't have the means to be spending like $18,000. You're just trying to figure out how to make due on rent or your student loans. But for sure, for sure, if I had known about this, I would have done this when I was a lot younger. Or even if I was in my midthirties, I would have just gone on and done it. But again, I kept hoping that, you know, Prince Charming would come and sweep me off my feet.

When I asked Tiffany what kind of man her "Prince Charming" might be, she was quite open to possibilities. Although she was clear that she wanted a Black male partner, she did not rule out working-class men, some of whom she had dated previously.

> I've been fortunate enough to date blue-collared guys. And the ones that I have dated, sometimes they are more put together than the white-collared guys! For me, "blue collar" was like a postal worker. And they make good money, you know what I mean? Because I'm in [the engineering] industry, I meet a lot of men. And some of them are owners of their businesses, you know? Electricians and things like that. And again, they make good money and are very stable. But unfortunately, they all happen to have, like, kids already or are in some situation and they don't want to, like, get married again or something like that. So you know? I don't have a problem dating blue-collared, what everyone calls "noneducated" people. I think it just depends on what you're looking for. But now, I realize, you know, the odds are kind of stacked against me. So, in order for me to meet my Prince Charming, I'm going to have to do a lot of the legwork

myself. I don't know. I think as I've gotten older, I've realized that I probably made some—I don't want to say bad choices—but I didn't date a lot
when I was younger. So I think if I was a little more receptive to just date,
I might have met some more people in my circle. But when I was younger,
I was of the opinion that my Prince Charming was going to find me.

On Tiffany's last online effort to find her Prince Charming, she had told
a potential suitor that she had frozen her eggs. "He was like 'Oh, okay. That's
cool.'" But then, Tiffany laughed, "Of course, things didn't work out with
him!" Still, Tiffany felt that egg freezing had "taken the edge off" dating.

[I'm] not like trying to rush, rush, rush to see if this guy's going to put a
ring on it! I found that, like, as I get older, it's harder for me to multitask.
So trying to keep up with my job and then not trying to stress out with
egg freezing and then trying to do the online dating, this is like, ugh, I
have to pick one. I can't do it all, so—but I will say, though, that it does
take the pressure off of dating, so that I'm not always looking at the guy
I'm dating as, like, the next baby daddy [laughs]!

In recent months, Tiffany had given more thought to going it alone
without a "baby daddy." With her stable job, significant salary, and a decade of home ownership, Tiffany was in a relatively good position to become a "single mother by choice," the term now used to describe women
who deliberately embark on motherhood through the use of donor sperm.
But money was still a concern for Tiffany. For example, she had put the
$18,500 for two egg freezing cycles on a zero-interest credit card, paying it
off over twenty months rather than dipping into her limited savings. The
thought of raising a child on her own in the expensive city of Washington,
DC, intimidated Tiffany. "It's like, do I have the resources to do it? Like,
do I have the financial means to do it? Because that is a big, big commitment, you know. When you're doing it with two parents and you take off
for maternity leave, there's someone else bringing in money to keep the
household afloat, you know? If I take off three months, I don't have vacation time. The bills aren't getting paid. You know?" Still, Tiffany had made
herself that vow: if she remained unmarried at the age of forty-two, she
would thaw her frozen eggs and "get on to the sperm bank!"

* * *

Three years later, I received an email from Tiffany. The COVID-19 pandemic had literally just begun, but Tiffany, now forty-three, had some extremely happy news to share.

Hi Marcia,
I hope you are staying safe in these uncertain times. I know you're still not doing the study anymore, but I wanted to let you know that I was successful with my frozen eggs and I delivered a healthy baby girl [this] January as [a] single mom. I have three more fertilized eggs remaining and not yet sure if I will try again.
All the best, Tiffany

The Minority Mating Gap and the Fertility Paradox

Tiffany was one of my most generous research volunteers, sharing her journey to, through, and beyond egg freezing, until the eventual arrival of her baby daughter born from a frozen egg. Clearly, Tiffany's primary reason for egg freezing was her inability to find a committed partner—the "Prince Charming" who she had always hoped would sweep her off her feet. Tiffany voiced many of the same gender laments found in other women's stories we have heard—namely, the skewed gender ratio in Washington, DC, the missing men in the dating pool, and men's unreadiness to marry and have children, especially if they were already fathers. Like many other women, Tiffany also blamed herself for her singleness, pointing to the "bad choices" she had made by not dating enough when she was younger, her inability to understand the social scene because she did not go out enough, and her flagging energy for the "second job" of online dating. Yet it seemed to me that Tiffany had tried so hard, for so long, to be so "good," in every sense of that term. She had clearly not produced the social situation she was facing.

Tiffany's pursuit of egg freezing is indicative of the role that this technology is now playing in the lives of educated Black women in the US, as well as professional women from other minority groups. As noted earlier, nearly one-third (31 percent) of the women who volunteered for my study identified as non-White, including women who are Black, Latina, Asian American, mixed race, and of Middle Eastern backgrounds. Even though such diversity in egg freezing is rarely represented in media portrayals or the stereotypes they generate, it is actually not unusual, according to the IVF physicians I interviewed. For example, one IVF physician I interviewed in the Atlanta area wanted to challenge the 2016 *New York Times* editorial, which had questioned whether egg freezing was for "White women only."[3] "If one were to ask that rhetorical question here in Atlanta, then the answer is absolutely not! You know, because there is a pretty strong presence of an African American middle class; there's an African American managerial class and administrative class. . . . It's not the majority, but I would say a quarter to a third of our egg freezers here are women who are not White—and for all the same reasons. I mean, there's no race-specific reasons why White ladies would come and African Americans wouldn't. They're coming for all the same reasons."

The mating gap—caused by the massive undersupply of eligible, educated, and equal male partners—is the main reason that educated American women of *all* backgrounds are freezing their eggs, as we will see throughout this book. But the mating gap is a special problem for educated Black women in the US. Today, nearly two-thirds (64 percent) of all Black college graduates are women, compared to only one-third (36 percent) who are men.[4] At historically Black colleges, these disparities are even more pronounced. For example, at Howard University in Washington, DC, 71 percent of Black undergraduates are women, compared to only 29 percent who are men.[5]

This educational gender gap means that women like Tiffany, who wish to marry within the Black community, have little choice but to consider men who are missing the *e* of education.[6] Studies show that Black college graduates are less likely to marry others with college degrees, and this is especially true for Black women, who generally marry "down" with regard to educational achievement.[7] Indeed, one-third of married Black women have a spouse with less education, compared to about one-quarter of American women overall. Furthermore, marriage rates have been declining among Black women at all educational levels, meaning that today 62 percent of Black American women are unpartnered.[8] Black women with a college degree who are between the ages of thirty-five and forty-five—women exactly like Tiffany—are about 30 percent less likely to be married than White women with a college degree and about 15 percent less likely to be married than White women without a college degree.[9] This decline in marriage among educated Black women reflects the undersupply of educated Black men in the population. But the problem of "missing" Black men in the US goes much deeper than this, reflecting the major social

TABLE 3.1. Percentage of College Degrees Conferred by Race and Sex

Race	Female (%)	Male (%)	Overall college graduation rate, in rank order (%)
Asian American	54	46	59
Two or more races	59	41	44
White	56	44	42
Black	64	36	37
Latinx (Hispanic)	60	40	36
American Indian/Native Alaskan	61	39	24

Source: National Center for Education Statistics 2021.

injustices of high Black male incarceration rates and disproportionately high rates of Black male death, including during the time of COVID-19.[10]

Black women are not the only minority group facing a dearth of educated men within their communities. In the US today, women from *all* minority groups are outperforming men in higher education, leading to growing disparities between college-educated men and women. The National Center for Education Statistics shows that female-to-male education gaps occur regardless of race.[11] As shown in table 3.1, over half of all college graduates in every single census category are women, and, correspondingly, less than half are men. The highest percentages of female college graduates versus male college graduates occur among Black women (64 percent), American Indians and Native Alaskans (61 percent), and Latinas (60 percent). But even among Asian American and Pacific Islanders, who have the highest college graduation rates overall (59 percent), 54 percent of college graduates are women, versus only 46 percent who are men.

In short, across the US educational spectrum, women are doing considerably better than men with regard to educational achievement. This is especially true of minority women, who are significantly outperforming minority men in higher education. For minority women like Tiffany who are high achievers—succeeding educationally, attaining professional and managerial positions, fulfilling their families' hopes and dreams, and, in some cases, also performing as cultural role models within their communities—their success has been double edged. High-achieving minority women like Tiffany may face serious challenges in finding reproductive partners, particularly if they are looking for eligible, educated, and equal partners within their own communities.

This *minority mating gap*, as I call it, not only applies to Black women. It is occurring across minority groups in the US and is leading to what I call a *fertility paradox*. To wit, we might expect women's high levels of educational achievement to lead to high levels of personal achievement and the fulfillment of life goals, including marriage and motherhood. But that does not seem to be the case for many high-achieving minority women. Instead, minority women's *increasing* educational performance and over-achievement in comparison to men within their communities may paradoxically be *decreasing* their chances for marriage and parenthood with these same men. Or put another way, the most high-achieving women in minority communities may be the least likely to marry and bear children, a situation that is paradoxical and turns high achievement itself into a tacit *fertility penalty*—one that has historically applied to well-educated professional White women as well but that is now accentuated in minority communities.[12]

Furthermore, given that some minority groups may hold so-called traditional family values, women who cannot meet cultural motherhood imperatives, for whatever reason, may experience profound feelings of failure or shame for being perceived as "racial outliers."[13] Indeed, narratives of *fertility shame*—or painful feelings of distress and humiliation caused by the inability to become pregnant "correctly," meaning within marriage, through the heterosexual sex act, without overt technological assistance, and within a normal reproductive time frame (say, the thirties, as opposed to the forties or fifties)—were apparent *across* minority groups in my study.

As we will see, fertility shame was especially apparent among minority groups *underrepresented* in egg freezing, including Black, Latina, and Middle Eastern American women, with religion often fueling that shame and leading to egg freezing stigma and reluctance. But it was also present among minority women *overrepresented* in egg freezing, including Asian American and Jewish American women, whose religious and cultural traditions exerted motherhood pressure and made egg freezing feel imperative as a shame-reducing intervention. These issues of under- and overrepresentation will be examined in turn, so as to understand the complex intersection of race and religion in the fertility paradox that is leading more and more minority women to egg freezing.

Tiffany herself confronted this situation. Coming from a traditional Catholic family, Tiffany felt considerable trepidation over her inability to find a mate and how her lack of marriage and motherhood might disappoint her aging parents. Furthermore, Tiffany was all too aware of the negative stereotypes surrounding Black single motherhood, and given the politics of respectability within her educated Black circles, she worried about what others might think if she chose this option.[14] Only with her mother's unexpected but explicit approval could Tiffany move forward. Yet she felt quite alone on her journey. She could not find a Black IVF physician. She saw few other Black women in the IVF clinic. Nor was she able to connect with an online community of Black egg freezing women, as such a community simply did not exist. Tiffany wanted the comfort of others who "looked like her." But, Tiffany asked, where were other Black women who had "been through this before"?

The Underrepresented

Tiffany's question is exceedingly important, because it points to the issue of Black women's *underrepresentation in egg freezing*. Black Americans make up 12.4 percent of the overall US population. In New York City and Washington, DC, where I recruited many women for my study, Black Americans make up 26 percent and 50.7 percent of the population, respectively. But in my study, only nine Black women froze their eggs, three because of cancer diagnoses. Healthy Black women like Tiffany constituted only 5 percent of the study population and were mostly African American, except for one woman whose family had immigrated from Ghana. This low percentage of participation was identical to that of Latinas, only ten of whom volunteered for my study, four of whom froze their eggs because of cancer diagnoses. Yet the Latinx (aka Hispanic) community makes up 18.7 percent of the US population, 26 percent of the New York City population, and nearly one-third of all residents in Silicon Valley, where I also recruited women for my study. Latinas who volunteered for my study primarily lived on the East Coast and had families who had immigrated from a variety of Central and South American countries.

In other words, Black and Latina women, including three who were biracial, were significantly underrepresented in my study, at only 10 percent overall, when on the basis of overall demographics, they should have constituted about one-third of the study total.[15] Only 2 percent of women in my study were of Middle Eastern background, compared to 4 percent in the US population. Native Americans, who make up 1.6 percent of the

US population, were not present in my study at all, an unfortunate consequence of the high rates of poverty in this community and the invisibility of Native women's reproductive health concerns in both scholarship and US medicine.[16]

Of the fourteen Black, Latina, and Middle Eastern American women in my study who had undertaken nonmedical egg freezing, their rates of educational attainment were impressive. All but one, or 93 percent, had earned advanced degrees, including nine master's degrees (64 percent), two medical degrees (14 percent), two law degrees (14 percent), and one PhD (7 percent). Furthermore, half of these women had attended Ivy League universities or elite private institutions. Consistent with their high levels of educational achievement, all were gainfully employed in professional fields, including health care, law, engineering, information technology, economics, journalism, and business.

If such highly educated Black, Latina, and Middle Eastern women are significantly underrepresented in egg freezing circles, then what are the factors that might account for this lack of representation? Here I want to address some of the key concerns that emerged in my study—namely, the high cost of egg freezing and barriers to access, the role of religion in producing both reproductive pressure and shame, and overarching concerns about minority women's place and participation in US reproductive health care.

It is important to begin with the technology's high cost, which poses a major barrier. As noted earlier, egg freezing averages between $10,000 and $15,000 per cycle, costs that are rarely covered by health insurance. Thus, most women in this study paid for egg freezing on their own, feeling fortunate for the career successes that had allowed them to do so. But many of the Black and Latina women had come from less affluent families than did the White women in the study. Thus, they had often taken on significant student loan debt, sometimes over multiple academic degrees. Some women were also helping family members who needed financial assistance. As a result, egg freezing posed a significant financial burden for two-thirds of these women. To pay the egg freezing charges, they were forced to rely on credit cards, bank loans, small loans from family members, flexible spending accounts at work, and in one case, a trip overseas to purchase cheaper hormonal medications. One woman who ended up paying $30,000 for three egg freezing cycles described it as "lighting a match to tens of thousands of dollars," especially when her three cycles produced only three frozen eggs. Another woman, Renee, who told me that she made $120,000 a year as a federal attorney, struggled to pay nearly $25,000 for two cycles of egg freezing. Renee's parents were working class and her father a devout Christian; thus, she feared his disapproval, even though her mother supported her and gave her $1,000 to help defray the costs. A credit card was Renee's primary solution, as she explained.

> So what happened was both times I think I put it on a non-interest-bearing credit card and just paid it off over time, so I never got interest. I never went into debt for it. But, yeah, it was hard for me. Yeah, it was for me. I don't know if there are other women out there who maybe work in a private sector where it's not so much of an issue. But I was having a lot of difficulty paying for it, and I make that six figures a year, which isn't a whole lot of money, but, you know. I also have a student loan. So it was hard. I mean, it really put a dent in my ability to save and then purchase a home because I'm not a home owner. I'm trying to buy, but I'm just thinking, you know, if I had that money, it would've been helpful.

Beyond the economic stress of egg freezing, religion emerged as a crucial factor in shaping minority women's egg freezing considerations. All of the Black and Latina women and one Arab American woman in my study were raised in Christian households, nine of them Catholic and four of them Protestant. For most of these women, Christianity produced its own kind of fertility paradox—namely, pronatalist pressures to have children within marriage, coupled with stigmatization and shame for those who failed to do so. Fertility failure could take many forms: never reproducing, reproducing without a partner, turning to a reproductive technology for help, or using a reproductive technology deemed immoral.

This religiously fueled fertility paradox weighed most heavily on women who were raised Catholic. Catholicism continues to uphold the world's most restrictive reproductive regime, with the Vatican disapproving of all forms of reproductive technology—from birth control to abortion to IVF to egg freezing.[17] These technologies are considered "unnatural" and hence forbidden for use by practicing Catholics. Catholicism views procreation within marriage as a divine process. Thus, egg freezing, which usually takes place outside marriage, is seen as separating reproduction from the conjugal sex act. Egg freezing is also forbidden based on intention: a woman who freezes her eggs is intending to use them later in

IVF, a technology that is similarly prohibited. Perhaps most important to Catholic women themselves, frozen eggs, once fertilized, become human embryos, which, according to the Catholic Church, represent the beginning of human life. Thus, women who are asked to freeze embryos—either as part of an egg freezing cycle or later on when they return to use their frozen eggs—must decide what to do with any excess embryos, as embryo destruction is considered tantamount to murder.[18] The Catholic concern over embryos is shared by some evangelical Protestant groups as well.[19] But Protestantism, in general, has been much more supportive of IVF and related technologies than Catholicism, including egg freezing.[20] Thus, the Catholic Church stands alone in its unyielding moral opposition to reproductive assistance, while at the same time encouraging Catholic women to become married, fertile child bearers.

Many Catholic women in my study described how they faced this fertility paradox in their own lives. But it was especially challenging for Black and Latina women in my study, because three-quarters of them were raised in staunchly Catholic families. Although most of these women were no longer practicing Catholics, they nonetheless felt the moral weight of Catholicism, not only regarding egg freezing but for other deviations from the moral code.

Isabel was one of these women. Raised in a deeply religious Puerto Rican American family, Isabel described how her strict Catholic upbringing had influenced her. Even though she had graduated from two Ivy League universities, had earned two master's degrees, and had become a successful health care policy maker, Isabel had come to believe that "reproduction defines you as a woman." In secrecy, Isabel had volunteered for an early egg freezing clinical trial back in 2008, freezing half of her eggs and allowing the other half to be fertilized with donor sperm before freezing them as embryos. Eventually, Isabel become a single mother through IVF, using her new partner's sperm. But all of these reproductive decisions had been made in secrecy, for reasons that she explained to me.

> I was raised in a very Catholic household. I went to Catholic school until I was in college. And in college, I fell into a depression, and I lost my faith. . . . And I have to say, I respect my mother, I think my mother is an incredible woman. [But] I just thought about her kneeling in front of men and, in the Catholic Church, not having the ability for her to be viewed as holy. . . . And I just, I couldn't do it. So morality is very important to

me, but organized religion is not. I'm the only person in my family who doesn't go to church on Sunday. . . . I mean, my family is Catholic, really strong faith. And here I am, I am an unwed mother, and I still hold onto these things. . . . So, you know, when I was doing IVF, when I got pregnant, I couldn't—I didn't tell my mother.

Nina was also raised in a strict Catholic household in Puerto Rico, where marriage and motherhood were revered. But unlike Isabel, who chose secrecy in her turn to assisted conception, Nina felt the need to destigmatize herself through openness and candor. In Nina's Puerto Rican social world, fertility failure, or the ultimate inability to become a mother, was not an option. But she also ardently hoped to avoid feelings of fertility shame for becoming an "unwed mother." As an academic obstetrician-gynecologist now living and working in an East Coast city with a high rate of Black and Latina teenage pregnancies, Nina was extremely sensitive to the stigma of out-of-wedlock childbirth. She was thus most concerned about what her obstetrician colleagues might think, and she felt obligated to justify the nature of her son's post-egg-freezing conception.

It's funny. I was mortified to have people think I had just gone off and gotten pregnant. I'm very open about how I conceived—that this was very much planned, yeah. Like, I very openly tell people I tried very long to conceive my son—that I'm not the "irresponsible kid" that did this. This was very important, that my kid wasn't an afterthought. There are a lot of people who probably care about that. There's a lot of projection in that statement, but I do believe that a lot of my colleagues would care that it isn't a "random" conception, versus maybe in other socioeconomic groups, there isn't the same stigma there. But where I come from, I think most people do want children. I think in some ways it's actually socially driven. The expectation of an adult is to be a parent. I think it still takes guts to choose to be child-free. I think you will have to, uh, endure years of people telling you, "When are you having kids? When are you having kids? When are you having kids? When are you having kids?" I think you have to be very strong. This is in some ways very socially biased—the social expectation.

This social expectation to marry and have children was also felt strongly by minority women who had been raised in religious Protestant households.

Rita, an Arab American lawyer who had been raised in the deep South, described herself as a "very religious" Christian, one who shared the Catholic opinion that embryos are human lives to be treasured and saved (including, if necessary, through embryo adoption).[21] When Rita moved to Washington, DC, to work for the federal government, she was confronted by the dearth of eligible men to date, but she was also disappointed by the Christian men she met, who seemed ageist and did not want an equal partner. By the time I spoke with Rita, she had moved to Denver—sometimes called "Menver" for its surplus of men—because she hoped to make a fresh start there.

> I just wasn't happy living in DC. It's not a bad place to live. It just wasn't working for me. Because I was going to a church in Washington, and my friends and I were like, all these men in this church—and these are Christian men—like, all they cared about in dating was fertility and sex. That's it. . . . It's really basic, right? And maybe that just sheds some light on how men are, that they aren't—I think, men in general are not looking for intelligence or women with ideas or a conversation. I think they're looking for sex and fertility. . . . I feel women are judged for their age, generally, but I think women who are married may not feel it like women who are single. Because in a dating context, it's kind of like just a huge factor for men, and infertility is just like—it's huge for men, so they're always going to go for the younger woman who's, like, fertile. And for Christian men, I think it's huge, yeah . . . which basically boils down to, like, I need to do something different. So I did something really drastically different, and I moved to Denver.

Although Rita's frozen eggs were stored back in a Washington, DC, IVF clinic, she planned to keep this secret in Denver, including from men she might meet and date there. As Rita told me, sharing her egg freezing decision had already brought her moral censure.

> I will tell you, I have talked to some people about it who are, like, really kind of against it. And there's a stigma. And so my one friend was really judgmental about it, and she is religious. And so I don't know if it comes from that. And then I have another friend who's not religious at all, and she just thinks it's really weird. She's just sort of like, "That's a petri dish. That's like science. That's not how you have a baby!" And then once I

realized they were judgmental, I just stopped sharing. And that was sort of like the end. Because I think there is still a stigma about it.

The role of stigma in Christian women's lives was articulated most powerfully by Kendra, who had grown up in a Southern Baptist congregation. After attending a historically Black college and earning her master's degree in public policy from a prestigious university in London, Kendra moved to New York City, where she became the vice president of a communications firm. For Kendra, egg freezing was about keeping her options open. "I want the option to decide that if I'm in a relationship and I decide that we want to start a family, have children, that I have that ability," Kendra explained. "But also, if I decide that I don't want that, that's okay, too."

Kendra realized that her perspective on the optional nature of motherhood was quite different from many other women who had grown up in the Black Church, especially in the deep South. In fact, she was quite critical of the ways in which religion could be used against Black women who chose a different route, including freezing their eggs.

I think that there's just an increased shaming of women that is above and beyond anything that you can imagine. And I really don't think that it's anything to be ashamed of. So, you know, I've got so many women who would say, "I thought about doing it" or maybe "I did it, but I just didn't share my story." It was amazing to me, and I think that the sense of keeping it to ourselves is because there is an inherent shame attached to it, especially in the African American community. I think the shame for women is that you're expected to be married, to have a family, and to have kids by a certain age, and with no problems attached to it. I think that in the African American community, religion, especially Christianity—it plays a huge role there. And so the idea that you are trying to control something that is outside of God's plan, I think, is a big thing. . . . The shame is overwhelming. And I think the shame is related to just women making decisions on their own and for their own health. Their reproductive health care is on a whole other level. And if you take that and put it in communities of color, and then you put it in the South [*laughs*]! I mean, you just, you know—you're pushing a brick wall there.

As a mentor for other young Black women in her profession, Kendra opted for candor over secrecy, believing that she could be a voice for

Black women who might want to consider egg freezing. Kendra viewed egg freezing within a longer historical trajectory, in which Black women's reproductive choices and desires have been fundamentally denied and neglected.

> I think reproductive health care in and of itself is an issue among all women but has a very sensitive vibe in the African American community, from the historical ability to control our own bodies and our own reproductive health care. So, for me, it was very important to do the procedure but to also share it with someone who may be—who may need that voice or may need to see someone else doing it to know that it's okay and that it's our choice. Like, it's really our choice and our decision to make, and what it means to have, you know, bodily autonomy. I control what I do. So I wanted to share that message, not only with the young [Black] women that I mentor but the other women in my office. Interestingly enough, after I did the egg freezing, the young women at my office went crazy, you know, wanting to know more information on how they could do it. So . . . I want to be proud of myself for standing up and saying, "This is something I wanted to do, so I did it."

For Kendra, overcoming the silence surrounding egg freezing was vitally important, so that other Black women could begin to view egg freezing as a reproductive option, a way of claiming their reproductive rights. Given the long history of reproductive injustice faced by Black women in the US, including contemporary forms of racism within US reproductive health care, Kendra's concern to place egg freezing within a reproductive justice framework was of immense importance.[22] Furthermore, in Kendra's narrative, she identifies the fertility paradox facing Black and other minority women who have been raised in pronatalist Christian religious traditions. The enormous pressures to marry and have children—by a "certain age" and with "no problems," as Kendra put it—have contributed to shame, stigma, and secrecy surrounding egg freezing, which may serve as a potent barrier for minority Christian women who might otherwise consider this option.

It is also important to recognize that highly educated minority women like Kendra who have been raised in strong Christian religious traditions face not only a minority mating gap based on disparities between college-educated men and women but also a *religiously driven minority mating gap*, in which one's religious affiliation affects the very likelihood of ever receiving higher education. The Pew Research Center conducted a "Religious Landscape Study" in 2014 to assess levels of education among thirty US religious denominations, including historically Black Protestant denominations.[23] Among members of the African Methodist Episcopal Church, the National Baptist Convention, and the Southern Baptist Convention, only about 20 percent were college graduates. But women in these denominations had earned 66 percent of all the college degrees, versus 34 percent for men. American Catholics constitute a much larger group, as nearly one in five Americans have been raised Catholic. But Catholics fared only slightly better in educational achievement, with approximately one-quarter of adult Catholics finishing college, 54 percent of them women.[24]

In short, the intersection of race and religion truly matters with regard to educational achievement. Highly educated Black, Latina, and other women of color are clearly a distinct minority within their Catholic and Protestant religious traditions. In the US, college graduation rates are low overall, at only 36 percent of all American adults. But these graduation rates are lower for men than for women and lower among some religious groups than others. This leaves highly educated women like Tiffany, Isabel, Nina, Rita, and Kendra in a *double fertility paradox*, in which their educational outperformance of both men *and* their coreligionists leads to exceptional challenges in achieving the three *p*'s of partnership, pregnancy, and parenthood if they hope to form and maintain relationships within their own communities.

The Overrepresented

The intersection of race and religion, I argue, is also important in understanding the *overrepresentation in egg freezing* of women from other racial and religious minority groups in the US. In my study, fifty Asian American and Jewish American women volunteered to speak with me, or fully one-third of the 150 women I met. Asian American women represented 17 percent of the study total, although Asian Americans make up only 5.8 percent of the US population overall.[25] Jewish American women represented 16 percent of the study total, although Jewish Americans represent only 2.2 percent of the US population.[26] In other words, Asian American women and Jewish American women were substantially overrepresented in my study.

Before examining the reasons for this overrepresentation, it is important to describe these women's backgrounds. Among the twenty-six Asian American women in my study, twenty-two had completed nonmedical egg freezing, three had completed medical egg freezing (for a variety of conditions), and one had started egg freezing but then ovulated before her cycle could be completed. The heritage backgrounds of these Asian American women were diverse, with their parents immigrating from China, India, Japan, Pakistan, the Philippines, and Vietnam. Twelve women were of East Asian heritage: eight of Chinese ancestry and four of Japanese ancestry. Eleven women were of South Asian heritage: ten of Indian ancestry and one of Pakistani ancestry. Three women were of Southeast Asian heritage: two of Filipino ancestry and one of Vietnamese ancestry. Two of these women were of mixed Asian American backgrounds.[27] With regard to religious identities, the majority of East Asian American women had not been raised in any religious tradition; this was especially true of Chinese American women but also half of the Japanese American women. The majority of South Asian women had been raised Hindu, but three Indian American women and one Pakistani American woman were Muslims.

As a group, these women had achieved exceptionally high rates of education. Of the twenty-three healthy women who had undertaken nonmedical egg freezing, twenty-one, or more than 90 percent, had earned advanced degrees. These included eleven master's degrees (49 percent), nine medical degrees (39 percent), and one law degree (4 percent). Interestingly, one-third (35 percent) had attended Ivy League universities; another one-third (39 percent) had attended other elite private universities; and with only one exception, all the rest had attended highly ranked public universities. Given these women's high levels of educational achievement, it is not surprising that all were gainfully employed in professional fields, including health care, information technology, business management, entrepreneurship, government and law, academia, foreign service, and humanitarianism.

Similar numbers of Jewish women volunteered for my study. Of twenty-four Jewish women, nineteen had completed nonmedical egg freezing, and five had completed medical egg freezing, three for cancer or precancerous conditions. Two of these women were Jewish converts, but the rest were raised in Jewish households of Ashkenazi (European) ancestry. Two of these women were Orthodox Jews, but the rest were from Reformed backgrounds and were largely secular. As with Asian American women, these Jewish women were exceptionally well educated. Of the nineteen women who had undertaken nonmedical egg freezing, all but three, or 84 percent, had earned advanced degrees. These included ten master's degrees (53 percent), two medical degrees (11 percent), one law degree (5 percent), and three PhDs (16 percent). More than one-quarter (26 percent) had attended Ivy League universities, while nearly half (47 percent) had attended other elite private universities. The majority of these Jewish women worked in health care and scientific fields, but others were employed in law, academia, business, and a variety of other professions.

The question is, Why are so many Asian American and Jewish American women turning to egg freezing, not only in my study but in others as well?[28] Although Asian Americans are an ethnically diverse racial minority and Jewish Americans are an ethnically distinct religious minority, I would argue that they share some key characteristics, which are leading Asian American and Jewish American women to undertake egg freezing in particularly high numbers. These shared attributes include women's exceptionally high levels of educational achievement, among the highest in the nation; pronatalist scripts of cultural success that make motherhood seem imperative; and religious support for assisted reproductive technologies, which makes egg freezing acceptable, even encouraged, including among those who are religiously observant. Indeed, this latter attribute—the moral support for egg freezing provided by Hinduism, Islam, and Judaism—constitutes a key factor propelling women from these overrepresented minority groups toward egg freezing.

To begin with education, Asian American women and Jewish American women are two of the most highly educated groups of women in the US. As shown in table 3.1, Asian Americans have the highest college graduation rates of any US census group, at 59 percent overall. Furthermore, within the Asian American category, Hindus, who are primarily Indian Americans, constitute the top American religious group with regard to educational achievement.[29] More than three-quarters of Hindus (77 percent) have a college degree. American Jews rank third among religious groups with regard to educational achievement, with 59 percent of all adult Jews having graduated from college. Given the strong correlation between educational attainment and economic success, Jews and Hindus are also high earners, with 44 percent of Jews and 36 percent of Hindus living in households with annual incomes of more than $100,000.[30]

Both Asian Americans and Jewish Americans view educational achievement as a key to success, including for women, who are encouraged to pursue higher education. As a result, and in line with the gender-based educational disparities described earlier in this chapter, Asian American women have now outperformed men educationally, with 54 percent of all Asian American college graduates being women, versus 46 percent who are men. Similarly, Jewish American women's college graduation rates have risen over the generations to overall parity with Jewish American men (49 versus 51 percent).[31] However, Jewish women's educational achievement exceeds that of Jewish men as the educational level increases beyond the bachelor's degree.[32] Jewish American women are four times as likely to have completed a graduate degree than the broader population of White American women.[33] Indeed, Jewish American women are much more highly educated than most White Americans. Whereas the modal degree for non-Jewish White Americans is a high school diploma, the modal degree for Jewish women is a bachelor's degree.[34]

Given these exceptionally high levels of education, Asian American and Jewish American women who seek equally educated male partners may face a serious lack of options. Indeed, the minority mating gap may be taking a particularly heavy toll on highly educated Asian American and Jewish American women, who are much more educated than the vast majority of American men, including many men within their own communities. The great difficulties in finding educated male partners, particularly those with advanced degrees, was well described by Rebecca, a Jewish American PhD scientist working for a major US federal agency.

I work in a highly technical field with a lot of women, and I've watched them. It's very difficult to find somebody. And I've noticed it in the dating process as well. I noticed that there's a huge imbalance. . . . I mean, I must have been on over one hundred dates. And I think maybe five of the men—maybe—had any sort of professional degree. . . . I mean, I dated a few lawyers. But most of the time, people will be like, "Oh, you work for [federal science agency]?" Like a couple of guys were stupid enough to insult my job [*laughs*]! I think that's part of why I've been single for a long time. And I'm older now, and I'm less willing to compromise. I do like my own life, and it's a different thing than dating in your twenties.

For women who were looking only for Jewish partners, the pool of men was often even narrower. Fully 71 percent of non-Orthodox Jewish Americans marry outside their religion.[35] When a Jewish American man marries a non-Jewish woman, that means "there's one less eligible Jewish guy for the Jewish girls," as explained by the Jewish American author Melanie Notkin in her poignant book called *Otherhood: Modern Women Finding a New Kind of Happiness* (2014).[36] This dearth of eligible Jewish men was noted by Jewish women in my study; as one of them put it, "[It is why] all the Jewish girls of my age in this area are doing egg freezing."

Micah was one of these women. A highly successful Baltimore businesswoman, Micah had had no luck on online dating sites, including JDate.com, which advertises itself as the "#1 Choice for Jewish Singles." Thus, at age thirty-eight, she had spent $22,000 of her own savings for two cycles of egg freezing, telling me, with laughter, that she was now contemplating the purchase of a professional Jewish matchmaker's services. "Whatever! I have already paid $22,000 for something, and now I'm paying to, like, find a husband! Not that there's anything wrong with it. But it completely counters anything that my friends have done or anything I know, where you meet someone naturally, you have a kid, and, like, great! You know? And I don't know if I feel defeated, empowered, or otherwise by the egg freezing thing, in and of itself—having to go through it and paying that and whatever. And then the same thing with potentially doing that in a matchmaking setting."

The problem of finding partners within one's own community was felt by Asian American women as well. Suzi, a Chinese American academic physician who was a highly specialized surgeon, had always hoped to marry a Chinese American man, especially because her parents could not speak English fluently. But, as she lamented, the Chinese American men she met were inevitably intimidated by her accomplishments.

> If you meet me, and even when you talk to me, I'm not an imposing person. I'm actually very small and petite, and I'm very nice and friendly. So it's not like when you meet me, you're like, "Oh my gosh! She's an intimidating person." . . . It's almost like they're afraid of my accomplishments. So, when people now ask me what I want in a man, I was like, "I really honestly just want someone really comfortable in their skin. So they're not intimidated by me. So they are okay with who they are, and that has

nothing to do with me. And that's all I want." And then they're like, "But that can't be that hard to find." And I'm like, "Actually, you'd be surprised."

The male intimidation factor also affected Indian American women, many of whom had used Indian matchmaking services and speed-dating events in an attempt to meet potential Indian American partners. Although Indian American women were often appreciative of the "marriage-mindedness" of Indian American men, they often complained bitterly about the kind of men they were meeting. For example, Sita, a humanitarian health care worker, described her experience being "pinged a lot" on dating apps.

> I mean, I tried OKCupid, and yeah, I left that one because I actually got depressed. Like, the quality of men contacting me was just terrible. I mean, you know, a guy would write you a message saying, "hi sexy" or "you are hot" or you know "I love curvy women." And I'm like, really? This is how one guy—one guy that we actually matched and started to set up a date—I exchanged phone numbers with him. He said to me on the phone, "Let's meet at Victoria's Secret at the mall. I want to show you something." And I just said, "Well, is that going to work for you? Like, do women really go for that?" And then later, when I was telling my girl-friend this story, she was like, "Well, obviously it has. Because he's used it before." So, I mean, this is not the first time. And I was like, huh. It must work.

Sita's mother tried to intervene, putting her daughter through "online Indian matchmaking" and a number of "arranged introductions" with Hindu men. "And it didn't work out for her either [*laughs*]! I'm not your typical-looking Indian girl. . . . I have curly hair. I'm not very thin, you know, and not the stereotypical what you see in the movies. And it's not attractive to Indian men, because Indian men want that idealistic picture. So it really hasn't worked out with any of the Indian guys." Indeed, Sita never told her mother about her two "secret boyfriends in college," both of whom were Black. In her thirties, Sita also dated a Pakistani Muslim American man, resolving, "I'm just going to tell my parents." But when she did, her mom "just lost it," bespeaking the difficulties of interfaith and interracial dating within South Asian American communities.

Even within one's own faith, finding a partner could be excruciating. Nahla, a physician from the Indian American Muslim community, considered her chances of finding a "good Muslim man" to be "pretty bad." "It's hard to find those ones there [who] were also just like me, just kind of like career oriented for a while but happened to be really good guys and happened to find themselves, you know, single at a later age. And so they're there, don't get me wrong. They're there, but it's really hard to find them. . . . [It's] very slim, slim pickings to find a good guy." Nahla also pointed out that many Indian American men of all religious backgrounds were ageist, "screening out" any woman over the age of thirty. In her case, they would consider her current age of thirty-five to be a major deterrent. "They have no problem telling me that it's about, you know, it's about fertility. And, oh, like, they want to start a family. They don't use the word 'fertility' necessarily, but they're like, 'Oh, we want to take our time in having families and we want to have large families.' . . . They're very, like, open about that, you know. And I just don't like that [laughs]!"

Rajani, who was also Indian American but from a Hindu family, had encountered this problem as well. Working in international affairs for the US federal government, Rajani had had a cosmopolitan career but no luck finding a suitable partner. Thus, at age thirty-nine, she had decided to date "down," entering a mixed-collar relationship with a divorcé, who was already the father of two children. Rajani explained her decision to become engaged to him in this way:

> I think [if] you look for someone who's similar to you in education and income, maybe that pool doesn't exist in the way you would assume. So, then I'm finding in my friend circle and in my family—I have two sisters—most of us are married or dating guys who have less education and means than we do. And maybe if you're not willing to do that or you're trying to find someone who's sort of similar to you, you're limiting your pool. Because almost all of them, yeah, have less education. . . . I think because we have tried in our twenties and early thirties to find people who are, you know, also the same race, same religion. But for me, it wasn't working out. I think honestly, the people I was meeting, I was intimidating them in some way. So I feel like I'm quite lucky to have found my fiancé. But he's not good on paper [laughs], in the way that I would have wanted in my twenties.

All of these women—Rebecca, Micah, Suzi, Sita, Nahla, and Rajani—
were hoping to marry, but only Rajani seemed to be headed in that direction. Marriage is highly valued in both Asian American and Jewish
American communities in the US, where marriage rates are higher than
in the general population. Jewish Americans and Hindu Americans marry
more than their counterparts in any other religion, except for Mormons.[37]
Furthermore, 60 percent of Asian American adults are married, versus 54
percent of Americans overall.[38]

For women in these communities, becoming a married mother is considered a key marker of success. Indeed, Jewish women face what my colleagues and I have called the *Jewish maternal imperative*—namely, the
religious and social mandate for Jewish women to become mothers in
order to participate fully in Jewish culture, as well as to pass their maternal Jewishness to offspring, thereby "reproducing Jews" and helping to
perpetuate a religious minority community that was once devastated by
the Holocaust.[39]

For Asian American women, pressures to become married mothers
are less tied to minority group perpetuity than to larger "success frames,"
in which women are expected to succeed on multiple levels, including in
education, careers, marriage, and motherhood.[40] But as with Jews, Asian
American communities tend to support "traditional family values," in
which marriage and childbearing are highly valued and being unmarried
and childless are statuses rife with negative social, cultural, and emotional consequences.[41]

These pronatalist pressures weighed heavily on both Asian American
and Jewish American women in my study, as they described their marriage and motherhood desires and prospects. For example, Clara, a Jewish
American PhD clinical psychologist, explained why she had volunteered
to participate in an egg freezing clinical trial when she had barely reached
her early thirties. "My anxiety was so high about it. I felt this pressure to
meet someone. And at that point, I was much more involved in the Jewish
community, so I think the pressure was even more intense, because that's
sort of what it means to be a successful Jew. It's all about having kids and
family. And so, my anxiety was very high, and it was getting in the way. I
was really [thinking about] my own family of origin, and I was just really
anxious about it."

Similarly, Rhoda, the director of academic career services at a major
East Coast university, described how pursuing egg freezing had created

tremendous emotional angst for her as a Jewish woman, because it was a reminder of both her motherhood desires and her ongoing lack of a partner. She had attended a clinic's informational session on how to inject hormonal medications but realized that it was mostly for married couples who were undergoing IVF. Rhoda described how she felt.

> Being Jewish, you're from this tough Russian stock, and you know, I did it. I think I was—and I'm sure that people get emotional when you talk about this—you know, I *so* much want to be a mom. And I think the motivation—I mean, I was scared the first time. I was very overwhelmed when I went. It was really hard when I went to the information session, because everybody else is there with partners or rings on their finger. And you're there. And that's one of the hardest things, I will tell you, going through this as a single woman. It's like you see other people going through it, and they have partners with them. And that's really hard to be doing it by yourself.

For many Jewish women, the inability to find a partner was particularly bittersweet, because they looked to their own parents' happy marriages and the successful family lives they had created. Several women mentioned having especially close relationships with their fathers, who had always supported them emotionally and financed their educations. A physician, Dina, who described her relationship with her recently deceased father as "very, very, very, very, very strong," said she wanted "somebody who was going to be an amazing, amazing father": "like, you know, one-tenth of what my dad was . . . something special."

Interestingly, no Jewish American women in my study reported any explicit pressure to produce grandchildren for their parents. Thus, women were left alone to make their egg freezing decisions, even though parents provided support as needed. For example, Miriam, a lawyer running the business development section of her law firm, described how her parents reacted to her egg freezing decision. "I think my parents are—they're not your typical Jewish, overinvolved parents. They're more of, um . . . I want to say nonjudgmental. But they let me live my life with very little interference and sometimes too little interference and so little guidance. So, when I told them I was doing this, my mom said, 'That's very brave. I'm proud of you.' I don't think there was a sense of, 'Oh my God! I'm not going to have grandkids!' If there was, I didn't get that impression from her."

Second-generation Asian American women, on the other hand, more often faced explicit pressure from their first-generation immigrant parents to marry and have children. Almost all of the Asian American women in my study described how hard they had worked in their twenties to complete their education and establish their careers, hoping to add marriage and motherhood by their early thirties. Furthermore, no matter the ethnic background, these expectations were placed on women by first-generation, immigrant parents, who were often deeply involved in their daughters' lives. Sometimes these parents encouraged and supported them; sometimes they pressured them; and sometimes they criticized them for failing to live up to their filial expectations as devoted daughters to their parents.

For example, Suzi, the highly specialized academic surgeon mentioned earlier, described her Chinese immigrant mother in this way:

Like, my mother, nothing's ever enough. Yeah, you never satisfy them. I think it's cultural. Like you always have to want more. . . . It's terrible, because you grow up with that, and all of a sudden [they say], "We don't want you to advance your career anymore. We want you to now get married and have a baby." And I'm like, "You know, I spent like thirty years doing this. I can't switch it off now. You made me into the person I am, and now you don't like this person." . . . I don't know what the right balance is. I don't know what will make me happy at this point. . . . [But] I really want to be a mom.

Indian American women, too, described the pressures they felt from their families to succeed academically, professionally, and reproductively, although many described their own mothers as "strong feminists" who had always championed them. Yet, as these Indian American women approached their midthirties, they often began receiving "small comments," such as "Oh, you should start thinking about getting married." Sita, the humanitarian health care worker mentioned earlier, described the pressure both she and her younger sister were feeling to marry and produce children.

My parents are freaking out! Freaking out [laughs]! My mom calls my sister and me almost every other day to ask if we have any "good news," which means, "Have we met anybody?" No, there is immense pressure—immense pressure because of the culture that we're from. And, you know, the culture says that your responsibility is not over until your daughter is married. She continues to be your responsibility. No matter that I, you know, have a very nice job, a well-paying job, that I have bought my own place. . . . She openly says that "I really would like to see grandchildren." . . . She's ready for us to have children outside of marriage, which, as you know, is really not a thing for us Indians [*laughs*]! However, I have made the choice that that's not something I want to do. I'd like to do it *with* somebody.

Although Sita was stunned that her mother would encourage her to become a single mother, she was not alone. Half of the Indian American women in my study had been encouraged by their mothers to consider donor insemination because their mothers were "desperate" for grandchildren, making their thirty-something daughters feel "sad," even "bittersweet." As one put it, "very few women come to that conclusion on their own." Furthermore, no other Asian American parents forwarded this idea. Rather, Chinese American parents were more likely to offer to pay for egg freezing in the hopes of seeing future grandchildren.

The relative acceptance of egg freezing among Asian American and Jewish American women and their parents reflects pro-reproductive-technology stances in both of these communities. Asian Americans and Jewish Americans have among the highest utilization rates of IVF and other assisted reproductive technologies, because these technologies generally brook no religious or cultural opposition, as they do in the Catholic and Protestant Christian communities described earlier.[42] Instead, Judaism is *the* most supportive Abrahamic faith tradition, allowing multiple forms of assisted reproductive technology, including among Orthodox Jews in the US and Israel, the country with the highest rate per capita of IVF utilization in the world.[43] Islam, too, has been highly supportive of assisted reproduction, making the Middle East home to one of the most vibrant IVF sectors in the world.[44] However, today, Asia is the global epicenter of assisted reproduction. Together, China, India, and Japan boast nearly 2,500 IVF clinics, the majority of which are in India, where the country's two major religions, Hinduism and Islam, view these technologies as permissible fertility-enhancing interventions.[45]

With exceptional religious support from Hinduism, Islam, and Judaism, egg freezing has been made possible even for the most religiously observant women. For example, Nahla, the Indian American physician who still hoped to find a "good Muslim man," was able to freeze her eggs with encouragement and support from her large Muslim family. "Yeah. All the women in the family were totally aware," Nahla told me, "and they were checking up on me, and they were like, very good." Nahla's mother was particularly relieved that she had decided to undergo egg freezing. "She was happy about it. . . . I mean, I think it was bittersweet in some ways, because she was sad that I was in a position that I needed to do that. But she was happy that I was being proactive and doing it. You know what I mean?" Still a premarital virgin per cultural and religious expectations, Nahla underwent the various "transvaginal" (through the vagina) egg freezing procedures at the age of thirty-five, justifying her decision in this way:

> I do think "medical is medical." So I don't care about, like, my hymen or whatever being broken. I think that's like kind of old school. Like, it can probably bleed by riding or you know what I mean? I don't really—I don't care that much. Maybe for other people it would be. I don't. Not for me. And in fact, to be honest, it's kind of—this is kind of like TMI [too much information]—but I was happy that they did it, so I knew that there was no problem [*laughs*]. If that makes sense? Because I was like, "Oh, okay. Everything works here. Everything's good." You know?

Unlike the Catholic and other Christian women described earlier, Nahla suffered no religious guilt, instead describing this religiously permitted procedure, which produced twenty-eight frozen eggs in one cycle, as "magical."

> I don't have this sense of anxiety, of like feeling like I need to get married yesterday. I mean, I want to get married, and I want to get married sooner rather than later. But I don't—I don't feel like it needs to happen yesterday, because my clock is ticking. . . . It's kind of funny. I have this, like, magical thing in my back pocket that I can pull out, and you know. It's like it extends my fertility for all these years. I don't have to think about this clock at all. And so, yeah, it just puts me [at ease]. It makes me very relieved, and it makes me feel like I potentially might not miss out on the things that I wanted, which, like I said, were ideally like three kids or more. I really want more than just two kids. I mean, if God blesses me with one, I'll be happy. But like, if I can plan to have more than one or two, I would want that, you know?

Orthodox Jewish women in my study were also very grateful for their opportunity to pursue egg freezing, especially given the significant mating gap in the Orthodox Jewish community.[46] For example, Esther, a computer programmer who had reached the age of thirty-four without finding an appropriate partner, described the problem in this way:

A lot of men, they stay studying religious texts for a lot longer. Which is fine. That just means that they're getting, you know—if they're planning to get a career, they're getting a later start in life on a career. And meanwhile, the girl's been working since she was twenty. And he's just starting at the age of thirty. That ten years makes a huge difference in terms of— not in terms of the ability to start a family but the mentality of a person. Like, they're not necessarily on the same wavelength of understanding, you know, the world around them and to acting with people in the same way. Not to say that it can't work, but it just sometimes becomes a little bit more difficult when the girl has been out in the world and the boy hasn't. . . . [The women] outsmart the men, and sometimes the men can't handle it; or sometimes the girl doesn't feel like she's on the same wavelength as the guy.

Indeed, Esther herself had obtained a master's degree in computer science and had found a good job but never a partner "on the same wavelength." Thus, with the support of her older sister—a nurse and mother of thirteen children—Esther pursued egg freezing. Although her dream of ten children was no longer realistic, Esther was grateful for egg freezing, because it had taken some of the pressure off, "not in terms of getting married," Esther noted, but in holding out hope for future Jewish motherhood. "It's sort of like, you know, if I was going to go through this, I'd rather take care of half of it now, because it sort of jump-starts the process," Esther explained. "When I do get married and if we do have a problem [of infertility], I already have half of it taken care of."

Egg Freezing as a Self-Preservation Technology

Indeed, for Esther, Nahla, and most of the minority women who volunteered for my study, egg freezing served as a relief valve, significantly reducing the built-up pressure that these women felt over having to find a partner in order to achieve a pregnancy. Once they had frozen their eggs, women reported feeling calmer about their reproductive lives, without having to worry about the constant ticking of their biological clocks. In addition, many women experienced a sense of empowerment after egg freezing. Egg freezing made them feel agentive, that they had done something "for themselves" and within their "own powers" to preserve the possibility of future motherhood. As one Chinese American IT designer, Melinda, put it, "I actually consider myself lucky that I live in an age where this is an option, and I can do something about it, and I'm in a position to do something about it. I mean, I felt quite positive about the whole experience."

Beyond these psychological rewards, what does egg freezing offer to minority women in the US—be they Black, Latina, Middle Eastern, or Asian American, or Christian, Hindu, Jewish, or Muslim? What benefits might egg freezing confer *across* groups, especially as increasing numbers of minority women turn to this reproductive technology? Although this chapter has focused on the diverse experiences, expectations, and challenges that lead to under- and overrepresentation of particular groups in the egg freezing demographic, I want to focus here on the issues that unite these minority women in crucial ways.

First, for highly educated minority women who are raised in family- and child-centered religious and social environments, egg freezing may serve as a powerful *self-preservation technology*, literally preserving one's sense of personhood amid powerful pronatalist pressures. Being raised in cultural and faith traditions in which marriage and motherhood are mandated and celebrated, minority women who freeze their eggs may be able to retain some sense of normative fertility within their communities, because egg freezing allows them to reclaim the possibility of future motherhood, even as they reach their late thirties. In this way, egg freezing becomes more than a hope technology; it becomes a way for women to preserve maternal identity and dignity in pronatalist environments where motherhood is considered imperative.

Second, egg freezing may be a way to address the fertility paradox, in which minority women's outstanding educational achievements paradoxically diminish their chances of becoming mothers. High achievement itself may translate into a fertility penalty for the doctors, lawyers, engineers, scientists, government officials, and other kinds of minority women whose stories fill this chapter. This is especially true for high-achieving minority women raised in American Christian traditions, whose outperformance of both men *and* coreligionists may lead to a *double* fertility penalty, in which their options for motherhood with men from their own communities become extremely limited and their consequent feelings of fertility shame and failure especially strong.

The fertility paradox facing high-achieving minority women reflects the mating gap existing *across* minority groups in the US. Without exception, Asian American, Black, Latina, Middle Eastern, and American Indian/Alaska Native women are excelling in higher education at levels well beyond their male peers. This is resulting in critical challenges for highly educated minority women who hope to marry and raise a family with eligible, educated, and equal men. As we saw in Tiffany's opening story, she did her very best to find her "Prince Charming," including partnering "down" the educational and economic spectrum, including with divorced men who were already fathers. But, despite her best efforts, Tiffany could not bridge the minority mating gap and ultimately decided to pursue single motherhood by choice via fertilization of her frozen eggs by donor sperm.

Tiffany was not alone in this regard. As we have seen, women raised in conservative religious traditions are making these kinds of difficult reproductive decisions. Despite the stigma of out-of-wedlock motherhood, women's desires for children—and their parents' desires for grandchildren—may be trumping the propriety of marriage. As will be discussed later on, single motherhood via egg freezing seems to be on the rise across the US. That minority women like Tiffany, Isabel, and Nina are among the beneficiaries of this new option is an important trend that deserves to be studied further, as educated American women of diverse racial and religious backgrounds decide to pursue two of the three *p*'s, namely, pregnancy and parenthood, in the absence of men as partners.[47]

Ultimately, whether raised in religious traditions or not, highly educated minority women in the US are facing the dilemma of how to move forward with their reproductive lives, given the "men as partners" problem that they face. In the absence of a "Prince Charming"—that rare and special type of man that Tiffany had once hoped would sweep her off her feet—egg freezing is performing the triple labor of women's *fertility* preservation, women's *self*-preservation, and, in some cases, *cultural* and *community* preservation, where motherhood is expected and children are cherished for minority group survival.

4

The Fertility Threats

From Aging Ovaries to Cancer

Maya's Fertility Crisis

Of the many dynamic professional women I met in this study, six of them had worked at the highest levels of US government, serving in the political administrations of Presidents Bill Clinton and Barack Obama and Senators Hillary Clinton and Bernie Sanders. Maya was one of these women in politics. After the president for whom she worked left office, Maya joined a Washington think tank, then a federal agency. By the time Maya turned thirty, she had done more in Washington than most people could imagine in a lifetime.

But after a decade spent in politics, Maya yearned for a change of scenery. Having never left the East Coast, where she had been raised by her Taiwanese immigrant parents, Maya felt attracted by California's booming tech industry. Soon she and her fiancé headed westward to San Francisco, where Maya took a position as director of development for a tech firm. Although the move was good for Maya, it was not good for her relationship. "It wasn't the right thing. It wasn't going to work," Maya told me. So she ended her engagement shortly before her thirty-third birthday.

By the time I met Maya two years later, she had repartnered twice. Her new partner, Kevin, was eight years older and divorced, and unlike Maya, he had never wanted to have children.

> He's in his early forties, doesn't have kids, and doesn't feel like on his own he would ever have kids. But, like, he knows that in order to be with me, it involves having kids. . . . Um, so when I first started seeing him, you know, we talked really early on about it. Like, I made it clear that having kids was important to me. And obviously I wasn't going to put any pressure on him to commit to that or do that right away. And

we talked really early on about, like, I'm going to freeze my eggs. And he was very supportive of it. He's been very supportive of me through this whole thing.

Indeed, Maya was one of twenty women, or 18 percent of the study total, who were in a relationship at the time of egg freezing. In all of these cases, egg freezing was a way for these couples to put off immediate marriage and childbearing decisions, usually because male partners were unready to have children. In Maya and Kevin's case, their relationship was simply too new to predict its future outcome. So egg freezing allowed Maya to be proactive at the age of thirty-five in preserving her fertility while letting her relationship take its natural course.

Maya booked an appointment at a Bay Area IVF clinic for what she thought would be a simple fertility checkup. But the results were anything but expected. A female reproductive endocrinologist explained to Maya that her anti-Müllerian hormone (AMH) level was much lower than expected for a woman of her age. She also explained that AMH is the main biomarker of ovarian reserve, or the supply of eggs still remaining in a woman's ovaries. Along with two other reproductive hormones, follicle-stimulating hormone (FSH) and luteinizing hormone (LH), these tests are used to measure a woman's "egg reserve" and to indicate the relative status of her fertility. With Maya's low AMH score, her fertility was in jeopardy, as she was shocked to learn that day. "During the consult, I found out that my AMH is very, very low. So, it's like .467, bottom percentile for my age. And so that was the first time I knew anything about my fertility. All my reproductive history in terms of, like, I don't have any STDs [sexually transmitted diseases]. Like, all of that was healthy . . . [but] I had a very low AMH level. I got a second opinion. And the second opinion confirmed it." Indeed, the second opinion was even more unsettling, with regard to both its content and delivery.

I went to a doctor, a male doctor . . . and his second opinion came in the form of writing as a long report. And at the end, he said, "My advice to you"—he had two pieces of advice—"One, you should gain more weight, because your BMI is low. The second piece of advice," he said, "is—my advice to you is to work less and try to find—try to find some work-life balance so you can meet the right partner and have kids." That's what he told me. He put that in writing!

Maya was affronted by this physician's proposed solution and felt that other women would certainly feel the same way.

> This is why the space is so hard for women, because they're constantly coming up against these kinds of things, even from medical professionals. So this is why this issue is so emotionally charged. . . . So I looked him up. He's older. He's probably in his midseventies. He must just have this old-fashioned way of thinking. But at the same time, the reason I went to him is because he's considered a world-class doctor, from whom I could get a second opinion. And, you know, he's telling me, like, how to live my life. That's not a medical diagnosis or a course of treatment. That's unsolicited life advice.

This alarming news from two doctors, some of it delivered in an offensive written report, made Maya reexamine her entire life history. Like most American women, Maya had been put on birth control as a young adult, and nearly fifteen years later, she was still on the Pill. Throughout this long period of hormonal contraception, Maya had never received any specific form of fertility education, nor had she ever spoken to a physician about her fertility intentions or the age at which fertility begins to decline. "I'm thirty-five. I've been to the OB/GYN, let's just conservatively call it twenty times in my life. It's been more. They've tested me for HIV/AIDS more times than they've tested me for my AMH. And my statistical chance, thanks to expert public health work, of contracting AIDS is practically zero. But my chance of having fertility issues is much, much higher. And so, you know, the reason it was such a shock, especially the first several months, was because I didn't have years of accumulated knowledge to be able to navigate this issue. Everything was, like, from scratch."

Maya's shock over her poor fertility profile made her wonder whether she was somehow to blame for her lack of fertility knowledge. Did other women receive information about their fertility from their gynecologists? Had she somehow failed to ask the right questions? These issues troubled her, so she began digging into the existing research literature.

> It's interesting. There was a recent study in *Fertility and Sterility* [one of the leading reproductive medicine journals] where they actually surveyed, like, how women understand fertility and reproductive issues.[1] And over 90 percent of women said that their OB/GYN was their primary

source of information. But even though they said that their doctor was their primary source of information, engagement with their doctor on this topic was shockingly low. Less than 20 percent of women in their thirties actually talk to their OB/GYN about age-related fertility issues. So, like, people say it's their doctor, but no one actually has that conversation with their doctor.

This study of physician-patient fertility communication, or lack thereof, made Maya feel less alone. But the research findings also upset her.

You know, I really honestly am like every other woman. I didn't think about this issue until I walked into a fertility clinic and found out that I'm going to have some challenges. And it just caused me to really start thinking about, like, I am someone who is highly intelligent, has access to resources, access to information, and access to technology, and I've had excellent health care my entire life. Why is this happening to me? This is completely upside down and wrongheaded. And a lot of this is because of policy, what is covered and what is not covered. And a lot of this is because our education system in terms of sexual education, health education, [it] does not include fertility. It totally should. I also think there's so much in terms of public policy that needs to be done. Curriculums need to be changed. I mean, why nobody talks to you about this when they talk about sex ed is beyond me. Why is this any weirder or out of bounds or not appropriate?

Although Maya came to realize that her lack of fertility knowledge was probably not her fault, she now faced a number of pressing clinical decisions. Maya was suffering from premature ovarian aging (POA), in which the quantity and quality of her eggs had declined much earlier than expected based on her age.[2] Because women are born with all the eggs they will ever have, by their midthirties, not only do they have fewer eggs left, but their aged eggs tend to degrade and have more abnormalities, leading to higher rates of fertilization failure, abnormal embryos, and miscarriage. But in Maya's case, these processes had started early, leading to a POA diagnosis. POA affects about 10 percent of women and may be genetically based, with these women's mothers often experiencing early menopause. Because POA is also one of the major, but overlooked, causes of infertility, women with this diagnosis must decide what to do if they hope to conceive a child. They can try to get pregnant immediately (either "naturally" or through IVF), freeze their eggs, or fertilize their eggs to make embryos, either with a partner's or a donor's sperm. Frozen embryos are often considered superior to frozen eggs from a pregnancy standpoint, because they are already fertilized and assessed for their quality before being frozen.

Maya was thrown into this decisional matrix almost immediately. Physicians at the IVF clinic encouraged Maya to think seriously about getting pregnant now through IVF or at least freezing IVF embryos fertilized by Kevin's or a donor's sperm. But because Maya and Kevin had only been seeing each other for six months, these decisions about fertilizing and freezing embryos felt quite premature.

> So we talked about both. And I think . . . like, we weren't going to freeze embryos now. Like, I have to get my eggs now, because the sensitivity of the time. My ovarian reserve is very low. Like, I feel a lot of urgency to do as much as I can to preserve my eggs as fast as I can, just because of my personal situation. . . . It's possible that if we had waited like a year, I could go back, you know, and we could freeze embryos and use them maybe a couple years after that, but I don't feel like I have that time. So I feel like I have to do my own fertility preservation as quickly as possible. And then, you know, so that forces a trade-off. If I wanted to guarantee having a kid . . . what I would potentially do is either if he [Kevin] didn't want to do it, I could just use a sperm donor and have a kid right now. But, like, I've thought about the trade-offs and I don't want to do that.

Although Maya elected to undertake egg freezing, she began to be treated like a much older IVF patient facing age-related infertility problems. She was put on an ovulation tracker. She was prescribed several fertility-enhancing supplements, including dehydroepiandrosterone (DHEA) and Coenzyme Q10 (CoQ10), which are usually given to older women. And she was required to self-inject a demanding and expensive regime of hormonal medications, including Follistim, Ganirelix, and Menopur. To Maya, her treatment felt something like a medical emergency. "To think about it from this perspective, I'm doing what is considered 'elective' egg freezing, but I don't feel like it's elective, because my health situation is forcing me to do it. If I wait another year, it will have a measurable impact on my reproductive health outcomes. So even though it's like 'elective' and I don't have cancer and I'm not doing it because I'm undergoing chemotherapy, it doesn't feel elective to me."

To that end, Maya braved the two weeks of daily injections, in which the doses were raised to maximize the number of retrievable eggs in her ovaries. But the injections were only one part of the pressure Maya felt.

> You know, I don't think I'm unusual in dealing with this, but it's definitely very stressful. And there's a lot of anxiety around this procedure—not because it's a medical procedure that's particularly difficult or invasive. Frankly, like, the hormones didn't even have an impact on me. But I think there's like a psychological environment around it, because everything has a stigma attached to it. I have a friend who's a doctor. She's a doctor, and she had her eggs frozen. She did three cycles, and she was like, "I'm a doctor, and I felt shame. I felt all these emotional things that all other women felt, who were in their midthirties." But she's a doctor! You know, it's like psychologically and emotionally very charged, and financially, it's very expensive. The procedure costs like $12,000 a cycle and, for me, more like $15,000 because of the extra medications. And so it's very expensive. You know, I feel like I need to do this, [because] my fertility is in the bottom quintile, but my access to technology is in the top quintile. . . . But not everyone has that access and ability. So financially it is a lot. It's stressful. But that's the thing with fertility: when you're making decisions in a crisis environment, whether you're a single person doing egg freezing or you're a couple trying IVF, you'll pay whatever it takes. And they can charge whatever it takes. And, of course, you'll pay tens of thousands of dollars to get this done.

By the time I met Maya, she had just finished her first egg freezing cycle, which produced only three frozen eggs. Maya was preparing herself for a second cycle, having been told that approximately twenty eggs were needed to "optimize for two kids." She assumed that she might need a third cycle—in which case she would spend more than $40,000 on egg freezing.

Looking back, Maya regretted not having undertaken egg freezing earlier, when her ovarian reserve was larger. In most women, ovarian reserve begins to decline slightly in their early thirties (around age thirty-two) but then drops precipitously at age thirty-seven, which has been described as the "fertility cliff."[3] To be most effective, then, egg freezing should occur prior to reaching that cliff, sometime between the ages of thirty-two and thirty-seven. But because of POA, Maya's fertility cliff had already happened by age thirty-five. And because she had never had any hormonal testing—which is not offered routinely in gynecological exams among thirty-something women in the US—Maya had no way of knowing the state of her remaining fertility. She thought she was being proactive, only to find out that she was perhaps too late to freeze the number of eggs she needed.

Full of regret, Maya scoured the research literature, learning that feelings of regret were quite common. In one study published in *Fertility and Sterility*, more than 70 percent of women surveyed wished that they had undertaken egg freezing at a younger age.[4] From Maya's perspective, earlier egg freezing could prevent age-related infertility, the main reason why American women end up undergoing costly and repeated cycles of IVF.

It's totally true! And if you think about it from this perspective, a commercial perspective, most couples who do IVF are in their late thirties, early forties. And when you're doing IVF at that point with your own fresh eggs, you will probably have to do—I'm not an expert—but I think like three or four cycles in order to get a successful live birth. If that woman at forty was finishing an IVF cycle using eggs that she had frozen when she was thirty or twenty-five, like, that means she would probably be successful with one cycle. She'd be getting more and much healthier eggs with fewer chromosomal abnormalities. So, like, if you're looking at it from a whole system, one way to bring the costs down is to actually promote women to freeze their eggs early, if they think there's any reasonable chance of them using IVF down the road. . . . I think the sensitivity around this is like, "Oh, you're pushing this on people who don't want it. You're an egg freezing pusher." Well, no, people should have the tools and resources to make the best decisions for them. . . . Like, in some instances, it may actually cause a woman to choose to just have a kid on her own or with the partner she's with. Whatever. Egg freezing is not, like, by default advocating delaying having kids. It's giving people information that's actionable to make choices. . . . So I don't really think about it as a women's health issue; I think about it as a public health issue. These are technologies that should be affordable and accessible to everyone.

As we began to wrap up our conversation, Maya told me that her own fertility crisis had sparked an idea for a fertility tool, one that could potentially help other women.

You don't have any understanding of this issue until it becomes a crisis. You know, like, we don't have a universe of accumulated knowledge in understanding this in the way that we do now about contraception. Women are operating in the dark! We have not created tools for women to be able to understand their fertility. So that's when I started really thinking about trying to put together a product that can sort of meet this really unique moment. My goal is to create a product that is as easy to use and as elegant as any consumer product out there that's beautifully designed . . . like Pinterest or any of these really beautifully designed consumer tech products, and apply that to helping women understand fertility . . . because I do think there is an almost laughable lack of really beautifully designed tools for women to manage and understand their fertility. It's shocking.

* * *

Two months later, Maya emailed me to ask if I was planning to attend the American Society for Reproductive Medicine conference in Baltimore. Maya told me that she was becoming serious about her fertility tool idea and was looking for ways to enter the burgeoning "fem tech" market. She wanted to travel to Baltimore to listen to the cutting-edge scientific research, as well as to peruse the giant exhibition hall, where hundreds of fertility equipment manufacturers and pharmaceutical companies would be showing off their wares. And in an unusual role reversal, Maya asked if she could interview me as one of the "experts" in the field.

Maya and I did, indeed, meet in Baltimore, where we talked for an hour over coffee. Maya was already making significant headway with her fertility tool idea, and she hoped to meet a number of leading fertility experts at the conference. Maya was excited.

MAYA: I've never been to a fertility conference before!
MARCIA: Well, they're interesting. You're going to learn a lot!
MAYA: Are the sessions, like, super technical? Will I be able to understand?
MARCIA: Probably some of them are, but some of them aren't. . . . Either way, I hope you'll enjoy it!

As Maya and I parted ways, I reflected with admiration on Maya's initiative and verve. Having only recently recovered from the shock of her

POA diagnosis and the stress of her first egg freezing cycle, Maya was already turning her own fertility crisis into a preventive effort, so that other women would no longer have to "operate in the dark."

Fertility Benightedness

Maya's story is instructive, for we see that her fertility was a black box, having mysterious and unknown internal functions and mechanisms that had never been tested in her long history of routine gynecological check-ups. Without any type of fertility testing, Maya had blithely assumed that all was well with her ovaries. She had always been healthy, had no specific reproductive complaints, and was a conscientious contraceptive user and a compliant reproductive patient. Yet, in retrospect, she realized that she had been operating "in the dark," "from scratch," "without accumulated knowledge," leading her to ask, "Why is this happening to me?"

Only through careful research and reflection did Maya begin to arrive at an answer. Although she was highly educated, Maya realized that she had never received any specific fertility education as part of the normal sex-education curriculum offered in her East Coast public schools and the elite private university she attended. Despite excellent gynecological health care, Maya also registered the fact that those annual "well-woman" visits were entirely focused on pregnancy and STD prevention. And although Maya was placed on hormonal contraception in her teens and stayed on it over two decades, she had never talked with her gynecologist about her fertility intentions or the relationship between her age and fertility decline. Although she wanted children, Maya had not asked these kinds of fertility questions, because she honestly had no idea that her reproductive function was under threat. Furthermore, despite being proactive by seeking fertility testing at the age of thirty-five, Maya realized that fertility testing is not routinely offered in US reproductive health care. It must be sought out, usually through an IVF clinic with specialized reproductive endocrinological services. By the time Maya reached such a clinic at the age of thirty-five, her ovarian reserve had already significantly diminished. Without preexisting knowledge of a fertility cliff, Maya had no idea that she had fallen off.

Maya's story brings together a larger constellation of issues that I would characterize as *fertility benightedness*. To be "benighted" means to be over-taken by darkness or night—just as Maya felt that she was "operating in the dark" about her fertility. To be benighted also means to exist in a state of intellectual or social darkness. Maya believed that too many American women are in this state of affairs when it comes to their own fertility. As she pointed out, most women are taught to understand *fertility prevention* through the utilization of birth control, but most women lack knowledge of other crucial fertility dimensions, including *potential threats* to their fertility such as POA and the nature and pace of age-related *fertility decline.*

Indeed, potential threats to fertility and age-related fertility decline are salient for highly educated women, who are unlikely to marry and bear children in their early reproductive years. Yet, in interview after interview, women explained to me that they knew little to nothing about their own fertility until they arrived at an IVF clinic for egg freezing. Through no fault of their own, these women were fertility benighted—and for multiple reasons. First of all, like Maya, most of these women had never received any specific school-based fertility education, even though most had been exposed to sex education at multiple points in their academic careers. For instance, Ellen, a retired diplomat who was now working as an academic administrator, had attended an elite East Coast women's college. But she realized that fertility education was entirely missing from the undergraduate curriculum.

I was actually thinking about this recently, because I got a survey from my alma mater—right?—which is a women's college. And it was, you know . . . "Was there something that you wish, you know, that you didn't get out of your experience?" And I remember thinking, you know, we spent a lot of time talking about women's health issues as an undergrad. And that was great, you know, getting to know about your body and not being afraid to ask questions and, you know, questions about sexuality and birth control and wellness and all this kind of stuff, sexual assault and, you know, all kinds of things like that. I don't remember ever having any discussions about fertility—contraception, yes; fertility, no. And this was kind of a recurring theme at my—I had my twentieth—what was it, twentieth reunion? Twentieth? Yeah. And this was a recurring theme with a number of women that I talked to that, you know, we thought we could do everything. We didn't know that we were going to have trouble getting pregnant if we waited.

This focus on birth control and pregnancy prevention in school-based sex education meant that most of these women were committed to contraception. Their hormonal contraception had usually been initiated in adolescence to regulate heavy, painful, or irregular menses, as well as acne, but then continued by most women as a primary form of birth control. The Pill was the contraceptive of choice among women in this study, although women also used other hormonal methods, including the patch or vaginal ring.[5] Most women had been on hormonal contraception continuously for ten to twenty years, or as one woman put it, "I've been pretty much on it my entire adult life." Others had used it off and on, with small breaks in between. But because of their commitment to hormonal contraception, most women had no idea about their natural fertility cycles, including whether they ovulated regularly. One woman who had been on continuous contraception since the age of nineteen told me that she stopped the Pill at age thirty-five, because she "just wanted to make sure that everything was still working."

In some cases, women were in for upsetting surprises when they went off hormonal contraception. For example, Helen, a small business consultant who described herself as a "doer," decided to initiate egg freezing without realizing that she would need to go off the Pill first. "None of this was on my radar. . . . I was on the Pill, and if you do the testing, you have to be off the Pill. And then there was a test that for some reason sent me back in. I went back, and the ovarian reserve . . . well, I'm on this accelerated decline. There's, like, the normal declining, and then there's accelerated. . . . So my fertility, even though I'm thirty-five, is sort of declining and is already lower than some women who are forty."

Up until this point, Helen had no idea that she might be facing fertility problems, because, like Maya, she had always considered herself to be reproductively healthy. Indeed, few women in this study had ever considered their fertility to be under threat, because as a group, they reported very few known reproductive complaints. As fastidious adherents to contraception, few of these women had ever had unplanned pregnancies leading to abortions, and only one woman had sustained any known fallopian tubal damage.[6] Four divorced women had had miscarriages, but with no long-term ill effects. A dozen women had been diagnosed with common reproductive health conditions, including polycystic ovary syndrome (PCOS), endometriosis, uterine fibroids, and ovarian cysts. Four of these women had undergone reproductive surgeries, but their ovaries had been left intact. Thus, none of these women had reproductive conditions known to impair their reproductive function, even though some had found these conditions to be distressing.

When I asked the women if they had ever experienced any reproductive problems, I usually received responses such as "very uneventful," "nothing, nothing, nothing," or "a good easy run." Rose's response was fairly typical. The director of a broadcasting network, Rose explained how her irregular periods in adolescence had normalized once she went on the Pill and how healthy she had been over nearly two decades of continuous contraception.

> So I got my period when I was about thirteen. For the first four to five years or so, I would say it was pretty irregular, and initially when it started, it was so irregular that my mom took me into the doctor, because they were concerned there was something wrong. They had me do the basal temperature recording and stuff like that. Everything looked fine. Once I got on the Pill—I became sexually active when I was twenty, in college—once I was on the Pill for that, that really helped straighten things out. And so, I mean, I've only slept with three people, so I'm not, you know, whatever—just in committed relationships. And I was on the Pill for all of that. I've never been pregnant before. I'm sure I would have had no problems getting pregnant. I don't think I would have a problem getting pregnant now. I don't know, but I feel very normal.

Furthermore, as a competitive athlete who had once trained for the Olympics, Rose prided herself on being healthy and physically fit. "You know, I live a very healthy lifestyle, and most people think when they meet me that I'm ten years younger than I am. Like, my maturity level is not, you know—I have the relaxed look of somebody without children, I guess! So, you know, I've been very healthy. I don't drink or smoke or do any of that stuff, not a bit. If anyone can be a mom at like eighty-six, it's me [laughs]!"

Indeed, women in my study often connected their good reproductive health to their robust physical health, often priding themselves on their "healthy lifestyles." Many women assumed that because they were healthy, they would have excellent fertility well into their late thirties and even their forties. For example, Lily, the Manhattan art curator, described her penchant for healthy living. "I don't drink—I mean, not really. I used to smoke pot . . . in high school and college and whatever. But I really don't drink. I exercise, you know, as I can . . . except when I get sick and travel; then it doesn't happen. I don't smoke, you know. One glass of wine, I'm like exhausted or tipsy. I don't judge other people, but I just don't like it. I'm strong, but I have an equilibrium, and I keep that equilibrium in balance."

Like Lily, Simone, who was about to finish her PhD in law, was living a healthy lifestyle in Northern California, as were most of her graduate-school friends. Thus, when Simone learned that she was facing POA, she was shocked.

I've never had that conversation with any doctor or person. . . . And I think that to me, the most surprising thing is that I had never reflected on it, but it was an unstated assumption, that fertility is related to general health. And I'm sure my friends even think that. I was speaking to my friend who's a PhD student in immunology, and she was so surprised to hear that it's not related to general health. And she's like, "Oh, that's not true. It is." But no, you know, you can't improve your fertility, not your baseline. . . . If you don't take care of your health, you could decrease it, but you can't improve it. . . . It just does not align in that way. I think it's also that they don't—or I didn't know the limitation really. I think that other people probably don't know also. So they're probably not thinking, "Oh yeah, you should hurry up." I never had a female relative say that to me ever. I've never had anyone say that to me.

This belief in the power of healthy lifestyles was connected to another widespread but mistaken belief among women—one that I would call *fertility longevity*, or the belief in the ability of women to become pregnant well into their forties. To support this conviction, women in my study often relied on anecdotes, for example, of a grandmother, an aunt, or an older friend who had gotten pregnant in her early to midforties without difficulty. In addition, women sometimes mentioned celebrity pregnancies of women like Halle Berry, Madonna, Janet Jackson, Brigitte Nielsen, and Naomi Campbell, all of whom had late-in-life pregnancies that were highly publicized.[7] Yet, as Zoe, an academic obstetrician-gynecologist who had frozen her eggs, emphasized in her interview, this nonstop attention to the pregnancies of older women celebrities was ultimately harming American women.

We do talk about this whole celebrity thing and this belief that these celebrities are getting pregnant on their own at forty-two with their own eggs. And they're just not! Like, Halle Berry did not just have her own genetic child; she didn't, no matter who is saying what to whom.[8] And so that, I think, is a disservice, because we're seeing both personally in my friends and professionally at work that a lot of women are coming up to the age of thirty-seven, thirty-eight, thirty-nine, and no one's really impressed upon them that fertility is an issue. And even married people—I have a friend who's a midwife, and she had a patient who was married to the same person for like seven years and got to the age of thirty-seven and is now needing IVF. And her previous OB had never even mentioned to her, just, "Are you thinking about having kids?"—a nice, open-ended question, just to get people thinking about it.

These problems turned up in my interviews with women who had come to believe in fertility longevity through celebrity culture and who had never been dissuaded of this idea through a conversation with a physician. For example, Cecilia, the British-American California lawyer, wished that she had started egg freezing much earlier, rather than waiting until age thirty-nine at the end of her protracted divorce.

I try not to live life with regrets, but for me, what I really lacked is education and awareness. I think I just wasn't informed of two things: one, what the biological reality was-slash-is and, secondly, about the options. And just to drill down a little bit further about what the biological reality is, I knew conceptually that your fertility goes off a cliff at the age of thirty-nine or late thirties, but then, ever the optimist, you see those people, like celebrities, having beautiful babies and they're forty-two, forty-three. And everyone knows a friend who had twins that are gorgeous at the age of forty-four, and she wasn't even trying. So I wish I had known the reality. And not to say doom-and-gloom, but it's just better education around the reality of the situation. And what would have helped for me is not just "fertility goes off a cliff at thirty-nine" or whatever, but it's putting numbers to it. Like, if I had done a round of egg freezing when I was thirty-four, I would have been getting twenty eggs at a time, as opposed to getting three. That would have resonated with me. If you want to understand it, you need to know the actual reality of the situation. And I think people talk about it in abstract, conceptual terms, which then doesn't—it's easy to, not necessarily disregard, but to focus on the positive success stories and think, "Oh, well, you know, it goes down, but other people manage it" kind of thing. So I think the reality—that was a real turning point for me, because I was like, "Holy crap, I wish I would have known that. I wish I would have known that when I was thirty-six." But it was never communicated to me. People used to talk in general terms, like, "Well, if you want to have children, you better hurry up," like those sort of phrases. Couldn't be more general if you tried. Whereas, if someone had said to me and showed me a chart—because now I've seen the charts [of age-related fertility decline], and it's just pretty compelling. It's not even complicated [*laughs*]!

Fertility Silences

The question is, Why had Cecilia never been shown a fertility chart until the age of thirty-nine, when she initiated her first cycle of egg freezing? As she pointed out, doing so would have been "uncomplicated." But it would have meant discussing age-related fertility decline, which was "never communicated" to her by her physician. These physician-patient *fertility silences* were widely reported by women in my study. They told me that gynecologists rarely raised fertility decline as an issue, failed to ask about women's fertility intentions, and assumed that single women in their thirties would want to remain on birth control. The few women who were bold enough to raise these subjects with their physicians were sometimes callously brushed off, told not to worry, or given questionable advice. Indeed, some of the advice bordered on neglect or misguidance.

For example, Emma, who described herself as the "hippiest Republican" lawyer in Washington, DC, chose to see a young female gynecologist in the hope of having her fertility questions answered with up-to-date information. But after her first visit, Emma never returned.

I was like, "This is great! She's young. She has new perspectives on medicine." So I was thirty-three—this was like eight years ago—and I said, "Hey, I'm not looking to have a child, and I keep hearing about the increased rates of Down syndrome after thirty-five, and I don't know, like, I've just been wondering what is the latest," you know? And she said to me, "Well, you know, I would suggest to you if you're interested in having a baby, you should try around thirty-three and see if you can get pregnant, and that'll answer a lot of questions for you." And I walked out of there, and I was like, well, first of all, my next birthday was going to be when I turn thirty-three. So I was like, what kind of advice is that? To just go out and try to see if I could get pregnant? Like, first of all, that's exactly what we don't need in the world are women who aren't ready to have children having them. You know, it was such a—it's so ridiculous, and I mean, yes, it's very cavalier. So I stopped. I thought, "Well, I don't need the OB part, and my primary care physician can give me the GYN." So I quit going to that practice.

Fran, who worked as a federal health care regulator, also tried to be proactive by scheduling an appointment with her regular gynecologist before embarking on egg freezing. As always, her physician was reassuring, even though he was mistakenly sanguine about Fran's fertility prospects.

I mean, everyone's heard of when you hit thirty-five—you know?—tick tock, your biological clock is ticking, you know. . . . But what's crazy is that, like, I went and got my GYN stuff done, you know, because I wanted to get that done prior to starting this and just letting them know what I was doing and everything. And I came out of there totally fine! In the GYN office, I have actually never had any issues at all—like, I'm totally clean. "How's it going?" "Everything's great." And then I walked into [the local IVF clinic], and you're like, "Holy crap! Like, actually, I'm not good." And that's why I'm in a bad spot. . . . I mean, it would be great to have some level of testing, just to be aware of where you're at, you know? And when people are like, "Oh, yeah, you still have time. You're good." I'm like, "Well, okay." But in the back of my mind, I'm like, "Dude, I know too much now." And so I don't have a lot of time, you know?

The question for Fran and many other women in my study was why their gynecologists seemed unwilling to have these crucial conversations. I often ended up referring women to a study that my colleagues and I had conducted, which suggested that these fertility silences are endemic in US gynecology. In an online survey of 238 American OB/GYN resident physicians, we asked questions to assess their knowledge of fertility decline and their willingness to discuss this issue with their patients.[9] What we discovered was quite shocking: namely, one-third of those surveyed overestimated the age of slight fertility decline, and nearly half overestimated the age of marked fertility decline, believing that it occurred in the early forties (ages forty to forty-four), as opposed to the late thirties (age thirty-seven and thereafter).

We were also interested in ascertaining OB/GYN residents' knowledge of and attitudes toward egg freezing, including whether these residents felt comfortable initiating discussions with patients on this topic.[10] Again, the results were eye-opening: 60 percent of physicians surveyed believed that they should *not* be initiating these egg freezing conversations. These *non-initiators*, as we called them, were largely misinformed about age-related fertility decline, with two-thirds overestimating the age at which slight and marked fertility declines occur. Their own misinformation shaped their reluctance to discuss egg freezing, as did their fears of being seen as "pushing childbearing" on their patients or causing single patients to experience emotional distress. Given the high levels of misunderstanding about fertility decline among young OB/GYNs, we concluded our study with a stern warning: "Within the USA, there appears to be a critical need for improved education on fertility decline in OB/GYN residency programs."[11]

If gynecologists themselves are misinformed about fertility decline and reluctant to discuss egg freezing with their patients, how does this translate into clinical practice? As I was told by many women in my study, gynecologist noninitiators tended to offer reassurance about women's fertility rather than realistic expectations, and sometimes they offered quite questionable advice, steering women toward immediate pregnancy rather than egg freezing. For example, Marleen, a clinical social worker, had spent five years after her divorce trying to decide whether she should pursue egg freezing. Multiple conversations with a variety of gynecologists had been of little help. "When it comes to conversations I've had with practitioners . . . the OBs that I've seen in the past five years, they're very ignorant about egg freezing and the process. They're surprisingly uneducated on it. Certainly, it wasn't discussed. So I was not able to rely on either my GP [general practitioner] or my OB/GYNs for good information. They were asking me questions!"

Another woman who had gone through a drawn-out divorce, Aneela, was also trying to figure out her next steps. But when she visited a Bay Area gynecologist, her questions about egg freezing were considered almost amusing by the gynecologist. "I was thirty-four . . . and I remember asking a doctor, 'Should I freeze my eggs?' And she almost laughed at me a little bit, and she had to control her composure. And she said, 'I really wouldn't worry about that until you're thirty-seven.' And so, you know, in my head, 'cause I was so busy with work, I had this ticking time bomb at thirty-seven. However, now I've learned women are doing it much earlier. Look how things have changed."

Another deeply disturbing episode was reported by Dawn, a clinical psychologist in Texas who was contemplating egg freezing during the breakup of a ten-year relationship. When she asked her female gynecologist about egg freezing, she was advised, "Why don't you just get knocked up? You know, it's free. And you know, you know whether it takes or not right away. You don't have to inject yourself with hormones." Dawn left the office feeling "flabbergasted." Ultimately, she left her gynecologist, her partner, and the state of Texas. At the time of our interview, she was considering becoming a single mother with the support of her aging parents.

Gynecologist Initiators

So, are there up-to-date, caring gynecologists out there, who want to provide women with highly accurate information about age-related fertility decline, as well as the option of egg freezing? My study suggests that there are. Despite the bad experiences of women like Cecilia, Emma, Fran, Marleen, Aneela, and Dawn, other women had encountered younger-generation female gynecologists who could be characterized as *initiators*, or ones who were willing to discuss fertility concerns and egg freezing options with their thirty-something patients. Although the numbers were small, a dozen women in my study (10 percent) credited their clinicians for being the ones to initiate fertility conversations. In every case, these clinicians were young women, primarily gynecologists but also primary care physicians or physicians' assistants, who were roughly the same age as their patients and empathized with their patients' situations. In some cases, these clinicians had undergone egg freezing themselves and were willing to share their experiences and recommendations. Women who had been cared for by such clinician initiators were often grateful for their encounters.

For example, Louisa, who worked in environmental communications, described how repeated conversations with her gynecologist over the course of a brief and rocky marriage brought her decisional clarity, especially when she learned that her gynecologist had frozen her own eggs.

My gynecologist had started talking to me. . . . As soon as I got married, she started asking me, like, "Are you ready for me to take you off the Pill?" And you know, I was like, "No, no, no, no, no!" And so every time I saw her she was like, "Are you ready to go off the Pill?" and I said, "No, no, no!" So I guess it was when I was thirty-three, she said, "All right, what's the deal? Are you ready? Are you ready to go off the Pill?" And I was like, "No." And so she kind of took out a piece of paper, and she drew the graph for me of my fertility, and she showed me how, you know, at thirty-five it will start to decline and at thirty-seven it will sort of fall off the cliff. And it sent a chill down my spine. And she said, "You're running out of time, if you want to have kids." She was very nice about it. She's like, "I'm not telling you what to do. I'm not trying to pressure you, but I just want you to be aware of this." And then I was really grateful, and she told me that she had frozen her eggs. She was just, "Something to think about. You know, I just did this. It's awesome. I'm really good friends with the doctor. He's great. Just go in and, like, for a consultation." And I was like, "Uh, that seems like—okay, this is all very new. I'm very overwhelmed right now. Thank you for bringing this up. I'll think about it." And I just sort of filed it away in the back of my mind. But that all got me sort of thinking, like, if I want to have kids, I need to start sort of taking steps to get there. And so that's sort of where I started making moves to leave my husband, and so I finally did that when I was thirty-three.

Young female gynecologists seemed particularly empathetic toward the women in my study who were going through relationship traumas and heartache. For example, Mikaela, a DC-based federal lobbyist whose four-year marriage with an unfaithful husband was "spiraling out of control," was treated with acute sensitivity by her woman gynecologist.

When we got divorced, it was a very humbling process of having to go to my OB/GYN and get an STD test, because he had exposed me to other people. And it was at that time that my doctor kind of planted the seed about thinking about egg freezing if we were going to be getting divorced. And I wasn't really ready to hear that, and you can picture, you're in the stirrups, you're pretty overwhelmed. It's a very vulnerable moment. But her suggestion was somewhere in the back of my mind even though I wasn't ready to act on it yet. And then about a year later, actually, almost exactly a year later, because it was for my annual appointment, she really sat me down and said, "Do you want to have a family?" "And if so"—she kind of, you know, in no uncertain terms, kind of laid out for me, you know—"here's how long it's going to take to divorce, here's how long it's going to take to recover from that, here's how long it's going to take to meet 'the one,' and then you date for a couple of years, and all of a sudden you're forty. And, you know, today you're thirty-four, and you're healthy, and, you know, you're in a position to do something about it. So I think you should give some thought to this." And so I really credit my doctor, my OB/GYN, with opening the conversation. I didn't even really know much about it at that time. I mean, I'd heard of it, but I hadn't really known anyone who had talked about it with me. So it was really doctor driven.

When I asked Mikaela, "Why do you think she in particular was pretty directive?" Mikaela explained, "You know, I think she's a younger doctor. And, in fact, a number of my friends go to her, and I've even seen her at restaurants around town. I think—my sense is there is a lot of empathy from her for my situation. . . . I know that I said to her, 'I'm very concerned about what this means for me, having a family.' And I think, you know, she had a potential solution that could give me some peace of mind and help me medically."

Friends as Influencers

But it was not just young women gynecologists who were motivating their patients to think about egg freezing. With regard to influence, friends also played an important role—not only friends who had already undertaken egg freezing but especially friends who had not and regretted the age-related infertility problems they were facing. This latter group, which I came to think of as the *infertile influencers*, were mentioned by nearly 20 percent of women in my study. For example, when I asked Kendra, the vice president of the New York City communications firm, "Can you tell me the story of the egg freezing?" she described the importance of both types of friends, the egg freezing friends and the infertile friends, in her drawn-out decision-making process.

Wow! I don't know how I initially found out about it. Maybe just in reading or research or hearing it on the news and then, of course, having conversations with many of my girlfriends and family members and knowing some people who had done egg freezing. And I thought about it for a while, and then a couple of years went by, maybe two. I kept saying, "I'm going to do this. I'm going to do this." And hit thirty-seven and was kind of like, "Okay, I think I should go ahead and do this." Actually, one of the other things that prompted me to do it more rapidly than before was I had two very close girlfriends who were both having issues getting pregnant and had been married for a while and were just really saying kind of the torture and torment that they were going through with the inability to carry or to, you know, conceive a child. This sent me to the Google search to figure out what those options were. And actually, when I first spoke with the—when I had my initial consultation at the center, I inquired about donating eggs. So I wanted to know if it was possible that I could actually donate eggs to one of my friends who was having a really tough time. The doctor said [*laughs*] this was a great idea, but she didn't recommend donating them when I hadn't frozen my own or didn't have any, you know, off to the side for myself. Also, we talked about the age. So, as I began to do more research and exploring, she said, "You know, usually they go for younger eggs if it's someone that you don't know. Not that there's anything wrong with eggs at your age, but of course, if someone's paying for it, they want to get the best of the bunch. But if they're close friends or something like that, then it may be a situation where they are fine. But I definitely wouldn't recommend you giving eggs away if you don't have any saved for yourself." So I was probably thirty-six, [and] I didn't donate eggs. . . . Actually, during the process of researching and kind of dragging my feet and traveling all over the place, both of them ended up getting pregnant and having babies!

Another woman, Claudia, who was an ESL teacher, was also an egg freezing "foot dragger." But the experience of a close friend from college, who was now infertile, made her change her mind and initiate the egg freezing process.

She was like, "Yeah, this is not a joke! Like, you've been crying about this for years about how you're getting older, and it's not a joke. Like, it's happening to me." What finally pushed me to look into it more, and I knew it was only going to get—I wasn't going to get any better, so I needed to finally look into it more seriously and move on it. I mean, look, in my late thirties, I was already realizing that I'm aging, right? But it just really hit me—like, it hit close to home. Like, you can't just keep putting it off, you know.

Unfortunately for Claudia, by the time she started egg freezing at the age of thirty-seven, she was facing POA. Her ovaries did not respond to hormonal stimulation, and her first egg freezing cycle was canceled. Claudia became tearful as we talked, although I tried to console her.

> CLAUDIA: Oh my God! It was horrible. I was really—I'm probably going to cry at some point during this conversation.
> MARCIA: Oh, I'm sorry. I'm sorry.
> CLAUDIA: Oh no, it's all right. I'm just telling you. It's, like, to relive it is, like, ugh. But, yeah, but still really hard at first. And I was like, "Oh my God, this whole nine days has been for nothing. All—everything I went through was for nothing." And I can tell you now, like, in retrospect, it was just the tip of the iceberg. At the time, I was like, "This is all for nothing, and all that money was for nothing. My insurance isn't covering it. All the doctors' visits, logistically difficult—it's early in the morning, it's far away, whatever it is, like, on the weekends, the callback and all the research I put in." I'm like, "All this is for nothing." I have to do it, you know, again.

Seven egg freezing cycles later—with three midcycle cancellations—Claudia was able to bank sixteen frozen eggs, at a total cost of nearly $40,000. When I asked Claudia if she had any recommendations for other women, this is what she had to say: "Do it sooner, like early thirties, when you have a bigger ovarian reserve and a bigger chance at having a higher quality. Because for me, that was the biggest stress factor and the reason I had to end up doing it so many times. . . . So, I mean, if you have the resources, then why wouldn't you do it if someone could have all those results I did in one cycle, you know? That's my gut, my recommendation based on not having to relive my mistake."

Although Claudia blamed herself for waiting too long to undertake egg freezing, she had no way of knowing that her fertility was under threat. Like so many other women, she had never had any prior fertility testing or a conversation about fertility decline with her gynecologist. Ten other women in my study found themselves in the same situation—learning about their POA only when they arrived at an IVF clinic for egg freezing. Simone, who was in the final year of her PhD program, admitted to me, "I just didn't know much about my own body, and now I realize just how misguided I was. I can't believe how little I knew about fertility. But my fertility is much lower than expected. My doctor said, 'Your ovaries are acting older than they should be.' And I'm not used to being below the bottom tenth percentile."

Another woman, Ruth, who directed a mental health research unit, was told that she was in "the bottom fifteenth percentile" for her age. "It was awful. I was hysterical," Ruth confided. "I was hysterically crying, because something was terribly wrong. I was super stressed, and every cycle [of three] was very dramatic." Suzi, too, was told that her AMH levels were too low for her age. Although she was a highly specialized surgeon, she told me, "I was, like, crying like a stupid person. . . . I was like, 'God, this is really depressing.'" Another surgeon, Tina, sighed, "My ovaries were aging and almost in failure. It was devastating. It puts you in menopause. The doctor presented these terrible statistics, and it was all bad news."

Claudia, Simone, Ruth, Suzi, and Tina were not the kind of women who were accustomed to being placed in the "bottom percentile." As responsible professional women, they had all thought that they were being proactive in undertaking elective egg freezing in their midthirties. But in each case, these women were thrust into fertility crises marked by last-ditch efforts to preserve their remaining ovarian reserves. Their situations suggest that medical and nonmedical egg freezing are not poles apart; the boundary between these two categories can be quite blurry. Yet, despite the blurry boundary, women who undertake medical egg freezing receive a form of general sympathy that women undertaking nonmedical egg freeing do not. I would suggest that women who undertake *both* forms of egg freezing require our compassion. But as we will see in the next section, medical egg freezing for cancer moves beyond the realm of fertility preservation into a true rescue effort.

Fertility Emergencies and Salvation

Egg freezing for cancer deserves its own book, one that I hope to write someday. But in this chapter on fertility threats, it seems important to discuss, at least briefly, how cancer diagnoses in reproductive-aged women are, in fact, *fertility emergencies,* for which medical egg freezing has been designed to respond. This vulnerable population is the very reason why egg freezing was developed in the first place.[12] These courageous young women deserve our attention and respect, even though they are rarely described in the media and scholarly portrayals of egg freezing.

In cancer patients, it is the treatment, rather than the disease, that diminishes or destroys a woman's ovarian function. Many chemotherapeutic agents used in cancer treatment are toxic to women's ovaries, putting them at a high risk for premature ovarian insufficiency (POI), or what is more commonly called "early menopause."[13] In addition, some breast cancer tumors are endocrine sensitive, requiring women after chemotherapy to also undergo additional long courses (up to five years) of suppressive hormone therapy, during which time pregnancy may not be recommended.[14] Although a woman's menstrual cycle may resume after cancer treatment, her fertility may be compromised due to treatment damage. Age-related fertility decline may be accelerated in cancer survivors, especially women who are already in their late thirties when chemotherapy is administered. As a result, about one in six cancer survivors experience POI. Cancer survivors also have a 30 to 50 percent overall reduction in live births compared to the general population.[15]

Over the past decade, a dedicated field of oncofertility has emerged to address fertility preservation for young cancer patients and reproductive options for cancer survivors.[16] Current clinical oncology guidelines suggest that all cancer patients of reproductive age should be informed of their fertility risks and be referred for medical egg freezing whenever possible.[17] For cancer patients, only one egg freezing cycle can usually be performed, given the urgency of cancer treatment. Given the need for immediate postdiagnosis egg freezing, timely referral and scheduling remain ongoing challenges. However, many eligible cancer patients are not able to freeze their eggs before undergoing sterilizing cancer treatments, not only because of lack of timely referral but also because medical egg freezing is not covered by health insurance in the vast majority of US states.[18]

In my own study, I met thirty-three young women who had been able to freeze their eggs, usually because of heroic efforts on the part of their families to raise funds for medical egg freezing on an emergency basis.[19] Ten of these women had conditions other than cancer, primarily ones that had resulted in the partial or total removal of their ovaries.[20] The rest of these women had been diagnosed with cancer. Thirteen had breast cancer, five had blood cancer (leukemia or lymphoma), and five had other cancers (tongue, thyroid, muscle tissue, cervix, and vulva). About one-third of these cancer patients had advanced or aggressive forms. Three women had cancer that had metastasized to the lymph nodes, bones, lungs, and/or brain, and four women had recurrent or chronic cancer. In other words, a significant number of these women were seriously ill, even though they were young, at an average age of twenty-eight.[21]

Almost all of these women told me that their cancer diagnosis was utterly unexpected, catching them off guard and causing them to feel shock, confusion, and disbelief. Given their relative youth and their lack of family cancer histories, few were prepared for this unexpected and life-shattering news. However, it was not only the threat of death that scared them. Cancer was experienced by most women as a kind of double jeopardy—one that involved both the risk of death *and* the possibility that chemotherapy could damage their ovaries and lead to irreversible sterility down the road.[22] This latter news was considered devastating by most women, who explained to me that a permanent loss of their fertility would be radically life altering, jeopardizing their future happiness by destroying their vision of themselves as both women and mothers. They used terms such as "grave," "dark," "hard," "horrible," and "crushing" to describe the ominous weight of this potential fertility threat.

For example, Brittany, a lawyer, told me over coffee in a small New England café that her metastatic thyroid cancer diagnosis was both shocking and unfair. First of all, an endocrinologist had misdiagnosed the cancer in her thyroid gland, allowing it to spread. Next, Brittany's long-term boyfriend, with whom she had been discussing pregnancy, left her, because he could not "handle" her cancer diagnosis and treatment. Then Brittany, now single, was told by her oncologist that cancer treatment could lead to her early menopause. The last bit of news caused panic. "I was like, 'What am I going to do? I'm thirty-five.' And I was really freaking out. I was feeling so super anxious about it, like, to a point where I couldn't tolerate it I was so anxious. . . . I felt like if [pregnancy] couldn't happen, if it couldn't be mine, this would be the most devastating thing. Like, there would be no comfort to me. I would just be so devastated. And also just, like, the idea of having your own [children] . . . I was really intent on it."

At that point, Brittany was referred to a local university's IVF clinic, where medical egg freezing was now being offered. Brittany undertook a single egg freezing cycle, which produced only four viable eggs. Even though both she and her IVF physician were disappointed with the results, these four frozen eggs soon became highly meaningful to Brittany, giving her considerable peace of mind and a sense of control amid chaos.

> You know, it wasn't that bad. So I think it's worth it, considering what we're talking about. . . . There are so many things I can't control about what's happening this minute. But this is one thing I can do. So, if I look back and regret it, I can say, "Hey, I tried." This is the thing I could do, and I did that thing I could do at that time with the money I had, with the motivation I had. So at least I tried. Yeah, at least I did something. I think it also made me feel better at that time, with how I was feeling, to just do something. Also, this is kind of a dorky aspect of it, but I think I just liked the idea of—this is going to sound so horrible—I liked the idea of participating in something that's so cutting-edge, like, that's so modern and fascinating, what they can do now.

Other young cancer patients I met expressed these same feelings of excitement, gratitude, and luck for living in an age when medical egg freezing is now possible. Women often used exalted terms to describe their egg freezing, calling it a "gift," a "blessing," a "miracle," and a form of "empowerment." Beyond the gratitude, egg freezing brought with it a kind of double hope— hope for a brighter future *without* cancer and one *with* children. Indeed, these cancer patients told me that they imagined their frozen eggs as "my babies," "my kids," and "my future family." A few admitted that they sometimes drove past the IVF facilities where their frozen eggs had been stored, feeling hopeful that their future children were waiting for them inside.

That frozen eggs often took on such a heightened meaning in the lives of these young women, some of whom were still in treatment, while others were now considered survivors, suggests that medical egg freezing confers more than just hope. In the lives of cancer patients, medical egg freezing may represent a *technology of salvation*, literally saving one's fertility in the hope of a future life as a mother. Ultimately, medical egg freezing brings with it the life-affirming optimism of cancer survival and an imagined future in which one is fully capable of bringing new life into this world.

Egg Freezing as Infertility Prevention

At the end of this chapter on fertility threats, it seems quite important to re-ask the main question of this study: Why are so many American women freezing their eggs? As I have argued, the women who undertake egg freezing are not trying to *postpone, defer,* or *delay* their fertility. Although these three verbs are commonly used to describe women's egg freezing intentions, I believe that they are wholly incorrect. Rather, as we have seen in women's stories, egg freezing is about trying to *save, preserve,* and *extend* fertility among women who hope to become mothers but are concerned about real and imminent threats to their fertility. Women's fertility, as we have seen, may be destroyed by chemotherapy, fall off a cliff because of POA, or dwindle away because of inevitable age-related fertility decline, sometimes without sufficient warning. The technology of egg freezing thus offers these women the only means at hand to respond to their fertility emergencies, as well as to overcome the unintended consequences of their fertility benightedness.

As should also be abundantly clear, egg freezing is rarely, if ever, undertaken by women lightly. It is a frankly expensive and arduous process that women enter into with trepidation. Those who are most motivated have often witnessed the suffering of their infertile friends—friends who often warn and encourage them to try egg freezing as a form of *infertility prevention.* But in order to do so, these women must freeze their eggs in a timely manner.

So, when is the correct time to freeze one's eggs? According to most of the IVF physicians I interviewed, the twenties are too early (despite all of the questionable marketing being directed at this younger population).[23] During the twenties, most women's fertility remains remarkably stable, and many of these women will eventually find partners with whom to become pregnant. But once a woman reaches her early thirties, egg freezing is something that she should consider *if* she is still unpartnered yet knows that she wants to become a mother. According to the physicians I interviewed, the early thirties are the "sweet spot" for egg freezing for most women—especially between the ages of thirty-two and thirty-seven, when fertility slightly and then significantly begins to decline. The forties are too late, according to all of the physicians in my study. As one of them explained, forty-something women usually have the "double-barrel problem" of needing multiple cycles and producing chromosomally damaged eggs that will not yield normal embryos. Thus, "realistic expectations need to be set" for forty-something women, many of whom will pursue egg freezing, then IVF, with little hope. As one female physician remarked regarding women's expectations, "I sometimes feel totally amazed. I feel like we've done so much to try to talk about fertility every day. I feel like it's out there, but you know, I guess not, because I still see people who are surprised when they come in at forty, and they're like, 'You know, [I'm] having trouble getting pregnant, and nobody told me'—which boggles my mind, because we're not doing as good a job as we should be."

This lack of adequate fertility knowledge—or what I have described throughout this chapter as fertility benightedness—was one of the most troubling findings of my own study. And one final story should truly make clear how fertility benightedness can lead to heartbreaking outcomes. On a cold February afternoon in 2015, a Yale graduate student, Samantha, came to visit me in my office. She had been told that I was an infertility specialist, now studying the phenomenon of egg freezing. As soon as Samantha sat down, she began crying, her tears absorbing a full box of tissues as she told me her story. Samantha was now forty-three, married for fifteen years. Describing herself as "hyperresponsible," she and her husband had planned to have children once they became financially stable. As Samantha explained, she had taken "really good care" of her fertility, favoring condoms over hormonal contraception and undergoing regular gynecological exams. But as Samantha put it, "No one ever said anything. No one ever talks about fertility." Thus, she had incorrectly assumed that she could become pregnant in her early forties, because several generations of her hearty Canadian family members had already done so.

> SAMANTHA: So my grandma had a baby when she was forty. My great-grandmother had a baby when she was forty-three. A close friend of the family had a baby when she was forty.
> MARCIA: Okay. So you have this assumption, just from like family history, that it was easy to get pregnant in the forties?
> SAMANTHA: Yeah. It had made perfect sense. And then that stupid article came out in the *Atlantic*, which was like, "All the data about fertility [decline with age] is from, you know, French studies carried out in the 1800s, and it's bullshit."[24] . . . And so basically, it's fine if you want to get pregnant in your late thirties, early forties. Like, you're going to be fine.

But as Samantha was soon to learn, "the forties are the exception to the rule." When she and her husband tried to become pregnant, they had no luck, eventually finding their way to the Yale Fertility Center. At the age of forty-one, Samantha was diagnosed with extremely low ovarian reserve, making IVF her only option. Three IVF cycles later, Samantha was still not pregnant, and now she and her husband were $20,000 in debt. When I asked Samantha whether they might consider donor eggs or adoption, she called those options "impossible," as their finances were in ruin. As Samantha spoke, she wept openly in sadness, anger, and frustration.

> I'm absolutely screwed! This was so preventable, if someone three years ago had just encouraged me to have a baby then. . . . I had lots of dreams about what our kids would be like, how our genes might look like together. But I'm infertile now, and our lives are just so shitty. Our lives are in shambles. It's just like I've uncovered like this world of immense human suffering that I wish I had never had to be exposed to, you know? And it's just like—it's so fucking depressing, because it is, like, suffering so much pain unnecessarily. . . . It's like, somehow, I was magically supposed to know, even though nobody ever told me. Or was it just me fooling myself about my reproductive aging? It's like, "No, I'm a really smart person, really concerned with health issues. I've done so many proactive things in my life to live a healthy life, and had I known, I would have done everything in my power to not be in this situation." So, you know, if you have kids too early, you're a loser. If you try to have them too late, you're selfish. And it's just like, no matter what you do, as a woman, you're screwed. Like, if this happened to men, you know—like fucking sperm and the cellphone thing, like we hear about it, you know?—you know, there would be massive education campaigns.

At the end of our meeting, in which Samantha had literally poured out her broken heart to me, there was little that I could offer other than reassurance that she was not to blame for her plight.

SAMANTHA: It's hell. Yeah, and it's just like, you know, that I'll have to live with this for the rest of my life—you know, the thing that, like, if I had just done it one year or two years earlier, everything would have been different.

MARCIA: Yeah, but don't blame yourself. I mean, you *cannot* blame yourself.

SAMANTHA: Yeah, no. I mean, that's the thing is, I can't, and yet, like . . . because women get blamed so much for everything, it's just, like, you can't help but feel this like sort of self-hatred, even though I know it's not my fault. Like, I've relived the last four years of my life over and over and over again, being like, "This is where I fucked up. This is where I fucked up. This is where I fucked up."

MARCIA: You haven't fucked up anything, you know? You haven't. You haven't fucked up your life, you know? And it's not . . . you really are not to blame for this, you know? You were acting in a planful manner with the best information that you had, okay? And, you know, in the egg freezing study, I want to tell you, you know, most of these women, the problem is they don't have a partner, you know? And they're like, "Where did I fuck up? Where did I fuck up?" They're blaming themselves for not having a partner, you know? But like you, they're not to blame.

* * *

Indeed, Samantha was not to blame for the fertility benightedness that had led her to become infertile. If anyone was to blame, it was the gynecologists who had offered no such infertility warnings. And, for single women who are turning to egg freezing, they are certainly not to blame for the mating gap, which has led to a dearth of educated, eligible, and equal partners ready to marry and have children.

It is deeply disturbing that women are blamed—and blame themselves—for reproductive and relationship problems not of their own making. Instead of assigning blame, it is more useful to focus on the proactive ways in which American women are now turning to egg freezing as a potential solution. We shift now to part 2 of this book, which focuses on women's egg freezing experiences. In chapter 5, we will learn what it is like to go through the egg freezing process, particularly for brave single women who are entering couples-oriented IVF clinics on their own.

PART II

Experiences

5

The IVF Clinic

Single Women Braving a Couples' World

Leanne's Cautionary Tale

When I started this study, I had no idea that more than one-third of the women I would meet would be health professionals undertaking egg freezing. Eighteen of these women were physicians—some academics, some in private practices, and from a wide variety of fields. They included dermatologists, emergency room physicians, endocrinologists, gastroenterologists, hepatologists, immunologists, internists, nephrologists, obstetricians and gynecologists, oncologists, otolaryngologists, psychiatrists, surgeons, and transplant medicine specialists. In addition, I met thirty other women who were working in allied health care professions. They included nurse-midwives and nurse-practitioners; medical researchers and medical residents; pharmaceutical regulators and pharmaceutical representatives; health care administrators and health care consultants; health insurance strategists and health care finance attorneys. Public health professionals also volunteered for my study, including several women directing nonprofits or delivering direct public health services to vulnerable communities in the US and abroad. I also interviewed health and science reporters, two of whom also interviewed me for stories they were writing.

Leanne was one of these women in health care. With her master's degree in public administration, she had become deeply involved in the health care legislation arena, helping to introduce the Affordable Care Act (aka Obamacare) to US society. Although Leanne loved being a health policy maker, her demanding work schedule and travel obligations had put a damper on her relationship with her boyfriend, Peter. When I asked Leanne, "Are you single, partnered, divorced?" she chuckled, "I am pretty much single. Yep!" Leanne recounted her recent breakup, one in which Peter's dissatisfactions with Leanne's career commitments had played a major role.

> I guess I always assumed I would have kids . . . and you know, I started feeling more of an urgency and desire to have kids in the last couple of years. And I was in a failing relationship, and I was just starting to feel a lot of pressure that I needed to do something. . . . I wanted to at least understand what my options are. Being completely terrified of needles, I did not think I would ever do anything like freezing my eggs! But, in February, I decided to go to an egg freezing seminar . . . to at least learn a little bit more about my options. And, when I went to that, it was pretty clear that I'm kind of at the perfect age if I wanted to do this. And you know, I walked out of there feeling like I didn't know what was going on with my relationship to make this decision. Because what they said is, "If you're going to get pregnant in the next six months, don't do this. Just try and get pregnant." And I'd been on the Pill since I was like twenty-one or twenty-two, and I had gotten off of it about a year prior with my boyfriend. I had just changed jobs. And I said [to him], "I want to figure out what my cycle is, and I really want to start trying. I don't care that we're not married. This is what I want." And that just wasn't happening, and we were using condoms. And so the day after I went to the egg freezing seminar, I ended my relationship. . . . It was kind of a quick decision. I needed to feel empowered and control over something that I feel like I hadn't had control over for quite some time.

Curious about the reasons for Leanne's breakup, I then asked, "What would you say was the issue in that relationship that you ended?" Leanne laughed, saying, "I might as well tell you this."

> Like, we began the relationship, and maybe a year in, somebody approached me and said, "You know, your boyfriend is on Match." And I was like, "Really? We've been together a year, and he's on Match?" And I approached him and said, "What the hell are you doing?" And he's like, "You know, I just want to make sure I'm looking for the right things." I'm like, "You are in this relationship. What do you mean looking for? You're with me. You're either in it or out of it. Get out of it if you want." And that was the first time he told me he loved me [*laughs*]. I should have known

then that that should have ended. . . . You know, we just weren't able to get on the same page with the relationship in general, and the key factor was, you know, the fact that our relationship wasn't going well. It didn't feel like the right kind of relationship to bring a kid into, and I'm thinking about having children in our future. We were having trouble reconciling that together and that I was feeling these intense pressures that I needed, that I wanted to do something, and I wasn't going to do it by myself. . . . But I've had a couple years of therapy to think about this. You know, the truth is he felt like I had sort of dwarfed him professionally; and then I changed jobs, and he still didn't feel good about it. So he was really uneasy, and we had poor communication. So I think it's just, you know, it's a lot of things, and we both knew that introducing kids into the relationship, it wasn't going to make it work. I think he had these ideal notions of what a relationship would be like, what a family would look like. And at our age—we were both thirty-six when it ended—you know, it's just kind of like, "Come on, dude! Get practical here. I mean, like, we're not going to be perfect. We're never going to have, you know, millions of dollars. But we both have wonderful jobs. The salary is good. We have families. We're extremely healthy." I was being practical . . . and I think he didn't believe that I would actually be there. He thought he'd have to be the primary caregiver because of my commitment to my job, which I didn't agree with, and I think 90 percent of people who know me would feel the same way as I did [laughs]! . . . He saw me making more money, and therefore my work has to be a priority. You know, I do travel for work, but he was worried he'd have to be "on" all the time and I wouldn't be there, and he didn't believe that I would make changes upon having kids. So it's just like, you know, a lot of miscommunication, I would say, misconceptions. But that's just from my perspective. His perspective, you know, is obviously a different story!

Having ended her relationship with Peter, Leanne now found herself alone at thirty-six, entering the couples-oriented world of IVF. She chose a busy East Coast IVF clinic because of its decade of experience with egg freezing, including its early participation in clinical trials and its high volume of egg freezing patients. Leanne's mother, a fourth-generation Jewish Philadelphian, offered to accompany Leanne to her first appointment, even though she told Leanne that she was quite skeptical of egg freezing. But by the end of the consultation, Leanne's mother was convinced that egg freezing would be a good option for her now single daughter, and she and Leanne's father offered to pay for the procedure. Leanne thanked them but politely declined. "I was like, 'You know, I want to do my own thing in my own division. I don't really need any of that.'"

Although paying for egg freezing was not a problem for Leanne, her needle phobia was. At the first appointment, Leanne was told that she would require three daily injections of gonadotropins—hormonal medications designed to stimulate the maturation of eggs in her ovaries. Most of the shots were to be done with small needles inserted into the abdomen near the navel. But the final "trigger shot," designed to release the mature eggs for collection, would need to be injected with a long needle in the buttocks, a challenging procedure for any woman to manage on her own. Leanne was told that IVF clinics do not normally offer injection assistance, as they assume that women will learn to self-inject or seek their partners' assistance. Understanding Leanne's dilemma, the clinic told her that a visiting nurse could be hired, but the cost would be high, amounting to thousands of dollars over the two weeks prior to egg retrieval.

Leanne could not imagine injecting herself; thus, egg freezing without injection assistance would be a deal breaker for her. Fortunately, one of Leanne's married friends came to the rescue. Experienced with needles because of juvenile arthritis, this friend gave Leanne every single shot, sometimes late in the evening or very early in the morning on Leanne's way to the clinic. When Leanne needed the final trigger shot—"the one in my butt, which the idea of terrified me"—her friend was not available. Fortunately, her female cousin ran over at the last minute to do the grim duty. "And it was awful!" Leanne said, laughing. "But at least I did not do a single one," Leanne admitted. "I did not watch a single one!"

At the clinic, Leanne continued to face an array of invasive tests and procedures that challenged her needle phobia and sense of bodily integrity. "You know, I'm not psyched about any of it! But I actually found I have more issues with the blood draw than I did the needles. The blood draws take longer. The needles are pretty quick, although I feel like a human pin cushion [laughs]! And then you have monitoring, too. So, like, on my highest days, I have one shot before I go to the doctor. And I have a blood draw, [vaginal] ultrasound, and two shots at night. So it's a lot of getting poked!"

Overall, Leanne found the physical experience of egg freezing to be quite challenging. The hormonal stimulation phase, the two-week period of daily injections, led to feelings of abdominal pressure and "the discomfort you feel just from the follicles growing." Leanne never knew whether these feelings were normal, and she wished that the clinic would have provided more guidance. "It would be nice if they kind of—whatever the app is that people have for, like, you know, 'Your baby is now the size of a pea. Your baby is now the size of an apple'—if they could do a better job, like, 'All right, this might be what you're feeling now, and this is normal. And the strange surge that's happening, that's totally normal, too.' Like, weird stuff happens to your body, and they sort of don't prepare you for it."

When the time came for Leanne's egg retrieval, a surgical procedure conducted under general anesthesia, Leanne debated whom to ask, as IVF clinics usually require physical accompaniment after surgery. Leanne's mother volunteered, sitting in the waiting area with other women's husbands. "I don't care that the men are there," Leanne explained. "Like, as far as I'm concerned, there has to be a problem most of the time, so, you know, 'We need IVF because of his sperm. We need IVF because of me.' You know, whatever the situation is. . . . But I think that there could be a lot more done to be supportive with the women doing this."

In particular, Leanne thought that single women needed more support. Because of her background in health policy, Leanne had approached her own egg freezing experience with an astute observer's eye, assessing how services could be made more user-friendly. Telling me that someone "should do research on this," Leanne asked if I was interested in hearing her assessment. When I said I was, Leanne offered this analysis of the ways that she believed egg freezing could be made more accessible for single women.

Given how stressful this is and just how kind of time consuming and how different it is from anything else in your life, the customer service experience could be a heck of a lot better. It's just kind of absurd. . . . Like, I had my test this morning, and they weren't going to get the results until this afternoon on my estrogen. And then so at three o'clock, they call you, while you're in a meeting, and tell you your results. They tell me I have to go to the pharmacy, and I have to tell the pharmacy to fill the prescription. But you can't just go to any pharmacy. You have to go to a specialty pharmacy and go get the drugs. So you can't price compare.

You know, I found ways to save hundreds of dollars on individual drugs by comparing, and you just can't do it. I know that's not what you're looking at . . . but there's a business case for this, to be doing better on that front.

But beyond pricing issues, Leanne had much more to say about being a single woman in an overly busy IVF clinic catering mostly to married couples. As a single woman, Leanne felt that she was required to do extra work to ensure the quality of her own care.

I mean, it's amazing. They told me I had to watch all these videos, or they weren't going to let me do it [egg freezing]. But the videos were actually for—they went the whole way through IVF. And like, "Why didn't you just tell me to look into the first half or warn me that this is, you know, everything that features *you and your partner*?" And, you know, they create a written protocol for you, and then they don't volunteer to update it every day. It's just, like, I'm paying like $18,000 for this, and God, insurance is not covering it. . . . You know, I chose this clinic because it's a factory and, you know, they do this, and I didn't need the special kind of treatment with genetic testing and this and that. So I was like, I can deal with the factory. I've got the moral support outside. But you have to really be on top of your own situation with a lot of questions. Because I only half understand what the heck they're telling me. . . . You walk in, they're sometimes friendly, they're sometimes not. The nurses tell me really conflicting information. Like, the first nurse, this morning, they told me I was probably not going to trigger tonight. The second nurse I talked to ten minutes later told me I was going to trigger tonight, and I had to correct her. I'm like, "Come on, guys. You have electronic health records. I see you staring at the thing. This is what you do for a living. Do you not communicate with one another and the doctor?" You know, they pass you off between so many nurses. So it's just like, I mean, our health care system in general, it's transforming, and we're paying for more quality now. But I'm finding them kind of frustrating and feeling like I'm helping guide them, which is sort of silly as this is what they do every day.

Having registered her critique of the IVF clinic as an overworked factory, Leanne admitted to having some sympathy for the clinic's staff.

Well, to be clear, you know, we're all like completely hormonal women who—none of us, like, want to be there. I mean, I don't know what brought you to this issue in general, but you should go sit in [the clinic] [*laughs*]. I mean, in any given morning, there are tons, say, fifty-plus women who are cycling through in the time that you're sitting there . . . but none of us want to be there. Everyone's got something "wrong." So, I mean, I'm sure it sucks for them [the clinic staff], dealing with these completely hormonal, varying-degrees-of-fertility-issues women. But, I mean, I adjusted, because you walk in, and you don't even, like, tell them your name. You just hand them a piece of paper. And I didn't understand; I thought that was so weird at first. And now I'm like, "I totally get it. I'm here every day. I don't really want to talk to you either!" [*laughs*]. . . . You know, my nurse the other day was like, "If it makes you feel any better, the four women I saw before you were in this place, and you're in that place" [with more eggs maturing]. And I'm not really sure I care about the four other women who are on the same schedule as me. But, "Okay. Thanks."

Leanne had chosen this clinic because of its experience and reputation. But she realized that the clinic's high volume made the consistency of her own care suffer.

They do get that fair bit of experience because of so many patients, but in some ways, it can desensitize them. And I think that there's something to be said about greater continuity. I mean, I'm all about nurse-practitioners and PAs [physician assistants] and whatever. But it's like, I'd love for my team to be *my* team, and every time I come in, I don't want to have to tell every person that I'm afraid of needles. And like, "Please, just tell me when you're done" and "No, I do not want a Band-Aid over it. I just want the little piece of cotton that I can throw away when I'm finished."

Ultimately, Leanne believed that egg freezing patients at the clinic deserved better support and services directed specifically to them. She noted that the only special provision made for egg freezing patients was the initial seminar, which she "actually really liked."

There were all these women there, and I was like, "Wow! I'm kind of part of a group." I actually think it would be cool if they facilitated a little bit more. Like, I would have loved to have gone and gotten drinks with these women afterwards to talk about it, because I don't know other people in this situation. Like, they can certainly do some more supportive things. I mean, I do find that when I go in there, I'm always looking like, "Who's wearing a ring? Who's not? Why might they be here?" So I think that there could be a lot more done to be supportive with the single women doing this. Because it's a lot of money, too, that you're putting into this, so, like, you know, you want to get it right. Which is also why customer service could be better, like, you know, more support to make sure you don't screw it up.

By all objective measures, Leanne did not "screw it up." In the course of two cycles, Leanne was able to freeze sixteen eggs. At the time of our interview, she was contemplating a third cycle to bring the total egg count to more than twenty. When I asked Leanne how she was feeling with her eggs safely in storage, she was quick to respond.

Now that I've done this, I do have this feeling that "Gosh, my eggs are out. We can fertilize them. I can get genetic testing, reduce the risk of miscarriage. And we'll call it a day." I'd like to meet somebody who I want to spend my life with and then get interested in trying to get pregnant, you know. And I actually did not ever think that I would have to wait to find him in order to have kids. So it is a little disturbing to me to think about the possibility of having kids, you know, after forty, but for no other reason than they won't have siblings. If I had a kid, they might not have a sibling. . . . I always assumed that I would have two, but not sure if I can fit it in [laughs].

Still, Leanne felt relieved to have undertaken egg freezing, because it took the pressure off dating in the aftermath of her failed relationship.

I did it immediately after my breakup, intentionally, because I felt like I was basically going to put a pause on my life. I thought, now I have the ability to travel and all sorts of things, you know, really kick off like the rest of my life and feel like I have at least this as an insurance policy, a very expensive insurance policy, you know, because it doesn't mean I use it at all, but it's just insurance. So I feel good about it, and I'm glad I've done it. It's just kind of empowering, too, at a time when I felt that I didn't have a lot of control. So, yeah, I certainly think that it's the right thing for me. You know, I'm getting older, and I'd like to get married and have a kid.

As we wrapped up our interview, Leanne thanked me, telling me that she rarely took part in studies but that she felt the need to help overcome the egg freezing information gap.

I just felt like there's just such a dearth in information. So I just want to be able to share, like, what this is, what it really entails, and what you might expect out of it. I've told people, "Use me, please! If you know somebody, I'm happy to talk to them." I'm not, like, looking to publicize it on Face-book, but, like, you know, there's this piece of me that really wishes that I'd done it sooner. . . . I kind of wish in some ways that, like, egg freezing was something that people did when they just like, "Oh, you're eighteen. You're done with high school. You're going to college. Why don't you do it so you don't have to worry about it for a while?" That would be good [*laughs*]. I mean, there are certainly pros and cons to that, you know. I don't know how I feel about us all waiting until we're kind of old to have kids, if that really messes with things that much. And I'm curious about what it'll mean for the generation of children who are like from mothers who are forty-plus. But, you know, I guess we'll see.

* * *

Almost three years later, I heard from Leanne, who wanted to tell me the end of her egg freezing story. She had undertaken a third egg freezing cycle, bringing her total to twenty-five. But sadly, those twenty-five eggs did not deliver on their promise. Leanne saw her saga as a cautionary tale.

Marcia—not sure if you are doing any follow up with ppl who were part of your research, but I figured I would share since my recent experience drastically changed my feelings about egg freezing.
I was single when I froze my eggs. I met someone and due to my age (39) we decided to immediately go for the frozen eggs rather than trying naturally since we assumed higher chance of conception and a healthy birth with genetic testing.
Sadly, despite having 25 eggs, I only ended up with one embryo that they thought was usable with an AA rating and then I miscarried. So, all to say that after the empowerment I felt from freezing and $40k plus

investment, I have nothing other than emotional exhaustion and a slimmer pocketbook.

No one knows why this all happened but many suspect that using frozen eggs just is not ideal. Of course, I did not have a sense of this at the outset (or know I would meet someone), but it makes my advice to younger folks considering freezing a bit different. It just isn't quite the insurance policy I thought it might be.

I hope you are well. Sorry if this isn't something useful to you—but more info always seems better to me.

Leanne

Egg Freezing Bravery

Leanne's story, replete with fear, courage, critique, and failure, shows that egg freezing is never a true "insurance policy," even though it is often described that way, including by more than thirty other women in my study. Egg freezing is also not for the faint of heart. As Leanne's story reveals, egg freezing entails physical, emotional, and logistical challenges, as well as significant financial sacrifice. Indeed, most women who enter IVF clinics to freeze their eggs probably do not want to be there. Thus, egg freezing requires substantial bravery, of the kind that I witnessed time and time again among women in my study.

Leanne was one of these brave women—a true "badass," in the complimentary terms of my study subjects. Leanne's first act of bravery involved ending a relationship with a man who would not commit to her. She then willed herself into becoming a "human pincushion." And amid the not-so-subtle discrimination of being a single woman in a married space, Leanne stood up for herself in a busy IVF clinic to ensure her own safety. Leanne also managed to meet the urgent medical demands of egg freezing over three separate cycles, while working full-time and depleting $40,000 of her savings. Then, with the relief of eggs in storage, Leanne worked to "kick-start" her life again, finding a new partner who wanted to have children with her. Returning to an IVF clinic that had not served her well, Leanne nonetheless asked for her eggs to be thawed and fertilized. And despite the inexplicable loss of her eggs, Leanne tried her best to become pregnant with the remaining single embryo. Despite her heartbreaking miscarriage, Leanne mustered the courage to reach out to me, so that other women might learn from her example.

What Leanne's story clearly shows is that egg freezing cannot provide guaranteed outcomes, even in the nation's most experienced IV clinics. The insurance policy that Leanne *thought* she had purchased effectively expired prematurely, leaving her with nothing but "emotional exhaustion and a slimmer pocketbook." Indeed, when Leanne contacted me, I could not help but wonder, Had the IVF clinic done right by Leanne? Was her case handled carefully and correctly? Were her eggs frozen and rewarmed to the best of the clinic's ability? Could the final outcome have been any different? Or was Leanne simply one of the unlucky ones, given that twenty-five eggs frozen at the age of thirty-six should have yielded a better result?

These are important questions, as is the question of care. What could the IVF clinic have done to improve its customer service so that Leanne felt cared for as a patient? From the beginning to the end of her egg freezing journey, Leanne realized that the care that she was receiving was less than she deserved. It began with the informational video, which was designed for married IVF patients, not for single women freezing their eggs like her. Then the injection assistance she needed was not available at the clinic, nor was her fear of needles accurately acknowledged and addressed. The clinic's nurses were sometimes friendly, sometimes not. And the information they provided to Leanne about her case was not always up-to-date or accurate. With her health policy background, Leanne chalked this up to poor customer service in an overcrowded clinic "factory." But in a factory devoted to precious human eggs, Leanne's concerns were not only valid but deeply concerning.

Leanne was not alone in her critique. More than one-third (38 percent) of the women in my study had experienced adverse aspects of egg freezing care, with some women volunteering to speak to me precisely to register their complaints. The women I interviewed had attended a dozen different IVF clinics across the country, half academic, half private, and mostly in cities along the East and West Coast corridors. Large and busy IVF clinics seemed to provide the least favorable conditions of care. Smaller IVF clinics, where patients received more personalized attention and were usually seen by the same IVF physician over multiple cycles, were generally preferred.

It is important to emphasize that the majority of women in my study, almost two-thirds (62 percent), were relatively satisfied with their egg freezing care, sometimes developing close relationships with their IVF providers. But even when conditions were good, egg freezing itself was difficult because of challenges that are inherent to the process. These include choosing a clinic and clinician, entering the clinic alone, self-injecting medications (sometimes while traveling), and experiencing side effects, some of them serious. To endure this complicated and physically invasive process, women must draw on substantial reserves of stamina, willpower, fortitude, and courage, demonstrating their *badass bravery*, as we will see.

Clinic(ian)s

The first crucial decision that women must make is to choose an IVF clinic with well-established egg freezing protocols and services. Women must consider a number of different factors, including a clinic's location, its regional reputation, and the advice from knowledgeable friends who have already attended. Women are also influenced by clinics' websites and their egg freezing advertisements, which are increasingly appearing on social media outlets aimed at women in their twenties and thirties but which may exaggerate their egg freezing claims.[1] Although much attention has been paid in the media to so-called egg freezing parties, not a single woman in my study had attended one, even those living in major East Coast cities.[2] In fact, Leanne complained that the informational seminar she attended was devoid of any form of socializing, which she believed could have been a great facilitator of much-needed egg freezing support.

Leanne ultimately made her decision based on the clinic's reputation and experience with egg freezing. But as she would soon discover, the quality of her care was substantially diminished by the high volume of IVF and egg freezing patients being processed through the clinic at the same time. Women who had chosen other large IVF clinics often felt the same way. They reported inconsistent care due to a constantly rotating team of physicians and nurses. Harried physicians were often hasty or formulaic in their communication with women, sometimes making flippant, cavalier, or even sexist comments (for example, calling women "Fertile Myrtles"). Nurses sometimes relayed instructions that were wrong, with potentially serious consequences for women's egg freezing cycles. Large clinics also did not make scheduling accommodations for women, despite the logistical difficulties that single women faced as they juggled their professional responsibilities with the significant requirements of egg freezing.

With "dollar signs" hanging over almost every procedure, women also complained that egg freezing felt more like a money-making venture than a form of reproductive care. Indeed, some women said that they felt pressured by their physicians to pursue additional egg freezing cycles, and they remained skeptical about their clinicians' motivations. A few women also reported frank clinical errors being made in their cases, involving the misreading of charts, incorrect dosages of medications, prescription of expired drugs, timing errors leading to the unexpected ovulation and loss of eggs, and the breakage of eggs during retrieval.

By the end of the egg freezing journey, some women reported being quite upset about their experiences, with a few women being downright livid. The "factory" image that Leanne had used was repeated by others throughout my study, with women saying that they had been placed on an "assembly line," on a "conveyor belt," or "in a mill," where they were treated like "machines" by "robot" physicians and nurses. At other times, women used farming analogies to describe IVF clinics where they were treated like "cows" in a clinic's "cattle call." In fact, large and busy US IVF clinics seemed to be regarded by many women as equivalent to *factory farms*, where too many human bodies were being herded anonymously through routinized, impersonal, and occasionally harmful processes.

In my very last interview of this study, I spoke with Pauline, an executive director of an environmental organization who had previously worked in Congress for a US senator. With her substantial policy background and a mother who was a practicing physician, Pauline was an insightful analyst of the treatment she had received. When I asked my final question, "Do you have any final thoughts, insights or recommendations about what could be made better, or just anything that comes to mind?" Pauline reflected on her egg freezing experience.

There were just parts of the process that, you know, I think that they weren't really on top of. So, you know, I would hope and I'm sure that as more and more people do this, that kind of stuff will get better. Like, I was having to talk to a different nurse like every day. . . . There was one day where, like, over a weekend, they screwed up and told me not to take a dosage that my doctor had told me to take. . . . And I very clearly articulated to my doctor, like, "That shit ain't cool. Like, all the people who are doing this are committing, like, physically and financially to this. And, like, I'm sorry that your person, like, didn't read the computer screen right. Like, what is the solution there?" And, you know, your doctor isn't necessarily the one who actually performs your egg removal. And all of a sudden, you're, like, seeing this person for the first time. And look, it's like very personal and intrusive, and there's like a shit ton of emotional baggage associated with it, and all of a sudden, you're, like, meeting this person, which also adds the emotional sense of being treated like you're just in an assembly line, which just screws with you, as you're already, like, dealing with whatever you're dealing with as you're going through it.

Pauline hoped that egg freezing processes would be standardized over time to improve the quality of patient care and safety. But because US IVF clinics are self-regulating, without government oversight or inspection, each clinic is an island unto itself, accountable only for its own standards and practices. As Pauline concluded at the end of our interview, "They need to hire, like, some sociologists to help figure out how to make it better!"

Fortunately, some smaller academic and research-oriented IVF clinics seem to be doing a better job. There, women were more likely to develop consistent, one-on-one relationships with particular IVF providers. Building a trustworthy physician-patient relationship was especially important to single women, who were managing the complexities of egg freezing on their own. They wanted clear and open communication and considered themselves lucky if they found an IVF physician with excellent interpersonal skills.

To that end, women tended to be more satisfied with female IVF providers in academic IVF units than with male providers in large private centers. One academic IVF physician who had performed egg freezing for a substantial number of women in my study received the highest praise. Because of her calm demeanor and ability to provide encouragement to her single patients, she made women feel comfortable, confident, and supported throughout the egg freezing process. One of her patients, Yuki, who worked at a major Silicon Valley tech firm, had gone through a recent divorce. Thinking that she might have aged out of egg freezing, Yuki nonetheless met with this IVF physician, who succeeded in changing her outlook.

I'll never forget, because I was sort of doom and gloom about turning forty, and she did the ultrasound. And I'll never forget. She said, "You have a beautiful uterine lining" [*laughs*]. And I was like, "That is the highest compliment anyone has paid me in a long time." I remember walking out and feeling like . . . just absolutely fantastic about myself. And so, you know, I think that's what her job is. She sees a lot of uterine linings. So apparently at forty, I'm okay. So then I thought, "Okay, good, I'm in good shape." . . . And then I had to do a lot of travel. And so I asked her if it would be a problem if I scheduled it for a few months later, and she's like, "No, it's not going to make a big difference. So whenever you have the time and you're not traveling, you can put aside a couple weeks to do this." . . . Like, they weren't pressuring me, but it was, like, obvious that if I wanted to start it, I could. So I was like, "Oh yeah, maybe I just should." So then I was, like, off and running!

Female IVF physicians were not the only ones to receive praise from patients. Some male physicians, too, were beloved by their patients, making women feel comfortable and supported in their decision-making. Chiara, a ballerina turned ballet-store owner, described why she had switched from one IVF clinic to another due to contrasting experiences with two male IVF physicians.

I didn't like the first clinic at all. The doctor was—he was just—I don't know how to even explain it—just very cocky, and, you know, I didn't get a good feel from him, no bedside manner. It's just all ego. He was acting like he was, you know, Jesus. And, you know, it was just very uncomfortable. He was a little too secure in himself, and it was more about him than about me. And so then I found Dr. Smith [a pseudonym], and I adore him. He's probably one of the best doctors I've ever been to. Really wonderful! The other doctor, when I spoke to him, he just kept focusing on—he kept saying, "I know it's a lot of money, but you're going to be really happy at the end of this," and blah blah blah. And Dr. Smith was more about—he was more realistic with what he thought the outcome would be and how successful I would be. He was just more . . . more real. And I just felt really good going to him. He's unbelievable! I've never had a doctor take that much time with me, just for the consultation. I think I was there for like an hour and twenty minutes speaking to him. He kind of explained how it works, how the logistics worked and what I could expect, side effects from the medication and all that. And then he just kind of gave me some very loose numbers, and I think we kind of ended up with maybe a 40 percent chance of a live birth. And he was just very, very kind and gentle and talked me through, like, what the ultrasounds would be like and all that kind of stuff and how the procedure would feel. And, you know, it was scientific without being overwhelming and way over my head. My mom was with me, and she was just really impressed with his patience and how he presented it.

Partnerlessness

Even though Chiara and Yuki were enthusiastic about their IVF physicians, they were less excited about entering IVF clinics in their current state of *partnerlessness*. Egg freezing patients are fundamentally different from infertile IVF patients, who are mostly married with rings on their fingers and partners in tow. For single women, being forced to enter this couples' world can be a major challenge, especially because the lack of a partner is the very reason that most women are seeking egg freezing in the first place. As one woman put it, "You know, you go to these clinics, and everybody is there with their husbands. So it's like adding insult to injury."

To date, very few IVF clinics have made special provisions to separate the egg freezing patient population from IVF-seeking couples. But the mixed nature of the clinic can be very unsettling for single women, whose feelings of loneliness, stigma, shame, and envy can be quite intense. For example, Cynthia, the vice president of a California tech firm, described her trepidation over pursuing egg freezing at the age of thirty-six, when she had always hoped to be married by this point with children.

> For me, in all reality, I wish I was pregnant now. Like, I wish I was having a baby at this point in my life. So going through this alone, it sort of reminds you of how alone you are. So that's a little tough. And I think the first day I went in for my first ultrasound, you're sitting in the waiting room, and there's a lot of couples there, because they are doing IVF at the same facility. Certainly, I don't want to be in a position where I'm having such a difficult time getting pregnant I have to use IVF. That's not what I'm envious of. I'm just envious that they found someone to have a baby with.

For Danielle, a Manhattan-based fashion designer, the loneliness of egg freezing made her feel highly emotional throughout the process. Almost every step of the way, she received constant reminders of her singleness, which made her feel both stigmatized and lonely.

You know, one thing that I wanted to say about the egg freezing . . . that was one of the harder parts for me. I looked around, and, like, a lot of people were there alone. But then a lot of the time they're with partners. And that was, like, kind of a mind trip for me, just feeling like that aloneness and feeling by myself. I just thought to myself, "I just wouldn't wish this on anyone going through it alone." You know, when you're doing it out of "What choice do I have?" you know? It was just this very lonely experience in that sense. And they make you go to this clinic. . . . It's a mandatory three-hour clinic to learn about how to give yourself the shots and everything. I think I was like one of two people in the room without a partner. And, like, all the paperwork is actually preprinted. . . . So the last day, when they gave me the paper, and it was like, "Will your partner be picking you up?" And they're like, "Oh, not you." And they crossed it out with a big X. And they wrote, "No partner." And I'm just like, "Why don't you have a separate form for people who are egg freezing, who don't have partners?" And, like, the day that I had the surgery, I was crying on the table before they put me out. I was just crying. You know, it's very, very scary. And when you're coming in for egg freezing, you just feel single . . . and ashamed. I just want to share that, for what it's worth.

As Danielle's story suggests, injection classes are usually filled with married couples, under the assumption that husbands will provide injection assistance, particularly with the final trigger shot that is administered in the gluteal muscle (the buttock). Being a single woman in an injection class designed for married couples can be quite demoralizing, as Rebecca, a planetary scientist, lamented. "They did a little training course for the needles, the injections, and it was like me and two couples. And then at the end, when they show you how to do the big injection, they're like, 'Oh, well, your husband can do it. You don't have to do it.' And I just started crying. Afterwards, [the nurse] stayed, and she talked to me. She was very understanding and nice and said, 'Do you think we should have a separate course for people who are doing egg freezing?' And I said, '*Yes!*'"

Needlework

As suggested by both Danielle and Rebecca, the singleness of egg freezing is accentuated by the fact that women must engage in their own *needlework*—namely, self-injections of powerful and expensive hormonal medications, the dosage and accuracy of which are critical. Few IVF clinics offer direct assistance with these important injections. Nor do they host separate injection classes for single women undertaking egg freezing alone.

Some clinics now offer online injection courses that women can watch in the privacy of their own homes. But instructional videos may be hard to follow, since watching an injection on a computer screen is not the same as inserting a needle into one's own body, a process that is "not hard but not intuitive," as one woman put it. Even physicians who underwent egg freezing admitted having qualms about the self-injection process. Bridget, an internal medicine physician, told me, "I have more empathy for my diabetic patients now!" And Suzi, a surgeon, had much to say about how self-injection affected her both emotionally and physically.

> When I was injecting myself, just the fact that you literally have to poke a needle into yourself is just very hard. And the fact that you're on hormones makes you more emotional, and you're just, like—you're like a complete mess. It was really difficult. And the other thing was that when I went to go pick up drugs . . . it's like a fertility drug pharmacy, so everybody in line is picking up, you know, Menopur, Follistim, whatever. And the majority of people in line are men because they're picking up medication for their wives or partners. And it made me feel even more sad, because at least they have someone going through this with them, whereas I was doing it on my own. Does that make sense? And then so you feel really alone. You already feel alone having to do this, and then the fact that you see those men, it makes it even harder. It makes it even harder. You feel like there's something wrong with you, like, "How are you even still single?" or "What's wrong with you?"

Beyond the loneliness of self-injection, 10 percent of women in my study had to overcome *trypanophobia*, or fear of needles, which is one of the top-ten phobias and affects about 20 to 30 percent of all adults.[3] The needlework required in egg freezing may be a deal beaker for women with trypanophobia. Like Leanne, several other women told me that they almost backed out of egg freezing, because they were petrified of needles and could not imagine the self-inflicted terror.[4] Micah, a realtor, was one of these women, who described her deliberations.

> I talked with a doctor, and they're like, "Okay, so you're going to take an injection class." And I'm like, "No, I can't do that to myself." So they're like, "Well, you can have a partner." And I'm like, "Well, the reason I'm here is because I don't have a partner." And they're like, "Well, you can have a friend do it." So I said, "Okay, well, you know, I have to think about this and figure this out and whatever." So God forbid, like, if anything went wrong, I did not want to have somebody I knew and then, like, attach something bad to them. So I really struggled. [The clinic] doesn't have a nurse you can hire, but they have, like, a nursing company that I guess they refer people to if that's something that's of interest. But that was like a whole extra—it's a lot of money . . . an extra $2,000 that I'd rather not spend if I don't absolutely have to. And then they couldn't guarantee that it'd be the same person every day. And I just ended up not wanting to go that route. So then it happened that one of my best friends—she's actually a special educator, but she's always been kind of medically inclined—I kind of went back and said, "You know what? Maybe I'll ask her if she'd be willing to, you know, administer the shots." So I did, and she obliged.

A few women with trypanophobia somehow overcame their fear of needles to administer their shots on their own. Ariel, an art history professor, described the range of feelings that ensued. "I was petrified. I mean, when I think back on it, it's so ridiculous, you know, the drama that I had going into it. But once I started doing it, I thought, 'Wow, now I understand all those drug addicts who use needles. Now I understand,' you know? It was not painful, and I had such a rush from doing it. So that was pretty funny [*laughs*]. I don't love needles, I would just say, but it wasn't nearly as bad as I had imagined."

Overall, women in this study managed their self-injections, often taking pride in their ability to insert needles into their abdomens and even their own behinds. Sallie, a lawyer, became "really good with the needles": "I mean, I could poke myself with the needle right now. I mean, I've never done it before. I've never had a reason to inject myself . . . but all of it went fine." Women even learned to give themselves injections "on the go," carrying their needles, syringes, and medications in ice packs and coolers to work, conferences, and restaurants and even on dates. Women often had funny stories to tell about injecting themselves in strange bathrooms or creating suspicion among their peers that they might have developed a drug habit. In other words, egg freezing spilled over from the private realm to professional and friendship circles, as women managed both the timing and stigma of injecting themselves while in public.

Reprotravel

Women who faced the most difficult challenges, however, were those who were forced to travel in order to access egg freezing itself. *Egg freezing reprotravel*—or long-distance movements between cities, regions, or even countries for the explicit purpose of egg freezing—was undertaken by about 10 percent of women in my study.[5] Some of this reprotravel was necessary because women lived in places where they could not access local egg freezing services. Other women had visited local IVF clinics, only to switch to distant locations because of dissatisfaction with their local clinical encounters. Some women had moved from one city to another for work but needed to continue or complete the egg freezing process back home. And, in a few cases, women traveled to and from foreign countries simply to access care or to find more affordable egg freezing services elsewhere.

Perhaps the bravest group of reprotravelers were those who were deployed overseas on dangerous missions. These included several high-ranking military, foreign service, and intelligence officers, as well as women working for humanitarian organizations. Their high degree of professional mobility made both relationship formation and motherhood very difficult, so they were trying their best to keep their reproductive options open through egg freezing.

Tara, a military intelligence analyst, was one of these women. She had been stationed in Cairo and decided to purchase her hormonal medications there at a fraction of the cost, before heading home to Virginia to undertake an egg freezing cycle before redeployment. Tara told me her egg freezing story with both verve and humor, realizing that I would appreciate its subtleties because of my own long-term research in the Middle Eastern region. We laughed together, perhaps to reduce the tension surrounding the dangers she faced.

TARA: This Egyptian doctor wrote me a prescription, and I purchased it the night before I left to go back to the United States. A man showed up on his motorcycle—you know how delivery works there.

MARCIA: Oh, yeah.

TARA: Shows up and hands me a bag of the drugs, like the Gonal-F and all that. And I gave him $500 in cash, and he drove away into the night.

MARCIA: This is like a spy novel [*laughs*]!

TARA: [*Laughs*] And I said, "Thank you." And I put them in a cooler, and I carried them back from my assignment through Frankfurt, you know, back through New York. I had that cooler of Egyptian, you know—

MARCIA: Oh my God!

TARA: And hoping they were [okay], because I paid the guy in cash, you know. You can't—you don't know if they're good or not. But then I got back, and then I went to the clinic and went and learned about the process [of self-injection]. And then I ended up—I was going to Afghanistan, so I had to go through what's called this counterterrorism training course.

MARCIA: Yeah, yeah, yeah.

TARA: Learn how to, like, drive backwards and crash vehicles and fire guns. And they told me I wouldn't be able to do that [course] because while I was shooting myself up, it just wouldn't—it didn't work. So I basically—I did that [course], and we had to reschedule some stuff. . . . But I was in DC for a month, and I basically stayed in a hotel, shot myself up there, went in every morning for all of the procedures. . . . I had the procedure [egg retrieval], and two or three days later, I got on a plane for Afghanistan—or maybe a week later.

MARCIA: Oh my God! So a week later you were heading to Kabul or something?

TARA: Yeah, exactly.

MARCIA: Oh my God!

TARA: So I did it between Egypt and Afghanistan. But it worked! It went well.

MARCIA: Oh good. It went well. It worked?

TARA: Yeah. I got forty eggs.

MARCIA: *How* many eggs?

TARA: Forty.

MARCIA: Forty eggs! Wow. That might be a record. Oh my goodness. Wow!

TARA: Yeah. So I guess I'm fertile or something!

MARCIA: Yes. Yes. Gosh. They were probably really happy.

TARA: That was when the doctor was so cute, because I didn't realize. I was like, "Do you know how many we got?" And she was so cute. She's like, "It's forty." And I'm like, "Is that the most you've ever gotten?" And she's like, "Hmm, I think there may be one or two more, but that's one of the most."

MARCIA: [*Laughs*] Maybe we should attribute it to those Egyptian hormones.

TARA: I know, right [*laughs*]?

Indeed, Tara was quite unusual in producing forty eggs, or double the desired goal of twenty, in a single egg freezing cycle. And because she suffered no noticeable side effects, she was back on a plane to Afghanistan within days of the procedure. When she told me that she was just following in the footsteps of one of her "badass" colleagues who had frozen her eggs between Middle Eastern deployments, I could not help but think that Tara was a true badass herself.

Embodiment

Tara was lucky to go unscathed—suffering no ill effects of egg freezing and then surviving her dangerous posting in Afghanistan. Like Tara, the vast majority of women in my study (83 percent) experienced their *egg freezing embodiment* with no serious side effects beyond the mild abdominal pain, pressure, and bloating that is common during the hormonal stimulation phase, when eggs are literally being ripened in the ovaries.

However, for some women, this two-week period was physically intense. Some women experienced significant weight gain, with one petite woman gaining twenty pounds, or one-fifth of her entire body weight. Other women felt the painful enlargement of their ovaries, making it difficult to sit, walk, sleep, or eat, especially in the final days before egg retrieval. Women described their abdominal symptoms in various ways, including "incredibly painful," "one of the worst experiences," "I thought I was going to die," and "my body went insane." Several women reported "bawling" or "weeping" in both physical and emotional agony, with one woman describing the days before egg retrieval as "the longest days" of her life.

For most women, however, egg retrieval brought relief, once the eggs were "harvested" from the ovaries through transvaginal, ultrasound-guided aspiration. Because the procedure is performed under general anesthesia, women must be accompanied to and from the clinic and are required to rest at home for the remainder of the day. A few women experienced significant pain and bloating during this postretrieval period, causing them to take off additional, unexpected sick days from work.

For four women in the study, however, bloating was actually the sign of a serious complication called ovarian hyperstimulation syndrome (OHSS). OHSS is a rare but potentially life-threatening reaction to the hormones used to stimulate production of extra eggs in the ovaries. Although most cases of OHSS are mild, involving abdominal bloating, nausea, and slight weight gain, more serious cases involve marked abdominal bloating above the waist and shortness of breath due to pleural effusion, or the buildup of excess fluid in the lungs. This form of OHSS is a medical emergency, often requiring hospitalization and efforts to drain the fluid.

Barbara, an academic physician, was one of the women who developed OHSS. Because of her medical training, she was acutely aware of the signs and symptoms of OHSS after an otherwise unremarkable and successful egg freezing cycle.

They harvested twenty-six, and they were able to freeze nineteen. To follow up on what happened next, I was like, "Great! I made it through!" I didn't get too bloated or nauseated or whatever—definitely some bloating, but it wasn't horrible. I had the harvest on Saturday. Then literally on Monday, I looked like I was five months pregnant, and I think it was twelve pounds of water when they weighed me, twelve pounds of ascites [the accumulation of fluid causing abdominal swelling]. This happened over the course of days, because I went in to get checked, I walked in leaning over because it hurt so much, because I was expanding so quickly. I couldn't sleep because it was such pain. I was nauseated, and I couldn't eat because there was no room in my stomach. And I got admitted. Basically, what happened is—I laugh about it now—but really what happened was I had OHSS. . . . Anyway, I went in just overnight for IV [intravenous] fluids because I wasn't able to eat at that point. They admitted me for IV fluids and Lovenox [an anticoagulant to prevent blood clots]. . . .

So I stayed overnight and went home the next day. At that point, I was hydrated. It still took two weeks for the fluid to resolve. They had offered to drain it, but I did not want another procedure. I said, "It will go away. I just have to be patient." I just wore big clothes. I did look pregnant, which was odd. It was very uncomfortable, because it happened so quickly. And it was just uncomfortable to walk, sleep, anything. It went away in about two weeks, and obviously I started eating and feeling better. I was back to myself, in terms of my physical body, within probably three weeks. That was difficult.

Throughout Barbara's egg freezing cycle and the hospitalization that followed, she received exceptional care from her male IVF physician and several female IVF physicians in training. In fact, Barbara believed that they were giving her special attention because she was their physician colleague. Yet, like so many other women, Barbara did not enjoy her experiences at the IVF clinic, with its cold impersonality. In an animated tone of voice, Barbara recalled,

I totally felt like a cow, not because of bloating or anything but because you walk into the clinic, and you get a plastic number, and you sit in a waiting room in a row with all these women who have a number, and they're like "Number Niiiiiine? Number Niiiiiine?" I'm like, I know they do this for confidentiality, but do they have to call it like you're at the butcher's? We got called in, you get your lab stuff done, then you go back out, sit back out, and then, "Number Niiiiiine?" to go get your ultrasound. It was very much, like, we're all like cows. It felt pretty bad.

Patient-Centered Egg Freezing

Barbara and the many other women whose stories fill this chapter wished for but did not fully receive what my colleagues and I call *patient-centered egg freezing*.[6] To be patient-centered, clinics and clinicians must provide care that is "respectful of, and responsive to, individual patient preferences, needs and values," thus "ensuring that patient values guide all clinical decisions."[7] Patient-centeredness is now considered one of six key dimensions of quality health care, the others being safety, effectiveness, timeliness, efficiency, and equity of access.[8] All of these dimensions are of profound relevance to egg freezing, as the stories in this chapter clearly show.

Patient-centeredness has been considered crucial to the treatment of infertile couples seeking IVF care. In a large-scale study in Europe, researchers surveyed 925 IVF patients and 227 IVF physicians and conducted fourteen focus groups with 103 infertility patients.[9] What they uncovered were major discrepancies between physicians' and patients' attitudes toward patient-centeredness. Whereas patient-centeredness placed high on IVF patients' priority list, it was less valued by IVF physicians, who cared more about measures of IVF success. When patient-centeredness was lacking in an IVF clinic setting, patients often "voted with their feet," engaging in reprotravel, sometimes to other European countries.[10]

On the basis of these study findings, researchers in Europe developed a conceptual model, in which they enumerated the ten key dimensions of patient-centered infertility care.[11] Six of these dimensions were "system factors," including information, competence of clinic and staff, coordination and integration, accessibility, continuity and transition, and physical comfort. Four of the dimensions were "human factors," involving appropriate attitude and relationship with staff, communication, patient involvement and privacy, and emotional support.

Not surprisingly, these ten key dimensions of patient-centered care were also relevant to the women in my study. On the basis of their own egg freezing experiences, the women offered many astute observations about how to improve the quality of egg freezing care. Although they did not use the term "patient-centered," their detailed recommendations fit well into the ten key dimensions framework of patient-centeredness developed in Europe.

Table 5.1 summarizes women's recommendations, according to these ten dimensions. However, there is one key difference. In the US, "cost" must be added as an important system factor of patient-centered egg freezing. In the US, most patients must pay for their egg freezing cycles, just as most infertile patients pay for IVF. Out-of-pocket payment substantially diminishes the accessibility of these technologies in the US, whereas in Europe, IVF is usually covered by state health insurance, and discussions of coverage for elective egg freezing are also under way in some countries where medical egg freezing coverage is already offered.[12]

These issues of cost and insurance coverage for egg freezing will be taken up later when activist efforts to increase accessibility for single and

TABLE 5.1. Patient-Centered Egg Freezing: Women's Recommendations

Dimensions	Women's recommendations
System Factors	
Information	• National registries of clinics providing egg freezing services, numbers of cycles performed, and pregnancy outcomes • Information about egg freezing on clinic websites and advertising materials, which is both specific and accurate • Instructional media for home or office use (e.g., webinars, videos), which are specific to egg freezing, focusing on women only and not assuming the involvement of partners • Written materials on egg freezing (e.g., brochures, data sheets), including up-to-date clinical outcome data, provided during office visits • Consent forms, free of excessive legalese, for egg freezing patients only and not assuming the involvement of partners • Informational sessions on egg freezing, held in evenings and on weekends for increased availability among single professional women • Clinical consultations on egg freezing procedures, risks, and outcomes, provided face-to-face and in a timely fashion • Anticipatory guidance on ideal numbers of eggs and cycles • Expectation management for egg freezing outcomes, on the basis of women's age and fertility profiles
Competence of clinic and staff	• Training of all IVF clinical staff (i.e., physicians, nurses, ultrasound technicians, clinical psychologists) on egg freezing procedures and outcomes for delivery of accurate and consistent information • Hiring of diverse staff with expertise on egg freezing care for women of all kinds, including single, lesbian, and minority women from diverse racial and religious backgrounds
Coordination and integration	• Education of community-based gynecologists on women's fertility decline and egg freezing options, to raise patients' awareness during well-woman exams • Timely referrals to egg freezing services from community-based gynecologists • Coordination with pharmacies (on-site and community based) for ease of access to hormonal medications
Accessibility	• Convenient clinic hours for single professional women, ideally before and after work • Reasonable wait times for egg freezing appointments and procedures • Injection classes specifically for egg freezing, ideally during evening hours • Private areas within clinics devoted exclusively to egg freezing patients, apart from waiting areas for infertility patients • Specialty clinics devoted exclusively to egg freezing
Physical comfort	• Injection assistance, instruction, and support to address the fear of needles and self-injection among single egg freezing patients • Information on physical discomforts, including expectations about potential egg freezing side effects and days lost from work • Timely management of post-egg-freezing complications, including ovarian hyperstimulation syndrome (OHSS)
Continuity and transition	• Reliable transportation and home health care services for single egg freezing patients on the day of egg retrieval • Consistent follow-up for egg freezing patients postretrieval • Information on next steps, based on number of eggs retrieved and stored • Egg storage and disposition guidelines, including clear information on consent forms and annual renewal forms

Dimensions	Women's recommendations
Cost	• Egg freezing "packages," with discounts for multiple cycles • Financing options for egg freezing, including monthly payment plans • Credit card and insurance payment options for egg freezing services • Refunds for egg freezing cycle cancellations • Income-based discounts for low-income egg freezing patients • Price consciousness to reduce egg freezing fees and increase patients' access, especially for low- and middle-income patients • Stable annual storage fees and billing practices for frozen eggs • Egg freezing insurance coverage, provided by states and employers
Human Factors	
Attitude and relationship with staff	• Consistent relationships with providers, especially consultations with the same physician throughout the egg freezing process • Extra clinical support for single women, who are absorbing information and navigating egg freezing on their own
Communication	• Adequate screening and counseling prior to all egg freezing procedures • Appropriate bedside manner during all egg freezing appointments, to avoid information delivery that could be perceived as cavalier, overly optimistic, or doomsday • Compassionate delivery of postretrieval "bad news" (e.g., low numbers of eggs retrieved) • Adequate discussion of future egg-thawing outcomes, including potential loss of frozen eggs
Patient involvement and privacy	• Sensitivity to single women undertaking egg freezing, by not assuming or discussing male partners or husbands • Consent forms that are specific to egg freezing and do not require partners' consent • Postretrieval assistance for single women, including discussion of transportation and home health care needs
Emotional support	• Psychologists and social workers present within clinics to meet the needs of single egg freezing patients • Egg freezing support groups, especially within clinics serving large numbers of egg freezing patients • Extra emotional support for egg freezing patients who have gone through recent divorces and breakups • Special sensitivity to egg freezing patients' circumstances, including their potential loneliness and feelings of stigma in IVF clinic settings and their need for maximal social support

minority women are discussed. But suffice it to say here that they are important system factors in the US, especially given egg freezing's significant expense. Although the women in my study were all highly paid professionals, they still experienced the high cost of egg freezing as a financial burden, particularly when they had to pay for multiple cycles. Thus, women appreciated the ways in which some IVF clinics were already attempting to make egg freezing more affordable through egg freezing "packages" (such as reduced costs for additional cycles), various financing options, and income-based discounts, which are outlined in table 5.1.

It is important to focus on the final recommendation in table 5.1, "special sensitivity to egg freezing patients' circumstances, including their potential loneliness and feelings of stigma in IVF clinic settings and their need for maximal social support." Among more than one hundred egg freezing stories I gathered over the course of my study, it certainly became clear to me that this final recommendation is not being sufficiently met in US IVF clinics. Single egg freezing patients are still routinely lumped together with married IVF patients and their husbands, from the initial injection classes to the final request for partners' signatures on egg-storage consent forms. Adding insult to injury, IVF clinics have not adequately separated or addressed the particular needs of egg freezing patients, most of whom are single and braving the couples-oriented IVF world on their own.

Not surprisingly, then, women's recommendations for *egg-freezing-only services* wind their way through almost every dimension of patient-centered care listed in table 5.1. As seen under the "Accessibility" category, some women also recommended the development of "specialty clinics devoted exclusively to egg freezing." Such "boutique" egg freezing clinics, like Kindbody and Extend Fertility, have already begun to be opened in some major cities in the US.[13] Although they have been criticized for being more like "glam day spas" than medical clinics, their model may appeal to those who are seeking the various forms of patient-centered egg freezing care that women in my study recommended.[14]

Indeed, if we actually listen to women's voices and take their recommendations seriously, then the desire for specialized, stand-alone egg freezing services makes more sense.[15] As seen clearly through the stories in this chapter, single women are braving the various challenges of egg freezing alone in traditional, couples-oriented US IVF clinics. Even though they have their own special needs and concerns, they rarely receive the attention, compassion, and support they deserve. Thus, instead of being herded with IVF patients through a factory farm of human egg production, single women want *patient-centered egg freezing*, as well as *egg freezing safe spaces* to call their own.

6

The Supporters

Family, Friends, and Men Who Care

Holly's Helper

"Are you single, partnered, divorced, married?" When I posed this question to each woman in my study, I was usually met with a resigned "single." But sometimes the responses were more nebulous. Holly, the director of a federal energy office in Washington, DC, was a woman with a complex answer. On the one hand, she told me that she was "single," repeating the term for emphasis. But on the other hand, she told me about a man in her life, Brad, who was rarely available but whom she loved nonetheless.

As I would learn, Holly and Brad were former coworkers, who had known each other for more than a decade. Brad was married with two children and eventually left the federal energy agency for a more lucrative position in the private sector. Holly, for her part, had remained mostly single throughout her twenties and early thirties, emphasizing to me that DC was "*such* a hard dating town." Although she enjoyed a vibrant and demanding career, full of international travel, Holly was now thirty-seven and complained, "A lot of women my age are still single, unfortunately."

But as Holly went on to explain, she had bumped into Brad at a DC charity event years after they had stopped working together. It was then that she learned that he was now divorced, with joint custody of his two teenaged children. Sparks flew between them, and Holly and Brad began to see each other intermittently. Brad no longer worked inside the Capital Beltway, and his new job often took him out of state. Thus, Brad's absences made Holly feel like a single woman, even though, on an emotional level, she was deeply attached to Brad. Holly explained her dilemma in this way:

> I don't know how well it's going, even though I've been seeing him for over a year and a half. It's kind of complicated, 'cause he's not in town a

lot, which is the challenge we're facing now. Actually, his company has a work project down south, so he's in the South almost every other week. And then, when he's in DC, he has custody of his two kids from his first marriage. I don't know if right now I know how to make this work, because he's pulled in a million different directions. When he's with the kids, he wants to be with the kids, and that's great. And I haven't met them. No one's allowed to meet them until he's engaged to somebody.

Still, Holly considered Brad to be her "boyfriend," and she told me without hesitation that she loved him. Holly felt some hope for their future together, because unlike many of the men she had met, Brad wanted to remarry and have more children.

It was absolutely an issue, because I know that I want to have kids. And since he has two older children, I knew there was a good chance that he might not want additional kids. So it was funny, when I was talking to him three months into dating, we had the "Do you see yourself having more kids one day?" talk. And he made an interesting comment. He said, "I think people want the number of children that they grew up with. Like, I'm the oldest of four, so I always saw myself having a family of four. I'd like two more." And it's funny, because I always thought about myself having three as well, because I have two sisters. Probably, at this stage, two children, I think, is realistic. I always wanted more, I guess. But, you know, I think at this age, that would be pushing it for any number of reasons, honestly. So, you know, I'd be very, very happy with two. I'd be happy with one, too. I don't know. But originally, I would have said three.

Holly realized that Brad was a unicorn—that rare, middle-aged, divorced father who was still open to having more children. Holly, too, was exceptional, in that she had done all she could as a single woman to seek fertility testing and thus ensure her future childbearing potential. Yet, even with regular monitoring, Holly's sense of fertility security was ultimately shattered.

I'd been thinking about doing egg freezing for a number of years and had put it off. I thought I had been on top of things because I've had some friends who've had fertility issues, and so every year when I'd go to my annual gynecological visit, I'd have them look at my FSH. As of a year and a half ago, mine was great. I hadn't checked it in maybe fifteen months, but when I went to do the testing for egg freezing, I was really surprised. My numbers were horrible all of a sudden. So it turns out I had premature ovarian aging, which I wasn't aware of until I started this process. . . . I mean, it's funny, because I thought I was on top of everything, but I guess I wasn't. I didn't realize how quickly a woman's fertility can change. And I have a wonderful [IVF] doctor, and you know, she broke the news to me, and I was devastated. . . . I was just really shocked and devastated. That was a really bad day. And when I talked to the doctor about it, she's like, "Unfortunately, it's a little bit age and a lot of bad luck. It's just bad luck. Some women have this happen, and you're one of them."

Still, Holly's physician was encouraging, explaining to Holly that POA did not absolutely prevent her from undertaking egg freezing.

A lot of places I guess would have turned people like me away, and [this IVF clinic] amazingly wasn't one of them. So my doctor said, "This means you're likely not going to be as good a responder as women with levels where we would expect them to be." She said, "Um, you know, I don't think that's a deal breaker." She said, "If anything, this makes me think if this is something you're willing to pursue, that you need to do this now." And I absolutely agreed. I said, "Yeah, I know these numbers are pretty bad. I know I'm not going to have the outcomes you would normally see, even in a woman of my age, but this is something I feel strongly about. I really want to do it." And she said, "Wonderful!" And she's been great.

Yet Holly felt reluctant to share the details of her situation with her women friends and coworkers, most of whom were married and none of whom had been through egg freezing. As a born-and-bred southerner, raised in five different southern states, Holly also could not shake her sense of stigma, which her recent POA diagnosis and turn to egg freezing had somehow engendered. "There's something taboo about it. I think even with female acquaintances, I don't know that I feel comfortable talking about it, and I don't know why. It's just something that women don't really talk about. And even with my girlfriends, I'm a little leery. . . . I am going through this stuff, but I don't exactly feel like I could share it with them. I don't know why." Instead, Holly confided in her father, who happened to call when she was feeling particularly low.

Broaching it with my father was . . . interesting. It's not something I nec-essarily felt comfortable with, you know. I thought about maybe doing it [egg freezing] anyhow, but he happened to call, I guess, the night that I got the AMH blood work, and I was just so upset. So I told him I had been thinking about freezing my eggs, and it looks like it may be hard, if not impossible. And since then, we've had conversations. He asks, "Is this pricey? I figure it's probably pricey." And I tell him, "Yeah, you know, it's . . . it's $10–$15,000 per round." And he was blown away by that cost. He said, "I thought you were going to say like $2,000!" I said, "No! I'm budgeting to spend up to $30,000 on this." And he was just in shock. And I said, "Hey, maybe with luck you'll have the most expensive grandkids ever, right out of the box!" [laughs]. He's a very old-fashioned southern gentleman. We don't really talk about things like that, so it was a bit . . . you know, out of my comfort zone.

Nonetheless, Holly's old-fashioned, Irish American, Catholic father was very supportive, encouraging her to confide in her mother and sisters as well. Indeed, Holly felt the need to warn her thirty-two-year-old unmar-ried sister about POA and to encourage her to think about egg freezing, too. But her sister seemed reluctant. "At first, I thought she was maybe being a little bit dismissive, so I finally came right out and said, 'This is something you need to consider. That may be a situation for you as well. You should start making plans.' And she's like, 'I can't afford egg freezing. Thanks for this, but that's just not going to be an option for me.' Which is sad." Although Holly was able afford at least two egg freezing cycles, she admitted that it was a "big financial hit." She also felt that lack of insurance coverage for egg freezing was a form of discrimination against single women like her, for reasons that she explained.

For me, one round is costing . . . $14,000. The meds themselves were $6,000, because I'm basically taking, you know—my dosage is as high as they'll give women. It's kind of daunting to get all the vials. It's a lot of meds. So the second round . . . I think it will probably be more than that. I think I'm probably looking at $16,000. The only thing insurance would cover was the initial diagnostics. So doing the bloodwork to understand my fertility, that was covered by insurance. The funny thing about it is now that I know I have premature ovarian aging as a result of this process, I strongly suspect if I were married, this would be covered. But since I'm single, even though I have this diagnosis now, this is considered something voluntary. And I have this wonderful gynecologist who is my age and just had her first baby. She's great, and I've been open with her for many years about my concern. You know, "Is it time to freeze? What do I need to be looking at?" Stuff like that. She was telling me the coverage would apply if I were married. And I said, "Well, if I were married, I wouldn't need to freeze my eggs!" [*laughs*]. It's kind of ironic. But yeah, all out of pocket.

Unfortunately, Holly had depleted most of her savings when she purchased an old house on Capitol Hill, and most of her spending was now focused on fixing up this historic property. But with her fertility in crisis, Holly's priorities quickly shifted.

So I decided this year's big project isn't on the house; it's on me. So I looked into doing some financing, and there are some fertility financing companies where this is their main business, but their interest rates were crazy. I actually wound up taking out a new credit card that had a sixteen-month, you know, no interest if you pay off the balance before the date deal. Luckily, I have the credit, and with my situation, I'm going to be able to pay that off within that promotional period, which is lucky. But yeah, it's still a significant expense. . . . I had a little bit of savings that I could apply to it, but pretty much everything's gone on the card now. It's sad and kind of scary.

In addition to the financial planning, the logistical planning was difficult for Holly, because she needed to pursue egg freezing "rather quickly." In a matter of weeks, she completed her jury duty, rearranged her travel schedule, and learned how to give herself the injections. Holly also needed to find a friend who could take a day off from work to accompany her to and from the IVF clinic for the egg retrieval. Holly's close friend, who was married, agreed. "But then she found out I had to be there at seven a.m., and she's like, 'Oh, I'm not going to do that! I'm not even awake by seven a.m.!'" Holly admitted, "That kind of took me by surprise," as she was not expecting her friend to renege on her commitment.

With only thirty-six hours' notice, Brad came to the rescue. He canceled his upcoming work commitments and headed to Washington, DC. With Brad by Holly's side before, during, and after the egg retrieval, she learned that she had produced more eggs than expected. "For my situation, I was pretty pleased," she exclaimed. "They wound up—I think I had eight follicles. They were able to aspirate seven eggs, and of those seven retrieved, they froze six." At the time of our interview, Holly was in the midst of her second cycle. Nine egg follicles appeared to be growing in her ovaries, and Holly was hoping that Brad would make it to DC in time to administer the dreaded trigger shot. Holly offered to show me the needle, the length of which took me by surprise.

> HOLLY: The needle's huge! And it's intramuscular, so I had to give it to myself. Brad had offered the first time, but he was in South Carolina then. So I had to do it myself in the bathroom, like, twisting myself around so that I could see to my backside, to inject this needle that's—have you seen the needle?
>
> MARCIA: No, I haven't, but I've heard it's a very large needle!
>
> HOLLY: Oh, I actually have it.
>
> MARCIA: I would love to see your needle! Oh, let's see your needle.
>
> HOLLY: I'll get it. Hang on. It's been easier for me to keep my box of IVF crud in the dining room, so long as I don't have people coming over. I mean, I moved overseas at the age of twenty-three and have done some stuff that people find amazing. After this trigger shot, after giving it to myself, I've decided I can do anything!
>
> MARCIA: Oh! [*Laughing upon sight of the needle*] That's huge! It's like . . . the length of your neck.
>
> HOLLY: Yeah, it's not just the cap. That's how deep the needle has to go into your muscle. So giving it to yourself is just, uhh . . .
>
> MARCIA: Oh, that just looks horribly difficult. And it *has* to be in the backside, as I recall, right?
>
> HOLLY: It *does*. And you have to do it at exactly the right time.

Given the demonstrated challenges of the trigger shot, Brad told Holly he truly wanted to help her. In general, Holly found Brad to be "super supportive" of her egg freezing. When they were together, Holly loved Brad as a partner. "He's wonderful. He's wonderful! He's really, really supportive. You know, we're not in a great place right now, just because it's just difficult not having seen him so much recently. It's just hard to have a relationship in this context. So even though things are really strained right now, and I think we probably need to sit down and have a talk, we get along well. We get along *really* well, and he still *really* wants to go with me and do it."

Holly hoped that her second retrieval with Brad by her side would yield enough eggs to avoid a third cycle. If she had one regret, it was that she had not undertaken egg freezing sooner, with a potentially better outcome.

You know, when I was younger and probably until I found out about my situation, I probably would have said it's like insurance. And I didn't do it when I was younger because of the cost and the pain and the taboo. But also, you know, you kind of hope things will change. And I would love to get married one day, and I hope that will happen. I'm not ruling that out. But you know, at thirty-seven, you really have to start to think, "Okay, if you want to be able to try to have your own children biologically, you really need to consider this." So I think I did look at it more as insurance. Now I'm starting to realize this could be the only way I *could* have a child, knowing what I know now about my ovarian reserve. You know, even if I got married in a year, who knows what would happen? I wish I would have done it when I was younger, especially because I was thinking about it. And, you know, people just don't talk about it. It just seems like this big, overwhelming process. And also because there still is this stigma to it, I thought, "Oh, I really don't want to have to do it." And now that I've done it, it's not so bad, you know?

* * *

Almost three years later, I received this cheerful email from Holly, who had just turned forty-one and was about to marry Brad.

Hello Dr. Inhorn,
I hope that this e-mail finds you doing well. . . .
I'm happy to report that I am engaged to be married! My fiancé and I hope to try to start a family shortly thereafter, so I am *very* glad that we have those egg reserves. . . .
Very best regards,
Holly

As I read Holly's note, I reflected on the fact that Brad had proven himself to be much more than Holly's supportive egg freezing helper. He had become her true mate, committing himself to Holly and her reproductive dreams.

Egg Freezing Webs of Care

Holly's story is important on many levels, reinforcing and extending some of the core themes of previous chapters. Holly clearly experienced the precarity of her age-related fertility decline and the specific difficulties of POA, which forced her to turn to egg freezing under pressure. Pursuing egg freezing made Holly feel uneasy and stigmatized, partly because of her traditional southern Catholic upbringing, where conversations surrounding fertility were "taboo" and definitely well outside the normal "comfort zone." Furthermore, the financial stresses of egg freezing were daunting for Holly, who came to realize that marriage conferred certain health insurance benefits that both she and her single sister were denied. Finally, Holly bravely faced the bodily discomforts of egg freezing head-on, even managing during her first egg freezing cycle to self-inject the dreaded trigger shot, the needle of which was lengthy and imposing, as well as awkward to administer on one's own.

Yet Holly was never entirely alone throughout this process. Although Holly declared herself to be "single," she was, in fact, surrounded by an *egg freezing web of care*—a group of individuals who supported, assisted, and cared for Holly on her egg freezing journey.[1] Holly had seven egg freezing supporters by her side, helping her to overcome the medical, logistical, psychological, and moral challenges that she encountered during two egg freezing cycles with a difficult POA diagnosis.

Two of these individuals were female gynecologists, who took Holly's fertility concerns quite seriously and reassured her that egg freezing would still be possible, despite her POA. Holly was quite lucky in this regard. As we have seen, not every woman who freezes her eggs receives this kind of patient-centered physician support, including from their female gynecologists and IVF clinicians.

Four of Holly's supporters were her family members but especially the family's patriarch, Holly's dad. Although women's fertility issues are not the stuff of southern gentlemanly conversation, Holly's father nonetheless came through for her, consoling his daughter during her fertility crisis and condoning her egg freezing decision, even though he was a practicing Catholic. Furthermore, Holly's father urged her to reach out to her mother and two sisters. Although financial constraints prevented anyone in Holly's family from being there to help her, their knowledge and support were critical in convincing Holly to move forward.

Holly was particularly reluctant to share her situation with friends, and ultimately it was her friend who let her down, balking at the early-morning hour of Holly's egg retrieval. This then allowed Holly's boyfriend, Brad, to rise to the occasion. Not only did Brad support Holly's egg freezing decision, but he proved to be a "super supportive" egg freezing companion, who deeply empathized with Holly's desire to become a mother in their possible future together.

Holly's web of care was fairly typical, although the prominent role of her boyfriend stood out. Most of the women in my study relied on one or more family members or friends to see them through their egg freezing journeys. In general, other women played the leading roles as *egg freezing caregivers*. Fully 95 percent of the women in my study received support from other women, usually mothers, sisters, and often close female friends. But egg freezing also allowed men to demonstrate their caring capabilities. Nearly two-thirds (63 percent) of the women in my study received care from men, usually fathers but also brothers, male friends, and sometimes partners, past or present, as in Holly's case.

Virtually every woman in this study had someone to lean on in their egg freezing journeys. The fact that family members, friends, and occasionally boyfriends participated in these webs of care served to reinforce

TABLE 6.1. Types of Support for Women's Egg Freezing

Type	Support provided
Instrumental	Seeking/providing information Referring to helpful others Attending appointments Cosigning consent forms Seeking/providing information
Financial	Analyzing/budgeting costs Paying (for all or part) Offering to pay Loaning money Covering egg freezing in divorce settlements
Physical	Assisting with injections Accompanying to and from egg retrieval Providing postretrieval food and care Offering donor sperm or eggs Assisting with injections
Psychological	Suggesting egg freezing Encouraging egg freezing Providing emotional support Providing entertainment/humor

existing bonds of kinship, friendship, and romantic partnership, for which women who were freezing their eggs were often very grateful. Egg freezing support took many different forms, from simple messages of encouragement to injection assistance and postretrieval care. The diverse forms of egg freezing care that women received are outlined in table 6.1. They comprised four different categories—instrumental, financial, physical, and psychological—with certain types of support aligning with particular individuals. For example, fathers were more likely to offer financial support, while brothers provided instrumental and sometimes physical assistance. As we will see, sometimes men proved to be the most helpful egg freezing supporters, proving their love in wholly unexpected ways.

Webs of Kinship

When I asked the women in my study if anyone had helped them through their egg freezing process, I was most often told about the women's natal kin: the mothers who had flown across the country to be there on the day of retrieval, the fathers who had offered to pay, the sisters who were confidantes and injection assistants, and the brothers who were designated drivers. Occasionally, aunts, uncles, and cousins were also egg freezing helpers, as were stepmothers and stepfathers who lent their support.

In these webs of kinship surrounding women's egg freezing, parents played the most important role. Many of the women in this study maintained close relationships with their parents, often attributing their own successes to the support and guidance that they had received from their mothers and fathers. Thus, when the women embarked on their egg freezing journeys, they often consulted with their parents, many of whom were excited for their daughters, supportive of their egg freezing decisions, and ready to offer their assistance.

The women's primary egg freezing supporters were their mothers. In fact, mothers were sometimes the ones to suggest egg freezing to their late-thirty-something daughters, encouraging them to think about this as a fertility preservation option. When the women decided to move forward with egg freezing, their mothers were often there to help. About one-quarter of the women in this study ultimately relied on a mother's help, including financial assistance, injection assistance, and accompaniment on the day of egg retrieval. Although four women had very strained relationships with their mothers and another eight felt that they were being pushed, even "hounded" by their mothers to pursue egg freezing in the quest for grandchildren, the majority of the women felt no such maternal judgment. Most mothers instead played the role of moral supporters—expressing pride in their daughters for undertaking an arduous and expensive process with no guarantees.

For example, Maddy, who had followed her father into a military career, had been deployed four times to the Middle East. By the age of thirty-five, Maddy had become a colonel. But her biggest regret in life was "missing that college window of opportunity" to find a partner. Few men, she told me, could now understand her life as a high-ranking military officer. So, when her last brief relationship ended, Maddy decided to freeze her eggs with the help of her mother, an OB/GYN nurse, who drew on her professional network to arrange the complicated logistics. For Maddy, this involved beginning the ultrasound monitoring and hormonal medications on a military base in Colorado, then flying to her parents' home in the metropolitan DC area for the final week before egg retrieval. Throughout the process, Maddy's mother stood by her.

> My mom, she was definitely there for me. You know, I was calling her with updates from Colorado through the whole process. It was fantastic, I have to tell you. There's something extremely comforting in being able to bounce all of this off of her. And I have to say, she never pushed for it, but once I decided to do it, you know, she provided me with all the information and she was very supportive. . . . And she actually gave me the final trigger shot. She did [*laughs*]! And she did a wonderful job, actually! That's a reason why having a nurse for a mom is really handy in this!

On the day of the egg retrieval, Maddy's mother accompanied her to the IVF clinic and cosigned all of Maddy's consent forms, essentially stepping in as the "partner" in this regard. Her mother's cosignature was extremely important to Maddy, who was concerned about the safe disposition of her six frozen eggs. "I do remember that actually we asked them what happens if I die, and the reason for that is because I deploy to war zones, you know. So my mom actually asked that, because that's actually a possibility. I mean, I know it is for everyone else, but it's something that in my family we actually think about, like, their wills and instructions and things like that. And so my mother has my medical power of attorney, so I think she determines their fate."

Overall, Maddy considered her egg freezing experience to be "very positive," explaining that she was well taken care of. In fact, she laughed, "Compared to the military socialized medicine, the whole experience was very posh!" Yet, with only six eggs frozen, Maddy was told that she needed a second cycle, which would cost an additional $10,000 and possibly much more. Hearing this news, Maddy's ex–Marine Corp father stepped in, secretly loaning the money to his daughter. "My dad gave me a low-interest loan—and it's actually just between my dad and me. My mom doesn't even know about it. He's particularly—in a weird kind of way, he's particularly supportive. So, to cover the difference that I didn't have immediately in savings, he gave me a small loan, and I also used a no-interest, yearlong payment plan."

Maddy's father was not alone in being "particularly supportive." Fathers were often the first ones to offer their daughters financial support, occasionally paying off all or part of their daughters' egg freezing cycles or offering low- or no-interest loans, as Maddy's father had done. One-fifth of women in this study had parents who paid, offered to pay, or loaned money to their daughters, with some of these offers coming directly from fathers rather than mothers, as in Maddy's case. Although most of the women did not need their parents' financial support, they appreciated the ways in which their fathers and mothers offered to defray their egg freezing expenses.

Beyond financial support, one-fifth of the women in this study had fathers who supported them in other ways, encouraging them, helping them, and sometimes consoling them when things went wrong. For example, Ruth recalled the bitter day when her fertility tests came back in the "bottom fifteenth percentile." Not knowing what to do, she called her father, whose advice she had relied on many times before.

So I'm like hysterical that day, like, hysterically crying, because now it's like, "By the way, not only do you have to do three rounds . . . you have crappy fertility. . . . And, by the way, your meds cost twice as much." . . . So now my price has gone from, you know, expecting roughly $18,000 to $36,000, potentially $36,000. So now I've doubled my price. . . . And here I am, you know, now spending a lot of money to maybe never use them [the frozen eggs]. So there was a decision, you know, and I called my father. My father's a scientist, an engineer. So he's really good at like, mathematically, just being like, "This is how it is." And so he was like, "For your mental health and mental well-being and peace of mind, yeah, you should go ahead and do it. Yeah." So I decided to do it.

In general, when fathers were informed about their daughters' desires to pursue egg freezing, they were psychologically supportive, with several also accompanying their daughters to the IVF clinic. Not a single father was mentioned as placing undue pressure on a daughter to produce grandchildren through egg freezing. Instead, fathers sometimes told their daughters that they wished for them to have future children through egg freezing only because they believed that their daughters wanted children and would make good mothers.

In addition to the women's parents, siblings, too, were crucial allies in women's egg freezing trajectories. Like many mothers, sisters were often encouraging and supportive, helping their sisters with the injections, accompanying them to the clinic, and occasionally offering financial aid. For example, Stacey, an IT program manager, said that she felt lucky to have a pediatrician as a sister. When Stacey returned from an egg freezing informational seminar, she called her sister immediately.

I told her, "They didn't say anything too scary." So I was like, "Okay, I still want to do this. Now I just have to get the money together." So my sister, she was excited. She said if that's what I wanted to do, then I should definitely do it. She kind of wants me to be happy, so whatever I want. She actually—she talked to her doctor friends to see, you know, if she knew anybody that had done it. And she actually did. And so she was asking all types of questions to make sure that it was safe and all that stuff. My sister helped me out financially, too, because, after grad school, you know, I kind of had been in between jobs. And so she gave me some of the money, and then I came up with the rest.

Sometimes sisters encouraged each other to pursue egg freezing together—or vowed to donate their eggs to each other. About a dozen women in my study had discussed what might be called *sisterly egg sharing*, either offering to donate "leftover" eggs to a younger sister or being offered a younger sister's eggs when an egg freezing cycle yielded less eggs than desired. Sisterly egg sharing was also mentioned by women in the military, who hoped that their sisters would use their eggs in case they got "blown up" or died in Afghanistan. To my knowledge, no one in my study actually carried out such sisterly egg sharing, including women in the military. But this topic was brought up time and time again throughout my study, particularly among sisters who were single in their thirties and were contemplating becoming single mothers.

Cheryl, a pharmaceutical representative, was one of these women. Both she and her younger sister were hoping to marry but were not having any luck on the DC dating market, despite the large number of African American men appearing on dating apps. Thus, they had joked with each other about sharing the eggs that Cheryl had recently frozen. "She has been dating, but she's not married either. So it's funny, about a week or so ago, because she was saying the guy she thought she wanted to be with just wasn't working out, this, that, and the other. She's like, 'Well, if I don't hurry up and do something, I'm not going to have children either.' And I was like, 'Remember, we have our insurance policy. I can be the aunty mom, and you can be the mom aunty. It'll be great!' [*laughs*]."

In these familial webs of egg freezing care, sisters played a larger role than brothers. But brothers, too, occasionally lent their support. Several women had close relationships with their younger brothers, who looked up to their older sisters and wanted to see them become mothers. For example, Lakshmi, a psychiatrist, described how her younger brother encouraged her.

> You know, my brother, he's about six years younger than I am, and we're very close. He's one of my best friends. He's actually the one who sort of clued me in or sort of encouraged me to consider egg freezing. I actually had not even thought about it until then. So I was hanging out with him, and I was like, "Okay, you're going to have the babies for us, you know, because I'm a little bit older now." And he got dead serious, and he's like, "Because I really care about you, I want you to hear where this is coming from. I think you should really think about freezing your eggs."

Brothers also pitched in in very practical ways, helping with the various tasks of egg freezing. When humanitarian worker Sita was facing serious challenges in sourcing her hormonal medications, her twenty-two-year-old brother came to her aid, helping her to complete her egg freezing cycle.

> There were points where the clinic would call me and say, on a Saturday, "We want you to stay on the medicines one more day." And I didn't

have any. So then, like, I would have to run around and get medicine. I would have to, you know, figure out a way to get it. And it was just a very stressful concept. And I have a tendency to have anxiety as well, and so, with the anxiety of getting the medicine or the hormones themselves, I was having panic attacks. So I would sort of wake up in the middle of the night and feel like I couldn't breathe. So, luckily, my brother, who's quite a bit younger—he's sixteen years younger than I am, and he is waiting for med school to start—he hung out with me for two weeks. And it was really helpful. And he has a car. So we drove up to Maryland to get the meds. He was actually here to help me with the procedure, because I couldn't drive, you know, because they put you under and that type of thing. And I was supposed to have the procedure—you know, they would estimate that it would happen a week before, but because I went a week longer on the meds, he ended up staying for an extra week. So, yeah, it was great to have him here!

Another psychiatrist, Leah, was still mourning the death of her "amazing" father when she decided to pursue a cycle of egg freezing. Her younger brother pitched in over the Thanksgiving holiday, accompanying Leah and her mother to the IVF clinic on the day of retrieval.

He and my mom took me, and it was really cute. My brother was playing in the car a playlist of songs, of "happy songs," because he wanted the eggs to have happy songs. And I wanted him to come because I didn't know how out of it I would be. And so he's a big guy. I mean, my mom was coming, and then I made her just bring my brother, because I'm like five foot three and he's like six foot three, so it's like a bigger-brother type thing [laughs]! I haven't ever been put under or anything, so I was just like, "I don't know if I'm going to be drowsy, how I'm going to handle that." And so it was like a family event!

For many other women besides Leah, egg freezing was a "family event." Mothers, fathers, sisters, and brothers solidified their bonds of kinship by helping their daughters and sisters make it through the egg freezing process in ways that were both helpful and endearing. Family members often tried their best to make women's egg freezing journeys more acceptable, manageable, affordable, comfortable, and stress-free—a tall order but one that was taken quite seriously.

The women, for their part, sometimes told me that they hoped their frozen eggs would become new family members—nieces and nephews for their siblings, grandchildren for their parents, and, in a few cases, great-grandchildren for their grandparents. Four women had used inheritances from their grandparents specifically to finance their egg freezing cycles, attributing great meaning to this cross-generational extension of the family line. Two women had also used inheritances from their own deceased fathers, who had passed away before ever seeing their future grandchildren. Angela, a landscape architect, considered her egg freezing cycle an attempt to fulfill her father's dying wish. "When he passed away, he said he really wanted me to have children. And then he corrected himself. He was like, 'At least I think you want to have children, and I really don't see why you shouldn't have everything you want.' And I said, 'But I could always adopt. I could, like, have foster children.' And this was when he was dying . . . dying. And he shook his head so hard, and he said, 'You should be pregnant.'" Angela ended up spending $20,000 of the $60,000 inheritance from her father in an effort to achieve her own and her father's dream. "It's like all of what he had left to give me I'm spending to have children. So I feel somewhat bad. But half of me feels he would approve, because he did want me to do what I want. And I've always . . . well, I hope I can have kids now." For Angela and many other women like her, egg freezing was not only a family event. It was a way for these women to pay tribute to their families, too—extending the webs of kinship that ran from their grandparents through their parents to themselves and hopefully onto a new branch of the family tree.

Webs of Friendship

Just as many families supported their loved ones through the egg freezing process, so did women's friends. Friends, both male and female, appeared frequently in women's egg freezing stories, with friendship bonds sometimes outweighing kinship bonds when women needed egg freezing support. Women often talked with great affection about their "best friends," their "close friends," their "friend group," and their "friend community." Close friends were "like family," especially when women lived far from their natal families but needed immediate assistance.

Friends were often the first ones to encourage their single thirty-something friends to consider egg freezing. As noted earlier, infertile friends played a major role in this regard, warning women about fertility decline and the need for infertility prevention. Sometimes these warnings came from male friends, who were going through IVF with their infertile wives. For example, Eleanor, a thirty-five-year-old journalist, had been considering whether or not to freeze her eggs, but it was her close colleague at work who urged her not to delay.

> I knew that they had been doing IVF, but I'd never known any of the details. And he said to me, "Yeah, you know, we're doing IVF, and it's been really hard. And you know, if we were working with younger eggs . . . like, that would've been helpful." And so he was saying to me, like, "You know, you should do it, because we wish we could have younger eggs." And I kind of felt like it was a really powerful conversation, and as I thought about that conversation later on, I realized that I sort of felt like he was this voice from the future [*laughs*]. He was like, "You could be in my shoes or my wife's shoes in a few years, and I'm, like, telling you that you should do this because you could make your life easier."

Women's female friends also played a major role as egg freezing influencers, with certain women becoming *egg freezing bellwethers*, or the first ones to try egg freezing, to share their insider knowledge, and then to convince their friends of the technology's worth. *Egg freezing friend groups* would then emerge, with women freezing their eggs together or in close succession. Over the course of my study, I interviewed several members of these egg freezing friend groups, as women urged their close friends to volunteer for my study.

Nina, an academic obstetrician-gynecologist, was one of the first women I met. Following the breakup of a decade-long relationship, Nina had frozen her eggs at the age of thirty-five, then used donor sperm to become a single mother. Nina was the egg freezing bellwether for her group of close friends and colleagues, including the single female obstetrician who had delivered her baby. As Nina recounted,

> So it's funny. . . . I remember when I told her I was doing this, she goes, "Oh my God, you're so badass." That was her answer! I'm like, "What?" She goes, "Yeah, you're so badass!" And she pursued it since and actually has recently, about two months ago, delivered her daughter—a single woman. And stories like that, it was interesting, once I pursued it, how

many of my colleagues actually followed. I have a couple of colleagues that followed. Some have succeeded, some are in the process, some are trying to figure out the funds, because financially, it's not easy. But it was interesting.

Shortly after I interviewed Nina, I met Zoe, the one who had delivered Nina's baby. Zoe had frozen her eggs, too, at the age of thirty-five, before deciding to become a single mother like Nina. Zoe referred me to several of the women in their friendship circle, all of them single professionals. The next one was Priscilla, a thirty-seven-year-old nurse-midwife in the same OB/GYN practice, who told me that her ovaries were now "screaming," which is why she had decided to follow Zoe and Nina's path. I then met Sandra, a thirty-three-year-old obstetrician-gynecologist, who was completing her first egg freezing cycle before moving across country for a new job. I also met two of their nonmedical friends, a thirty-five-year-old lawyer, Iris, and a forty-two-year-old professor, Ophelia, who had each had an egg freezing consultation at the local IVF clinic but had ultimately decided against it, for both medical and financial reasons. Among the six women in this egg freezing friend group, four pursued egg freezing, and two did not. Three became mothers, including Iris, who became pregnant naturally with a new boyfriend, even though she was diagnosed with POA. Zoe, who had introduced me to most of these women, was described by her friends as their "pioneer"—the one who had gone before them, thus serving as their role model for both egg freezing and single motherhood by choice. Zoe, in turn, regarded these friends as her "chosen family," the importance of which she described to me. "I'm really lucky. I have a big community of friends and support here—my chosen family, as some of my friends like to say. I've been pretty open about everything. And yeah, people are fantastic. We have a close-knit group of women who hang out together. And we all rise to the occasion for each other for all of our issues. It's kind of fantastic. In fact, two of them are looking into buying a house, a fixer-upper, right now and looking into having kids by themselves and living in proximity to help each other out."

Beyond the influence of these egg freezing friend groups, friends were often crucial helpers during women's egg freezing cycles, performing many of the essential tasks, including injection assistance, accompaniment, and postretrieval care. Close friends sometimes made herculean efforts in this regard, taking time off work, flying across country, driving through blizzards, or staying in hotel rooms together the night before retrieval.

In a few special cases, women's friends offered to pay for their egg freezing cycles. Marta was one of these lucky beneficiaries. A school-based psychologist, Marta received a small income-based discount for her $8,000 egg freezing cycle, but she was hard-pressed to cover the full cost. Marta was able to pay for one-third, and each of her divorced parents volunteered to do the same. But at dinner with a wealthy friend, Marta received a surprise gift.

> Literally, at the end of the dinner, she was like, "I feel really uncomfortable about this. And I've thought about it for a while, and I'm not sure how you're going to react, but I really want to give this to you." And she literally, like, slides this check across the table for $8,000. And she was like, "I just—it just makes me so, so infuriated and sad. Like, I think that you would be such a good mother. I just don't want money to be the reason why that doesn't happen. And I have money. You know, I can help with that." So it was the most generous gift, and I could not have been more floored. . . . It was just a really beautiful thing.

Eventually, Marta was able to reimburse her parents, thereby allowing Marta's mother to "pay forward" the friend's gift, by helping a struggling woman friend in need. Marta also repaid her friend half the original amount when her financial situation improved.

Such generosity was not limited to women's female friends. Male friends, too, sometimes loaned or gifted money or served as financial advisers. Rhonda worked as the sales director of a small publishing firm and, like Marta, was very worried about paying for a $10,000 egg freezing cycle. She first asked a male friend to review her budget, which helped her to feel better about her decision. "He's very smart when it comes to business decisions. You know, he went to Harvard. I respect him. He's very like logical and analytical, so when I told him I was thinking about freezing my eggs and then I told him the cost, like, he didn't even think it was that big of a deal. And once he sort of signed off on it, if you will, the price of it, that helped me settle, because, you know, finances of a single person, I sweat over that a lot." Rhonda then took a loan for the full amount from another male friend, who offered her the money rather unexpectedly. "I did not have it in savings. And I didn't want to go, you know, take a credit line or credit out or something. So I borrowed it. And I'm actually still paying it back, but I'm almost done paying it back to a close friend of mine who loaned me the money. I don't like owing people money, so that's why I'm trying to pay it back, you know, as quickly as I can. But you know what I tell people? That you never know who might be a support."

Male friends sometimes offered other forms of assistance, including help with injections, accompaniment, and postretrieval care. Often, they also brightened the mood through healthy doses of humor. In IVF clinics, male friends were often mistaken for women's husbands, which these friends could later laugh about. A filmmaker, Gail, felt lucky to have a special male friend like this, who accompanied her to and from the clinic on the day of egg retrieval, joking all the way. "I felt weird asking people, because it was so intimate and it made me feel vulnerable. But my close guy friend came. We made so many jokes about it, it was actually funny. Because I felt fine afterward, we went and had lunch at a diner. And so we ordered omelets, and he kept making egg jokes. He was actually a perfect person to come with me. And we're close friends. I helped him produce an event, actually. So he owed me a few favors."

Another "favor" that occasionally arose in friendships of this nature was the offer of donor sperm, from both gay and straight male friends. Jia, a physician working for a global health organization, received such an offer while her friend drove her to her retrieval. "I've known him for twenty years. In fact, we actually joke about it. But, you know, he was like, 'If you want a sperm donor, I'll be the sperm donor.' So that's kind of cute, you know. He's just open to the idea. I was like, "Maybe . . ." [laughs]. Like, he—he had a crush on me when we first met like over twenty years ago. But that, you know, went nowhere. And he's not really my type. So yeah, we're just friends."

At least five other women told me about male friends who were in love with them and hoped to take their relationships to the next level. For example, Sasha, one of the women described earlier, who had been abandoned by her "tech guru" boyfriend after she had borne their son, told me about a male friend who very much wanted to be her partner. He had helped her on multiple occasions and had joked about "using the eggs together."

He's a potential coparent. He's a great guy, really attractive. He went to Stanford undergrad, too. He's from the East Coast, and he lives in New

York. He just—he checks off all the boxes. He's six foot two. He's a tech retiree at my age [*laughs*]! But, um, honestly my head's not in it. . . . We've been friends, and we talk on the phone every day. And he's been really great. There was a time when I needed some money, and he's probably given me at least $50,000. He's just so great. He's just my biggest cheerleader. I'm so lucky. . . . You know, he wants me to move to New York, but I said no. I'm sure I could have that relationship if I wanted it, but I guess I'm truly not over my ex. And until I feel like I'm 100 percent over it, I don't really want to move on with someone else. So he's just a great, perfect guy, and he's single. People would think I'm foolish for not being with him, but yeah, yeah, he's a great friend.

I never found out whether Sasha's friendship blossomed into a romance, even though it was clear to me that Sasha's friend loved her very much. As we will see in the next section, romantic love is sometimes present in egg freezing webs of care, too, as male partners, both old and new, show up to support their loved ones in unexpected ways.

Webs of Romance

As we know from the many stories in this book, the absence of a male partner is the primary reason why American women are freezing their eggs. The vast majority of women who freeze their eggs are single, including 82 percent of the women in my study. But as seen in Holly's story at the beginning of this chapter, some women are in a slightly different situation. Although Holly declared herself single, there was clearly a man in her life. Holly's relationship with Brad developed over time, with her feelings of love for him being strengthened by his "super" support of her egg freezing process.

That men like Brad *do* show up as women's invested partners is an unappreciated aspect of the egg freezing story, one that deserves to be examined.[2] Ex-partners, current partners, and new partners are sometimes intimately involved in women's webs of care, accompanying women to appointments, helping them with injections, and delivering tender loving care before and after the egg retrieval. In fact, almost one-third (30 percent) of the women in my study reported some form of care delivered by a current or former male partner at the time of egg freezing.

Men's involvement in women's egg freezing seemed to vary according to the state of the current relationship. First there were the amicable relationships between former partners, whose romantic love had turned into solid friendship. Second were relationships that had ended, but male partners had been supportive through the egg freezing process. Third were the current relationships with partners who, for one reason or another, were not ready to commit to having children. And fourth were the brand-new relationships, in which partners seemed hopeful but the outcomes were hard to predict.

Regarding the first category, egg freezing care delivered by women's former partners is somewhat surprising, given that these men had no formal obligation to participate. But sometimes failed romances turned into loving friendships, as was the case for Gretchen, a software financial director. Gretchen had been the one to leave her marriage, a decision that had angered her parents but not her ex-husband. Gretchen now considered her ex-husband to be her best friend, and she told me how he had helped her through a rough patch in her final egg freezing cycle.

It could just be that I wasn't the right partner, I don't know. But, I mean, he is great with kids, and he would make a great dad. He was very supportive of it [egg freezing]. Everyone was like, "Oh, does he know you're doing this?" and I said, "Yeah, he's actually very supportive." So I started the process while we were still married, but basically, we had separated before I ever had the first egg retrieval. . . . So I did three retrievals. The first two, my mother came up and helped me for the actual procedure. But the third one, my mother came up and basically the night before told me that—that I'm not a good person [for initiating the divorce] and all of this kind of stuff, and I asked her to leave. And I called my ex-husband, and he got on a plane at like nine o'clock at night and got here in time for my six a.m. retrieval the next day and was there with me for a couple of days, recovering. We were separated at that point, but he was kind enough to help me at a time when I needed it because I just couldn't have my mother be there.

Unlike Gretchen, April, a career diplomat who was always on the move, was in a current relationship at the time of egg freezing with a partner who was kind and supportive. But like Gretchen, April decided to leave, for reasons she explained. "He was really on board. He paid for half of it, because he was, like, thinking, 'Okay, I'm really serious about this. We're not ready to have kids yet, but, you know, I really do want to show you that I'm really serious about doing this with you later.' . . . Honestly, he's an amazing person, and I love him very much. But I'm not physically attracted enough to him, and that was unfortunate. It was the career thing, and then it was the lack of physical connection."

April was not alone. A number of women had supportive boyfriends who helped them through the egg freezing process, even though their relationships ultimately ended. On the other hand, a small group of women, ten to be exact, were in quite stable relationships with men who were committed but not ready to marry and have children. Men's reasons for delay were varied and included graduate school, new jobs, career moves, financial considerations, or as in Holly and Brad's case, waiting for children from a previous relationship to accept a new stepmother. Because these men were the ones to delay, they were generally enthusiastic about the reproductive postponement afforded by egg freezing.

Mei, an academic dermatologist, found herself in this waiting-for-the-partner-to-be-ready situation. Her partner, Aaron, was excited about Mei's egg freezing, becoming her biggest cheerleader.

> The funny thing is he actually ended up thinking it was a really cool process, after we were done. And he started telling his friends! He thought of me in a pioneer kind of way. He actually thought it was a very empowering, cool thing that I did. So I was like, "God, who are you telling?" [*laughs*]. He had dinner with a bunch of his friends [from college]. I'm like, "I don't even know those people, and they know that I've frozen my eggs." For a second, I was like, "I don't know." Then I was like, "Whatever." I mean, I have nothing to hide. And the relationship is going well. And the eggs are successful. So there wasn't anything that I didn't want told. So that was fine.

In Mei's case, she attributed Aaron's eventual readiness for marriage to the egg freezing process itself. In fact, Mei had been married for six weeks by the time she told me her story.

> I had a couple girlfriends that were saying, "Don't you think [egg freezing] is a bad sign in terms of your relationship?" But I actually think I was being very realistic about it. We were two years in, and he still hadn't proposed. I think I thought about it, about breaking it off. I really had. And that was part of the reason I didn't do the embryos, like, "Well, if he

can't commit to me in two years, I don't know what that means, if we do embryos." And then I don't know—I don't know if it was the egg freezing that made him realize that I was just going to still do what I wanted to do, with or without him. I'm not sure. But I asked him what changed. He's like, "I don't know." To me, it seems like a switch just flipped, and he was like, "Okay, I'm ready." It was just really weird. So I don't know. I can't explain it. It just made sense to him one day. I'm like, "Okay!" [*laughs*]. He was very proud of me for doing it. It was interesting. It was a good dynamic that we had. So the whole thing was very positive for us. And maybe it just made him think a little bit more about having children and the fact that I really wanted it and that I was going to do it with or without him. So maybe that helped. I don't know.

Mei surmised that her egg freezing at the age of thirty-seven had actually released the mounting pressure on Aaron, as it had on her. "Well, it's funny," she said. "I think this whole egg freezing thing was good for our relationship, because I stopped being so focused on deadlines and reminding him of my age and kind of freaking him out a little bit."

This pressure-relieving function of egg freezing served new relationships as well. Instead of "freaking out" over a new partner's reproductive potential, both men and women could feel calmer, putting these childbearing considerations on hold. Several women in my study found new boyfriends in the midst of their egg freezing cycles. Like Aaron, most of these men found the idea of egg freezing to be intriguing or, as one new male partner put it, "the most brilliant thing." Indeed, most new boyfriends became eager to help, realizing the potential benefits to them of this fertility preservation technology.

Such was the case with Tracy and Colin, who bonded as a couple over egg freezing. Both Tracy and Colin were highly specialized federal security agents, who had "traveled the world and carried a gun." But on their second date, Tracy had to give herself the difficult trigger shot. As she told me, with humor, she excused herself to "do an injection," thus piquing Colin's curiosity.

We were supposed to have dinner the first night, and we got caught up talking. So dinner didn't work out. So, on the second night, it's literally like forty-five minutes before I'm supposed to give myself the trigger shot injection. So I'm looking at him, and I'm like, "I'm starving, but I now can't go out to eat because it's nine thirty on a Sunday, and I have no idea where we would go, because I've got to give myself a shot, you know?" I just kind of left it at that. But I said, "But I'm happy to cook." So I make dinner, we're sitting down, and I was like, "Well, crap. I need—I need to do this before we sit down. Do you mind waiting a few more minutes?" And again, he's very kind. He's a better person than I am. He's like, "No, no, it's okay!" And I was like, "Okay, well, if you happen to hear a thud in the next couple of minutes, please do come in." And he's like, "Do you need any help?" And I'm like, "I don't think so. But this is supposed to be the biggest shot I have to give myself, and so I think it'll be okay. But, you know, if you do hear a big thud, like please do come in because I probably passed out, you know? [*Laughs*] I don't want to hit my head on something and end up killing myself." So he's like, "Cool." So it goes without a hitch. I come back out. Like, we *are* federal agents, so he's sort of like, "What was that all about?" And I'm, you know, "I'm not a drug dealer, you know?" [*laughs*]. And he was actually very interested. Like, he never had an opportunity to have the conversation. . . . And so then he got very concerned about like, "Well, who's taking you?" And I was like, "Well, my cousin has, you know, graciously offered. She's going to go with me. Well, she has to go with me to the appointment. She's going to drive me home and drop me off, and then, you know, then she's got a lunch meeting that she has to make." And he's like, "Well, is she going to come back and check on you?" And I was like, "No, I had shoulder surgery. I've been under anesthesia. I'm not super concerned about this. So, you know, I don't think so. She's got the rest of her workday to do." And he was really very sweet. He was like, "Well, do you mind if I check on you?" Literally, like, we've had one lunch, and we were having dinner for the first time, you know? So I said, "Sure, if you want to. That would be nice, yeah." And so sure enough, he comes over at like two o'clock with soup from Whole Foods!

Family, Friends, and Men Who Care

This chapter began with the story of Holly and Brad and ended with the story of Tracy and Colin. I chose these stories to show that men *do* become the partners of highly accomplished women, proving that not all men are uncommitted, uncaring louts. In a book on the mating gap, these stories of men who are caring partners need to be told, and I hope that this chapter will move the conversation forward in this direction.

Ending with Tracy's story shows once again how women who freeze their eggs are enmeshed in webs of care. Although Tracy was a highly independent person, who had been deployed several times to war zones, she still required some egg freezing assistance, which she received from a female cousin and her new boyfriend, Colin. Although Tracy told me how difficult it had been to find an equal partner, saying, "Woe is me. My career, I chose this," she *did* manage to meet a man who understood her career and who was also kind and helpful.

One-third of women in my study were like Tracy in that they received some form of egg freezing care from a partner, past or present. Another one-third received care from men in their own families, as well as their male friends. Although men's support of women's egg freezing remains deeply hidden in both media and scholarly accounts, it is definitely present, constituting a new, powerful, and intimate form of male participation in women's reproductive lives.

Finally, almost every woman in this study received some form of care from another woman, usually a mother but also sisters and female friends. In some cases, women's female friends were their "chosen families," even closer than kin, both geographically and emotionally. Ultimately, as we have seen, *no woman is an island in the world of egg freezing.*[3] Women are buoyed by webs of care from family, friends, and (ex)partners, who, through egg freezing, demonstrate their investment in the reproductive futures of the women they love.

7

The Empowered

From Reluctant Feminists to Egg Freezing Activists

Judith's Vocal Feedback

Judith was one of those Americans whose childhood had been spent moving from state to state as her scientist father pursued his career in the pharmaceutical industry. But when she eventually moved to California to attend one of the state's fifteen Catholic colleges, she never left. Judith quickly established a career as a Silicon Valley IT security specialist—a job that she loved, with the added benefits of significant upward mobility and a substantial salary.

But even though the tech industry was literally brimming with unmarried men, Judith found herself single at the age of thirty-five. When I asked about her opinion of men in Silicon Valley—especially the saying that "the odds are good, but the goods are odd"—Judith laughed, then launched into her own analysis of the local dating scene.

> There are definitely some very, very unique personalities in this field! And I could talk to you for hours about the "diversity in tech" issues and how different people look at that or how they see that. But I have a lot of friends who don't work in tech who are my age and single as well, so I don't think it's just necessarily a factor of being in the tech field. I think it's actually the Bay Area, which is pretty overrun by tech, but it is definitely a much different environment, dating here. I would say that dating in the Bay Area is a very surreal environment. It is hard. It is incredibly, incredibly hard. I've tried Match, and I've tried different dating sites. They were never for me. I just never liked them. I think I went on one date on Match and pulled myself off and went on one date on eHarmony and pulled myself off. To me, I've always just much more enjoyed the organic way that these things develop. And I'm also not a person who

just dates to date. I always said, "My free time is precious, and I want to spend it with somebody that I saw a future with." I would never just get into a relationship with somebody if I didn't think there was some sort of future. I really hadn't had a boyfriend since I was twenty-three. I had dated some people, but I just didn't want to end up there. I was also of the mind-set that if by a certain point in time I hadn't met anyone, you know, I talked about the fact that I would do this [motherhood] on my own. So that was kind of my thought in my head when I was thirty-five. I wasn't ready to throw in the towel that I wasn't going to meet anybody, but I also recognized that my fertility was on the downswing and wanted to do what I could to protect that. . . . And I have no doubt—and I have always said this—I have been very successful in my career and I love my job, but I have always said, even back to the time I was in high school, I have always said that I wanted to be a mother. But I also wanted to wait for a partner—somebody that I wanted to spend the rest of my life with, not just somebody who was going to be able to give me a child.

With no partner on the horizon and not knowing what to do, Judith spoke with her mother, a nurse, who asked, "Have you ever thought about doing egg freezing?" At the time, egg freezing was brand new, its experimental label having just been lifted. Judith searched on the internet to find out about the procedure, as well as where she could head for a consultation. She settled on an academic IVF clinic that had participated in the early egg freezing clinical trials. There, a highly regarded female IVF physician diagnosed Judith with polycystic ovary syndrome but reassured her that her hormonal values were much better than expected for her age.

In inquiring about the costs, Judith assumed that egg freezing would be covered by her employer's insurance. She had been working in Silicon Valley for more than a decade, where most major tech firms subsidized part or all of their married employees' IVF expenses. But she was surprised to learn that her egg freezing would not be covered by insurance on two major grounds: first, her lack of a partner and, second, her lack of an official infertility diagnosis. This made Judith angry. Here she was, a thirty-five-year-old woman with legitimate fertility concerns, who was undertaking a clinical procedure that was literally half of an IVF cycle. Why, Judith wondered, was egg freezing for single employees not covered, when IVF for married employees was? Furthermore, egg freezing was intended to prevent future infertility and the incumbent expenses of repeated IVF cycles.

Feeling quite irked by this disparity in coverage, Judith began arguing to her company's internal benefits office that egg freezing cycles should be covered, too, just as IVF was.

> I know there's a lot of information out there now about how [her company] covers egg freezing. They did not three years ago, when I did it. I would actually like to think that my very vocal feedback to our internal benefits group around it maybe played some sort of a role in them eventually moving to this. . . . I was incredibly vocal going through that entire time. . . . Just the entire way it happened, I felt like the insurance company really didn't know how to deal with a situation like mine. I mean, even the questions they were asking about infertility and having a partner . . . you could tell it was just something that was completely foreign to them and they didn't know how to respond. And I remember that I said [to someone] I work with, I said, "God, it's actually funny. I actually feel like I'm in a situation where I kind of walked away feeling like there was something broken with me or something wrong that I'm thirty-five and single and that I'm even thinking about doing this."

Beyond the feelings of stigma, Judith began to see this lack of insurance coverage as a form of discrimination against single women, as well as LGBTQ employees of her company.

> I'll be honest, even three years ago, going through this, it was all about your male partner. . . . I was even thinking on the flip side, you know, if I had a female partner at that point in time, how would they have approached that and looked at it? And it was funny. Not only on the insurance side but even when I was going through the classes to learn how to inject myself and all of that, I mean, I was the only single person in there, you know. And I even remember one of the women saying to me, "Well, you know, don't worry; my husband didn't come with me to the first class, either." And I said, "Well, I'm actually not married. I don't have a partner. I'm actually going through this because I'm going to be freezing my eggs." It's already an emotional time and an emotional issue. And, like I said, for a lot of people it can feel like, "What's wrong with me?" You kind of feel like this is something that you should be able to do. You should be able to reproduce, and this is how it should be happening. And just all of their questions! I mean, they are, "How often are you having sex?" Really? Is this really necessary? "How

many doctors have you seen?" Just the way that they ask the questions and phrase the questions to go through this, it's incredibly invasive at a time when you are already feeling emotional, overwhelmed. It's a very sensitive topic, and there's just no sensitivity in how this is handled.

Still, Judith persisted in her vocal advocacy, and soon thereafter, her firm began to subsidize egg freezing for its single women employees, although Judith never personally benefited from the company's largesse. She forked out $16,000 for her own egg freezing cycle, an amount that was never reimbursed by insurance. But what really bothered Judith was the negative media attention that her company's decision to offer egg freezing as part of its "fertility benefits" package attracted. What Judith saw as a major win for women in tech, one that she had fought for so vigorously, was being attacked on both the left and the right as a major setback for women. Judith was stunned by this backlash, which she saw as inherently misguided.

It's funny to me, even now. Obviously, there's been a lot more coverage of it recently and especially with both Apple and Facebook announcing that they cover it as a benefit for their own employees. But it's really interesting for me to see and listen to how different people talk about it . . . and how things get blown out of proportion as well. All these stories came out that said that Apple and Facebook are paying female employees to freeze their eggs and that then, in turn, "Well, they're paying you because they don't want you to have kids, because they don't want you to walk away from the workforce." And it just made me laugh so hard, because I said, "They're not paying to freeze your eggs! They're saying that they're going to cover it if you decide to do that." They're not offering any financial incentive.

For her part, Judith felt that the growing chorus of egg freezing opponents were being highly judgmental of a reproductive option from which single women like her could benefit. "You know, for me, what I always say is, 'Who am I to judge how somebody determines what their family looks like or what their family structure is going to be?' Probably a lot of it is the influence of both my parents being in the sciences and my mom on the medical side. But I have always been a big proponent of science, [which] can really help and improve our lives and offer us a lot of great opportunities, and we should take advantage of that where we can."

When I asked Judith how she felt personally about her own egg freezing cycle, which had rendered a total of forty-one eggs, she was pleased and excited. "It might very well turn out to be the best decision I've made in my life! I'm a planner by nature, and so I've always looked at it as my insurance policy."

Indeed, by the time of our interview, Judith's relationship fortunes had turned for the better. A friendship at work had blossomed into an office romance, leading to the biggest company benefit of all.

> He actually referred me for my job, and I got hired. And then our desks were in a very open environment, and our desks were diagonal from each other. So we were looking at each other all day. We became very good friends. I would say we were really, really good friends for about eighteen months. I always say we were "friend-dating." And then it kind of turned into more than that, and we started officially dating. And we got engaged about ten months after we started dating-dating. It was totally organic, totally from work. . . . And I am incredibly blessed that I met this wonderful and loving man and that I am now married.

Judith's husband, Gary, was also keen on having children. But after a year of trying and two failed IVF attempts using Judith's thirty-eight-year-old "fresh" eggs, they decided to try Judith's frozen eggs in storage. Of the thirty-six eggs that were successfully rewarmed (with five lost in the process), twenty-four were successfully fertilized (or twelve total lost in the process). Two grade-A embryos were transferred to Judith's uterus just two weeks prior to our interview, and the rest (twenty-two embryos) were returned to the freezer, with Judith calling them "our own sports team!"

Again, Judith had to fight for egg freezing insurance coverage. She was the first employee at her firm to undertake the second half of the egg freezing process, which involved the rewarming of her frozen eggs, their fertilization with Gary's sperm, the transfer of two embryos into her uterus, and the cryopreservation (frozen storage) of the twenty-two embryos that she did not use. Judith argued that these costs should be covered, as they were for any routine IVF cycle. Again, her advocacy was convincing.

By the time I met Judith, all aspects of egg freezing, from the initial fertility testing to the final embryo storage, were now covered by her company's health insurance plan, including for single women who might choose to become a mother using donor sperm. Through her very "vocal feedback," Judith had helped to initiate a comprehensive egg freezing pol-icy at her leading tech firm, one in which single women could hold onto their motherhood dreams without having to worry about the costs.

* * *

Judith's own motherhood dreams, too, were becoming a reality. At the end of our long conversation, Judith received a phone call from her IVF physician. Excusing herself for about five minutes to take the call, Judith returned with tears in her eyes and a smile on her face.

> MARCIA (READING JUDITH'S EXPRESSION): Congratulations!
>
> JUDITH: Thank you!
>
> MARCIA: Do you seem to be pregnant?
>
> JUDITH: Yes! Well, I will tell you. . . . We were kind of expecting this be-cause I took a home test on Saturday, and it came back, but we were waiting for the actual number to make sure they were good. Success!
>
> MARCIA: Oh, that's so exciting! I had that feeling that this was good news. Oh my God, that's so exciting. Are the numbers high, like maybe there are two?
>
> JUDITH: She said they are very happy with the numbers right now. She said we'll want to keep seeing, the next couple of days, where they go, but she said I'm definitely in that mid- to high range.
>
> MARCIA: Wow, that's so exciting. Gosh, congratulations! You probably need to go. So go and share your happy news with your husband. It's wonderful!
>
> JUDITH: Thank you. And if there's anything, any follow-up or anything you need, you have my email. Please feel free to reach out at any time. . . .
>
> MARCIA: What an exciting ending to the story. Yay! What a great deci-sion you made, my gosh.
>
> JUDITH: Yes, yes it was!

Egg Freezing Benefits

Judith's story is important on a number of levels, from the social to the clinical to the political. From a social perspective, Judith's struggle to find a loving partner in Silicon Valley meant that she spent a dozen prime reproductive years, from the ages of twenty-three to thirty-five, on her own. Eventually, an "organic" relationship developed for Judith as she gazed across her computer screen at her coworker Gary. Although not "love at first sight," Judith and Gary's relationship took the most common route, namely, the "friends-to-lovers" pathway, in which a long-term friendship turned to romance and then to marriage.[1]

On a clinical level, Judith and Gary's story is also important, for it shows that the "second half" of an egg freezing cycle can be successful. Frozen eggs are never a foolproof guarantee of pregnancy. But in Judith's case, she considered those eggs to be her "insurance policy," one that, in her case, truly paid off. Because Judith had stored her younger, healthier eggs at the age of thirty-five, she was able to draw on them at the age of thirty-eight when she had already begun to experience infertility and the disappointment of two failed IVF cycles. In retrospect, Judith deemed egg freezing to be the best decision she had ever made in her life. And the proof came from the doctor's office, with a call confirming her pregnancy, possibly with twins.

Beyond this clinical success story, Judith's story is important politically, for it shows how the efforts of one woman made a difference in instigating policy change. Judith fought hard for egg freezing insurance, because she found the differential treatment of employees on the basis of their marital status to be unjust. Soon after Judith pressed her case, her firm added egg freezing to its fertility benefits package. By the time I met her, almost all of the major tech firms in Silicon Valley—Apple, Facebook, Google, and Intel among them—were offering similar coverage. The policy change that Judith and probably other women in these companies had inspired seemed to have ripple effects, with more and more tech firms and other Fortune 500 companies beginning to join the egg freezing benefits bandwagon.

Judith is what I would call a behind-the-scenes *egg freezing activist*— someone who took creative action to change a policy in a way that would make egg freezing technology more available for women in tech through the provision of *egg freezing fertility benefits*.[2] By the time I undertook my study, virtually all of the women I spoke with in tech had had their egg freezing cycles covered this way, a fertility benefit that they greatly appreciated. For example, Yuki, recently divorced and newly hired as an instructor at one of the big Bay Area tech firms, was thrilled to be offered this coverage.

I think between aging and getting out of a marriage that wasn't working and getting out of a job that wasn't working, like, a lot of these things pointed toward a greater focus on health, you know. The other thing that I think is really important to mention is that—and you might already know this from your other interviews—but [her company] introduced a new benefit which supports egg freezing. So I had considered it in the past but was a little reluctant, based on the financial commitment. But this was huge! I mean, if it wasn't the deciding factor, it was pretty close, along with turning forty [*laughs*]!

Sydney had also taken a job at the same company, but Sydney's situation was different from Yuki's in a number of ways. At age thirty, Sydney was a decade younger than Yuki and the second youngest woman in my study. Sydney was the only woman in my study—out of a total of 114—who was undertaking egg freezing specifically for career-planning purposes. With degrees from two Ivy League universities, Sydney was hoping to delay childbearing in order to achieve her entrepreneurial dream of founding a company that would be "deeply impactful in the world" and where she could do her best "to be a leader." Egg freezing, she told me, would allow her to pursue her goals without having her "professional and life ambitions kind of encroached upon." This would be appealing, she believed, for other women in Silicon Valley.

You know, women my age know about this for sure. Maybe it's just a Silicon Valley thing, but I think everybody has heard of it. And all the personal drivers are making me want to do this right now. It's that, like, triumvirate of pressure that I feel at age thirty to begin compromising life decisions because now is the time to, like, prepare for a family, on the relationship front, on the professional front, and then just, like, personally, when really, I don't want to be doing that. I want to stop the clock. I want to buy myself more time, kick the can down the road, you know? And maybe find somebody that I more sustainably want to be with for reasons that are more attuned to my personality and less attuned to, like, my life needs. You know?

Sydney was one of only three women in my study who identified as bisexual, and she told me that a more "sustainable" relationship for her meant finding a female partner. In fact, after our interview in my office in New Haven, Sydney was heading to New York City to meet a "lesbian CEO," the kind of highly successful woman that Sydney wanted to be with but had found it difficult to meet. In Sydney's view, egg freezing could be quite helpful for lesbian couples who could use their frozen eggs with donor sperm. In general, Sydney saw egg freezing as a "fantastic option" for all professional women of her age but felt that women needed company coverage to make this happen.

> I'm so lucky. I don't know how many women have like ten thousand bucks to literally roll the dice on ten eggs, you know. Cryopreservation is only eight to ten [thousand]. But it's still like eight to ten thousand more dollars than I probably wanted to spend on this on my own. . . . Honestly, I have enough savings that I think I would probably want to do something like this in the next one to two years. . . . But they offered it to me. They offered it now, and now is a good time, you know? Because in life, you literally never know what's going to happen.

Like Judith, Sydney was very puzzled about why her company's decision to fund egg freezing had been so hotly contested in the media. She described it as "the craziest thing" she had heard, a view that was shared by many other women in my study. For example, Victoria, who had spent her entire career in climate-change politics before joining a tech start-up, was disappointed that her own firm was too small and thus unable to provide egg freezing benefits for its women employees. Victoria was also upset by the media critique of egg freezing benefits, which tended to misrepresent women's motivations for pursuing this technology.

> One of the things that I really kind of thought was upsetting was when, you know, Facebook and I think it was Facebook and Google paid for this for their female employees. And there were all these articles saying, "Oh, women are putting off having children for career reasons." And that kind of upset me, because no one I know who has done this, it's not been for career. . . . I would never put my career above my personal life! I would actually never do that! It drives me crazy, because I just feel like a lot of people don't get why women are doing this at all. I really wanted to do it, but I felt like a lot of the articles written at that time, when Sheryl Sandberg [COO of Facebook] came out in support, there was this flood of articles, and I didn't really relate to any of them. And it wasn't just me but me, Patricia, my friend Betsy, my friend Janet, our friend Monica, like, all these people, like, everyone I talked to. I know a lot of women who have

done this, and not one of them related to that. So that's not what we're talking about at all. You know, I find that most women are doing this because they want to have children with a partner, they don't quite have that partner yet, or they have doubts about their partner. And they don't want to be in a situation where they're unable to get pregnant or feel like you're pressured into getting married because of this. Right? Like, you're feeling there's a clock on your back, kind of deal. That's the people I know.

Victoria's portrayal of egg freezing was extremely accurate for the women in my study. To reiterate this important point, more than 90 percent of these women were freezing their eggs either because they could not find a partner (82 percent) or because they were in unstable relationships that were too new or uncertain (9 percent). As single women, most of them were forced to bear the high costs of egg freezing on their own, and they told me that insurance coverage would have come as a great relief.[3]

For example, Efua, an internal medicine physician, laughed when she told me, "If I worked for Apple, that would be 'Yay!' Who would say no?" Efua had spent more than $20,000 to cover two cycles of egg freezing. "It was something I wanted to do," she said, "and it didn't matter how much it was going to cost. I was going to do it." But given that egg freezing was a measure to prevent the infertility that she was probably now facing at the age of forty-four, Efua called the lack of egg freezing insurance coverage "unfair." She was cautiously optimistic that this situation would change over time, telling me, "Everything that's new starts out very expensive. But the cost will go down within the decade, and insurance will start paying. Then everyone will do it!" Efua, as we will see, was more optimistic than most women, who complained about the high cost of egg freezing and the lack of insurance coverage as a form of discrimination against single women.

Egg Freezing Discrimination

If there was one overarching recommendation among women in my study, it was that the cost of egg freezing be brought down and also covered by insurance so that the technology would become available to more women, including their own sisters and friends who could not easily afford it. Some women argued that egg freezing's inaccessibility represented a form of gender discrimination. "If guys tried to freeze their eggs," one woman remarked, "companies would pay for it." Another woman complained, "I think if men were able to freeze their eggs, it would be free, it would be included in insurance plans, and it wouldn't be such a, you know, new technology. This would have come up a zillion years ago." Or as another annoyed woman put it, "If I were a dude, I could still have twelve grand in the bank!"

What bothered women most was the sense of discrimination based on their marital status. As single women, they were disqualified from the fertility insurance sometimes offered to married couples. This was a particularly sore point for divorced women who had lost these marital benefits. For example, Cecilia, the thirty-nine-year-old British American attorney who had just emerged from a bitter divorce, was maddened to learn that egg freezing was not covered by her insurance. "Insurance is skewed against single women," Cecilia fumed. "Why does marriage have any relevance? It makes me so angry! Let's be honest, it's discrimination." Ariel, an art history professor who had once "rushed recklessly into marriage and didn't want to do the same [again]," faced a similar situation. "I wouldn't have been eligible anymore, and of course, that made me very angry," she recalled. "It's horrendous! I can't believe that this kind of policy exists in this day and age. It's very patronizing."

Some of the strongest sentiments regarding marriage-based discrimination came from obstetrician-gynecologists who practiced in the so-called mandate states. In the US, fifteen states "mandate" some form of health insurance coverage for married couples facing infertility. In eight of these states—Arkansas, Connecticut, Hawaii, Illinois, Maryland, Massachusetts, New Jersey, and Rhode Island—IVF costs are partially or fully covered for those couples. Nina, who worked as an obstetrician-gynecologist in one of the most generous mandate states, was happy for her infertility patients but very concerned about all of the single women like her who had effectively been excluded from the state's mandate, even though they were facing age-related infertility concerns. "So [our state] mandate [applies] if you work for an organization bigger than sixty employees. But guess what? You have to prove that you have infertility. You have to prove you've had sexual intercourse with a partner for over a year. So that means same-sex relationships or single women do not qualify. I'm waiting for somebody to tackle this politically, because I will be the first one to help them. It is *huge* discrimination. If you ever decide to tackle it, let me know, because I'm coming with you!"

In an interview I conducted with Lydia, the director of an organization that had helped to champion the state mandates, she argued that egg freezing should constitute "the next wave" of insurance coverage.

> Let's get everybody covered with IVF, and then, you know, we can start dealing with the elective egg freezing. It's funny, because when all the media came out about Google and Facebook adding fertility preservation, not for cancer, and people were calling me and they were like, "You know, what does that say? These companies just want these people to work their butts off and never have kids." And I go, "How do you know that this wasn't an employee asking for it?" Because my experience has been—and we have data to prove this, Marcia—that the majority of companies that even have IVF and infertility coverage have it because an employee asks. And so I wouldn't be so quick to make some sort of negative judgment. And then, secondly, you know, "Who's to say this wasn't a great idea? Why are you looking at it negatively?" Because when we look at data that's out in the media space—on *HuffPost*, they did a survey on women in their twenties. And what was their number-one health issue, the number-one health concern? It was infertility. And so, you know, it kind of makes me mad when people automatically assume that these benefits are offered in some negative way versus thinking maybe employees asked for it. And secondly, maybe this is what women in their twenties and thirties are demanding today.

Kendra was exactly the kind of person that Lydia was referring to—an employee in her late thirties who had "asked" for egg freezing benefits. When Kendra pursued egg freezing at the age of thirty-eight, she was working as the director of communications for an international reproductive health organization. Given her organization's focus, Kendra was shocked to discover that egg freezing was one of the few reproductive technologies *not* covered by her employer's health insurance plan.

> You know, we had great health care coverage! But what it didn't cover was the egg freezing process. And a couple of the people that I talked to, one who froze her eggs for the similar reasons that I did and another who had done the IVF process, [I came to the] understanding that the IVF process was the same with the exception of actually fertilizing the egg. And my

health insurance would have covered the process if I was doing IVF and if I could have shown a pattern of having a fertility issue, showing that I tried to get pregnant for six months and was unsuccessful. I was like, "No. That's not exactly what I'm doing here." . . . I think Google and some of the other kind of very progressive organizations were offering that as a lifestyle bonus to their employees. And so my thing was, "Come on! This is [a reproductive health organization]! So, if everything else is covered, then you guys definitely need to get behind this as well." I was the one [*laughs*]! I was the one who was like, "Listen, if I'm on the road all the time, this is the part of my lifestyle, then my insurance should cover it to the same extent that [they cover IVF]." One of the great things about [the organization] is they cover unlimited IVF for their employees—unlimited IVF, which is unheard of. . . . And so, you know, my response to our HR [human resources] department was, "If you guys are covering all of these great procedures and we are [a reproductive health organization], then you should support my decision." So now [they] will cover egg freezing! They had to do some negotiating with the insurance companies and were able to get it covered. So I'm pretty proud of that—pretty proud of it. To have unlimited coverage for egg freezing is just above and beyond—pretty amazing!

As we saw earlier, Kendra also wanted to be a "voice" for egg freezing in the Black community, partly to counter the effects of fertility shaming, which she believed came from many different sources, including the media.

I understand kind of the negative tone that's often framed on women who make a choice about their body, period. So, whether it's freezing your eggs, whether it's choosing to have an abortion, whether it's choosing not to have a child, whether it's choosing to have twelve kids, it's always the woman [who] is always the problem. So I think that the ability to make that choice for yourself and/or with your partner is each person's individual space. It's unfortunate that the media kind of, to me, feeds into the stigma and the shaming tone. And I think that it—I think it's going to be some time, but I do think that women are beginning to find that space of, "Wait, wait a minute! You don't get the ability to define me for me. I'll tell you who I am." And if speaking up or speaking out or controlling my health care makes me selfish, then I'll be that. That's okay.

Given Kendra's strong advocacy of reproductive choice, I asked her if egg freezing should be considered a "feminist technology," one that helps women to plan their own reproductive futures. Kendra felt ambivalent about the "feminist" label, for reasons that she explained to me.

So I think that many times, especially in the feminist narrative, the voice of the African American woman is missing. I tend to shy away from the term "feminist" mostly because it doesn't feel as inclusive as I would like it to be. At times, it can be very alienating. The narratives that they use are noninclusive. But I understand that by definition, you know, it is about equality. So I'm okay with it, but I don't know that I would use it. I think that, you know, you don't have to be a feminist to want to make your own decisions. Like, you know, when are we going to say women should not have access or the ability to control their own bodies? Because I think at the end of the day, there's a larger fear of us having the power, understanding that we have the power, to make those decisions. I think that when we look at the egg freezing, it's a luxury right now. So, you know, we want people to have choice and all of that, but even though it's available, it's still not a choice for many women. And I think about that when we think about birth control. Although it's available, if a woman can't afford birth control and her insurance doesn't cover it and her employer's not fighting for it, it's not an option. It's crazy. It's almost just incomprehensible, just kind of the gap and the lag and the delay of how we are really still fighting for a grown woman to make her own health care decisions without being criticized or, you know, just shunned for making those choices. We're lagging behind. And when you say that it's legal or when you say that it's out there, to your point, if you cannot get access to it because of financial restrictions or geographic restrictions or religious restrictions, then it's not available.

Clearly, Kendra could be considered an egg freezing activist, who had changed the policy of an international reproductive health organization and had become a vocal advocate for egg freezing among Black professional women. Yet Kendra was reluctant to call herself a feminist because of the exclusion of Black voices or to consider egg freezing a feminist technology because of injustices in access. Furthermore, she found the growing feminist opposition to egg freezing in the media to be "skewed." Why, Kendra wondered, would a technology that offers women increased reproductive choice be viewed so unfavorably by some feminists? Kendra's question, as we will see, is at the heart of the contemporary *egg freezing debate*, which questions whether egg freezing offers women reproductive choice or oppression.[4]

The Egg Freezing Debate

Egg freezing has engendered a significant amount of debate since the moment of its inception. When egg freezing's experimental label was lifted in the US in late 2012, it was initially heralded as a "reproductive revolution," comparable to the 1960s introduction of the birth control pill.[5] However, over the past decade, most feminist scholars and commentators have been reluctant to embrace egg freezing as a positive development, given its significant expense, its potential for employer coercion, and its inability to guarantee the birth of a future child. Indeed, there have been four major strands of feminist thought regarding egg freezing, ones that I would call *liberal feminism, structural feminism, intersectional feminism,* and *technocritical feminism*—only the first of which has been supportive.

Liberal Feminism

This supportive strand of liberal feminism emerged early, arising even before egg freezing's experimental label was lifted. Liberal feminists are pro-choice and have argued that egg freezing offers women reproductive empowerment by freeing them from their biological clocks and allowing them to defer, delay, and postpone their motherhood until they are ready. While men routinely postpone their fatherhood well into their forties and beyond, egg freezing confers this same reproductive advantage on women. Furthermore, egg freezing promotes women's reproductive autonomy by allowing them to decide when and how to have children, with or without men as partners. In general, pro-choice liberal feminism regards egg freezing as liberating—increasing women's reproductive choices, control, timing, autonomy, and ultimately gender equality with men. This view is widely espoused by some feminist bioethicists who have theorized about egg freezing's potential, as well as by IVF physician-scholars who offer egg freezing services to their patients and who have also written extensively about this technology.[6]

In my own study, this pro-choice liberal feminist view was widely shared by the dozen IVF physicians I interviewed in cities across the US. One-third of these IVF physicians said that they would endorse egg freezing for their own daughters. An Indian American female IVF physician, who was practicing in a large midwestern city, had this to say about egg freezing's emancipatory potential:

> I think from the perspective [of] a woman who would potentially want to childbear but perhaps isn't in a point in her life where she has even found someone, or perhaps they're not ready to proceed with that, I think it's a wonderful way to freeze the clock. I mean, it sounds funny, because my daughter's nine, but that is one thing I'm going to be talking to her about later in life, that I'll be, like, look, when she's in her twenties, perhaps this is something worthwhile, absolutely. I mean, before I felt, just looking at reproductive medicine in general, the birth control pill was this amazing advancement for reproductive rights, sort of just choice and options. And now I feel that this is the next huge wave. It just provides so many potential opportunities, better than the Pill. The Pill allows you to choose when to have a child, but so does this in a way. It's even more revolutionary that way.

This pro-choice liberal feminist view, articulated so well by this female IVF physician, is not the view shared by most feminist scholars writing about egg freezing today. Three other strands of feminism, all of them quite critical of egg freezing, have become the dominant forms.

Structural Feminism

Structural (or materialist) feminism has been especially pronounced since the tech industry's egg freezing announcements. Structural feminists, who tend to have neo-Marxist orientations within the fields of sociology and philosophy, are concerned about society's material conditions, including the state of the economy, the labor market, the workplace environment, and the aspects of employment that disadvantage women in their work-life balance.[7] Structural feminists see egg freezing, and especially employer-sponsored egg freezing benefits, as a way for companies to exert a "moral imperative" on women to freeze their eggs and to postpone their fertility indefinitely while "climbing the corporate ladder." That women may be forced to use egg freezing to "put off" marriage and motherhood in order to achieve career advancement suggests that women cannot "have it all."[8] Furthermore, structural feminists argue that egg freezing represents a "quick fix" or a "Band-Aid" solution for underlying structural conditions that make women's work difficult to reconcile with their reproduction. The promotion of egg freezing by employers' policies may serve to reinforce both neoliberal corporate hegemony and patriarchy by leaving various forms of gender inequality in the workplace intact. These forms of inequality include lack of subsidized parental leave, lack of affordable child care, existence of a "glass ceiling" for women on the "mommy track," and a variety of other employment conditions favoring men.

This structural feminist critique is the one that women in my study were aware of, primarily through the egg freezing debates circulating in the media. But like Judith and Kendra, many women in my study were slightly or moderately offended by this critique, arguing that it did not align with their personal experiences or perceptions. Their egg freezing motivations, as we have seen, reflected partnership problems, not desires for career advancement. And even if career planning was a woman's primary motivation—as it was for Sydney, who wanted to become an entrepreneur and business leader—some women asked, what would be wrong with that? In fact, many women in my study saw egg freezing as advancing work-life balance by allowing them to become mothers while maintaining careers that were important to them. For example, Violet, an engineering manager in Silicon Valley, explained how egg freezing could broaden her ability to become a mother, not restrict it. "Egg freezing gives people more choices to do what they want with their lives, when they want it, without that pressure. I don't have to put my career on hold because I want kids. I don't have to put my life on hold because I want to do this or do that. I can do it when I'm ready and when I want it and on my schedule. . . . I always feel like you should bring kids into this world when you're ready to, when you're capable of taking care of that child financially and emotionally."

Intersectional Feminism

Intersectional, as in Intersectional feminism focuses not on women's workplace pressures to pursue egg freezing but rather on women's exclusion from egg freezing on the basis of intersectional forms of oppression faced primarily by poor and minority women. Derived from Black feminist theory and promoted by feminist legal scholars, intersectional feminist critiques focus on unequal access and reproductive injustice.[9] Given the unaffordability of egg freezing for most women, egg freezing reinforces the hierarchy between affluent White women who can purchase these services and minority and low-income women who cannot. Intersectional feminist critics argue that this hierarchy reinforces "stratified reproduction," in which some women are seen as less deserving of fertility preservation than others.[10] Furthermore, egg freezing may lead to the worrisome "colonization" of poor and minority women's bodies and reproductive futures, if they are asked to donate their eggs in order to reduce the price of their own fertility preservation. Such *egg sharing* arrangements, which have been promoted in some European countries, represent a haunting future specter in which some women's bodies become "bioavailable" for coercive egg donation.[11]

Very few women in my study were aware of this intersectional feminist critique, but in some ways, it resonated with their concerns. Like Kendra, most pointed to the high cost of egg freezing and worried about how this excluded many women who could never afford it. As we have seen, women in my study who came from underrepresented minority groups did have greater difficulty financing their egg freezing quests. They were more likely to rely on small loans, credit cards, and payment plans to cover their expenses, as few of them had employer-sponsored fertility benefits. Having said that, minority women were quite well represented in my study, comprising one-third of the study total. This included Nina (Puerto Rican American), Efua (Ghanaian American), and Kendra (African American), as well as Sydney (a sexual minority woman who was the daughter of a poor single mother), all of whom were glad to have undertaken egg freezing, deeming it an empowering reproductive tool for women in their respective communities.

Technocritical Feminism

Women's positive view of egg freezing is very much at odds with technocritical feminism, which questions whether egg freezing is a useful technology at all. Skepticism about egg freezing reflects a Luddite orientation in which new technologies are seen as inherently oppressive. This strand of technocritical feminism has a long history, emerging in the 1970s with the rise of second-wave feminism and then the birth of IVF, a technology that radical feminists immediately condemned as harmful.[12] Forty years on, technocritical feminist critiques are still quite reminiscent of those early anti-IVF screeds. Interestingly, today's technocritical feminists come primarily from my own field of anthropology and our sister discipline of sociology.[13] They argue that egg freezing is inherently oppressive, because it reinforces societal pronatalism, the formation of heteronormative family structures, and the imperative for women to become mothers to biogenetically related offspring. Egg freezing, they argue, also promotes unhealthy biomedical intervention into women's reproductive bodies, with the potential to induce bodily harm, now and in the future. Women who undergo egg freezing may also develop a false sense of security about their reproductive potential, when, in fact, egg freezing can provide no such future guarantees. Unwarranted technological optimism is thus being promoted by a for-profit fertility industry that is more interested in commercial exploitation than in women's health. Through false advertising, this industry has sold women a bill of goods, luring them onto "fertility vans" or inebriating them at egg freezing parties designed to dupe and dazzle.[14]

In my view, each of these feminist arguments does have some merit. But they also miss the most important point. A more accurate feminist critique, one based on the actual empirical realities of women's lives, would focus on the troubled nature of gender relations. As my own study shows, women turn to egg freezing not to participate in a reproductive revolution or to stop the biological clock for the sake of their careers or to submit their bodies naively and willingly to a for-profit fertility industry. Most real women are undertaking egg freezing today because of the mating gap—the absence of men as stable and committed reproductive partners. And until that significant gender problem is solved, educated American women will continue to pursue egg freezing as a prudent form of fertility preservation. Egg freezing for them is a technological solution to a gender problem that feminist critics have barely begun to consider.

In defending egg freezing against some of these more abstract feminist critiques, I am not arguing that egg freezing is an unambiguously positive technology. In my very first published opinion piece on egg freezing, written for *CNN Online*, I pointed out both positive and negative attributes of this technology, while also explaining why I might have used it (had it been available), given my own very difficult entrance into reproduction as a young professor.[15] Since then, with the empirical findings of this major egg freezing study behind me, I can now see how my earlier feminist assumptions about egg freezing as a career intervention were naive and how current feminist critiques of egg freezing are similarly off the mark. Only by appreciating women's real struggles to develop meaningful and committed reproductive relationships with men will we begin to be able to offer a compelling feminist critique, one that will resonate with egg freezing women themselves. It is the mating gap, not egg freezing, that women are largely upset about.

Egg Freezing's Reluctant Feminists

This disconnect between feminism and women's lived experiences is one of the reasons why many women in my study were reluctant to adopt the feminist label or to view egg freezing as a feminist technology. Just as egg freezing has engendered deep *feminist reluctance* in the scholarly community, women who turn to egg freezing are *reluctant feminists*. They tend to feel quite ambivalent about identifying with feminism or viewing egg freezing in feminist terms, even though, as we shall see, they associate egg freezing with significant empowerment.

Furthermore, just as feminist scholars have adopted four major stances toward egg freezing, three of them highly critical, women who freeze their eggs regard feminism in one of four different ways, three of which are ambivalent or dismissive. I learned this by asking two-thirds (64 percent) of the women in my study two questions: Do you consider yourself to be a feminist? And do you consider egg freezing to be a feminist technology? Women often had much to say, providing responses that were both thoughtful and persuasive.

Committed Feminists

The first group of women, comprising more than one-third (38 percent) of the total, were committed feminists, who were "absolutely" or "definitely" proud to claim the feminist title. Some women pointed to their own feminist mothers as their main influences and role models, the ones who had inspired them to view themselves as equal to men and capable in every way. Others attributed their feminism to their all-girls' high schools or women's colleges, where gender studies and feminist commitments were de rigueur. A nurse-midwife, Priscilla, laughed as she answered my question: "I mean, I went to a women's college. I will have my alumnae rights revoked if I don't say I'm a feminist!" But Priscilla also cautioned that the fight for gender equality was far from complete. The very term "feminism," she noted, is now deeply contested. "It's hard to know what that word means these days. But do I believe in women having control over their bodies and taking charge of their physical and life experiences? Absolutely!" This focus on women's bodily autonomy and control was reiterated by many other women, including Grace, who had left her position in the US Department of Health and Human Services to pursue a degree in health counseling. "Yes. I absolutely identify as a feminist. I am a huge advocate of gender equality and the movement away from patriarchal norms towards an egalitarian society, which I think would improve health and well-being for everyone. We need to do away with these damaging gender norms and socialization that traumatizes people."

Conflicted Feminists

A second group of women, about 15 percent, clearly believed in gender equality and expressed their feminist ideals. But they often answered my question, "Do you consider yourself to be a feminist?" with a "yes, but . . ." response, in which they attempted to qualify their feminist credentials. Violet, the engineering project manager in Silicon Valley mentioned earlier, was representative of this group of conflicted feminists. She believed in gender equality and was troubled by blatant sexism at work. But labeling herself as a feminist was more an outgrowth of her workplace experiences than an orientation to which she was firmly committed.

> There's so many meanings of "feminism." I think for me, I guess, I definitely want to empower women to have more choices and to not have to worry about societal pressures and things. So I guess you can call me a feminist that way. It also derives from the fact that I'm surrounded by so many men, all day, and listening to their comments and stuff, some of them just don't get it. . . . It's like, I want to be an equal. They just don't see it from my point of view, and I get very frustrated with these guys like that. So I guess I'm a feminist that way. Yeah, I'm a feminist, apparently.

Uncommitted Feminists

A third group of women, comprising nearly one-third (32 percent) of the total, did not feel encouraged to identify with the feminist label, often arguing that they were not part of any feminist movement or organization. But despite distancing themselves from feminism, these uncommitted feminists wanted gender equality and wished that feminist values were more mainstream. Their answers to my feminist question often took a "no, but . . ." form, in which they rejected the feminist label but then went on to explain their support for women's rights and "having it all." Many of these uncommitted feminists were clearly bothered by male privilege in the workplace, where, as one woman put it, "so many men are at the top." But they were also cautious about alienating men, including those who were their allies. Kayla, whose story opened this book, explained her concerns in this way:

> I don't think most of my friends, we don't want to be deemed feminists. None of us want to go to women-only events. I think women professionally do not help one another. And we work here in venture [capital]; it's an old boys' network. You have to be part of that old boys' network. You need men in your career to pull you through the ranks. . . . You just— you alienate yourselves, and you make men feel awkward, and I don't think you want to do that either. You have to figure out how to play, be a female in their world. Like, clearly, I want equal pay. I get really pissed off because I have much more experience than a lot of my male peers, and yet they seem to be the ones getting promotions to partner, even though they work half as hard as I do, and they're getting paid three times as much, because they have families. You see that sort of crap all the time. And you can't really do anything about it. So rather than complain about it, you just say, you know, it is what it is. So how do I make the most of what I'm doing?

Not Feminists

Fears of male alienation were also prominent among the final group of women, who comprised about 15 percent of the total. The word "feminism" for them had a very negative connotation. It was a "dirty word," one associated with "bra burners" and "man haters." Some of these women who were not feminists came from religious or cultural backgrounds that they identified as more "traditional." Others believed that their desires to marry and raise a family precluded any identification with feminism. For example, Chloe, a senior buyer at a California wine firm, was clear on this point. "Sometimes when I hear the word 'feminist,' I hear 'man hater' or something. And I actually love guys! I want to get married, have a husband, and have an amazing family. And so I don't see myself as a male hater or something."

Overall, only about one-third (38 percent) of the women I interviewed clearly identified with feminism. Almost two-thirds (62 percent) did not. But of the total, nearly half (48 percent) were what I would call *reluctant feminists*—women who did not immediately identify with the feminist label but still believed in gender equality and a woman's right to control her own body and her future. Although I was surprised by so many reluctant feminists, given my own long-standing feminist scholarly commitments, my study findings are in no way unusual. In fact, extensive research undertaken with Gen X and millennial women shows that most are reluctant to identify with feminism.[16] The term "feminism" for them sparks negative reactions, particularly of being a "radical" or a "man hater." The public declaration of feminism is also seen as carrying negative repercussions for women in the workplace, and feminism is perceived as contradicting normative femininity, including women's desires for heterosexual marriage and biological motherhood. Yet, even as Gen X and millennial women reject the feminist label, they still feel strongly entitled to gender equality and "having it all."

In other words, Gen X and millennial women, the two generations most represented in my study, feel great reluctance about feminism, while still wanting the gender equality that older generations of feminists have fought so hard for. As the sociologist Rosanna Hertz has argued in her book *Single by Chance, Mothers by Choice: How Women Are Choosing Parenthood without Marriage and Creating the New American Family* (2008), second-wave feminist achievements are now like "fluoride in the water" for younger generations of American women.[17] Feminism has provided the backdrop for these women's educational opportunities and professional successes. Yet it is no longer a "catalyst"—motivating most younger women to become revolutionary change agents in their reproductive lives and beyond.

Egg Freezing Empowerment

Given women's reluctance toward feminism, it is not surprising that views of egg freezing as a "feminist technology" are considerably divided. In my study, the majority of women were either opposed to the idea (44 percent) or unsure about it (13 percent). They often emphasized that egg freezing increases women's choices and gives them a measure of reproductive control. But they did not necessarily see egg freezing as a tool for women's advancement. Such views were expressed across the feminist spectrum, even among women who identified as committed feminists.

Mei, an academic dermatologist, was one of these women. She told me, "I am a feminist. I mean, I believe in equality. I believe in equal opportunity." But Mei then went on to explain why egg freezing for her could not be considered a feminist technology. "I actually don't think of egg freezing as a feminist tool or revolution. I don't. I think a lot of times it's women who ultimately want to get married, find happiness, have children, and are unable to find that person and are just doing the very prudent thing that is now available to them—well, to people who have the means. And I see it as very practical and a smart thing to do. But I don't necessarily think of it as a feminist thing. I don't think of it as a power-struggle tool."

Other women who were more conflicted about feminism often shared this view. Eva, a career diplomat in the US Foreign Service, argued that egg freezing could not be seen as a feminist technology because it serves a more "protective" role than a "proactive" purpose.

> I see feminism as when you want to proactively assert something in a feminine light and proactively assert your rights. I don't think this is a proactive thing. I think this is a protective thing. . . . I think it's something more natural and basic. I wouldn't relate it to feminism, I guess. I've thought of it at times like, it's something that can address women's needs because biologically we are just—we were dealt a different hand than men, which I hate, you know? But it's something that it's helping to make the situation a little more equal, giving us a little more power over our things that we can have power over.

Some of the strongest opinions came from women who were not feminists but who voiced positions interestingly reminiscent of the critical stances of feminist scholars. For example, Lucy, a nonprofit educational consultant who was also a practicing evangelical Christian, answered my feminist technology question with a resounding "No."

No, I mean, actually, pardon, frankly, it sounds like complete bullshit to me! And I think this is part of what is problematic to me and in my experience is, like, egg freezing's actually a pretty difficult and time-consuming and resource-intensive thing, you know, and we're all doing pretty complicated things to our bodies. . . . And I don't know. And the chances of it working out are not that great, right? So the notion that it's like, you know, some kind of breakthrough that everybody should be using and, you know, gives people more choices—like, yes, it gives people more choices, particularly people that are in a much worse situation than I am, right? Like, people who are going through cancer treatment, and that's obviously amazing and wonderful that that's available. . . . But I don't know. I almost feel like people are trying to sell women a good to, like, make it feel like, "Well, it's okay that we live in a society that's still not gender equitable, that still doesn't have affordable child care." You know? "It's okay we're still not terribly work-life friendly, because you can do this." And, like, I am worried that, like, it's going to become an expectation for women in some social group to where it's being oversold as, like, the solution, as opposed to dealing with the actual problem. So, not particularly, no. I mean, I just—I guess I felt a sense of accomplishment in that I learned how to do new things I hadn't been able to do before, like with the shots and stuff. It was pretty cool that I figured out how to do this well. And there is, like, something at the end that is, like, an actual thing [frozen eggs].

Lucy's rather bleak assessment of egg freezing was not shared by most women in my study. Nearly half (43 percent) of the women I interviewed agreed that egg freezing *is* a feminist tool, one that advances women's position by widening their reproductive choices. Most women, too, argued that egg freezing *is* empowering, because it helps women to take control of their reproductive lives in a way quite similar to birth control. This belief in *egg freezing empowerment* was widespread and shared by women across the feminist spectrum. For example, Cheryl, a pharmaceutical sales representative, laughed when she told me, "I'm not one of those burn-your-bra type people." But then she offered her positive view of egg freezing's empowering potential. "I think it does give women choices. And it gives you almost control of what you'd like to do, where you're not at the will of someone else, as far as just getting married prematurely, because you do want the marriage, the white picket fence, and the children. But then you don't choose as wisely because you're working against the clock, right? So egg freezing just gives a sense of empowerment."

Sasha, a legal professional, also had trouble with the feminist label but said, "even though, I mean, obviously, I model for equality and all that." Sasha believed that egg freezing could "level the playing field" in an era when men are no longer so committed to marriage and family-making.

It's being credited as important as the birth control pill. So I would say it could be revolutionary, and the reason I modify that is really because nothing's certain. There's not—I mean, it's not like a guarantee that if you freeze your eggs, you're going to have a baby. And so I think it's awesome that this technology exists and that women don't have to feel like their time has passed, because especially in this day and age, men are less commitment-minded than they were thirty years ago. . . . Men are just, you know, not getting married until later and later. But it's hard for the women who are in the same age group and really want to have a child, and they feel like maybe their window's closing. And this just gives them a playing field that's equal, possibly, to men. So the women I talked to, I kind of feel the same way that they did. They felt like empowered and hopeful. I would say those would be good words to describe how I've felt, too. Because I just wanted the chance, especially if I met someone and he wanted to have children, I wanted to still—I didn't want to close a door.

Theresa, a health care management executive, told me that she came from "a very strong lineage of women who were always told you can do whatever you want to put your mind to." Theresa argued that egg freezing was empowering for women who, in previous generations, would never have been able to reproduce.

I mean, I definitely think of the word "empowering," because I think it gives women the ability to have children a little bit later in life, when they wouldn't have been able to—so empowering from the perspective that they still have the ability to have children later in life, whereas women didn't have that ability before. And it allows women, I think, the choice factor, whether to have them later or to have them without necessarily having to have a partner. And I love the fact that lesbian women now have the option of having children, which is phenomenal.

Brenda, a psychologist who had majored in gender studies in college, called herself a committed feminist, although "maybe less of an active feminist" as she has "gotten older." Brenda went on to articulate egg freezing's feminist potential, as a tool for empowerment on both a personal and societal level.

> I definitely feel like it is a technology that gives women more choices. And I do think that that's the best part of feminism, you know. Across whatever area of their life, giving them more choices is like the best of what feminism is about. So, yeah, I guess it does resonate with me. And when thinking about the experience [of egg freezing], when I started, I was like, "I'm really not sure. This seems totally overwhelming and kind of crazy and whatever." And then kind of going step by step and getting through it in a very positive way. Honestly, I'm not sure that I would be living here now in DC if I hadn't frozen my eggs, because, even though that's kind of indirect, it was kind of that combination of like—it gave me a real sense of empowerment, I think, and that translated into making other really large decisions in my life that I had been percolating but that I hadn't really acted on. Once you get it moving, things kind of tend to fall into place, but it's like, making that decision and deciding to act is sometimes the hardest part. And I felt like the sort of empowered feeling that I got from going through the egg freezing process just kind of carried over into other parts of my life. It was empowering for me. It was *very* empowering for me.

Brenda's feelings of personal empowerment were shared by the majority of women in my study. "Power," "empowering," and "empowerment" were three of the most common words that ran through women's narratives. Egg freezing, they told me, made them feel agentive, of doing something "for themselves" and within their "own powers." Egg freezing allowed them to "take control" of their fertility and "invest" in their future as mothers. Egg freezing also provided them with powerful psychological relief, reducing the tremendous pressure that they felt over having to find a partner in a hurry. Once they had frozen their eggs, women felt calmer about their dating lives, without having to constantly worry about running out of time and scaring away men who might become fearful of a woman's reproductive panic and obsession.

Overall, women's assessments of egg freezing were overwhelmingly positive: 93 percent of women in my study expressed one or more measures of happiness, gratitude, pride, relief, and comfort for having undertaken egg freezing, even if they did not enjoy the clinical process itself. Most women were deeply satisfied with their decisions, offering a virtual outpouring of positive sentiments regarding egg freezing and its benefits. These are recorded in detail in table 7.1, where they are listed accorded to the major categories of satisfaction articulated by women in this study. Women perceived egg freezing as giving them choices and options; increasing their control and decision-making; empowering them; providing insurance and safety; preventing future regrets; providing them with psychological relief; facilitating their relationships; allowing them to invest in themselves; creating a sense of success; promoting their technological optimism; and extending their reproductive time.

By reading through the lengthy lexicon in table 7.1, we can truly begin to appreciate egg freezing's importance for women on both an emotional and tangible level. In fact, I would argue that egg freezing, once completed, is characterized by another set of *three e's*: *enthusiasm*, *endorsement*, and *empowerment*. Given women's positive assessments, it is almost impossible to accept the feminist critique that egg freezing is inherently bad for women. Egg freezing women themselves would most definitely disagree. Their lexicon is a heartfelt testament to what egg freezing benefits mean to women, who stated their hopes and satisfactions in more than two hundred different ways.

TABLE 7.1. Egg Freezing Benefits: Women's Lexicon of Positive Assessments

Category	Positive assessments (in alphabetical order)
Choices and options	Adding to a pile of options
	Advances women's ability to have as many choices as possible
	Allows for more choices
	Backup option
	Backup plan
	Choice to decide
	Exercised that right
	Fantastic option
	Feeling I have options
	Gives women a choice
	Giving myself options
	Having an option
	Leaving the option open
	Maximizing different options
	More options

Category	Positive assessments (in alphabetical order)
	Opportunity
	Opportunity of maybe having kids
	Optimizing choice
	Option of using them if I find somebody
	Preserve the possibility
	Privilege more women should have
	Still have this option
Control and decision-making	Contingency plan
	Control of situation
	Done something while life is working itself out
	In charge of my destiny
	Kind of family planning
	Not forcing me to make a decision right now
	Puts you back in the driver's seat
	Really proactive
	Right decision
	Right thing for me
	Right thing to do
	Taking charge of my situation
	Taking control back
	Taking fertility and future into your own hands
	Took control of my fertility
	Wasn't the victim anymore
Empowerment	Emotionally empowering
	Empowered me to feel like life wasn't happening to me
	Empowered me to fight for the family I don't yet have
	Empowering
	Empowering for family
	Empowering for men and women
	Empowers women
	Liberating
	Made me feel empowered
	Really empowering
	Sense of empowerment
	Sense of empowerment and agency
	Their mere existence [frozen eggs] is so powerful
	Very empowered
	Weirdly empowering
	Wildly empowering
Insurance and safety	Creating an extensive insurance policy for having a family someday
	Grateful they're available if needed
	Helps insure future pregnancy

(Continued)

TABLE 7.1. (*cont.*)

Category	Positive assessments (in alphabetical order)
	If needed, nice to be there
	Insurance
	Insurance policy
	I've got these things in my back pocket, or ten things
	Just an insurance
	Magical thing in my back pocket
	Pretty great insurance policy
	Protective
	Prudent
	Put away for safekeeping
	Safety net
	Security
	Something in the bank
	Something to fall back on
	To be on the safe side
Preventing regret	At a point where I don't want to have regrets in life
	At least I did everything I could
	At least I tried everything
	Better safe than sorry
	Don't want to foreclose having a kid
	Don't want to have missed the boat
	Don't want to regret
	No regrets
	Not closing doors
	Prevent regret
	Zero regrets
Psychological relief	Alleviating stress
	Almost immediate relief
	Amazing how much it takes off your mind
	Big relief
	Bit of my own pressure off
	Bit of relaxing
	Breathing room
	Certain calm and comfort
	Closed off that hole in my life
	Comfort that it's there
	Don't have to agonize
	Don't have to worry about ovaries wasting away
	Easing my anxieties
	Eliminating grief and worry

Category	Positive assessments (in alphabetical order)
	Feel absolutely zero pressure
	Feel calm
	Feeling relaxed
	Feel so much better
	Feel so much less anxiety
	Gives me a little bit of relief
	Huge peace of mind
	Huge relief
	Huge weight off my shoulders
	Little bit of a deep breath
	Little bit spiritual
	Made me feel better
	No shame
	Not pressuring myself
	Peace of mind
	Relief of all the heartache and stress
	Relieved of anxiety
	Sense of calm
	Sense of relief
	So relieved and so happy
	Takes any and all pressure off the table
	Takes away anxiety
	Takes pressure off
	Taking worry off the table
	Took the weight off my shoulders
	Unclenching
Relationships	Almost feel kind of bad for guys—"we really don't need you!"
	Better relationship decisions
	Choose the right partner at the right moment
	Clarity in dating life
	Don't have to compromise
	Don't have to feel like I'm in a desperate situation
	Giving back control of my dating life and love life
	Good for men, too
	Makes men and women a little more equal
	Not settling to have a baby
	Prevent bad choices

(Continued)

Table 7.1. (*cont.*)

Category	Positive assessments (in alphabetical order)
	Takes pressure off dating
	Take the time to meet someone
	Wonderful for people who are not in a relationship
Self-investment	Best decision I ever made
	Doing it for my future
	Doing it for myself
	Doing the right thing for myself
	For my own personal self
	For nobody else but me
	Helping me a little bit
	Investment in my future
	Investment in myself
	Investment in myself contributing to my self-esteem
	Journey of self-discovery
	Kick off the rest of my life
	Leaving myself opportunities
	Long-term investment
	Money well spent
	My thing
	One of the best investments I ever made
	Part of health maintenance
	Proud of myself
	Put myself first in life
	Really proud of myself
	Taking care of myself
	Trying to invest in some part of my future
	Worth it to me
	Worthwhile investment
Sense of success	Best chance of success
	Definitely glad
	Do it again in a heartbeat
	Done something so good and positive
	Ecstatic
	Elated every day doing it
	Extraordinary privilege
	Extremely glad I did it
	Feel good about it

Category	Positive assessments (in alphabetical order)
	Glad I did it
	Happy with outcome
	Have that little basket
	Incredibly positive experience
	My future unborn children
	One of the best things I've ever done
	One of the greatest blessings of my life
	Positive experience
	Quite happy
	Quite positive
	Really just pleased
	Really lucked out
	So grateful and just appreciative
	That was great
	Through-the-roof happy
	Very glad
	Very happy
	Very pleased
	Well worth it
	Wonderful happy time
Technological optimism	Amazing
	Awesome that egg freezing exists
	Change life as we know it
	Excited for women to embrace this technology
	Extraordinary
	Fabulous
	Fortunate that the technology came out
	Given a gift
	Great technology
	Gung-ho attitude
	Incredible
	Love it
	Lucky to live in an age where this is an option
	Practical technology
	Rewards far greater than risks
	Thankful that I can do it
	Very lucky it was an option
	Wonderful thing now available

(Continued)

TABLE 7.1. (*cont.*)

Category	Positive assessments (in alphabetical order)
Timing	Bit more control over time frame
	Bought myself time
	Buys a little time
	Don't have sense of anxiety that I need to get married like yesterday
	Don't have to worry about the biological clock
	Don't need to rush
	Giving myself more time
	Hopefully extend the clock a little bit
	Keep the hope alive longer
	No rush to find a partner
	No rush to make a bad decision
	Pause button on the body
	Took the pressure off my limited fertility

Egg Freezing Activists

Given this virtual outpouring of positive sentiments, it is not surprising that some women go on to become egg freezing activists. Judith, whose story began this chapter, was what I would call a "behind-the-scenes" activist, in that as an early adopter of egg freezing, she saw the need for this technology in her own life and then worked to make egg freezing more accessible to other women in the tech industry. Kendra, too, was a behind-the-scenes activist in her workplace, where she fought to make egg freezing completely available to employees of her international reproductive health organization. But Kendra also went on to became an outspoken advocate for egg freezing, employing Instagram and Facebook to become a social media spokesperson for egg freezing in her Black professional community. Although Kendra had clearly distanced herself from mainstream White feminism, she displayed the kind of "badass feminist politics" that some authors are attributing to a new generation of feminists and their forward-thinking communication and activist agendas.[18]

Like Kendra, nine other women in my study demonstrated badass feminism by becoming public egg freezing activists largely on their own terms. These women's methods were varied, but their major goals were to make egg freezing more visible, understandable, accessible, and beneficial to other women. Two of these women pursued egg freezing start-up ideas, including one whose award-winning MBA project became a successful venture to introduce egg freezing protocols into private clinics and then assign a "good housekeeping seal of approval" to clinics demonstrating best practices in patient-centered care. Another woman, who was an academic physician, decided to promote egg freezing as a health educator. She assembled recent studies on egg freezing into an accessible packet of online materials, which she then distributed to her friends and acquaintances, encouraging them to pass it on to others who might be interested. Three women worked as radio, newspaper, and magazine journalists and began publishing human-interest stories about egg freezing, drawing on their own experiences and interviews with experts, including me. One woman who worked as a sales director at a small publishing firm began blogging about her own egg freezing experiences. Eventually she cofounded an egg freezing podcast, for which I was again interviewed. Then she published a small book for women on how to make the most informed egg freezing decisions, a book that I was asked to endorse. Finally, two women were filmmakers, who began posting about their egg freezing experiences through blogs and vlogs. Again, I became involved in their projects, in one as an interviewee and in the other as an appreciative fan.

In the final case, Jenni (her real name, used with her permission) was the first woman I ever met who had frozen her eggs. Her enthusiastic involvement in egg freezing and the eventual production of a film provided a major impetus for my own study. Over the years, we have stayed in touch, and I was able to fly to Los Angeles for the premiere of her egg freezing documentary, *Chill*, at a Los Angeles women's film festival. There, this talented, multiracial (Black and Filipino) actor-producer also took questions from an appreciative audience, including young women potentially interested in egg freezing.

Looking back, when I first met Jenni, she had just broken up, calling herself the "queen of three-year relationships," one whose "picker might be broken." But, in a most happy turn of events, Jenni, then forty, met one of those rare Angeleno "unicorns," a man named Ari, whom she married in a beautiful Jewish wedding. Without having to use her frozen eggs, Jenni and Ari went on to become parents of a stunning baby boy named Remy. As of this writing, gorgeous Remy is now three years old, and Jenni's frozen eggs are still in storage—the "backup plan" in place for a second child.

It is these kinds of happy endings that need to be told, as they prove that auspicious outcomes do sometimes happen for egg freezing women. Not all women's stories end with a film, a wedding, and a baby. But most women find egg freezing to be well worth the struggle, as they dream about and sometimes birth their frozen egg babies.

8

The Banked and Thawed

From Frozen Eggs to Egg Babies

Hannah's Egg Baby

Like most women in my study, Hannah could only be described as a high achiever. The US-born daughter of a Canadian oil executive, Hannah had lived around the world before attending a top US liberal arts college and earning a degree from an Ivy League law school. Taking her first job in international management consulting, Hannah eventually made her way to DC to work for a US president. But what distinguished Hannah most to me was her enthusiasm for egg freezing and her subsequent eagerness to participate in my study. When I asked Hannah to share her egg freezing story, she launched in with gusto.

> I was really excited to talk to you about this! Because I found it, like my personal experience with it, was so wildly empowering! I was probably like, I guess, thirty-six going towards thirty-seven and like had been starting to get pretty anxious about family and kids, and "What am I doing?" and "I think I want a family, but how do I do that?" But, you know, I didn't feel prepared at that time, because I didn't want one by myself. And I had mentioned to my OB/GYN when I was just there for an annual checkup, "Gosh, I'm sort of worried about this. It's an issue. How do I think about it?" And she's like, "Well, you know you can get your eggs frozen." And obviously I had heard about it in passing maybe five years before or something, but I heard it was pretty experimental, didn't work pretty well, you really have to freeze an embryo, blah blah blah. And she's like, "No, the technology's really changing. It's available now, and there's a great place that does it, and here's the address." I was like, "Oh, wow, great!" So information presented itself to me in an incredible form at a moment when I, like, was really receptive to it. And so then particularly

because I was thirty-six going on thirty-seven and they sort of recommend you get it done before thirty-eight, I started to move. I looked into it and started to move pretty quickly.

In less than a year, Hannah completed three egg freezing cycles in rapid succession, for reasons that she explained to me.

I didn't have a partner to do it with. So egg freezing just allowed me to have an option, which is great. The thing that then became a bit of a dance with it was, you know, how many eggs then do you freeze? If it's not an insurance policy but you're then saying it's your whole plan, you know, how many cycles do you do? How many eggs do you freeze to feel comfortable that if you want to have two kids, you'll have that option? And because I didn't really have a reproductive history, because I never tried to get pregnant before, I really didn't know, you know. So you're freezing these eggs, unlike when they freeze embryos, you know, they can tell pretty quickly in a couple of days when they freeze real embryos, four, five cells or whatever, if the embryos are good. With eggs, they just really don't know. Like, they can tell if they're really bad, I guess, is what my doctor indicated to me. But they can't really tell how much success you're going to have when you unfreeze them and try to undo that. So then you get into crazy math around like, "Okay, well you lose X percent in the freezing and like Y percent in the defrosting, and then you have this kind of risk rate, and then does it pay?" So I ended up doing three cycles, which in hindsight . . . was probably way, way too many eggs in storage at this point. But, you know, that was life.

With thirty-two eggs now in storage, Hannah reflected on the many ways in which this experience had improved her morale and general outlook on life.

My net on the experience, though, was it's so emotionally empowering, right? Because I went from a state of sort of panicked, that I was probably, like, in denial of and trying desperately not to have, to all of a sudden, I'm in control of this situation. Like, as I talked to my friends about it while I was doing this, I felt like, "This is revolutionary like the invention of birth control, in terms of giving people, empowering people to have their life and have choices and all the rest of it." And so I was able to make plans in my own head and stuff like, "Hey, if I don't find the right guy in X number of years, I'll make sure I'm in a financial position and I'm in a professional position where I can have kids, so that's a real option for me. If I find the right guy, then I can do this." It's extraordinary, right? Because it really was. It, like, puts you back in the driver's seat versus someone's who's sort of, I mean . . . I suppose without egg freezing and if I really had my act together, I could have been planning to figure out how to be a single mom at thirty-eight or, you know, forty. But I was not. At thirty-seven, I was not psychologically, financially, or professionally prepared for it. Psychologically, that's where I was and what I sort of needed to get where I needed to be, I guess [laughs]. . . . But again, the whole process ended up being weirdly empowering, but it also made me sort of very, um, very aware of how challenging it is for plenty of people to have a baby. And again, I'm really lucky. I had sort of the financial resources so I could be like, "Oh yeah, this is a great way to spend $30,000" [laughs]. . . . But, oh, it was well worth it! It was extraordinary. You know, $30,000 and like four years of therapy might have gotten me to a similar point. Like, it basically gave me back a sense that I could make choices for the next six, seven years of my life with a plan. I wasn't sort of dependent on either finding a mystery partner or having a baby by myself immediately. And that was pretty extraordinary. Again, it's like, ah, those are privileged people problems, but still, it's a real solution to that.

Although recognizing her own privilege, Hannah admitted that coming up with the full $30,000 in a matter of months had been quite challenging. With her government job, she had not been "rolling in cash," nor were her parents, who nonetheless helped her out financially.

I had been talking to my mom throughout the process and talking out loud, "Do I do a third cycle? And here are the pros and the cons." And she showed up and said, "Well, let us help." Actually, she personally wanted to cover it for me. Like, a lot of her Social Security, she just cashed it in to do that, because I think she had seen how much it sort of mattered to me. And they certainly had not ever been the type of parents to be like, "Oh, your sister has had three kids." They don't feel like I need to have grandchildren for them. I think this just came from, you know, sort of wanting to be supportive and seeing the way the process was impacting me. So yeah. I think they wrote a check for like $5,000 or something.

Hannah was also accompanied to two of the egg retrievals by her mother and to the third one by a friend. Hannah undertook the rest of the egg freezing procedures on her own, including the difficult trigger shots.

You know, it's the *Pulp Fiction* movie, right? Where they like slam the needle into her chest [*laughs*]. Like, I do have a very visceral and vivid memory of the first time I did the trigger injection. And it was like—there was an important dinner I had to be at or something. So I basically had to go, you know. And they only tell you a day in advance exactly what time you need to do the trigger injection. So I'm in the bathroom of this really fancy restaurant, in a stall! And this was the first one I did. I was like, "All right, here we go! Yep, right on into the spot!"

With three trigger shots behind her (literally and figuratively) and nearly three dozen eggs in storage, Hannah's life began to head in new directions. Egg freezing, as she described it, had "freed her up" to make different choices. One of them was to abandon DC's stuffy online dating scene.

I have always talked to my friends about how I would be really excited about a "passionate plumber," I think was my phrase. Like, give me someone who is like engaged in life and whatever he loves to do. I would be totally into that. But the search process, you know, when you're in your online dating website, the screening costs are so high that it's just so much easier to be like, "Well, where did you go to school and where do you work?" And go on those criteria. So that's what I did for all the online dating, because having to figure out over a dinner, you know—this might all be about my lack of imagination, you know—but having to really figure out if this guy is your passionate plumber, or is he just, you know, another guy, slightly less well educated than I am.

Hannah made an even bolder move by quitting her job in DC and joining a four-month, transcontinental bike tour.

I had had a lot of time as I went through both the egg freezing process and everything else associated with it and the training for the trip to really reflect on what I wanted and who I was and what I was looking for. I think having the time and space on this bike trip to really get to know who someone was was a real privilege. And what was amazing for the trip was that it felt like you really get to see who people were, right? This is not some fancy bullshit over a really nice dinner in a DC restaurant. It's like, "How does somebody actually behave after they've cycled eighty miles in the desert and are trying to put up their tent in a windstorm?" And you get to see who people really are.

The person who caught Hannah's attention was Lucas, a West Coast firefighter. In addition to being impressively fit, Lucas was helpful and kind, caring for Hannah when she contracted a giardia infection from contaminated drinking water. "He's a sort of extraordinarily patient and generous and brave man," Hannah told me. "And it was just easy then to sort of trust him and fall in love with him, and it really was quite special. It was really neat. He's a good guy. He's a *really* good guy."

After the bike trip ended, Lucas returned home, "packed up his puppy," drove cross-country to Hannah's, and never left. Hannah was thrilled, after working through some initial trepidation.

You know, I was really, really nervous to introduce him to my friends, because all my friends in DC—I mean, which is all my own issues, right?—my friends in DC are extraordinarily loving and thoughtful people who were so excited to meet this incredible man in my life. But they all went to like Harvard Law School or Yale Law School or wherever, right? And so I was really uptight about it until I realized it was all my own issues. But when I got back from the bike ride, I had to unpack and work through a fair bit of, like, that anxiety again, which mostly is me carrying it around because years of a bit of a model of like, "Oh yeah, I'm going to marry this kind of guy."

With her friends' love and support and her own mental recalibration, Hannah and Lucas's relationship soared. Hannah took a job in a small town outside New York City, a place where she could "downshift" her heavy workload and reduce her amount of business travel. Lucas also began retooling his job skills, as well as their bikes, so that they could enjoy the area's verdant back roads together on their weekend rides.

Only a few months after their move, Hannah learned that she was pregnant. When I spoke to her for my study, she had just turned forty and had delivered her baby daughter, now two weeks old.

It's been great! It's been really great. The whole thing has been quite a whirlwind! In February, we found out we were pregnant, and we looked at each other and we're like, "This is supposed to happen in June at the earliest" [*laughs*]. It caught us a little—again, I mean, it's weird trying—but it caught us off guard. Because I read all the fertility stuff, and I read, "Oh, maybe six months, maybe a year, maybe we're going to need to do IVF, and there'll be big drama." And so, yeah, not so much. We're lucky. Just lucky, yeah.

When I established with Hannah that no frozen eggs had been used in her daughter's conception, she went on to tell me what she planned to do with those eggs in storage.

This is where the other privileges of the frozen eggs come in. If we didn't have those, I think we would both feel if we want another child, we need to make that call within a year, versus like some of our other goals for the future and what we want to save for and what we want to do and things like that. Which, for me professionally, for me physically, for us, like still a relatively young and close couple, I don't think that would be great. We would do it if that was our only choice if we wanted to have another kid. But having the eggs frozen really means we can be like, "Yeah, let's have one in two and a half years, three years." So it's another sort of privileged perk of that.

Overall, Hannah wanted to express how much her egg freezing decision had changed her life for the better.

I feel very, very lucky. And I mean, again, a piece of it was it worked out, because psychologically, I had the faith to allow it to work out. It was sort of an unclenching that came as a result of the whole process, right? So, one, there was a bit of a relaxing, and then there was another piece of freezing the eggs [that] was a recognition of like, "Okay, my plan when I was twenty or my expectation of my life when I was in college was that I would sort of, you know, grow up and meet a nice guy, go to grad school, get married, and then we would have kids in my early thirties, okay?" That kept getting like, "Wait, why am I not and all my other friends get to be on this path? Why am I not on this path?" And the process of egg freezing I think for me was also a sort of my life isn't necessarily going to follow the "normal" path or what I expected. It can follow whatever path I want, and I'm going to choose one. And I think that psychological shift as well opened up a lot of, you know—it wasn't just around freezing the eggs; it was around how I built and structured the rest of my life. And the freezing the eggs was sort of fundamental to that psychologically. Again, it was almost a kind of peace of mind, like, having the eggs is nice, you know. And if I really wanted to have a kid at forty-five, there are only so many different ways I could do it if eggs weren't frozen. So, if my own eggs were frozen—so that's for bonus points that they are my own eggs—but there's something psychologically about being able to take control, right? And not only over your own fertility, but also it felt like I was given back control of my dating life and love life, because I didn't have to, like, figure it out on the first day if this was a guy who needed to be the father of my children. I could take time and invest in myself and choose to date or not date. It gave me that flexibility on both those fronts, absolutely. . . . So I'd recommend it quickly and easily to anyone, you know, who had the appropriate, you know, who was in a circumstance where they may have to spend [money]. But, yeah, yeah, I just feel it's been an extraordinary privilege that I'm so grateful to have had, and again the options it has created for me, even without having to use them. Their mere existence is so powerful, although you know, [Lucas] trembles every time the checks come in to keep them frozen [*laughs*]! Like, now it's like, because I did three rounds, it's like $1,500 a year to maintain them, and they charge every cycle separately. So it's not a cheap insurance policy to hold for a long period of time. But, yeah, I would do it again in a heartbeat. I got very lucky that it was an option.

* * *

Exactly three years later, I heard from Hannah with more exciting news.

HANNAH: Since I spoke with you (after birth of our first, conceived naturally), we've actually used the eggs. I gave birth to our second child in May.

MARCIA: That is just terrific news! So your second child (son or daughter?) is a "frozen-egg baby"? If so, then I think that you are one of the first in the study! So happy for you.

HANNAH: Yes, he is an "egg baby"!

Egg Freezing Ideals

I chose Hannah's story to begin this final chapter because in many ways, her egg freezing journey represents the "ideal," incorporating the kinds of experiences and outcomes that most women in my study hoped for. Hannah was quite typical of the egg freezing demographic, as a highly educated, successful, professional woman who wanted to become a mother but lacked a male partner with whom to form a family. Teetering on the edge of her late-thirties fertility cliff, Hannah was lucky to meet a female gynecologist who initiated the egg freezing conversation. Immediately receptive, Hannah viewed egg freezing as a viable "solution" to her dilemma. Hannah's family also pitched in, lending her their emotional, physical, and financial support. As a result, Hannah banked an enviable number of eggs, without experiencing any notable side effects (other than the initial *Pulp Fiction* terror of the trigger shots).

For Hannah, the egg freezing experience itself was exceptionally uplifting. She expressed more positive sentiments than perhaps any other woman in my study and for a multitude of reasons. Hannah felt that egg freezing had given her increased choices and options, improved control and decision-making, feelings of empowerment and insurance, psychological relief, a sense of self-investment in a successful outcome, technological optimism, and facilitation of her romantic relationship, partly through the extension of her reproductive timing.

By "unclenching" her reproductive anxieties, egg freezing provided Hannah with a temporal reprieve, one that allowed her to relax while still looking for that "mystery man." She found him on a bicycle journey, one that would have never happened if she had stayed within her comfort zone. Hannah and Lucas were certainly a "mixed-collar" match—an East Coast, Ivy League–trained lawyer and a West Coast, state-college-educated firefighter. But Hannah quickly realized that she had met an extraordinary person, a man who was patient, generous, brave, and special in every way.

Lucas, for his part, had no anxieties about committing to Hannah. He was ready to spend his life with her and become the father of their children. Within a year of being together and within only two months of trying, Hannah and Lucas became pregnant the "natural" way, with Hannah giving birth to their daughter at the age of forty. Hannah's frozen eggs were then available for their second child. Having the eggs frozen allowed them to space the births, while also meeting Hannah's internal mother-hood deadline of age forty-five.

In all of these ways, Hannah was a true *egg freezing beneficiary*, a woman for whom the technology worked exceptionally well. Hannah achieved the *egg freezing ideal*—namely, a successful egg freezing journey without complications, a large number of eggs placed safely in cold storage, a future romance that became a stable partnership, a natural pregnancy and delivery, and then a frozen *egg baby* as her second child at the age of forty-three.

But embedded in between the lines of Hannah's story are other possible trajectories, including ones that often make egg freezing veer off this ideal course. First of all, Hannah's story speaks to the uncertainty of numbers. To be more specific, she was quite unsure of how many egg freezing cycles were truly called for, so she ended up undertaking three at a high cost to herself and her family. Then, when thirty-two eggs were safely stored, she wondered if there were too many for her needs, especially after she met Lucas and became pregnant without difficulty.

A second concern for Hannah had to do with frozen eggs versus frozen embryos (with donor sperm) and whether the latter were a better bet. She felt more reassured about egg freezing after speaking with her gynecologist. But she knew that some IVF physicians encouraged women to freeze both, assuming that frozen embryos would yield a superior chance of pregnancy.

Third, Hannah realized that if she could not find a partner, she would need to use donor sperm to make a baby. Becoming a single mother was Hannah's plan B, one that would require some serious financial and logistical planning. Having frozen eggs in storage would give her more time to prepare herself well for this eventuality. When the time came, she could then use her own eggs rather than donor eggs if she found herself infertile. For these reasons alone, Hannah considered the "mere existence" of frozen eggs to be powerful, allowing her to hold open the possibility of mothering a biogenetically related child.

Finally, Hannah wondered about the eventual disposition of her frozen eggs. How many eggs would be lost in the thaw? And because she had stored so many eggs, what would she do if they were no longer needed? This became an issue when the annual $1,500 bill for storage came rolling in, making Hannah and Lucas reassess this pricey long-term proposition.

Hannah's questions about egg cycles, egg counts, egg storage, egg thawing, egg donation, and egg disposition are ones that all women who freeze their eggs must ponder. Eggs, once frozen, are viewed by women as precious assets—the very substance of their future unborn children. Yet, as we will see, frozen eggs are no guarantee, leaving women to worry about whether they have banked enough eggs to produce a future child.

Post-banking, women also contemplate whether they should pursue pregnancy on their own using donor sperm.[1] Furthermore, women must decide post-banking whether they should keep, donate, or destroy any unused frozen eggs and at what point. Those who end up meeting a new partner, as well as those who decide to become a mother on their own, may end up thawing all of their frozen eggs, but to no avail, feeling disappointed, even despondent over a costly endeavor that did not come to fruition.

Ultimately, Hannah was one of the lucky ones, a woman who found a loving partner and became a mother of two children, one of them a precious egg baby. But, as we will see, such children conceived and born from frozen eggs are not the most common outcome of women's egg freezing journeys. A decade on, most frozen eggs remain in cold storage, with pregnancy and disposition outcomes that are yet to unfold.[2] In other words, although egg freezing has taken off, most women, especially single women, have not returned to use their frozen eggs, for reasons we will now explore.

Egg Cycles and Counts

How many cycles? How many eggs? These are questions that all women embarking on egg freezing must ultimately address. Unfortunately, there are no easy answers to these questions. The number of eggs produced in any given cycle is highly dependent on a woman's age and her remaining ovarian reserve. In fact, research shows that age is the main predictive factor for the number of eggs produced and for becoming a mother using those eggs, or what is referred to in the clinical literature as the chance of a "live birth outcome."[3]

But what is a sufficient number of frozen eggs to make a baby? One of the most important studies shows that women ages thirty-four, thirty-seven, and forty-two would need to freeze ten, twenty, and sixty-one eggs, respectively, to achieve a 75 percent chance of at least one live birth.[4] The same study shows that a thirty-four-year-old woman with twenty frozen eggs would have a 66 percent chance of achieving two live births, making egg freezing in the early to midthirties and a total of twenty eggs seem ideal. However, most women are already in their late thirties by the time they undertake egg freezing, and very few of them are able to produce twenty eggs in a single cycle. Thus, knowing how many eggs to expect and whether additional cycles are needed (and worth the cost) becomes a difficult decision for many women.

One of the IVF physicians I interviewed spoke at length about this issue. He explained how he and his colleagues had used their existing clinical data to develop practice guidelines and a financial package designed to assist women confronting these very difficult questions.

> From what we see, if you're under thirty-eight . . . at least 70 to 80 percent of the group should have one child, if you reach fifteen to twenty eggs. That's what our thaw data looks like. . . . So we recommend people freeze fifteen to twenty mature eggs. And we want people to get to that number, because then 70 to 80 percent of women should go home with at least one baby. So we kind of design our financial programs around that. . . . We created this program where we realize that the average person gets thirteen mature eggs per cycle. So, if you need to get to twenty mature eggs, how the numbers fall out: 20 percent got there in one cycle, 45 percent needed two cycles, 25 percent needed three, and a little less than 10 percent needed a fourth cycle in order to get to twenty mature eggs. And we share that with everyone, because we want to be transparent about it, have the expectations about it. Because thirteen mature eggs is our average number, and that's kind of a large data set. And we appreciate, when we start going about that, it's difficult for people to make decisions. It can't be this open-ended financial endeavor for them. They have to be able to afford this. . . . So we created this program that—not everyone elects to be in it, but it's truly designed for people's best interest. So it's $12,500, and it covers four cycles or twenty eggs, whichever comes first. . . . If you need two, three, or four cycles, you're automatically ahead with this program. It's essentially to contain their cost, so they know if they're going into it, this is what I'm looking at. That will cover me to make sure I get to a spot where at least from my perspective people are going to do very well. The medications are not part of the program. Meds cost somewhere between

$3,000 and $5,000 per cycle. So that's a variable cost in there. But they can at least put their arms around it, because it's hard to make these decisions.

Per this IVF physician's remarks, only 20 percent of the clinic's patients were able to produce twenty frozen eggs in a single cycle. In my own study, only 12 percent of women were able to do so. Not surprisingly, the relatively few women who did reach an egg count of at least twenty on the first try tended to be the most satisfied with their egg freezing experiences and outcomes. For them, egg freezing was a one-time, one-month, intensive affair, but one that ended with positive feelings and tangible results. Bethany, an international banking attorney, was one of these lucky women. Although she had already reached the age of thirty-nine when she decided to freeze her eggs, her ovarian reserve was still quite good, and she produced twenty mature eggs in a single cycle.

Ah, it was really great! It was not the most comfortable for me towards the end. I was like, "We gotta get these things out of me!" But when I went, they were like, "For your age, you have the amount of eggs of someone ten years younger." And so she said, "I think this really is going to be a positive experience for you." So I was really encouraged just to be told how many eggs I had. I mean, this was all new to me. I was completely ignorant, never given any thought about how many eggs I might be producing. . . . I know that there're people that it's seared into their brain, this process. It's not seared into mine. But every time I went in, they were like this, "It's great! You look good!" It's like, once they took the eggs, I just moved on with my life. I mean, I shouldn't assume, but I assume I had a pretty positive experience.

Although most women in my study were not as sanguine as Bethany, their overall experiences and outcomes were quite positive. Women's *egg counts*, or the number of eggs they had stored by the time of their interviews, ranged from one to fifty-five, with an average of eighteen. Although most women in my study were already in their late thirties (average of 36.6 years) by the time they froze their eggs, their egg counts were well within the desirable range mentioned by the IVF physician. As shown in table 8.1, more than half (55 percent) of women in my study had banked sixteen eggs or more by the time of their interviews.

TABLE 8.1. Women's Egg Freezing Cycles and Banked Eggs

Characteristics	No.	%
Age at egg freezing		
25–29	1	<1
30–34	19	17
35–39	83	73
>40	11	10
Total	*114*	*100*
No. of egg freezing cycles		
1	65	57
2	35	31
3	10	9
>3	4	3
Total	*114*	*100*
Total no. of eggs banked		
<5	7	6
5–10	25	22
11–15	20	17
16–20	25	22
21–25	18	16
26–30	7	6
31–35	6	5
36–40	3	3
>40	3	3
Total	*114*	*100*

However, as also shown in table 8.1, nearly half (43 percent) of the women in my study required more than one cycle in order to achieve these results. And some women strained, both physically and financially, to achieve a desired count. In fact, nearly one-fifth (19 percent) of the women in my study faced disappointing results at the end of their first egg freezing cycle, with egg counts in the one- to nine-egg range but generally between three and seven. Women were especially upset when the number of eggs retrieved was less than what they would have expected based on their preretrieval ultrasound monitoring. The terms "crushed," "shocked," "devastated," "disappointed," and "very sad" were used by women to describe their reactions to low egg counts and lower-than-expected results.

Feelings of postretrieval disappointment were conveyed by women in a variety of ways.

"Shit, did I just waste all this time?"

"I don't feel a ton of relief right now. It opens more questions than answers."

"It's not the be all and end all. It may be a whole lot of nothing."

"A month of your life, with no running, no sex!"

"It threw me over the edge. I'm not really glad. It's kind of a waste."

"All that struggle."

"It just made me feel like I was infertile."

"It was a weird feeling, like I had failed, messed up, or underperformed."

"It is not a continued approach for me."

"I don't feel that optimistic about them [frozen eggs], though I haven't written them off."

Carla, an academic nurse-practitioner, was one of these women under egg-count stress. She had received one cycle of egg freezing as part of her divorce settlement, a divorce that she described as costly, complicated, and "soap-opera-ish." But during this single cycle, Carla learned that she was suffering from POA, which threw her "over the edge," as she put it. Furthermore, she was "extremely disappointed" by an egg count of only five, especially because she could not afford to pay for an additional cycle after the divorce. "I'm not really glad, because it was kind of a waste," Carla told me. "I really wish I never did it. I really do." But then she added, "I really see the value in it. I just wish that I didn't. It's a poor solution, and it makes me feel sad for women in a tough spot."

Perhaps the two saddest women in my study were ones who found out during the egg freezing process that they were facing *premature ovarian failure* (POF). POF is a condition even more severe than POA, in that it involves the loss of ovarian function before the age of forty. Sometimes mistakenly called "early menopause," POF is not the result of a woman's normal aging process.[5] Rather, women with POF may continue to menstruate but not ovulate, and most have no idea of their condition.

Such was the case with Fran, a federal health regulator, who was also undertaking egg freezing in the midst of a bitter divorce. To add insult to injury, she learned from her physician that she was facing POF, which resulted in only one viable egg being retrieved. "The bottom line is that it didn't go well at all. It was only one full cycle, but with lots of starts and stops. And I ended up really bummed. Seriously, this sucks. It's traumatic, a roller-coaster ride. And now I'm so worried about the numbers, I don't know if I can put myself through it again. The whole process is overwhelming, and I paid $15,000 for one egg. My money ran out, so it's a sunk cost. It's very sad, you know?"

Olivia, a nanoscientist, who also worked for the federal government, received similar news, even though she was trying to be proactive by undertaking egg freezing at the age of thirty-four. "I started doing the backwards math, and it was clear I was on my way to early menopause. It was a bad feeling altogether, because the doctor said, 'You just don't have any eggs left.' So I did one cycle, then I stopped, and that was it, because I was in shock after retrieval. I only had one mature egg, and one immature.[6] I thought, 'Maybe you have the wrong person.' I felt horrible." Olivia told me that she stopped dating for several years after her egg freezing experience. "How could I explain?" she asked. "I actually feel really bad about this. It feels horrible." But by the time I interviewed her, she had achieved some kind of peace, even a glimmer of hope.

> [*Laughs*] You know, it's funny because I thought about like, "Why do I even keep that one egg if it's not going to survive unfreezing?" And then, of course, you hear the random story of, like, somebody's neighbor who only had two embryos and they both, you know, survived. And so, like, you hear these stories, and you just don't know. I mean, I feel like even with what I call "my one and a half eggs" that I have frozen, I feel like logically, I should not, in any way, that I should not put any hope that anything will happen with those two eggs. And yet I know there's just this part of me that hopes maybe they'll survive thawing, and maybe it'll start fertilization, and maybe it'll survive a pregnancy. And like, the odds are like nothing. It's like .oo, you know. It's like some tiny number. And yet there's a little part of me that really hopes that they survive.

Egg Banking and Postmenopausal Motherhood

Olivia and Fran had real concerns, given the low probability of one or two frozen eggs resulting in a future pregnancy. Yet both women were paying hefty annual storage fees to bank their eggs—another part of the overall "sunk cost" of an unsuccessful egg freezing cycle. The term "egg banking" is often used to refer to this long-term storage of frozen eggs. However, "banking" may not be the most appropriate metaphor. Rather than being stored individually in their own kind of safety deposit boxes, frozen eggs are stored in pipettes, or tiny straws, which are then kept together with other pipettes in large, steel, cryopreservation tanks, usually tucked away in the back rooms of IVF clinic laboratories.

Furthermore, frozen eggs stored this way are not kept indefinitely, unlike money in the bank, which sometimes grows with interest over time. Some countries have imposed strict *storage limits* on frozen eggs—for example, five years in Denmark and ten years in the United Kingdom, the latter of which was challenged by activists and eventually overturned by the government.[7] In the US, with its private health care system, storage limits are not imposed by federal law. Nonetheless, US IVF clinics have reached a professional consensus on storage limits, with the cutoff defined as the age of menopause (from fifty to fifty-five, depending on the clinic). Women are required to sign consent forms agreeing to these storage terms, as well as the payment of annual storage fees. In my study, the average annual storage fee seemed to hover around $500, although it ranged from $200 to more than $1,000, particularly when separate storage fees were charged for multiple cycles.

Women sometimes complained about the burden of long-term storage, especially when IVF clinics increased their storage fees over time. For example, in one IVF clinic, fees had increased annually from $360 to $480 to $560, making one woman wonder, "What did they do? Upgrade their freezer?" In another IVF clinic, the storage fees mysteriously lapsed for several years, probably due to an accounting error. Although women were relieved of this annual payment, they were also concerned about the fate of their eggs. "It's the one thing I worry about," a woman told me. "I hope they're still there."

Beyond these cost and storage concerns, the fact that US IVF clinics bank women's eggs until the age of menopause raises important questions about the limits of motherhood and particularly whether women in their fifties should be allowed to become *postmenopausal mothers*. The American Society for Reproductive Medicine cautions against postmenopausal pregnancies—whether with one's own frozen or donor eggs—because of increased risks for both pregnancy and delivery.[8] Yet there is no law against this practice in the US. Furthermore, modern medicine has made postmenopausal pregnancy quite possible, given that egg age, not womb age, is the main determinant of a woman's ability to conceive and carry a pregnancy. Through various forms of hormonal stimulation and other medical interventions, postmenopausal women *can* give birth to very healthy children, although the long-term effects of hormone induced and sustained postmenopausal pregnancies on both mothers' and children's health needs to be assessed.

Yet, by creating this possibility of postmenopausal motherhood, egg freezing could be said to level the playing field, providing women with the kind of reproductive extension that men have had for ages, as they father children well into their fifties and beyond. Carmen, an international economist, had been contemplating this very issue, given that her close friend had been dating a man who was twenty years her senior.

> This means that he's like fifty-seven or fifty-eight. He doesn't have any problems with having kids, right? And so it got me thinking a lot. It's just, like, nature. They can have kids any moment, right? And we don't. And one of the things that I went through when I was thinking through this is, Why do I have to think about it? . . . And I don't think that I will go and try to be pregnant, like if I'm forty-eight, because even then, you have certain years for your body. But you can keep the eggs until you are fifty-one or until you stop paying the storage. So it's still not that you can delay a lot, but yeah, it's kind of an equal opportunity to women.

Yet Carmen and many other women saw extending motherhood well into the fifties as inherently risky. For one, it significantly widens the age gap between mothers and their children to half a century or more. Children of older mothers may be orphaned early or be forced to care for their aging mothers while still in their childhood or teenage years.[9] Furthermore, postmenopausal mothers may be less effective as parents, due to decreased energy reserves and increased generational differences from their children.[10] Mothers who are the age of other children's grandmothers may create feelings of confusion, stigma, and resentment among their children, with potentially long-lasting psychological consequences for their offspring.

Women in my study worried about these kinds of issues. Most had no desire to become new mothers in their fifties, instead giving themselves a midforties motherhood cutoff, with the age of forty-five often being cited as the upper limit. Women sometimes noted that the age of motherhood was shifting upward. But even so, older motherhood was not considered desirable or normative, as Gail, a Manhattan filmmaker, explained to me. "I sort of gave myself the five- to ten-year range deadline. And maybe that's just my own limit. I never really considered that I would be someone who would be forty-five and a new mother. But now at thirty-five and thirty-six, I feel like I'm twenty-five. So maybe I would reconsider. And I think socially, this will become a little bit more of the norm. But, I mean, it will never be wholly mainstream."

The few women in my study who had already reached their early to midforties were often worried about their own parenting abilities and potential. For example, Isabel, a forty-five-year-old health care policy maker, shared her perspectives on how older motherhood could be quite difficult.

> The whole freezing your eggs, unless you go through it, nobody has an idea of how hard it is. The other thing is, I just think, being an older mother is not ideal. There are also reservations about that, where I think, "Am I too old to be having a kid? Am I going to die sooner?" All of that is not necessarily true, but I do think about, like, the moral consequences of being an older mother. . . . I think that people, you know, they think of [egg freezing] as empowering, and it's also another reason why it's empowering is it gives you the chance to choose this later, whenever. It gives you the chance to determine when you're going to do this later—this whole sense of security and all of that. But I also think women don't know what it is to get pregnant at forty-two, forty-five, forty-nine. People really think that you are making a bad decision and that it's unfair to your children. And not that that matters to me, but it's definitely harder to be an older parent, and I think again when you're thirty-four years old, you don't know what it's like to feel forty versus fifty, even if you take great care of yourself. And no matter how you look from the outside, it's just different.

Similarly, Regina, a forty-one-year-old climate expert, had frozen her eggs four years earlier but was now wondering what to do without a partner. Although she hailed from a large Catholic family in which women had given birth well into their forties, Regina was feeling skeptical about waiting much longer to become pregnant.

> I feel like most women my age, very legitimately, are nervous. And I was nervous, and finally I'm like, "Why am I freaking out?" Like, nothing

about my body is saying I'm old. Everything has looked good. I just need to calm it down and then decide if I want to have a kid or not. I mean, at some point, you don't want to. Like, personally, I see some disadvantages to waiting until I'm fifty to have a baby, you know? I just, like, I would like to be alive longer with the kids. But who knows? I don't know. I said that when I was thirty-three, too, you know? But, I mean, you know, I feel so tired now [*laughs*]! Like, I totally can see how it's evolutionary advantageous to, like, have your babies in your teens and twenties, where you can stay up all night and be fine the next day. I mean, I did that all the time for graduate school, and now it doesn't matter how much it means, I'm like, "Sorry, I got to go to bed!"

At the time of our interview, Regina was seriously thinking of pursuing motherhood on her own.

I'm not ready to make this decision yet, and I don't want to make the decision, because frankly I want to have kids with a partner. Mostly, I mean for all the normal reasons, and frankly at a totally practical level, I'm the person who goes and visits everybody and their children. I love kids. I love being with them, and I have seen, like, every version of parenting joy and hell—not every version but a lot of them. Even if you're a stable person, isn't it easier to go through this with two people? And so I'm like, "Oh my God! One person!" Doing this, just at a practical level, seems really not ideal.

Having said this, Regina realized that she would be surrounded by support, given her "huge, enormous clan" of married brothers, close cousins, and parents who were alive and healthy.

Before I even started saying anything about this, my brother and his wife said to me, "We think you will be an amazing mother. So, if you want to have a baby, you just come here. Move and we'll help you do it." He was like, "We're there for you. We want you to have kids. . . . You can come and have a baby. And we'll help you get through it." So, I mean, it doesn't say, "Okay, I'm going to do it," but it's huge. It's pretty amazing. Like, if I do this, I'm not in it alone. At least I have people either cheering me on or physically helping me, or, you know, if I get in a hard time, having my own kid financially, I've got some help, you know?

Egg Freezing and Single Motherhood by Choice

Regina was not alone in considering the option of single motherhood. Single motherhood was one of the pathways to parenthood that hung in the balance for women in my study, even though most, like Regina, had yet to make this decision. The "choice" to become a single mother is not a new phenomenon among professional women. In fact, the term "single mother by choice" (SMC) was coined in the mid-1980s to describe women who were educated, middle class, and "midlife" and pursuing parenthood on her own, either through adoption or donor insemination.[11] Today, the term also includes women who employ IVF directly without having first frozen their eggs, as well as women who freeze their eggs, then use donor sperm to conceive, employing a variant of IVF called ICSI (intracytoplasmic sperm injection) to do so.[12]

In my own study, there was an appreciable openness to the SMC option, although, at the time of my interviews, only two women, Nina and Zoe, had frozen their eggs on the pathway to single motherhood. Both were obstetrician-gynecologists who were part of the same professional circle discussed earlier. They were also supported by a large group of women friends who were happy to help as needed. As financially stable physicians, both women also had the means to pay for child care. In fact, Zoe had hired a live-in nanny after giving birth to her first child, and eventually she went on to have a second child, both daughters cared for at home when Zoe returned to work.

Many other women in my study were considering becoming single mothers like Zoe and Nina. About one-third of the women with whom I spoke had already given single motherhood serious consideration, often because they had friends who had done it or had family members who were encouraging it, including their own mothers. Yet many of these same women also admitted that becoming an SMC was a difficult move, made more by "circumstance" than by "choice" in their own cases. Women's biggest concerns were often pragmatic, revolving around the high costs of housing and the difficulties of finding good child care in the expensive cities in which they lived.

Dawn, a thirty-seven-year-old clinical psychologist, was doing what she could to make the logistics of single motherhood more possible. She told me how her opinion of the SMC option had evolved over time, from initial reluctance to more recent acceptance.

I hope to have kids soon, so I want to be nearer to my folks. And that happens especially if I end up being a single mom, which isn't my preference, but, you know, you can only do so much about that. So, yeah, this is a big life change to try and put myself in a position where family could be—where kids could be possible with grandparents. People are like, you know, at first shocked, but it's a great thing, a great opportunity to get to talk more about what the situation is. Even my grandmother, who's eighty-nine, since day one, she was all about it. She was fantastic. I explained it to her, and yeah, she was all on board. This dates to Thanksgiving a year ago. I went to my first appointment about egg freezing in October, and as a product of that appointment, I came out of there with the login and password information for the website where I would review the men's profiles and pick the sperm. So I went home for Thanksgiving and said, "Okay, Mom and Dad, here we go. I'm going to be doing the freezing, and then I'm going to pick the sperm, and let's look at these." And ten minutes into it, I said, "No way!" We were laughing hysterically, like, "There's no way I'm doing this. I'm just going to freeze. I'm not going to fertilize." It was extremely off-putting to the point of just being outlandish. Because, you know, the profile is like Match.com—the profiles where like, you know, the guy has this degree, and he likes math, and he has brown hair. And how on Earth would you ethically ever pick any of these? So I just said, "I'm out. I'm just going to freeze. I know the statistics aren't as good for an unfertilized egg, but I'm just going to freeze the eggs, because that's all I can wrap my head around."

A year later, Dawn's thinking and circumstances had shifted. She had taken a new job to be closer to her parents and had just moved across country, still surrounded by boxes as we spoke. Dawn's decision to become a single mother was clearly fortified by her "really wonderful family," including her parents, grandmother, and a younger married sister, who was uncertain about having children. Dawn's own motherhood desires were not a "craving," as she explained, but rather a desire to extend her family's lineage and traditions. "I think about our family relationships, like heading into Christmas now and being with Grandma and my mom's generation and wanting that in the future, those kinds of traditions and those kinds of relationships. And I would say they're really honoring whatever I would want to do. They would be okay regardless, but I would really like to bring a new child into our family."

Other women in my study, about one-third of the total, had thought about single motherhood but were less ready than Dawn to move forward. Many were still holding out hope for their "mystery man" to materialize. For them, the SMC option was more of a "last resort," only to be pursued if they could not find a partner. Pauline, who had spent her entire career in Washington politics, was representative in this regard. She was giving herself two more years to search for a mate but using her frozen eggs was her definite plan B.

I went into this [egg freezing] knowing that in the next years, I want to use them [frozen eggs]. So, you know, that's in my plan. Like, I haven't given up on finding a real live, you know, mate [*laughs*], to pursue this plan with. But, if that doesn't pan out, I'm not going to, like, not do it. So, yeah, my time frame is the next two-ish years, kind of roughly, I guess. I mean, to be clear, it also scares the shit out of me! Like, mostly, when I think about, like, you know, providing at the level that I was provided for. Like, I will never be able to do that as a one-income parent. So that means things like my kid will probably have to pay for her or his college. Literally, that gives me panic attacks! But I recently went and saw a financial adviser about, like, figuring out how I cannot have debt, when I think about it. But I have a great, a very solid network of very close friends, and obviously, I can't just pawn this off on people. But the flip side, it's not as if I would just be an island dealing with this. Like, I definitely would have other people who would be, you know, supportive and who would help and all that.

Dawn and Pauline were both moving in the SMC direction—Dawn in the active planning stage and Pauline in a kind of reluctant preparatory mode. But there were a substantial number of women in my study, the final third to whom I spoke, who rejected the SMC option altogether. These women were clear that they would never become single mothers, preferring to forgo children altogether if they could not find a partner. Their reasons for rejecting single motherhood clustered around six key concerns.

First and foremost, women were concerned about the *financial requirements* of raising a child on their own. "I think I would be a good mom," one woman told me, "but I'm not financially or emotionally capable of doing it on my own." Another explained, "I've finally established a lifestyle just within my reach, so it's really scary to contemplate being a single mom." A second tangible worry was about having *sufficient time and support* to be a good single parent. As one woman lamented, "I just think that between my job and having to raise a kid by myself, it would be insane." Another worried, "I don't want my mom to have to raise another child, because on my own, it would just be really difficult." A third issue revolved around the stigma of creating a *nontraditional family*, especially for women who came from religious backgrounds. "The idea of family is important to me," one Catholic woman told me. "So it's a big internal debate for myself, because my child is not going to have a dad." Another woman, who came from an Indian Muslim family, put it more bluntly: "I couldn't do it without a husband because people would grill the hell out of me!"

Beyond these pragmatic issues of time, money, and family forms, women expressed existential concerns about the ethics and emotions of raising a child on their own. For example, a fourth concern raised by some women was about perceived *selfishness*. "It's a bit egoistic, women having children because they don't want to be by themselves. I don't think it's fair," one woman argued. Another told me, "It's a selfish act. It's better to adopt a child who's already there." Some women also expressed a fifth concern about *loneliness* as a single mother. "I just keep picturing myself coming home from a hospital to an empty house with no one to hand off to," one woman admitted, while another shared, "It would be kind of empty and lonely, because a child brings only one type of fulfillment." Finally, some women considered single motherhood to be a sign of *desperation or failure*. "Using a sperm donor is kind of a desperate thing people do," one woman opined, while another woman summed it up by saying, "I could do it, but it still feels like a failure."

Given that many women in this study had close relationships with their own fathers, the thought of bringing a child into the world without a loving father was seen by some women as the ultimate failure, the issue that bothered them the most. One woman, thinking about her own father, lamented, "I have a wonderful father, and it just kind of felt like a failure. Like, my baby is not going to have a dad? I love my dad! How could I not provide? I'm not providing a father!"

Despite these kinds of pragmatic and ethical concerns, the majority of women in my study were considering single motherhood, and a few like Dawn and Pauline were moving in the SMC direction. Others were adopting a wait-and-see approach, hoping for the right man to come along but contemplating the SMC option if he did not. In either case, frozen eggs were women's reproductive backstop, a way to hold onto their fertility in the intervening period.

Egg Disposition

But what if a woman's eggs are never used, either because she partners and becomes pregnant or because she does not and decides against single motherhood? What becomes of those frozen eggs? This is a question that all women, whether single or partnered, must answer on IVF clinics' consent forms. Their responses, which must be recorded even before eggs are stored, often feel quite premature. But choosing the fate of one's unused eggs is a mandatory and often ethically fraught part of the process.

"Egg disposition" is the technical term used to signal the destination of women's unused eggs. The term "disposition" invokes a legal meaning, in that it refers to the final outcome of a case that has already been settled. With regard to the settlement of unused eggs, there are three possible disposition options: disposal, donation to research, or donation to other persons.[13] At the time of egg freezing, women are asked which option they prefer, and they must commit to one, usually by checking a box on an IVF clinic's consent form. However, the ease of checking a box belies the difficulty of making a decision. Women are often conflicted, debating whether they have made the right choice and whether it can be changed later on.

Perhaps not surprisingly, the first form of disposition, *egg disposal*, was the least popular option among women in my study. They often referred to disposal as "destroying," "discarding," or "dumping" their frozen eggs, and they found this outcome very difficult, given the herculean efforts and money they had put into producing these "golden" entities. Only 20 percent of the women I interviewed had chosen the egg disposal option. Women who did so tended to view egg disposal as comparable to the loss of eggs during menstruation. As they put it, "It's like a mass period. I mean, I shed an egg at least once a month, right?" "It's kind of like my period. They go in the toilet." "I mean, I hate to discard them, but I guess the reality is I discard one every month."

But some women chose egg disposal for other reasons. These were women who were worried about what might become of their frozen eggs if they were left to the clinic's discretion. For example, Carmen, the economist, worried about her unused eggs being sold by the clinic for profit.

"So here's the thing: I don't trust the system. I really think they're doing it for money, etcetera. And I really don't trust it because there is not enough regulation. So I wouldn't trust what they would do with them. And because of that—because I am all for [organ] donating, etcetera—I don't trust the system, and I would prefer to throw them away." Similarly, Tracy, a federal security specialist, felt that the IVF clinic should be willing to pay her back for her unused eggs, if they intended to use them in ways that would increase their own profit margin.

> My issue was, "Wait a minute! I just spent $24,000 to harvest and collect these." If [the IVF clinic] wants them for their own purpose, they're welcome to buy me out of them. I'm not just giving them to them, you know, because I went through this process and not personally used them. So there were the three options. I chose disposal, because I don't know who would be getting my eggs—not that I'm opposed to somebody else if I knew and had personal investment in them. But while I'm all about scientific research, I'm not about providing free genetic material for [the IVF clinic's] profit margin!

An even greater fear was that IVF clinics might use a woman's eggs to make babies for other women. This fear of losing connection to one's own offspring was a major reason for disposal. Diane, a Capitol Hill lobbyist who was also a practicing Mormon, was one of those concerned about this possibility. "I chose they would be disposed of because I—because I have a little bit of discomfort. While I'm an organ donor [*laughs*], I have a little bit of discomfort about, I don't know, what part of me it would be used for. Like, there's maybe a lack of control on my part or something like that. Like, I couldn't think of having part of me out there that I wasn't, like, taking care of."

Yet most women did not share these discomforts regarding clinics' ulterior motives and intentions. Many women were willing to donate their unused eggs to IVF clinics, so that their eggs could be used for the greater good. *Donation to research* was the second most popular option—chosen by 30 percent of women, particularly those in health, science, and engineering. As one Silicon Valley computer engineer put it, "For me, being a scientist, if they can use those eggs in some way to help cure cancer or whatnot, like, with stem cell research and stuff, I love being part of the greater good." Another woman in Silicon Valley quipped, "Well, I was going to make a joke, like about starting a genetic army of clones, and then I was like, one should not make jokes, like, on the record for medical research! Like, I would totally give them to medical research if I wasn't going to use them."

Per the computer scientist's remarks, stem cell research was often mentioned as the specific form of medical research to which women wished that their eggs be donated. In fact, at least one IVF clinic on the West Coast provided a list of medical research options that women could choose from, with stem cell science included on that list. Faith, an economic consultant, was one of these stem cell enthusiasts. "I would totally donate to science! I don't think I would have wanted them to be turned into a human. . . . But for science purposes, I'm very open. Stem cell research I think is totally brilliant, and I would love more stuff like that."

Interestingly, the most popular egg disposition option, expressed by half of the women I interviewed, was to *donate to others*, particularly to designated family members. As we have seen, women were often keen to have their unused eggs gifted to older or younger sisters who might need them. Women did not want their eggs to "go to waste," and so they thought about particular family members, including sisters, nieces, or cousins, who might benefit as future donor-egg recipients or who would make the best possible egg disposition decisions on their behalf, in case of their untimely deaths (which was of special concern to women in the military).

Some women included their "chosen families" in these disposition decisions. A popular option was to donate to gay friends, especially gay male friends who might otherwise face great difficulty in pursuing parenthood. Several women wrote their gay male friends directly into their egg donation consent forms. Some also pledged that they would use their eggs to have a child but then enlist their gay friends as "guncles," or gay uncles, to their children. Mei, the Bay Area dermatologist, explained why she preferred to donate to a close gay friend rather than to a stranger. "So I have a good friend in West Hollywood who's gay, and he's just dying to get married and have kids. He can't find a good man that wants to settle down in West Hollywood. I don't think I would donate to a stranger, because I couldn't handle not knowing if the kid was okay. But if it was someone I knew needed it and trusted me to have somewhat of a relationship, then I would."

Jenni, the Los Angeles actor who made a documentary film on egg freezing, chose the best of both worlds—donation to a family member and donation to a close gay friend—but with further instructions about her willingness to have her eggs passed on.

> So, after I froze them, I had to fill out some paperwork. And I also had realized that I didn't have a will, and so if I died, what would happen to those eggs? So I actually got a will, and I put specific instructions on what should be done with the eggs if I die. I actually left them to two people. One is a family member, and one is like my sister, but we're not blood related. And she happens to be a lesbian, so I put specific instructions in the will that they could either use them or donate them to an infertile couple, as long as they just weren't destroyed. They needed to be used for good, I guess you could say [laughs].

Jenni was not the only woman who felt this way. Nearly 20 percent of the women I interviewed wished that their leftover eggs could be donated anonymously to infertile women in need. However, egg donation to others—either altruistically, for a fee, or to reduce the cost of one's own egg freezing cycle—was never practiced, unlike in some European countries, where women who freeze their eggs can reduce their costs through so-called freeze and share programs.[14] In the US, IVF clinics often maintain their own egg donation programs, and most women who freeze their eggs are too old to qualify as donors. But even if they did, they are often dissuaded by their physicians, who are more concerned about each woman freezing a sufficient number of eggs for her own use.

Such was the case with Sabrina, who was one of the youngest women in my study at the age of thirty-three and whose egg freezing decision was somewhat related to her future career. After passing the difficult US Foreign Service exam, Sabrina froze her eggs before heading to her first posting in Latin America. Although Sabrina satisfied the age requirements for egg donation, her IVF physicians discouraged her from doing so. "I was so happy, because I got nineteen eggs! Like, oh my God, that's more than enough! I told them I could donate some of my eggs, because I'm not going to use all nineteen of them. But they told me not to donate them now, to wait until I actually use them, because they don't know which ones will actually survive."

Egg Thawing

The fact that Sabrina's IVF clinicians did not want her to donate any of her eggs, even though she had almost achieved the magical number of twenty, is clearly related to their concerns over survivability, or how many frozen eggs will ultimately survive the thaw. Some of a woman's eggs are unlikely to survive the thawing process. This is why Sabrina's physicians wanted her to keep all of her eggs, thereby increasing her chances of a future pregnancy. Many of the IVF physicians I interviewed felt the same way. They spoke about the technical difficulty of successful egg thawing, which is "user dependent" and thus highly reliant on skilled embryologists and consistent laboratory protocols. Even if done correctly, eggs may be lost in the thawing process, and eggs that survive may not become viable embryos once fertilized.

I spoke with a physician at one of the largest US IVF clinics about what women could do to increase their chances of egg freezing success. He encouraged women to do their research and to ask questions in order to make the most informed decisions.

> We feel real strongly that people who do this should interview their clinic, should make sure they're comfortable. They should be very clear and very frank about what the expectation of pregnancy is, based not only on the patient's age but with that clinic's own experience in egg thaw and embryo transfer, right? People confabulate in our field a lot. . . . I mean, they're loose and goosey with their denominators and pregnancy rates. So these numbers become gobbledygook, and patients don't know. They leave your mind numb. I mean, it does require some patient research. Testimonials are good to read in the blogosphere, because on the whole, they tend to be an accurate depiction of what's going to happen when you're in the clinic. But if the patient really wants to know what's the clinic's experience, they have to ask, "How long have you been vitrifying? Do you vitrify eggs? How many vitrification cases did you do last year for eggs? How many thaws did you do? What's the average age? What's the pregnancy rate ongoing?" You know? If they do that, they're going to get the information in.

I conducted another interview with an IVF clinic laboratory director, who is highly regarded in his field as one of the pioneers of egg freezing in the US. He explained to me that the chances of successful egg freezing and thawing increase substantially with an IVF laboratory's experience. IVF clinics with large egg donor programs or ones that handle a high number of egg freezing cycles are more likely to generate superior outcomes. Using his own laboratory as an example, he explained why the "everydayness" of freezing and thawing eggs is so important.

> We do not only the freezing of the eggs, the vitrification of those eggs, but we are warming those eggs every day, every day, you know? We are basically having very, very strict control, and we get feedback on, you know, how the technology is working. So it's not like we are vitrifying eggs and then we don't use [them] for the next five years. We are freezing eggs, but we are also warming eggs, thawing eggs. So we have immediate feedback, you know, if everything is going well. So, you know, basically, we can give a much better assurance for fertility preservation patients if they freeze their eggs with us, because they have a much better chance that it's going to work well, you know? If that makes some sense.

According to this laboratory director, if egg freezing and thawing are done correctly, the process is now 90 percent "efficient." In other words, if one hundred eggs are frozen through the vitrification process, ninety of those eggs should survive the thaw. This is compared to the older method of slow freezing eggs, for which only a 10 percent efficiency rate could be achieved. Embryo freezing, by comparison, is 70 percent efficient, a process that has worked well since the early days of IVF. Thus, when egg vitrification was still considered new and experimental, many physicians advised women patients to freeze both embryos and eggs, in order to increase the chances of a future pregnancy.

Bridget, an Irish American Catholic physician practicing in a New England hospital, was one of seven women in my study who had followed her physician's advice. Concerned about the "high egg fallout rate" of the new vitrification procedure, Bridget's physician recommended that she freeze three embryos from the thirty eggs she produced during her four egg freezing cycles. For Bridget, the process of selecting a sperm donor was "very awkward," partly because she was thirty-nine and the sperm donor she selected was an eighteen-year-old, basketball-playing, university student. But when I interviewed Bridget nearly four years later, she told me that her three embryos in storage now haunted her.

It probably is my background in Catholicism and just in general, but one thing I did have a lot of conflict with was doing the fertilization, of "do it or don't." And he really kind of encouraged me, in case I didn't have a partner, to do some eggs fertilized, which I really wasn't prepared for, and that was an emotional decision. I did it, but I was kind of conflicted about it. I mean, obviously, if it's an unfertilized egg, there's no Catholic association of anything. It's potential for life, but it's not life—versus a fertilized egg. I only have three . . . but I know other people have had issues with "What do you do with your own child leftover?" I don't know. I mean, that's also something that does create some pause for me . . . because I think of sanctity of life.

At the age of forty-two, Bridget was now feeling an intense desire to become a mother. But like most of the women in my study, she had had no luck finding a partner and was clearly feeling disheartened.

I don't know. I mean, being a mother is important to me. I mean, just going back to my own family and my own values, I had such a wonderful, supportive, loving, crazy family, but we're very close. . . . So it's something that's very important to me, to be a mother and have children and have a family. I mean, I would like it all the way it's supposed to be, with meeting someone, having a partner, going through with a husband who can help me, and do it together. . . . But, I mean, I haven't dated for the last couple of years. It's difficult to date, because men are very intimated by you being a doctor. You might have made more money than them. You have more education than them. Relatively speaking, a greater potential income.

In so many words, Bridget was describing her own personal mating gap, or the lack of an eligible, educated, and equal partner to help her achieve her motherhood dreams. When I asked Bridget if she might find a fellow physician to marry, she told me that her chances were quite slim. "It's ridiculous," she said, "but a majority of your male colleagues in med school are married by med school. So anyway, there's just not a pool of colleagues that are still single. And then I work seventy hours a week on a good week, and that doesn't mean I don't make any effort, but that's another issue."

Three years after egg freezing, Bridget was worried that she was "running out of time, body-wise," and she was still fretting over her next steps.

In this regard, Bridget was not alone. Most of the women in my study had yet to find a partner by the time I interviewed them, and most had yet to use their frozen eggs, a reality that is repeated in other studies in the US, Europe, and Australia.[15] Having said this, there were some women in my study who had returned to use their frozen eggs and an even greater number who had conceived children naturally with their new partners. Indeed, I discovered women's post-egg-freezing trajectories heading in several different directions, with a lucky few like Hannah conceiving and birthing the egg babies of their dreams.

From Frozen Eggs to Egg Babies

Although my study was not designed to follow women over time, I did learn a fair amount about women's post-egg-freezing trajectories, especially those who had undertaken egg freezing several years before I interviewed them. Women existed at many different points on an egg freezing continuum, with some having just completed their first cycle, while others had done so more than a decade before. Table 8.2 attempts to capture these varied trajectories, including the number of years elapsed since women's first egg freezing; women's relationship status at these two different points in time; and their pregnancy and birth outcomes, including with frozen eggs. These numbers are revealing, shedding light on both the positive and negative aspects of partnership formation and pregnancy outcomes in the era of egg freezing.

On the positive side, a substantial number of women in my study were able to find partners after egg freezing. Whereas only 9 percent of women were in stable relationships at the time of egg freezing, 15 percent were partnered and 7 percent were married by the time they were interviewed. Many of these relationships did not fulfill the "educated" and "equal" criteria that most women were hoping for. Instead, partners tended to be middle-aged men with children from prior relationships or younger men with considerably less education and career advancement. Yet these men met the "eligible" criterion, in that they were loving companions committed to family building. Indeed, ten of these couples went on to have children, and three were currently pregnant at the time of the interviews, mostly through "natural" conceptions.

On the negative side, natural conceptions did not always come easily, usually due to women's advancing age. Ultimately, ten women were

TABLE 8.2. Post-Egg-Freezing Trajectories of Women in the Study

	No.	%
Years elapsed since egg freezing		
Same year	40	35
1 year	28	25
2 years	21	18
3 years	12	11
4 years	7	6
5 or more years (5–11)	6	5
Total	*114*	*100*
Relationship status at the time of egg freezing		
Unpartnered		
Single	59	51
Divorced or divorcing	19	17
Broken up	16	14
Total	*94*	*82*
Partnered (unstable)		
Relationship too new or uncertain	6	5
Partner refuses to have children	2	2
Partner has multiple partners	2	2
Total	*10*	*9*
Partnered (stable)		
Partner not ready to have children	10	9
Total	*10*	*9*
Relationship status at time of interview		
Single	89	78
Partnered	17	15
Married	8	7
Total	*114*	*100*
Status of those women partnered/married at time of interview		
Equal partnership (education, age, no children from prior relationship)	6	5
Partner divorced without children	1	1
Partner divorced with children	7	6
Partner significantly younger	3	3
Partner significantly older/retired	2	2
Partner significantly less educated	1	1
Partner significantly less educated/divorced	1	1
Partner significantly less educated/divorced with children	1	1
Partner significantly less educated/younger	1	1
Partner with alcohol or legal issues	2	2
Total and % of total N	*25*	*22*

	No.	%
Pregnancy and live birth outcomes at time of interview		
Child born from frozen egg conception	1	1
Child born from natural conception (no frozen eggs used)	3	2
Child born from donor sperm (single mother by choice, no frozen eggs used)	2	2
Child born from IUI, IVF or surrogacy (no donor sperm, no frozen eggs used)	4	3
Currently pregnant from frozen eggs	1	1
Currently pregnant from natural conception	2	2
Total and % of total N	*13*	*11*
Women who had used frozen eggs at time of interview		
All oocytes thawed, one live birth, one embryo remaining	1	1
All oocytes thawed, currently pregnant, 22 embryos remaining	1	1
All oocytes thawed, no fertilization	8	7
Total and % of total N	*10*	*9*

encouraged by their physicians to use their frozen eggs, when their "fresh" eggs failed in repeated IVF cycles. Sadly, eight out of ten women lost all of their frozen eggs, with no eggs surviving to the point of fertilization. These results suggest that egg freezing's "efficiency" cannot be guaranteed and that frozen eggs are no "insurance policy" for women who desire a baby. Only two women in my study—Judith, whose story began chapter 7, and Janet, a Silicon Valley tech entrepreneur—were able to share their positive results with me, Janet while on maternity leave with her four-month-old egg-baby son.

Yet these rather discouraging results are in no way definitive. Because my own study was not designed as a follow-up, where I could track women's frozen egg conceptions over time, I have no way of knowing how many frozen egg babies were ultimately born. But occasionally, happy news and darling baby photos would grace my inbox. This is how I learned that Tiffany became the single mother of an egg-baby daughter and that Hannah became the mother of an egg-baby son with her partner, Lucas. For these two women, both age forty-three, egg freezing worked exactly how it was supposed to, extending their motherhood potential and making the birth of their precious egg babies possible.

Conclusion

The Future of Egg Freezing

The Ongoing "Men as Partners" Problem

My goal throughout this book has been to highlight the voices of the more than one hundred American women who shared their egg freezing stories with me. Oscillating between pain and empowerment, these stories reveal the complexity of American women's lives as they struggle in their late thirties to preserve and extend their fertility. Egg freezing is a costly, logistically complicated, and physically invasive reproductive technology, not for the faint of heart. But its use is increasing among the most educated American women because they face a mating gap, or a dearth of eligible, educated, and equal partners committed to reproduction and family life. In the midst of this inexorable mating gap, egg freezing is a reproductive backstop, a way for

- single women to attempt to stop the clock while searching for an available partner;
- previously partnered women to rebound after a breakup or divorce;
- unstably partnered women to assess whether a relationship is still viable;
- partnered women to pause and potentially resolve differences with men who are unready to become fathers;
- newly partnered women to test a relationship's potential; and
- unpartnered women to decide if parenting alone is financially, logistically, and emotionally feasible.

That egg freezing is being used to "hold on" while waiting for heterosexual relationship troubles to abate is not the dominant narrative of egg freezing circulating in US popular culture. But it is an accurate narrative, one true to the lives of egg freezing women themselves. As we have seen, these women face a "men as partners" problem, one that is quite widespread. The inability to find a committed male partner with whom to form a family is effectively preventing some of the most talented American women from achieving their reproductive goals.

It would be easy to blame this problem solely on men, who have been roundly criticized in recent years for their toxic masculinity, misogyny, and heterosexism.[1] Indeed, the anthropologist Matthew Gutmann argues that modern masculinity "sells men short" by encouraging them to act like "animals" instead of admirable men.[2] Men's toxic masculinity can be seen in a wide range of US settings, from "bro" culture on college campuses to the vitriolic "incel" movement of *in*voluntarily *cel*ibate men, to the cases of sexual predation, harassment, and assault witnessed at the highest levels of US business, government, and academia.

Women themselves have much to say about men's toxic behavior, including in their stories of infidelity, sexual rejection, controlling behavior, and unreadiness to commit. But the women in this study also described their positive and loving relationships with men, including their fathers, brothers, male friends, and current and ex-partners, who stood by them throughout the egg freezing process.

Listening to these women's stories, I find it difficult to condemn all American men as intractable cads or to view heterosexuality as a fatally flawed institution. Like the women in my study, I benefit from many positive relationships with men in my own life, including as a wife, mother, daughter, sister, aunt, cousin, friend, colleague, teacher, mentor, and anthropological researcher. So, as a social scientist committed to empirical research, I find it necessary to step back and to examine the broader social forces that seem to be affecting the lives of *both* men and women in the US and increasingly in many other societies around the globe.

From my reading of this situation, two key issues stand out. The first one is what I call *reproductive waithood*, a form of female reproductive suspension that I define in greater detail in the next section. The second is the *mating gap*, which, as I have argued throughout this book, involves the educational disparity between American men and women that is growing ever wider and that underlies the egg freezing phenomenon. As recent research shows, educational gender disparities have intensified over time, meaning that millions more American women in the current and future generations will be waiting for educated mates who may never materialize. Furthermore, this phenomenon is not limited to the US. Educational gender disparities are increasing around the globe, leading to significant mating gaps and the rise of egg freezing among the world's most educated women.

Reproductive Waithood

Egg freezing, as we have seen, is primarily motivated by women's singleness—a social status that is on the rise for both women and men in the US. Today, according to the Pew Research Center, almost two-thirds (61 percent) of American adults under the age of thirty-five are living without a spouse or a partner.[3] Of these unpartnered adults, more than half (58 percent) have never been married. Furthermore, about two-thirds (61 percent) of American adults between the ages of eighteen and forty-nine are childless, with nearly half (44 percent) saying that they never expect to have children.[4] In other words, two-thirds of Americans in their prime reproductive years are unpartnered and/or childless, with nearly half never expecting to become parents.

These rather startling statistics are indicative of the major declines in marriage that are occurring across the US and in many other societies around the world. In a study using a variety of international data sets, the demographer Philip N. Cohen shows that marriage delay, as well as an overall reduction in the marriage rate, is occurring worldwide, particularly in high-income nations such as the US, France, Italy, Germany, and Japan.[5] However, marriage declines and delays are not just found in the Global North. Today, 89 percent of the world's population lives in a country with a falling marriage rate, part of what Cohen calls a "package of demographic changes," including higher education, higher incomes, and lower rates of fertility.

The global decline in marriage has been characterized as "one of the most fundamental social changes that [has] happened in human history."[6] But the question is, Why are so many young people around the world waiting to marry and, in some cases, never marrying and never having children at all? Are these delays intentional, for example, due to years of extended education, and positive, for example, providing a sense of individual autonomy and personal fulfillment? Or are there obstacles in the way, for example, lack of employment for young men or lack of social supports for women in the workplace, that lead to prolonged waiting and accompanying frustration?

In a recent volume titled *Waithood: Gender, Education, and Global Delays in Marriage and Childbearing* (2020), my colleagues and I have examined the multifarious experiences of young people around the world who are living in a state of *waithood*, which, in the most general sense, refers to an extended period of young adulthood in which both men and women are waiting to marry and to have children, sometimes delaying indefinitely and sometimes opting out altogether.[7] In its original meaning, "waithood" refers to unintentional delays in marriage and childbearing, due to political and economic realities that force young people into a state of deferred adulthood.[8] However, not all waithood is unintended and unwelcome or due to untoward political and economic circumstances. Waithood may, in fact, have aspirational elements, as young people delay marriage and childbearing as a matter of choice. Waithood, then, may be intentional, unintentional, or some combination of both, and it may have a different impact on men and women.

For many young American women, waithood today involves the personal choice to pursue education, develop a career, engage in travel, and enjoy the single life. Increasingly, single women are being celebrated in US popular culture, as reflected in numerous movies and television series (think *Sex and the City, Girls, Broad City, Insecure,* and *Younger*), as well as in a spate of best-selling nonfiction volumes, including *All the Single Ladies, Singled Out,* and *Spinster: Making a Life of One's Own.*[9] Women who define themselves as "single at heart" have found a comfortable, if still slightly stigmatized, place in US society, with the "spinster" label giving way to the ambitious "career woman" label as an acceptable alternative for a woman who chooses a child-free lifestyle.[10] (I must note, however, that there is no equivalent "career man" label, nor a need for men to justify their own child-free status.)

For those single women who wish to have children, they can now opt to become single mothers by choice with the help of a variety of reproductive technologies. Indeed, egg freezing may represent a particularly powerful path to reproductive autonomy and fulfillment for single women, by allowing them to pursue reproduction on their own terms and at their own pace. Such intentional use of egg freezing bespeaks the revolutionary potential of this technology to decouple women's motherhood desires from men and from the constraints of reproductive biology.

But what about the many women who are not single by choice but rather hope to experience the three *p*'s of partnership, pregnancy, and parenthood? For these single women who have always hoped to become married mothers, they may find themselves in a frustrating state of *reproductive waithood.*[11] Reproductive waithood, as I define it, is an unintended and undesired period of reproductive delay, in which women are prepared to become mothers and feel a strong desire for children but are forced to wait because they are single and do not wish to embark on parenthood alone. Reproductive waithood of this type does not represent a manifestation of women's own desires to "delay," "defer," or "postpone" their fertility, the three verbs most often used to describe educated women's later childbearing behavior. Instead, women who experience reproductive waithood are already well into their thirties, with the dreadful feeling that their reproductive chances are beginning to dwindle. Furthermore, reproductive waithood has little to do with women's desires for reproductive autonomy, or individual control over their future childbearing intentions. Rather, women in reproductive waithood are hoping to make joint reproductive decisions within the context of a loving relationship. But without committed male partners with whom to reproduce, these women have no choice but to wait. Reproductive waithood, then, characterizes

- women who want to become mothers of biogenetically related offspring
- and are facing fertility decline, usually in their mid- to late thirties
- but are unable to find reproductive partners
- who can help them to achieve their reproductive dreams.

That a substantial portion of well-educated American women are experiencing reproductive waithood of this kind is reflected in the Pew Research Center's statistics. In the US today, more than half (51 percent) of women between the ages of eighteen and forty-nine are single, including nearly one-fifth (19 percent) of women ages thirty to forty-nine.[12] About half of these women who reach their thirties without a partner will not conceive a child in the following six years. Moreover, in corporate America, nearly half of high-earning women who reach their forties are childless, even though 86 percent of them indicate that they want, or would have wanted, to have children.[13]

Harking back to an earlier point, it is often assumed that high-achieving American women decide not to have children because of their demanding jobs and the "difficult choices about what to prioritize at different times in their lives—children, education or career."[14] In a US workplace culture that makes little room for motherhood, some women are experiencing a "fertility penalty" simply by caring about their jobs and trying to be good workers.[15] But by now it should be clear that this is far from a complete picture. This is a point that I tried to make forcefully in a 2018 *New York Times* piece titled "Lots of Successful Women Are Freezing Their Eggs. But It May Not Be about Their Careers."[16] And this is my main argument here. By listening carefully to women's egg freezing stories, it becomes clear that American professional women are also facing a serious "men as partners" problem, one that has not been given sufficient credence, especially when compared to the many critical analyses of US work-life culture.

As we have seen, the "men as partners" problem is forcing some of the United States' most talented women into reproductive waithood well beyond their individual control. For women stuck in reproductive waithood, egg freezing now offers a partial response. As a technology designed to extend women's fertility through preservation of their younger eggs, egg freezing can be used to bridge the waithood period, relieving women's feelings of reproductive tension and providing them with substantial hope. In this regard, egg freezing is single women's *new hope technology*, offering the kind of tantalizing reproductive promise that IVF once offered when it was first introduced to infertile British couples more than forty years ago.[17]

The Mating Gap Redux

Although egg freezing is a promissory technology, offering dreams of motherhood, it cannot begin to solve the fundamental human problem at the heart of the egg freezing phenomenon. To understand this issue, it is necessary to return to the mating gap, or the dearth of educated heterosexual American men who are willing to become women's life mates and reproductive partners.

From my reading of the situation, two primary issues stand out. On the one hand, many college-educated American men no longer seem to share women's vision of marriage-plus-parenthood as a joint partnership project or even as a fundamental life goal. Many men in the US no longer face a masculine marriage imperative, or any kind of social mandate requiring them to become a father. Furthermore, they do not face women's reproductive time pressure. As a result, more and more American men are waiting to settle down, sometimes remaining single well into their forties (and beyond). But if they do partner, they often choose younger women on the basis of the latter's perceived youth and beauty (as privileged in media, fashion, etc.), rather than choosing their female age-mates, who are viewed as too old, less attractive, and no longer fertile.

In other words, men's *intentional and desired* waithood is imposing *unintentional and undesired* reproductive waithood on American women. Men's lack of reproductive commitment has been shown to be the primary determinant of women's later childbearing behavior.[18] Moreover, men's lack of fertility awareness has meant that women are being forced into reproductive waithood well beyond their most fertile years. While American men are *waiting to mate*, American women are *waiting for them*, with ramifications for the latter's fertility that are serious and profound.

Not surprisingly, men's own waithood is becoming an exercise in frustration for many educated women. Women in my study complained bitterly about men's "unreadiness" to become fathers, including among the "Peter Pans," who valued their personal freedom so much that they had no intention of "growing up" and settling down. A woman might invest valuable time and energy in a fun-loving Peter Pan, but in the end, she might run the risk of running down her own biological clock, while waiting for a man-child to convert into a committed life partner and father.

Having said this, not all the blame for women's reproductive delay can be placed on Peter Pans. A second issue fueling the mating gap is of a quite different nature. This one involves men's retreat from higher education, a problem first captured in a 2013 Massachusetts Institute of Technology working paper titled "Wayward Sons." As the authors, the economists David Autor and Melanie Wasserman, wrote, "It is widely assumed that the traditional male domination of post-secondary education, highly paid occupations, and elite professions is a virtually immutable fact of the U.S. economic landscape. But in reality, this landscape is undergoing a tectonic shift. Although a significant minority of males continues to reach the highest echelons of achievement in education and labor markets, the median male is moving in the opposite direction."[19]

Indeed, men's educational underachievement in the US is proceeding at a stunning pace. According to data from the National Student Clearinghouse, a nonprofit educational research center, 59.5 percent of students enrolled in college in 2020–2021 were women, as opposed to only 40.5 percent who were men.[20] This was an all-time high for women but a generational decline for men. Of the one and half million fewer students who enrolled in college in 2021 compared to the previous five years, 71 percent of the decline occurred among men. If men continue to give up on college at these growing rates, then there will soon be only one college-educated male for every two female college graduates.

This path out of college has affected men of all races and has been exacerbated by the COVID-19 pandemic. In 2020–2021, many young men stayed out or dropped out of college to help their struggling families. Although young men in minority communities were especially hard hit, young White men, too, have struggled with a "hope deficit" that is turning them away from higher education in record numbers.[21]

Men's retreat from college education is also affecting their marriageability, according to Pew Research Center statistics. Because college-educated people display an "elite commitment" to marrying one another, non-college-educated American men are more likely than women to be single—not only because there are more of them but because their "financial fragility" makes them poor prospective mates.[22] Without stable and well-remunerated employment, almost one-third of all single men live at home with their parents. Among these singles are middle-aged men between the ages of forty and fifty-four, one-fifth of whom still live in their parents' homes. Overall, more than one-third (38 percent) of American men between the ages of twenty-five and fifty-four are unmarried and unpartnered, harking back to the original concept of waithood, in which economic malaise prevents men from establishing their own married households and achieving other normative markers of adulthood, including fatherhood.[23]

Given this rising proportion of uneducated men in the US, the newest generation of Gen Z women will face what might be called the *mating gap redux*, or an even shorter future supply of eligible, educated, and equal partners to marry. This intensified mating gap may well force highly educated, thirty-something women into egg freezing in higher numbers, meaning that egg freezing may solidify its position in US society as a technological means for educated women to preserve their fertility, while waiting for an eligible, educated, and equal partner to appear.

But as the pool of such men shrinks considerably over time, those American women who wish to marry will need to recalibrate, entering into a new generation of "mixed-collar mating."[24] As an anthropologist, I predict that we will see more and more women engage in *hypogamy* (marrying "down"), while more and more men will engage in *hypergamy* (marrying "up"). These marriage patterns are a clear departure from traditional conjugal norms. But I believe that they are here to stay, as Hannah and Lucas's example illustrated.

Hypogamy and hypergamy will require some substantial attitude adjustment on the part of both men and women, as Hannah described so eloquently for herself. For highly educated women, hypogamy will mean rejecting the notion that marrying a less-educated man is a sign of "settling." Intelligence, kindness, and loyalty do not directly correlate with a man's level of educational achievement. Frankly, in a world where most men will be less educated than most women, searching for a highly educated "mystery man" will become an increasingly futile proposition for most women. Instead of looking up in the air for a "unicorn" who may not exist, women may need to keep their eyes on the ground. There they might find a real-life partner who is willing to go the distance as a devoted husband and father.

For men, on the other hand, they will need to shed their feelings of inferiority when enacting hypergamy with more-educated women. In a world where women are reaching ever higher levels of educational achievement, men will need to see women's advanced degrees as signs of success, rather than as an ego-deflating form of emasculation. In other words, for men who hope to marry and raise a family, they will need to become much more comfortable with impressively educated women, like the high-achieving women I met in my study. By shedding their feelings of intimidation, men should come to realize that marrying a highly educated woman may be a source of good fortune instead.

All told, if men and women are to continue the very American tradition of marriage, then both parties will need to make significant accommodations, forgoing the traditional gender dynamics of marriage and making an unconventional marriage work. In a nation where the mating gap is growing ever wider, freezing one's eggs while waiting for an eligible, educated, and equal partner to materialize may be a stopgap measure. But finding that partner may become an increasingly futile proposition. Thus, searching for a different kind of mate may be the key.

Global Iterations

The scenario that I have just described is not limited to the US. Gender-based educational disparities are growing ever wider globally, with women now outperforming men in more than half of the world's nations. Evidence of women's educational achievement is found in the *Gender Parity Index* (GPI), a metric that compares men's to women's rates of participation in higher education.[25] The appendix provides a detailed list of the

GPI percentages in every region and nation where women now outnumber men. But let me summarize some of the most important findings.

Overall, there are 13 percent more women than men in higher education in the world today. Positive GPI scores for women are found in 132 of 217 nations, or fully 61 percent. Furthermore, women's positive GPI scores are found in every region except sub-Saharan Africa. These positive regional GPI scores include central Europe and the Baltics (29 percent); East Asia and the Pacific (14 percent); the European Union and the United Kingdom (20 percent); Latin America and the Caribbean (24 percent); the Middle East and North Africa (9 percent); North America (27 percent); and South Asia (4 percent).

Interestingly, some of the highest GPI scores, where women are outnumbering men at the highest levels, can be found in Western countries, including most of the nations of Europe and North America. In the US as of 2019, there were 28 percent more women in higher education than men. Canada was close behind at 24 percent. Many European Union countries also have GPI scores in this range or even higher, including Denmark (28 percent), Italy (26 percent), Norway (32 percent), Poland (34 percent), and Sweden (37 percent), among others. Although the United Kingdom is no longer a European Union member, its GPI score is only 1 percent lower than the US, at 27 percent.

Other high-income nations have similar GPI scores, including Australia (26 percent), New Zealand (35 percent), Israel (33 percent), and France (20 percent). But even in the low- and middle-income countries, GPI scores are mostly positive for women, including in Brazil (28 percent), Jordan (18 percent), Russia (14 percent), Thailand (29 percent), and South Africa (33 percent), to name only a few of the positive regional examples.

All around the world, women's advancement into higher education is an achievement to be celebrated, signaling, as it does, the reversal of some age-old forms of gender discrimination. Having said this, women's outperformance of men in higher education has not necessarily translated into advantages in their employment, their pay, or their ability to juggle work-life balance and equitable relations in the domestic sphere. Women's educational outperformance of men also seems to be leading to mating gaps in many countries. Take China, for example. Gender imbalances produced by the one-child policy have meant that millions of "excess" Chinese men with few opportunities to marry now abound in rural areas. But in urban areas, there are now millions of "excess" women, too, who, as only daughters, have been pushed by their parents to study hard, gain entrance to prestigious universities, find lucrative professional paths, and succeed in their careers, as if they were sons.[26] As a result, highly educated Chinese women now outnumber men by many millions in a country with a population of 1.4 billion people and a GPI score of 16 percent.

But despite the remarkable achievements of millions of highly educated Chinese women, they are being rejected as marriage partners because they have excelled beyond expected measures and Chinese men feel threatened by these women's overachievement. In fact, a variety of denigrating labels have been applied to these educated-but-unmarried Chinese women, including "leftover women," "surplus women," "unmarketable women," or, if they have their PhDs, the "third gender."[27] As a group, they are also being blamed for failing to marry and waiting too long to conceive, when in fact a huge mating gap problem is the basis for their unmarriageability.[28]

Unfortunately for these highly educated "leftover" women, China is one of the few countries in the world that has decided to ban elective egg freezing. This ban seems to be based on the mistaken assumption that egg freezing will incite more women to delay marriage and childbearing, when, in fact, egg freezing is the one way in which single Chinese women can hold onto their fertility during the interminable waithood period. But single women in China are beginning to fight back. The Chinese egg freezing ban has attracted considerable media attention, with Chinese celebrity women traveling abroad for this service and at least one Chinese woman initiating a lawsuit against a hospital for denying her access to egg freezing services.[29]

China's egg freezing ban represents an important case study of the ways in which governments can react to egg freezing quite negatively. At least three Asian governments (China, Malaysia, and Singapore) have prohibited egg freezing, although Singapore decided to lift the ban in 2023 for single women ages twenty-one to thirty-five, with the caveat that the frozen eggs must be used in a future legal marriage.[30] Having said that, India—with its 1.3 billion people, a GPI score of 11 percent, and the largest IVF sector in the world—has allowed egg freezing with open arms.[31] And Japan is beginning to encourage egg freezing as one measure to combat population decline, given its position as a society with "ultra-low" fertility.[32]

The opening of the world to egg freezing is reflected in table C.1. Of the eighty-two countries surveyed in 2018 by the International Federation

Table C.1. Countries in Which Egg Freezing Is and Is Not Practiced

Frequently practiced	Practiced	Infrequently practiced	Not practiced
Argentina	Armenia	Belarus	Austria
Barbados	Australia	Bulgaria	Bangladesh
Bolivia	Belgium	Cameroon	China
Chile	Botswana	Ghana	Malaysia
Guatemala	Brazil	Iceland	Norway
Kenya	Canada	Ireland	Senegal
Panama	Colombia	Japan	Singapore
Paraguay	Czech Republic	Latvia	Slovenia
Sweden	Ecuador	New Zealand	Togo
Switzerland	Egypt	Nigeria	
United States	El Salvador	Romania	
Uruguay	Finland	Russian Federation	
Venezuela	Georgia	Uganda	
	India	United Arab Emirates	
	Italy	Zimbabwe	
	Jordan		
	Kazakhstan		
	Lithuania		
	Mexico		
	Mongolia		
	Montenegro		
	Namibia		
	Netherlands		
	Nicaragua		
	Peru		
	Philippines		
	Portugal		
	Republic of Korea		
	Serbia		
	South Africa		
	Spain		
	Taiwan		
	Thailand		
	Trinidad and Tobago		
	Turkey		
	United Kingdom		
	Vietnam		
13 countries	37 countries	15 countries	8 countries

Source: IFFS 2019.

of Fertility Societies (IFFS)—a professional organization that tracks assisted reproduction services around the world—sixty-eight countries (83 percent) now allow egg freezing for medical fertility preservation, and fifty-six countries (68 percent) also allow egg freezing for nonmedical purposes.[33] Nearly half of these countries (43 percent) report frequent performance of egg freezing cycles in their countries' IVF clinics, especially in Latin America, where an active IVF and egg freezing sector is now in place.[34]

The IFFS, for its part, has taken a stand on egg freezing, calling it "one of the most significant recent advancements in assisted reproduction technology."[35] It notes that fertilization and pregnancy rates are similar between fresh and frozen (and then rewarmed) eggs, and preliminary safety data are quite reassuring. No increases in chromosomal abnormalities, birth defects, or developmental deficits have been noted in the children born from frozen eggs. Furthermore, as egg freezing has continued to develop substantially in countries around the world, it is finding "wider applications and use," according to the IFFS, "potentially extending [women's] reproductive lifespan in optimal circumstances."[36]

Once egg freezing technology becomes routinely available in IVF clinics around the world, women themselves will have to decide on the potential costs and benefits of this reproductive technology. Although the future is difficult to predict, I want to offer my own final thoughts on the future of egg freezing, including my own sense of who should be using it and who should not and also how access to the technology could be made more widely available and equitable.

The Future of Egg Freezing

Egg freezing from its very inception has been heralded as a *reproductive revolution*—equivalent to the 1960s introduction of the birth control pill. Shortly before dying in January 2015, ninety-one-year-old Carl Djerassi, the former Stanford chemistry professor who was widely known as the "father" of the birth control pill, made a bold prediction.[37] Djerassi opined that by the year 2050, egg freezing would be as routine among young professional women as oral contraceptive usage is today. He envisioned twenty-something women heading to IVF clinics to put their eggs on ice, returning years later to retrieve their eggs once their educations and careers had been sufficiently well established.

Djerassi's vision of egg freezing as a mainstream career-planning strategy has been promoted by some segments of the fertility industry through aggressive marketing to young women. This, in turn, has created a "moral panic" among feminist scholars, who have been eager to critique both the fertility industry and egg freezing technology itself. I do not align myself with those feminist critics. But I do *not* believe that young, fertile women are the appropriate users of this technology.[38] Women in their twenties not only have many years of healthy fertility ahead of them but also have many years in which to meet a partner and to decide more generally whether they want to become a mother with or without costly technological intervention. In my view, any twenty-something woman should think twice—and then think twice again—about putting her healthy reproductive body on the line for this physically invasive procedure, which offers no guarantees. As a mother, I would never recommend egg freezing for my own twenty-four-year-old daughter, and I believe that most mothers would agree.

At least for now, the evidence appears to bolster my position. In every single study conducted to date, it is women in their mid- to late thirties, not in their twenties, who are turning to egg freezing in societies ranging from Australia to Korea to Turkey to Israel to the United Kingdom.[39] Almost invariably, egg freezing women are thirty-something professionals who wish to become mothers but who "lack a partner," as the research always shows. I anticipate that single professional women in their thirties—ideally their early thirties rather than their later thirties, when fertility rapidly declines—will always be the main users of egg freezing technology, especially as the mating gap widens in the US and intensifies in many other countries around the globe.

Closing that gap between men and women, not only with regard to their educational achievement but also with regard to their egalitarian commitments to reproduction, will be a critical policy challenge in the decades ahead. But until we "fix men," as one of the women in my study put it, egg freezing will remain educated thirty-something women's single best reproductive option—a techno-medical solution to a fundamental gender inequality that provides them with some hope and allows them to retain their motherhood dreams. If I were a thirty-something woman today and found myself without a partner, I know that I would turn to egg freezing. And for this reason, I talk about egg freezing with my own graduate students, suggesting to them that they consider it if they are single in their thirties and know that they want to birth a child, as I did.

The problem is that egg freezing is far too expensive for most graduate students and for many other middle-class women as well. Cost is a major barrier to access in the most expensive country in the world in which to make an "egg baby." Furthermore, with the exception of France, no country, including the US, has provided insurance funding for nonmedical egg freezing, even though recent surveys show growing support among young women, including those who self-identify as feminists.[40]

Women in my own study, some of whom identified as feminists and some of whom did not, were generally deeply disturbed by what they saw as the economic injustices of egg freezing access, leading to the race- and class-based underrepresentation of certain groups of women. Furthermore, as we saw, many women in my study felt discriminated against as single women. In the US health care system, being married and infertile can confer certain forms of health insurance benefits. But egg freezing cycles are rarely covered by health insurance, even though most single women are desperately trying to prevent their own future infertility. Educated women's singleness is a societal issue, not their own fault. But they are being penalized through insurance policies that are simply unfair.

Clearly, the exorbitant costs of egg freezing need to be brought down. In addition, discriminatory insurance policies and inequitable state insurance mandates need to be revised to eliminate the bias toward married women. In this regard, access to egg freezing is an important reproductive justice issue among single women, both straight and gay, White and non-White, who are holding onto their dreams of becoming pregnant and bearing children. Although egg freezing is not a straightforward reproductive panacea for any of the issues described in this book, the barriers to egg freezing access are furthering disparities based on gender, race, class, age, sexual orientation, and marital status, all off which end up privileging reproduction for some women at the expense of others.

As egg freezing becomes increasingly globalized and normalized in educated women's circles—and hopefully made more accessible through substantially reduced costs and mandated health insurance coverage—it will be important to follow the technology's path well into the future. As long as women's accelerating educational achievement and men's spiraling educational decline perpetuate the mating gap, egg freezing will remain single women's most viable option, giving them time to figure out their next best steps in a world of partnership troubles.

So *is* egg freezing a reproductive revolution? Probably not. But is egg freezing the future of reproduction for educated women without partners? Probably yes. Of course, we will have to wait and see, for only time will tell.

ACKNOWLEDGMENTS

I am deeply indebted to the 150 women who so generously shared their egg freezing stories with me. I hope that this book has done justice to their courage and candor. I think of these women often, hoping that most have found their unicorn partners and birthed the egg babies of their dreams.

The research on which this book is based was generously supported by the US National Science Foundation. I am very grateful to both the NSF Cultural Anthropology and Science and Technology Studies programs for supporting my research projects now over four decades. In this regard, both Deborah Winslow and Jeffrey Mantz were abundantly helpful as the Cultural Anthropology Program directors, past and present, as was Frederick Kronz in the Science and Technology Studies program.

This project received its inspiration from Dr. Pasquale Patrizio, once the medical director and my main research colleague at the Yale Fertility Center, before he left to take over the IVF and fertility preservation program at the University of Miami. It was Pasquale who suggested that I embark on this study, joining me as my coprincipal investigator and helping me connect to other IVF clinics and women volunteers. Dr. Daphna Birenbaum-Carmeli, our medical anthropology colleague at the University of Haifa, enhanced the comparative power of the project by conducting a portion of it in Israel and then coauthoring more than a dozen articles with us, some of which are referenced in this book. I thank Pasquale and Daphna for being such generous, responsive, and good-natured research partners over the past decade.

At Yale, my smart and talented undergraduate students Mira Vale and Ruoxi Yu became my NSF research assistants, carrying out all of the interview transcriptions and some of the data analysis. Mira went on to pursue a PhD in medical sociology, and Ruoxi went to medical school. I am very proud of their achievements, including four papers that we coauthored from this project together. Similarly, Rose Keimig, one of my Yale PhD students, played an invaluable role, introducing me to Dedoose and its ethnographic data analysis functions, before going on to publish a pathbreaking book on elder care in China, based on her own NSF-supported research project. I also thank Jennifer DeChello, our Yale Anthropology faculty assistant, who helped me with my literature review, and Francesco D'Aria, who managed my grant budget. Jeannine Estrada of the Yale Fertility Center served as a wonderful study recruiter, also sending tokens of appreciation to my study participants.

Without the support of a number of IVF physician colleagues and clinics, this project would not have been so successful. I am particularly grateful to Dr. Joseph Doyle in Washington, DC, Dr. Norbert Gleicher in New York City, and Dr. Lynn Westphal in the San Francisco Bay Area. Dr. Kristina Austin, my childhood best friend, was instrumental in connecting me to Lynn, an IVF physician who is beloved by her patients. Thanks also go to Sandee Murray and Tasha Newsome, who played invaluable roles in study recruitment in the Washington, DC, and Baltimore areas.

An important "aha" moment occurred in the midst of this study when I read Jon Birger's book *Date-onomics*, about the "man deficit" facing educated American women. Since then, Jon has become a valued colleague and coauthor, and I thank him for introducing me to Melanie Notkin, whose book *Otherhood* was also instrumental in my thinking. The New York–based journalist Anna Louie Sussman has also been a major influence, as she wrote her own book called *Inconceivable*. I am truly grateful to Anna for the ways in which she has encouraged me and for the key editorial advice that she has provided.

My biggest thanks go to Zeynep Gürtin, a medical sociologist and prominent egg freezing scholar at University College London, who has provided inspiration, incisive insights, and wonderful friendship over two decades. I am deeply grateful to Zeynep for her careful reading of this entire manuscript, improving its content in many important ways. Remarkably, she read chapters 6 and 7 during her final trimester of pregnancy and chapter 8 and the conclusion following the long-awaited birth of her gorgeous baby, Sammy. He will never know how his impending birth provided the perfect inspiration to get this book written!

Along with Zeynep, I am very privileged to know most, if not all, of the social scientists studying egg freezing around the world. They include Lucy van de Wiel, Kylie Baldwin, Lorraine Culley, and Nicky Hudson in the United Kingdom; Yolinliztli Pérez-Hernandez in France; Charlotte Kroløkke, my very special friend in Denmark; Lauren Jade Martin, Rosanna Hertz, Rajani Bhatia, Khadija Mitu, Eliza Brown, and Mary

Patrick in the US; and Karin Hammarberg and Catherine Waldby in Australia. I have also met Azer Kılıç, one of two scholars studying egg freezing in Turkey, as well as Priya Pramod Sataklar, who works on egg freezing in India. As the technology continues to spread around the globe, it is my hope that others will follow in their footsteps.

I am truly fortunate to be part of a global network of IVF ethnographers—amazing anthropologists and sociologists who study key aspects of assisted reproduction around the world. Several are my dearest friends and coauthors, including Soraya Tremayne, who works in Iran; Aditya Bharadwaj, who works India and Nepal; and Andrea Whittaker, who works in Thailand and South Africa. Soraya and I are in constant contact about our lives, our writing, and our coeditorship of the Berghahn Books series "Fertility, Reproduction, and Sexuality"—making her, for me, a rare "unicorn" of an intellectual companion. Other close friends and colleagues in this IVF world include Trudie Gerrits (who works in Ghana, Mozambique, and Uganda), Sandra González-Santos (Mexico), Tsipy Ivry and Nana Gagne (Japan), Venetia Kantsa (Greece), Sebastian Mohr (Denmark), Michal Nahman (Israel and Romania), Sharmila Rudrappa (India), Charis Thompson (US), and Ayo Wahlberg (China). Along with Daphna Birenbaum-Carmeli (Israel) and Zeynep Gürtin (Turkey), we are fortunate to be part of a major international research collaboration called "Changing (In)Fertilities," funded by the British Wellcome Trust and directed by our brilliant colleague at the University of Cambridge, Sarah Franklin. I am honored to co-direct this project with Sarah and to interact with the project's postdoctoral fellows, who have included over the years Mwenza Blell, Julieta Chaparro-Buitrago, Katie Dow, Karen Jent, Kathryn Medièn, Noémie Merleau-Ponty, Robert Pralat, Marcin Smietana, Lucy van de Wiel, and Sigrid Vertommen. I must also thank Sarah immensely for her exceptional public support back in 2013, when I published a then quite controversial editorial arguing that thirty-something women facing reproductive, relationship, or career difficulties should consider egg freezing.

In 2018, our group held its first international conference, "Changing (In)Fertilities—in Asia and Beyond," at Yale-NUS College in Singapore. I will always be grateful to Joanne Roberts, now president of Yale-NUS, who made this conference possible and who is both an extraordinary leader and friend. I spent one of my happiest years at Yale-NUS, where I served as the head of studies for Anthropology. There, I was privileged to work with a dynamic group of junior colleagues, including Zachary Howlett, Ting Hui, Gabriele Koch, Neena Mahadev, Anju Paul, and Stuart Strange. I will always be thankful to Jane Jacobs for her friendship and hospitality that year, including delicious Indonesian meals for me and my daughter in a truly exquisite poolside setting. Boon Ping and Ah Hock Ee were our generous Singaporean hosts, connected as we are through the friendship of our sons, Shaun and Carl. I will always look back on that year in Singapore with great affection and nostalgia. It is also where the seeds of this book were planted, as I began to produce my first writing on this subject.

The year in Singapore ended with a delightful summer spent in Melbourne, Australia. There, Andrea Whittaker, who is an exceptional scholar of IVF in Southeast Asia, generously hosted me in the Department of Anthropology and Health and BioFutures program at Monash University. Andrea and her husband, Bruce Missingham, went beyond the call of duty to make me and my family feel welcome. So did Karin Hammarberg, a pathbreaking scholar of IVF and egg freezing in Australia, and her husband, Alan Trounson, the "father" of IVF in that country. In Australia and New Zealand, I had the pleasure of meeting many wonderful colleagues who work on IVF and other medical anthropological topics. They include Linda Bennett, Sarah Ferber, Hannah Gibson, Vera Mackie, Nicola Marks, Susanna Trnka, Catherine Trundell, Narelle Warren, Lisa L. Wynn, and our longtime *Medical Anthropology* journal editor, Lenore Manderson. I am glad to know them all and to have been invited to their universities to speak.

Good friends in Europe also extended invitations, including Nefissa Naguib at the University of Oslo, Merete Lie at the Norwegian University of Science and Technology, Charlotte Kr. lkke at the University of Southern Denmark, Rayna Rapp and Séverine Mathieu at NYU Paris, and Kylie Baldwin, Nicky Hudson, and Lorraine Culley at DeMontfort University in the United Kingdom. In Europe, I also gave keynote addresses on egg freezing to the British Fertility Society, the European Society of Human Reproduction and Embryology (ESHRE), and the UK Progress Educational Trust. All of these presentations, especially the one given at the 2018 ESHRE annual conference in Barcelona, generated significant global media attention, proving the worldwide interest in egg freezing from Latin America to the Middle East to Asia.

My initial foray into the media, however, occurred closer to home. My Yale colleague Laura Wexler, a faculty leader in the Women's Gender and

Sexuality Studies program, invited me to participate in The Op-Ed Project, designed to elevate women's and minority scholars' voices as media commentators and opinion leaders. It was through The Op-Ed Project that I wrote my first editorial on egg freezing for publication in *CNN Online*. Since then, I have written for *Slate* and the *New York Times* and have been interviewed about egg freezing for NPR and the BBC. I want to thank Laura, as well as The Op-Ed Project coordinators and mentors, for bringing this important and influential program to Yale and including me in it.

At Yale, I have had the pleasure of speaking about egg freezing to many young women, not only my own graduate students but MBA students at the School of Management (through the student-run FEMPIRE conference) and undergraduate members of the Reproductive Justice Action League at Yale (RALY). Helena Hansen, Yale's first medical anthropology MD-PhD, now a professor at UCLA, invited me to give my first talk at the Yale School of Medicine, with reproductive medicine faculty, fellows, and medical residents in attendance.

Indeed, one of the very best parts of being at Yale is the students. I have loved working with the Yale undergraduates, from their first uncertain days on campus to their final semester, when they turn in their senior theses before graduation. My world has also been expanded by a wonderful group of graduate students, including nearly forty PhDs, postdocs, and visiting doctoral candidates whom I have mentored since I arrived at Yale in 2008. These students include Naysan Adlparvar, Ainur Begim, Elizabeth Berk, Suriyah Bi, Dominic Bocci, Sarah Brothers, Roy Celaire, Jessica Cerdeña, Siran Chen, Beth Derderian, Abigail Dumes, Hatice Erten, Rachel Farell, Ge Guo, Chelsea Jack, Anne Jorgensen, Rose Keimig, Verena Kozmann, Mehmet Kurt, Sebastien Libert, Henry Llewellyn, Emily McKee, Kristen McLean, Gabriela Morales, Jessica Newman, Sara Omar, Tina Palivos, Aunchalee Palmquist, Haesoo Park, Fiona Parrott, Candas Pinar, Gabrielle Printz, Adriana Purcell, Mikaela Rogozen-Soltar, Aalyia Sadruddin, Vish Sakthivel, Chloe Sariego, Nahid Siamdoust, Emma Tran, and Emily Wentzell.

Many of these young scholars work in the Middle East, the area of the world where I have conducted most of my research on infertility and assisted reproduction. I am lucky to have Middle East studies friendships dating back to my graduate-school days at Berkeley. There, Ira Lapidus was my wonderful Middle East studies professor and mentor; Mia

Fuller was my Arabic study partner; and Sandra Lane was my first co-researcher in Egypt. Thirty years on, these friendships are still strong, as are my ties to my beloved anthropology mentors, Joan Ablon and Nelson Graburn. My Middle East anthropology circle includes fabulous friends and scholars: Sa'ed Atshan, Gustavo Barbosa, Ellen Gruenbaum, Hsain Ilahiane, Konstantina Isidoros, Robert Myers and Miriam Ayres, Nefissa Naguib, Sallama Shaker, Diane Singerman, Susan Slyomovics, Stanley Thangaraj, Lucia Volk, and Lisa Wynn. Special thanks go to Mia, Nefissa, Susan, and Lucia for cheering me on as I wrote my first non–Middle Eastern–focused book and to Stan for reading two of the most critical chapters. I am truly lucky to have such a special community.

At the Yale Council on Middle East Studies, which I direct, I am very grateful to Cristin Siebert, Marwa Khaboor, Kaveh Khoshnood, and Jonathan Wyrtzen for keeping things running so smoothly during the sabbatical semester in which this book took shape. At Harvard, my medical anthropology colleague Arthur Kleinman is a scholarly beacon and encouraged me to write this book for a general audience. My Boston University colleague Nancy Smith-Hefner helped me to further the "waithood" concept—first proposed by our good colleague Diane Singerman—through a scholarly volume we coedited on that topic. And the sweet and gentle Stan Brunn, a retired University of Kentucky geography professor, sent weekly poems that made me think and smile.

My wonderful NYU Press editor, Jennifer Hammer, believed in the importance of this book even before I imagined how it might take shape. She also read the full manuscript within a week of its submission, offering incisive comments. I thank Jennifer and all the editorial staff at NYU Press, including Ellen Chodosh, Andrew Katz, Veronica Knutson, Mary Beth Jarrad, and Alexia Traganas, who helped bring this book to fruition. I am proud for this book to be part of the Anthropologies of American Medicine: Culture, Power, and Practice series, ably edited by my colleagues Paul Brodwin, Michele Rivkin-Fish, and Susan J. Shaw. I also thank Rosanna Hertz and the other anonymous reviewers of my proposal and my book manuscript for such positive feedback and helpful suggestions. The reviews made me aim for both balance and critique when needed. And the index was skillfully prepared by Larry D. Sweazy.

I wrote this book from the comfort of an overstuffed red bedroom chair, during the ongoing COVID-19 pandemic. Zoom made possible what was lost in 2020–2021, especially visits to my parents, Stan and Shirley Inhorn (then ages ninety-three and ninety-five) in their congregate senior community in Madison, Wisconsin. But our weekly family Zooms, including with my brothers, Lowell and Roger Inhorn, and my niece Meredith Penthorn, allowed us to stay connected and to occasionally talk about my progress on this book. I am also grateful to all my other friends for our pandemic Zoom dates, including Robert Myers and Miriam Ayres, Mark Lazenby and Jodi Olshevski, Vanessa and Pasquale Patrizio, Clo and Stephen Davis, Leslie Jacobsen, Jane Edwards, and Kaveh Khoshnood. Truly special thanks go to Jonas and Afaf Elbousty, whose friendship, encouragement, and weekly food exchange made the pandemic period bearable. To Afaf, who arrived as a new bride from Morocco the month before the COVID-19 pandemic struck, you will never know how much your savory couscous and other mouthwatering Moroccan delicacies sustained us.

My days of writing were nurtured by my family—my husband of thirty years, Kirk Hooks, and my millennial children, Carl and Justine Hooks, who never imagined that they would "come home to roost" instead of living in their apartments in New York City and Los Angeles, respectively. Occasionally, egg freezing has made its way into our nightly dinner table conversations. I thank Justine in particular, who "got my mind going" most mornings through a word-expanding game of Scrabble and who has cared about this egg freezing project from its very inception. Justine, I thank you for all that you do to make our lives better. You are my inspiration. I also thank my talented and tech-savvy son, Carl, for his kindness in helping to put the various pieces of this manuscript together into one coherent document. I will miss you and your tech skills, Carl, when you return permanently to your life in the city. And my final thanks go to our elderly cat, Kira, who decided to sit on my lap as I wrote this book, proving to be a very comforting feline companion. She passed away on the day I submitted my final manuscript. Her spirit lives on in these pages.

APPENDIX

The Gender Parity Index (GPI)

Region/country	Year	% more women than men in higher education
World	2020	13
Central Europe and Baltics	2020	29
Albania	2020	37
Armenia	2020	31
Azerbaijan	2020	16
Belarus	2020	12
Bosnia and Herzegovina	2020	35
Bulgaria	2020	20
Georgia	2020	14
Kazakhstan	2020	17
Kyrgyz Republic	2020	20
Moldova	2020	27
Montenegro	2020	26
North Macedonia	2018	24
Russian Federation	2019	14
Serbia	2020	29
Ukraine	2014	13
East Asia and Pacific	2020	14
Australia	2018	26
Brunei Darussalam	2019	36
China	2020	16
Fiji	2019	32
Hong Kong SAR, China	2020	11
Indonesia	2018	13
Lao PDR	2020	12
Macao SAR, China	2020	26
Malaysia	2019	23
Marshall Islands	2019	11
Mongolia	2019	32
Myanmar	2018	29
New Zealand	2019	35
Palau	2013	34
Philippines	2017	24
Samoa	2020	29

Region/country	Year	% more women than men in higher education
Singapore	2019	12
Thailand	2016	29
Tonga	2020	60
Vietnam	2016	20
European Union and United Kingdom	2020	20
Austria	2019	18
Belgium	2019	26
Croatia	2018	28
Cyprus	2019	6
Czech Republic	2019	28
Denmark	2019	28
Estonia	2019	33
Finland	2019	16
France	2019	20
Germany	2019	2
Greece	2019	2
Hungary	2019	19
Iceland	2019	48
Ireland	2019	13
Italy	2019	26
Latvia	2019	28
Lithuania	2019	29
Luxembourg	2019	14
Malta	2019	29
Netherlands	2018	12
Norway	2019	32
Poland	2019	34
Portugal	2019	14
Romania	2019	22
Slovak Republic	2019	34
Slovenia	2011	31
Spain	2019	18
Sweden	2019	37
Switzerland	2019	4
United Kingdom	2019	27
Latin America and Caribbean	2020	24
Antigua and Barbuda	2012	55
Argentina	2019	41
Aruba	2016	48
Barbados	2011	55
Belize	2020	41
Bermuda	2018	33

Region/country	Year	% more women than men in higher education
Brazil	2019	28
British Virgin Islands	2019	49
Cayman Islands	2008	55
Chile	2019	14
Colombia	2019	14
Costa Rica	2019	18
Cuba	2020	45
Curacao	2013	56
Dominican Republic	2017	44
Ecuador	2019	14
El Salvador	2018	12
Grenada	2018	20
Guatemala	2019	14
Guyana	2012	49
Honduras	2019	28
Jamaica	2015	43
Mexico	2019	5
Nicaragua	2002	10
Panama	2016	36
Paraguay	2010	30
Peru	2017	5
Puerto Rico	2013	31
Sint Maarten	2015	70
St. Kitts and Nevis	2015	50
St. Lucia	2020	51
St. Vincent and the Grenadines	2015	40
Suriname	2002	40
Trinidad and Tobago	2004	21
Turks and Caicos Islands	2010	34
Uruguay	2019	41
Venezuela	2008	41
Middle East and North Africa	2020	9
Algeria	2020	41
Bahrain	2020	42
Egypt	2018	4
Israel	2019	33
Jordan	2020	18
Kuwait	2020	47
Libya	2003	10
Morocco	2020	5
Oman	2020	38

(*Continued*)

Region/country	Year	% more women than men in higher education
Qatar	2020	86
Saudi Arabia	2020	8
Sudan	2015	2
Syrian Arab Republic	2019	11
Tunisia	2019	46
United Arab Emirates	2020	30
West Bank and Gaza	2020	39
North America	2020	27
Canada	2019	24
United States	2019	28
South Asia	2019	4
Bhutan	2020	6
India	2020	11
Maldives	2019	73
Nepal	2020	4
Sri Lanka	2020	38
Sub-Saharan Africa	2019	−32
Cabo Verde	2018	33
Lesotho	2018	35
Mauritius	2020	31
Namibia	2018	49
Sao Tome and Principe	2015	4
Seychelles	2020	58
South Africa	2019	33

Source: World Bank 2021.

NOTES

PROLOGUE

1. The Vatican continues to forbid all forms of reproductive technology, from contraception to abortion to assisted reproduction. Egg freezing is included in this Catholic prohibition.
2. I have written six books on Middle Eastern gender relations and assisted reproduction (Inhorn 1994, 1996, 2003, 2012, 2015, 2018), including *The New Arab Man: Emergent Masculinities, Technologies, and Islam in the Middle East* (Inhorn 2012). *Motherhood on Ice* is my first study focused solely on American women.
3. The "waithood" concept was forwarded by Diane Singerman (2007), who studied the frustrations of marriage delay and deferred adulthood among educated Egyptians.
4. Adely 2012.
5. Ward 2020.

INTRODUCTION

1. The University of Cambridge medical sociologist Sarah Franklin (1997) coined the term "hope technology" in referring to IVF and later called it the "platform technology" for all of the other assisted reproductive technologies, including oocyte cryopreservation (i.e., egg freezing), that have followed in its wake (Franklin 2013).
2. On early feminist responses to IVF, see Thompson 2002; and on both the religious and media reaction, see Dow 2019.
3. ESHRE 2018.
4. Franklin 2013.
5. Setti et al. 2014.
6. Based in Tokyo, the Japanese embryologist is Masashige Kuwayama, who introduced a technique for successful oocyte vitrification to the world in 2005. See Kuwayama et al. 2005.
7. Cobo et al. 2016.
8. IFFS 2019.
9. Ethics Committee of the ASRM (2005).
10. Yu et al. 2016.
11. The term "oncofertility" was coined by the clinical oncologist Teresa K. Woodruff, who has begun an Oncofertility Consortium of clinicians who are dedicated to preserving the fertility of young cancer patients. See Woodruff 2010.
12. Inhorn and Patrizio 2015.
13. Birenbaum-Carmeli 2016; and Birenbaum-Carmeli et al. 2021.
14. The ASRM issued its report lifting the experimental label on oocyte cryopreservation in October 2012. The report was then officially published in the widely read reproductive medicine journal, *Fertility and Sterility*, in January 2013. See Practice Committees of the ASRM and the SART (2013).
15. ESHRE Task Force on Ethics and Law 2012.
16. Lampert 2019.
17. Dockterman 2021.
18. Guzman 2020.
19. See, for example, Goold and Savulescu 2009; Hughes 2012; and Wyndham et al. 2012.
20. See, for example, Lockwood 2011; and Shkedi-Rafid and Hashiloni-Dolev 2011, 2012.

21. Gibbs 2010.
22. See, for example, Argyle, Harper, and Davies 2016; Cobo and García-Velasco 2016; Donnez and Dolmans 2017; Goldman and Grifo 2016; and Gunnala and Schattman 2017.
23. Ethics Committee of ASRM 2018, 1022.
24. The British sociologist Kylie Baldwin (2019) has retained the term "social egg freezing" to indicate the many social dimensions of this emerging reproductive technology.
25. On the basis of my own study of American women, I have argued against the use of the term "social egg freezing," because of women's own critique of that term. In my first major publication on egg freezing (Inhorn et al. 2018a), I forwarded the term "elective egg freezing" to indicate women's preferred terminology for the procedure.
26. Ethics Committee of ASRM 2018, 1022.
27. Gootman 2012.
28. Richards 2012.
29. The *New York Times* stories questioning egg freezing's success include Belluck 2018; Grose 2020; and North 2015.
30. La Ferla 2018; Caron 2019. See also Patrizio, Molinari, and Caplan 2016.
31. Miller 2014.
32. For examples of *New York Times* editorials written by women who regretted freezing their eggs, see Ackerman 2019; and Rosemberg 2019.
33. Allen 2016.
34. Mertes 2013.
35. Mertes 2013, 141.
36. Sandberg 2013.
37. Many of the Washington, DC, women actually lived in the Maryland and Virginia suburbs. Silicon Valley women lived in such communities as Burlingame, Menlo Park, Mountainview, Palo Alto, Redwood City, San Jose, and Santa Clara. Some of these women also lived in San Francisco.
38. I also interviewed one British woman, not part of the 150 total, who was one of the first women to freeze her eggs in the experimental period, traveling to both Japan and the US to do so.
39. The study was carried out in the heart of egg freezing's first decade, from June 2014 through August 2016. In these prepandemic years, online research methods had not yet converted to Zoom, so Skype was mostly used.
40. The American anthropologists Robert I. Levy and Douglas W. Hollan (2015) have most clearly articulated the importance of person-centered interviewing methods.
41. Completed interviews were then transcribed verbatim by two research assistants at Yale University. All interview transcripts were uploaded into a qualitative data analysis software program (Dedoose) for thematic content analysis, and detailed interview synopses were written and summarized by the author. Sociodemographic information was transferred into Excel files by a third research assistant for descriptive statistical analysis. The research protocol was approved by the Yale Institutional Review Board and by the ethics committees of all the collaborating IVF clinic sites. The study was generously funded by the US National Science Foundation's Cultural Anthropology and Science and Technology Studies programs.
42. Inhorn et al. 2020.
43. Pew Research Center 2014c.
44. These studies come from a number of different countries, including Australia (Hammarberg, Kirkman, et al. 2017; Pritchard et al. 2017), Belgium (Stoop et al. 2015), Korea (Kim et al. 2018), the United Kingdom (Baldwin 2019; Gürtin et al. 2019; Waldby 2015), and the US (Brown and Patrick 2018; Carroll and Kroløkke 2018; Greenwood et al. 2018; Hodes-Wertz et al. 2013). In all of these studies, women are turning to egg freezing in their late thirties to early forties, when age-related fertility decline (i.e., the so-called fertility cliff) begins to impact their reproductive function (Waldby 2019).

45. In Turkey, a study by İpek Göçmen and Azer Kılıç (Göçmen and Kılıç 2018; Kılıç and Göçmen 2018) showed that the average age of egg freezing was closer to forty.
46. Ben-Rafael 2018.
47. Kagan 2021.
48. Goldman et al. 2017.
49. Only three women did not have college degrees, because of their early successes in the performing arts or US military.
50. Kime 2019.
51. For a list of the many international studies in which "lack of a partner" was women's main motivation for freezing their eggs, see notes 44 and 45.
52. With former graduate students Matthew Dudgeon (Dudgeon and Inhorn 2004) and Emily A. Wentzell (Wentzell and Inhorn 2014), I have written extensively about the "men as partners" problem in the Global South, including the problematic ways in which scholarship often tends to dehumanize these non-Western men.

CHAPTER 1. THE MATING GAP

1. Brigitte Adams became the face of egg freezing in 2014, when she appeared on the cover of *Bloomberg Businessweek*. But her frozen eggs did not result in the birth of a baby. To read her full story, see Cha 2018.
2. US Census Bureau 2020.
3. World Bank 2021.
4. Birger 2015, 83.
5. Birger 2015, 7.
6. Birger 2015, 3.
7. Birger 2015, 180–181.
8. Greenwood et al. 2018.
9. Notkin 2014.

CHAPTER 2. THE END OF ROMANCE

1. This chapter is a significantly modified and expanded version of Inhorn et al. 2022.
2. Carroll and Kroløkke 2018, 992; Brown and Patrick 2018, 959.
3. Carroll and Kroløkke 2018, 1000.
4. Becker 1994, 383.
5. Centers for Disease Control. 2017. On marriage and divorce dynamics in the United States, see Lehrer and Son 2018; and Pessin 2018.

CHAPTER 3. THE MINORITY CONCERNS

1. Although Tiffany used the term "African American" to specify her racial identity, I use the terms "Black" and "White," which are now most commonly used in critical race studies scholarship.
2. Immature eggs can be frozen, rewarmed, and fertilized, leading to successful live birth outcomes. But as explained to me by an IVF laboratory director, the best pregnancy outcomes occur when eggs are already mature when frozen. Ideally, any immature eggs that are retrieved should undergo a process of in vitro maturation in the IVF laboratory before being frozen, rather than trying in vitro maturation once they are thawed. See also Brambillasca et al. 2013.
3. Allen 2016.
4. National Center for Education Statistics 2021.
5. College Factual 2021.
6. Birger 2015.
7. Reeves and Guyot 2017.

8. But see also Minda Honey's provocative Valentine's Day essay, "Single Black Women and the Lies about Our Love Lives" (2022), which argues that even though 62 percent of Black women are unmarried, that is "not a 'problem' that has to be fixed."

9. Reeves and Guyot 2017.

10. Alexander 2020; Shiels et al. 2021.

11. National Center for Education Statistics 2021.

12. For discussion of the fertility penalty, see Lockwood 2011; and for an empirical example of this phenomenon among mostly White women in corporate America, see Hewlett 2002.

13. Lee and Zhou 2015.

14. Black feminist scholars have written powerfully about the "controlling images," or deleterious stereotypes, surrounding Black women in the US. For an analysis of these controlling images, see in particular Collins 2008; and for an analysis of the controlling images of Black women as mothers, see Roberts 2014. Roberts also provides a powerful analysis of the ways in which Black women's infertility concerns are ignored and their access to assisted reproductive technologies impeded.

15. Two women were White-Latinas, and one woman was Black-Filipina.

16. Two relatively recent books on Native American reproduction include Gurr 2015; and Theobald 2019.

17. Inhorn, Patrizio, and Serour 2010.

18. Inhorn et al. 2020.

19. Traina et al. 2008.

20. Protestant denominations—from Anglicans to Methodists to Baptists to Mormons—have generally condoned assisted reproductive technologies since their introduction in the late 1970s (Office of Technology Assessment 1988).

21. Cromer 2018, 2019.

22. Davis 2019.

23. Pew Research Center 2014b.

24. C. Murphy 2016.

25. For a detailed discussion of egg freezing among Asian American women, see Inhorn, Yu, and Patrizio 2020.

26. For a detailed discussion of egg freezing among Jewish women in both the US and Israel, see Birenbaum-Carmeli et al. 2021.

27. One woman was White-Japanese, or "Eurasian," and one was Black-Filipina, or "Blasian," as these interracial categories are sometimes called.

28. The overrepresentation of Asian Americans in my study is similar to that in other egg freezing studies, in which Asian Americans made up the second largest group (after White women) and represented between one-fifth to one-quarter of all study participants. See Brown and Patrick 2018; Carroll and Kroløkke 2018; Greenwood et al. 2018; and Hodes-Wertz et al. 2013. There are no comparable studies yet on Jewish American women.

29. C. Murphy 2016.

30. C. Murphy 2016.

31. Pew Research Center 2014a.

32. Hartman and Hartman 2009.

33. Fishman 2015.

34. Lugo et al. 2013.

35. Heilman 2013.

36. Notkin 2014, 136.

37. Pew Research Center 2014a.

38. National Healthy Marriage Resource Center 2017.

39. Birenbaum-Carmeli et al. 2021. See Kahn 2000; and Remennick 2000.

40. Lee and Zhou 2015.

41. Wu 2015.

42. For Asian American ART utilization rates, see Deomampo 2019; for Jewish Americans, see Birenbaum-Carmeli et al. 2021.
43. Birenbaum-Carmeli 2016.
44. Inhorn and Tremayne 2012.
45. IFFS 2019. For an analysis of Hindu perspectives on ARTs in India, see Bharadwaj 2016. It is also important to note that some Indians are Christian, for example, the mostly Catholic Malayalee population.
46. For an in-depth analysis of this phenomenon in the Orthodox Jewish community, as well as among Utah's Mormons, see Birger 2015, chap. 6, "Mormons and Jews."
47. See the special issue of *Medical Anthropology*, titled "Centering Race and Racism in Reproduction," coedited by Natali Valdez and Daisy Deomampo (2019).

CHAPTER 4. THE FERTILITY THREATS

1. Lundberg et al. 2014.
2. Gleicher, Kushnir, and Barad 2015.
3. Yu et al. 2016. The "fertility cliff" is described best by Catherine Waldby in *The Oocyte Economy* (2019, 65). The best general overview of reproductive aging can be found in *Freezing Fertility* by Lucy Van de Wiel (2020a). And Lauren Jade Martin (2010) was the first to write about the ways in which egg freezing could be used by women in "anticipating" their own future infertility.
4. This is an early study by Hodes-Wertz et al. (2013), in which 79 percent of 183 women surveyed reported that they wished they had undergone oocyte cryopreservation at an earlier age.
5. Only a dozen women relied on other methods, primarily condoms but also intrauterine devices (IUDs), diaphragms, sponges, or withdrawal.
6. Only seven women had had abortions following unplanned pregnancies. One woman who had borne a child in her early twenties had placed the child for adoption.
7. For a list of thirty celebrities who had children after the age of forty, see Decker 2019 . On Naomi Campbell's pregnancy at age fifty, see also Gürtin 2021.
8. It is impossible for me to confirm or disconfirm whether Halle Berry used donor eggs.
9. Yu et al. 2016.
10. Peterson et al. 2018.
11. Yu et al. 2016, 403.
12. Ethics Committee of the ASRM 2005.
13. Ethics Committee of the ASRM 2013a.
14. Baysal et al. 2015.
15. Chung et al. 2013.
16. Woodruff 2010.
17. Oktay, Harvey, and Loren 2018.
18. Inhorn et al. 2018b.
19. Inhorn et al. 2018b.
20. Ten women who underwent medical egg freezing did not have cancer, but seven required partial or full removal of their ovaries (oophorectomies) due to benign tumors, precancerous BRCA-positive genetic mutations, and severe endometriosis leading to a condition called "frozen pelvis." Thus, they were clearly placed in the medical category, as their ovarian function had been significantly impaired or was about to be impaired by surgery. Three others suffered from chronic conditions—such as Type 1 diabetes and autoimmune disorders—which affected their overall health and well-being and prompted their turn to medical egg freezing.
21. These cancer patients ranged in age from sixteen to forty-one.
22. Inhorn, Birenbaum-Carmeli, and Patrizio 2017.

23. Two of the IVF physicians I interviewed advocated for egg freezing in the twenties, partly based on their experience with a successful egg donor program. But their perspective was quite different from the rest of the IVF physicians I interviewed.

24. In the *Atlantic* article titled "How Long Can You Wait to Have a Baby?," the San Diego State University psychology professor Jean M. Twenge (2013) used her own reproductive story to argue that "the decline in fertility over the course of a woman's 30s has been oversold." She claimed that an oft-cited fertility statistic on the rate of childlessness (30 percent) in women ages thirty-five to thirty-nine is based on ancient French birth records dating back to the 1670s.

CHAPTER 5. THE IVF CLINIC

1. For an analysis of the ways in which egg freezing may be falsely advertised on IVF clinic websites, see Beilby et al. 2020; and Gürtin and Tiemann 2021.

2. For example, a *New York Times* article described some clinics as hosting "'lets chill' egg-freezing parties, inviting guests to take in facts and figures along with Champagne and canapés" (La Ferla 2018).

3. McLenon and Rogers 2019.

4. Several women in my study with STEM backgrounds had decided not to pursue careers in medicine because of their fear of needles.

5. "Reprotravel" is a term I coined in my book *Cosmopolitan Conceptions* (Inhorn 2015). It refers in the broadest sense to any cross-border movements undertaken in search of assisted reproductive technologies.

6. Inhorn et al. 2019.

7. Van Empel et al. 2011, 589.

8. Institute of Medicine 2001.

9. Dancet et al. 2012.

10. Van Empel et al. 2011.

11. Dancet et al. 2011.

12. See, for example, Mertes and Pennings 2012; and Shenfield et al. 2017.

13. For the best analysis of stand-alone egg freezing clinics, their financialization, and marketing, see Van de Wiel 2020b.

14. McMahon 2018.

15. Dancet et al. 2011.

CHAPTER 6. THE SUPPORTERS

1. The term "web of care" was coined by my former doctoral student Laura Heinemann (2016) in her study of organ transplant patients. The term has also been forwarded by another one of my former doctoral students, Elana Buch (2018), in her study of home health care workers who assist the elderly.

2. Inhorn, Birenbaum-Carmeli, and Patrizio 2020.

3. The phrase "no man is an island" has been used in multiple literary works but generally refers to the fact that no one is truly self-sufficient. We all rely on the companionship and help of others in order to lead meaningful lives. Here, I want to emphasize that no *woman* is an island in the world of egg freezing. At least one other supporter must be involved in the process on the day of egg retrieval.

CHAPTER 7. THE EMPOWERED

1. Stinson, Cameron, and Hoplock 2021.

2. Inhorn 2021.

3. Besides the women in tech, only three other women in my study had egg freezing benefits offered by their employers. These included a law firm, a management consultancy, and a reproductive health organization.

4. For an overview of some of the issues at stake in this egg freezing debate, see Inhorn 2018; and van de Wiel 2020a.
5. For this comparison of egg freezing to the birth control pill, see McDonald et al. 2011. For an analysis of the Pill's revolutionary impact on women's lives, see also Gibbs 2010.
6. Pro-choice liberal feminist views have been espoused most prominently by European bioethicists, including Imogen Goold and Julian Savulescu (Goold and Savulescu 2009; Savulescu and Goold 2008) and Heidi Mertes and Guido Pennings (2011). They have argued that egg freezing represents a form of "reproductive affirmative action" in the absence of gender equality. Feminist IVF clinicians who have been prominent advocates for egg freezing include Gillian Lockwood (2011) in the UK and Ana Cobo in Spain (Cobo and García-Velasco 2016).
7. Structural feminist critiques of egg freezing have been forwarded most powerfully by Jude Browne (2018), Lisa Campo-Engelstein (2020), Angel Petropanagos (2010), and Catherine Rottenberg (2017). Rottenberg in particular has critiqued the liberal feminist position on egg freezing as being, in fact, "neoliberal" in that its advocacy for egg freezing aligns with corporate interests in retaining women workers through egg freezing benefits.
8. The argument that women can "have it all" has been forwarded most prominently by Sheryl Sandberg (2013), the chief operating officer (COO) of Facebook (now Meta). A counterargument has been offered by Anne-Marie Slaughter (2012, 2016), who left her pressure-cooker position in the US State Department to become a Princeton professor and more "hands-on" mother. See also Sylvia Ann Hewlett (2002), who examines the personal price corporate women may pay for their high-powered careers.
9. Intersectional feminist analyses of egg freezing are more recent than liberal and structural feminist analyses. They have been forwarded by Michiel De Proost (2021), Michiel De Proost and Gily Coene (2019), Karey A. Harwood (2018), and Lisa Ikemoto (2015).
10. The term "stratified reproduction" was introduced by Shellee Colen (1995) in the feminist anthology *Conceiving the New World Order* (Ginsburg and Rapp 1995).
11. Bracewell-Milnes et al. 2018. The term "bioavailability" was introduced by the medical anthropologist Lawrence Cohen (2007). Erica Haimes, Ken Taylor, and Ilke Turk-mendag (2012) have argued that egg freezing may make some women more "bioavailable" than others, if they agree to egg donation in return for discounts on their egg freezing cycles. Such "freeze-and-share" schemes are beginning to be offered in some European IVF clinics.
12. Charis Thompson (2002) has provided the best single review and analysis of the early feminist critiques of IVF and assisted reproduction more generally.
13. The feminist sociologists Kit C. Myers and Lauren Jade Martin (2021) have provided a recent survey of the sociological literature on egg freezing, including the various critiques of the technology. Anthropologists have not studied egg freezing to the extent that sociologists have. Nonetheless, the anthropologists Lynn M. Morgan and Janelle S. Taylor (2013) forwarded an early critique of egg freezing in their opinion piece "Egg Freezing: WTF?," published in *Feminist Wire*. In particular, they took issue with my own more measured approach to egg freezing published in *CNN Online* (Inhorn 2013). As part of their critique, Morgan and Taylor questioned my own scholarly and feminist credentials in a rather mean-spirited ad hominem attack. See also Alana Cattapan et al. (2014)—self-defined "young feminist scholars of reproductive politics"—who joined Morgan and Taylor in their egg freezing condemnation.
14. O'Brien 2018.
15. Inhorn 2013.
16. Scharff 2016.
17. Hertz 2008, 15.
18. Blithe and Bauer 2022.

CHAPTER 8. THE BANKED AND THAWED

1. Tober 2018.
2. To date, most studies have shown that women are not returning in large numbers to use their frozen eggs, many frozen eggs do not survive the "thaw," and thus the success rate of egg freezing with regard to live birth outcomes is still negligible. See Argyle, Harper, and Davies 2016; and Balkenende et al. 2018.
3. Doyle et al. 2016; Goldman et al. 2017.
4. Goldman et al. 2017.
5. An excellent description of POF is offered by the Center for Human Reproduction (2019), an IVF clinic and research center in New York City that specializes in the treatment of women with POA and POF.
6. See note 2 in chapter 3 above.
7. Baldwin 2021a.
8. Ethics Committee of ASRM 2013b.
9. Shkedi-Rafid and Hashiloni-Dolev 2012.
10. Mertes and Pennings 2012.
11. Jean Renvoizé (1985) introduced the term "single mother by choice." For a more recent study, see Hertz 2008.
12. The increasing popularity of the SMC pathway is clearly reflected in a dozen recent books on the subject, most of them written by women who have chosen this path. Some of these books are "guides" for other women who are considering becoming SMCs. At least four books are for the children of SMCs to better understand their nontraditional family form.
13. Mertes et al. 2012.
14. For example, the London Egg Bank, which boasts the largest number of egg freezing cycles in the UK, offers a freeze and share program in which a young woman can undertake one egg freezing cycle for free, along with two years of free egg storage. But she must also donate half of her eggs to the London Egg Bank for use in its egg donor program. See London Egg Bank, n.d.
15. For the US, see Bakkensen and Goldman 2021; and Blakemore et al. 2021; for Europe, see Varlas et al. 2021; for Australia, see Hammarberg, Kirkman, et al. 2017; and for Israel, see Tsafrir et al. 2021.

CONCLUSION

1. Ward 2020.
2. Gutmann 2019.
3. Fry 2017.
4. Brown 2021.
5. P. Cohen 2013.
6. Roser 2016.
7. Inhorn and Smith-Hefner 2020.
8. The term was first forwarded by my Middle East political science colleague Diane Singerman (2007). Viewing the rates of education and marriage across the Middle East and North Africa region, Singerman used the term "waithood" to refer to a widespread pattern of marriage delay in societies where marriage is otherwise highly valued and culturally linked to full adulthood.
9. See Bolick 2015; DePaulo 2007; and Traister 2016.
10. DePaulo 2020.
11. Inhorn 2020.
12. Brown 2021.
13. Hewlett 2002.
14. Goold and Savulescu 2009, 50.

15. Lockwood 2011.
16. H. Murphy 2018.
17. Franklin 1997.
18. Hammarberg, Collins, et al. 2017.
19. Autor and Wasserman 2013, 7.
20. Belkin 2021.
21. Belkin 2021.
22. Carbone and Cahn 2014; Luscombe 2021.
23. Singerman 2007.
24. Birger 2015.
25. World Bank 2021.
26. Lake 2018.
27. Gutmann 2019.
28. Shosh Shlam and Hilla Medalia (2020) have made a PBS documentary film on the subject, called "Leftover Women," which explores the lives of three highly educated Chinese women, including a lawyer, a professor, and a public radio journalist.
29. Wee and Chen 2019.
30. Bach 2021; Tan 2022.
31. Allahbadia 2016.
32. BBC News 2016.
33. IFFS 2019.
34. Inhorn and Patrizio 2015.
35. IFFS 2019, 50.
36. IFFS 2019, 81.
37. Djerassi 2015.
38. See also the commentary by the sociologist Kylie Baldwin (2021b) on this topic.
39. See the introduction, notes 44 and 45, for a representative list of these global egg freezing studies.
40. Kaplan, Hashiloni-Dolev, and Kroløkke 2021.

REFERENCES

Ackerman, Ruthie. 2019. "Don't Put All Your (Frozen) Eggs in One Basket." *New York Times*, July 19. www.nytimes.com.

Adely, Fida. 2012. *Gendered Paradoxes: Educating Jordanian Women in Nation, Faith, and Progress.* Chicago: University of Chicago Press.

Alexander, Michelle. 2020. *The New Jim Crow: Mass Incarceration in the Age of Colorblindness.* 10th anniversary ed. New York: New Press.

Allahbadia, Gautam N. 2016. "Social Egg Freezing: Developing Countries Are Not Exempt." *Journal of Obstetrics and Gynecology India* 66:213–217.

Allen, Reniqua. 2016. "Is Egg Freezing Only for White Women?" *New York Times*, May 21. www.nytimes.com.

Argyle, Catrin E., Joyce C. Harper, and Melanie C. Davies. 2016. "Oocyte Cryopreservation: Where Are We Now?" *Human Reproduction Update* 22 (4): 440–449.

Autor, David, and Melanie Wasserman. 2013. "Wayward Sons: The Emerging Gender Gap in Labor Markets and Education." Working paper. https://blueprintlabs.mit.edu.

Bach, Sara. 2021. "Is Freezing the Future? Investigating Interest of Elective Oocyte Freezing Amongst Singaporean Women." *Journal of Fertility Biomarkers* 1 (2): 21–38.

Bakkensen, Jennifer B., and Kara N. Goldman. 2021. "After the Thaw: When Patients Return to Use Cryopreserved Oocytes." *Fertility and Sterility* 115 (6): 1437–1438.

Baldwin, Kylie. 2019. *Egg Freezing, Fertility and Reproductive Choice: Negotiating Responsibility, Hope and Modern Motherhood.* Bingley, UK: Emerald.

———. 2021a. "From Ten to 55 Years: What Does the Extension in the Storage Time on Frozen Eggs Mean?" *BioNews*, September 13. www.bionews.org.uk.

———. 2021b. "The Moral Panic over Egg-Freezing and Older Parents Is Irrational." *Independent*, September 8. www.independent.co.uk.

Balkenende, Eva M., Taghride Dahhan, Fulco van der Veen, Sjoerd Repping, and Mariëtte Goddijn. 2018. "Reproductive Outcomes after Oocyte Banking for Fertility Preservation." *Reproductive BioMedicine Online* 37 (4): 425–433.

Baysal, Ö., L. Bastings, C. C. M. Beerendonk, S. A. E. Postma, J. IntHout, C. M. Verhaak, D. D. M. Braat, W. L. D. M. Nelen. 2015. "Decision-Making in Female Fertility Preservation is Balancing the Expected Burden of Fertility Preservation Treatment and the Wish to Conceive." *Human Reproduction* 30 (7): 1625–1634.

BBC News. 2016. "Japanese City Helps Women Freeze Eggs to Boost Birth Rate." June 16. www.bbc.com.

Becker, Gay. 1994. "Metaphors in Disrupted Lives: Infertility and Cultural Constructions of Continuity." *Medical Anthropology Quarterly* 8 (4): 383–410.

Beilby, Kiri, Inrid Dudink, Deanna Kablar, Megan Kaynak Sanduni Rodrigo, and Karin Hammarberg. 2020. "The Quality of Information about Elective Oocyte Cryopreservation (EOC) on Australian Fertility Clinic Websites." *Australian and New Zealand Journal of Obstetrics and Gynecology* 60 (4): 65–69.

Belkin, Douglas. 2021. "A Generation of American Men Give Up on College: 'I Just Feel Lost.'" *Wall Street Journal*, September 6. www.wsj.com.

Belluck, Pam. 2018. "What Fertility Patients Should Know about Egg Freezing." *New York Times*, March 13. www.nytimes.com.

Ben-Rafael, Zion. 2018. "The Dilemma of Social Oocyte Freezing: Usage Rate Is Too Low to Make It Cost-Effective." *Reproductive BioMedicine Online* 37 (4): 443–448.

Bharadwaj, Aditya. 2016. *Conceptions: Infertility and Procreative Technologies in India.* New York: Berghahn.

Birenbaum-Carmeli, Daphna. 2016. "Thirty-Five Years of Assisted Reproductive Technologies in Israel." *Reproductive BioMedicine & Society Online* 2:16–23.

Birenbaum-Carmeli, Daphna, Marcia C. Inhorn, Mira Vale, and Pasquale Patrizio. 2021. "Cyropreserving Jewish Motherhood: Egg Freezing in Israel and the United States." *Medical Anthropology Quarterly* 35 (3): 346–363.

Birger, Jon. 2015. *Date-onomics: How Dating Became a Lopsided Numbers Game.* New York: Workman.

———. 2021. *Make Your Move: The New Science of Dating and Why Women Are in Charge.* New York: BenBella Books.

Blakemore, Jennifer. K., James A. Grifo, Shannon M. Devore, Brooke Hodes-Wertz, and Alan S. Berkeley. 2021. "Planned Oocyte Cryopreservation—10–15 Year Follow-Up: Return Rates and Cycle Outcomes." *Fertility and Sterility* 115 (6): 1511–1520.

Blithe, Sarah Jane, and Janell C. Bauer, eds. 2022. *Badass Feminist Politics: Exploring Radical Edges of Feminist Theory, Communication, and Activism.* New Brunswick, NJ: Rutgers University Press.

Bolick, Kate. 2015. *Spinster: Making a Life of One's Own.* New York: Crown.

Bourlon, Maria T., Antoinette Anazodo, Teresa K. Woodruff, and Eva Segelov. 2020. "Oncofertility as a Universal Right and a Global Oncology Priority." *JCO Global Oncology* 6:314–316.

Bracewell-Milnes, Timothy, Srdjan Saso, Hossam Abdalla, and Meen-Yau Thum. 2018. "A Systematic Review Investigating Psychosocial Aspects of Egg Sharing in the United Kingdom and Their Potential Effects on Egg Donation Numbers." *Human Fertility* 21 (3): 163–173.

Brambillasca, Fausta, Maria Cristina Guglielmo, Giovanni Coticchio, Mario Mignini Renzini, Mariabeatrice Dal Canto, and Rubens Fadini. 2013. "The Current Challenges to Efficient Immature Oocyte Cryopreservation." *Journal of Assisted Reproduction and Genetics* 30:1531–1539.

Brown, Anna. 2020. "A Profile of Single Americans." Pew Research Center, August 20. www.pewresearch.org.

———. 2021. "Growing Share of Childless Adults in U.S. Don't Expect to Ever Have Children." Pew Research Center, November 19. www.pewresearch.org.

Brown, Eliza, and Mary Patrick. 2018. "Time, Anticipation, and the Life Course: Egg Freezing as Temporarily Disentangling Romance and Reproduction." *American Sociological Review* 83 (5): 959–982.

Brown, Louise. 2015. *Louise Brown: My Life as the World's First Test-Tube Baby.* Bristol, UK: Bristol Books.

Browne, Jude. 2018. "Technology, Fertility and Public Policy: A Structural Perspective on Human Egg Freezing and Gender Equality." *Social Politics* 25 (2): 149–168.

Buch, Elana D. 2018. *Inequalities of Aging: Paradoxes of Independence in American Home Care.* New York: New York University Press.

Campo-Engelstein, Lisa. 2020. "Reproductive Technologies Are Not the Cure for Social Problems." *Journal of Medical Ethics* 46 (2):85–86.

Carbone, June, and Naomi Cahn. 2014. *Marriage Markets: How Inequality Is Remaking the American Family.* Oxford: Oxford University Press.

Caron, Christina. 2019. "Wait, Is That Another Ad for Egg Freezing?" *New York Times*, April 27. www.nytimes.com.

Carroll, Katherine, and Charlotte Kroløkke. 2018. "Freezing for Love: Enacting 'Responsible' Reproductive Citizenship through Egg Freezing." *Culture, Health & Sexuality* 20 (9): 992–1005.

Cattapan, Alana, Kathleen Hammond, Jennie Haw, and Lesley A. Tarasoff. 2014. "Breaking the Ice: Young Feminist Scholars of Reproductive Politics Reflect on Egg Freezing." *IJFAB: International Journal of Feminist Approaches to Bioethics* 7 (2): 236–247.

Center for Human Reproduction. 2019. "Premature Ovarian Failure (POF)." December 3. www .centerforhumanreprod.com.

Centers for Disease Control. 2017. "Marriage-Divorce." www.cdc.gov.

Cha, Ariana Eunjung. 2018. "The Struggle to Conceive with Frozen Eggs." *Washington Post*, January 27. www.washingtonpost.com.

Chung, Karine, Jacques Donnez, Elizabeth Ginsburg, and Dror Meirow. 2013. "Emergency IVF versus Ovarian Tissue Cryopreservation: Decision Making in Fertility Preservation for Female Cancer Patients." *Fertility and Sterility* 99 (6): 1534–1542.

Cobo, Ana, and Juan Antonio García-Velasco. 2016. "Why All Women Should Freeze Their Eggs." *Clinical Obstetrics and Gynecology* 28 (3): 206–210.

Cobo Ana, Juan Antonio García-Velasco, Aila Coello, Javier Domingo, Antonio Pellicer, and José Remohí. 2016. "Oocyte Vitrification as an Efficient Option for Elective Fertility Preservation." *Fertility and Sterility* 105 (3): 755–764.

Cohen, Lawrence. 2007. "Operability, Bioavailability, and Exception." In *Global Assemblages: Technology, Politics, and Ethics as Anthropological Problems*, edited by Aihwa Ong and Stephen J. Collier, 79–90. New York: Wiley.

Cohen, Philip N. 2013. "Marriage Is Declining Globally: Can You Say That?" *Family Inequality* (blog), June 12. https://familyinequality.wordpress.com.

Colen, Shellee. 1995. "'Like a Mother to Them': Stratified Reproduction and West Indian Childcare Workers and Employers in New York." In *Conceiving the New World Order: The Global Politics of Reproduction*, edited by Faye E. Ginsburg and Rayna Rapp, 78–102. Berkeley: University of California Press.

College Factual. 2021. "Howard University." www.collegefactual.com.

Collins, Patricia Hill. 2008. *Black Feminist Thought: Knowledge, Consciousness, and the Politics of Empowerment*. New York: Routledge.

Cromer, Risa. 2018. "Saving Embryos in Stem Cell Science and Embryo Adoption." *New Genetics and Society* 37 (4): 362–386.

———. 2019. "Making the Ethnic Embryo: Enacting Race in US Embryo Adoption." *Medical Anthropology* 38 (7): 603–619.

Dancet, E. A. F., T. M. D'Hooghe, W. Sermeus, I. Van Empel, H. Strohmer, C. Wyns, D. Santa-Cruz, L. G. Nardo, D. Kovatchki, L. Vanlangenakker, J. Garcia-Velasco, B. Mulugeta, W. L. D. M. Nelen, and J. A. M. Kremer. 2012. "Patients from Across Europe Have Similar Views on Patient-Centered Care: An International Multilingual Qualitative Study in Infertility Care." *Human Reproduction* 27 (6): 1702–1711.

Dancet, E. A. F., I. W. H. Van Empel, P. Rober, W. L. D. M. Nelen, J. A. M. Kremer, and T. M. D'Hooghe. 2011. "Patient-Centered Infertility Care: A Qualitative Study to Listen to the Patient's Voice." *Human Reproduction* 26 (4): 827–833.

Davis, Dána-Ain. 2019. *Reproductive Injustice: Racism, Pregnancy, and Premature Birth*. New York: New York University Press.

Decker, Megan. 2019. "30 Celebrity Moms Who Had Kids after 40." *Harper's Bazaar*, March 18. www.harpersbazaar.com.

Deomampo, Daisy. 2019. "Racialized Commodities: Race and Value in Human Egg Donation." *Medical Anthropology* 38 (7): 620–633.

DePaulo, Bella. 2007. *Singled Out: How Singles Are Stereotyped, Stigmatized, and Ignored, and Still Live Happily Ever After*. New York: St. Martin's.

———. 2020. "Single at Heart: The World's Most Joyful and Unapologetic Single People." *Fourth Wave* (blog), December 17. https://medium.com.

De Proost, Michiel. 2021. "Integrating Intersectionality into Autonomy: Reflections on Feminist Bioethics and Egg Freezing." *DiGeSt: Journal of Diversity and Gender Studies* 7 (2): 21–33.

De Proost, Michiel, and Gily Coene. 2019. "Emancipation on Thin Ice: Women's Autonomy, Reproductive Justice, and Social Egg Freezing." *Tijdschrift voor Genderstudies* 22 (4): 357–371.

Djerassi, Carl. 2015. *In Retrospect: From the Pill to the Pen*. London: Imperial College Press.

Dockterman, Eliana. 2021. "Data Show More Women Are Freezing Their Eggs during the Pandemic, Defying Doctors' Expectations." *Time*, January 13. https://time.com.

Donnez, Jacques, and Marie-Madeleine Dolmans. 2017. "Fertility Preservation in Women." *New England Journal of Medicine* 377:1657–1665.

Dow, Katie, 2019. "Looking into the Test Tube: The Birth of IVF on British Television." *Medical History* 63:188–208.

Doyle, Joseph O., Kevin S. Richter, Joshua Lim, Robert J. Stillman, James R. Graham, and Michael J. Tucker. 2016. "Successful Elective and Medically Indicated Oocyte Vitrification and Warming for Autologous In Vitro Fertilization, with Predicted Birth Probabilities for Fertility Preservation According to Number of Cryopreserved Oocytes and Age at Retrieval." *Fertility and Sterility* 105 (2): 459–466.

Dudgeon, Matthew R., and Marcia C. Inhorn. 2004. "Men's Influences on Women's Reproductive Health: Medical Anthropological Perspectives." *Social Science & Medicine* 59 (7): 1379–1395.

Eckel, Sara. 2014. *It's Not You: 27 (Wrong) Reasons You're Single*. New York: Pedigree.

ESHRE. 2018. "More than 8 Million Babies Born from IVF since the World's First in 1978." www.eshre.eu.

ESHRE Task Force on Ethics and Law (W. Dondorp, G. de Wert, G. Pennings, F. Shenfield, P. Devroey, B. Tarlatzis, P. Barri, and K. Diedrich). 2012. "Oocyte Cryopreservation for Age-Related Fertility Loss." *Human Reproduction* 27 (5): 1231–1237.

Ethics Committee of ASRM. 2005. "Fertility Preservation and Reproduction in Cancer Patients." *Fertility and Sterility* 83 (6): 1622–1628.

———. 2013a. "Fertility Preservation and Reproduction in Patients Facing Gonadotoxic Therapies: A Committee Opinion." *Fertility and Sterility* 100 (5): 1224–1231.

———. 2013b. "Oocyte or Embryo Donation to Women of Advanced Age: A Committee Opinion." *Fertility and Sterility* 100 (2): 337–340.

———. 2018. "Planned Oocyte Cryopreservation for Women Seeking to Preserve Future Reproductive Potential: An Ethics Committee Opinion." *Fertility and Sterility* 110 (6): 1022–1028.

Fishman, Sylvia Barack 2015. "Gender in American Jewish Life." In *American Jewish Year Book 2014: The Annual Record of the North American Jewish Communities*, edited by Arnold Dashefsky and Ira Sheskin, 91–131. American Jewish Year Book. Cham, Switzerland: Springer.

Franklin, Sarah. 1997. *Embodied Progress: A Cultural Account of Assisted Conception*. London: Routledge.

———. 2013. *Biological Relatives: IVF, Stem Cells, and the Future of Kinship*. Durham, NC: Duke University Press.

Fry, Richard. 2017. "The Share of Americans Living without a Partner Has Increased, Especially among Young Adults." Pew Research Center, October 11. www.pewresearch.org.

Gibbs, Nancy. 2010. "The Pill: So Small. So Powerful. And So Misunderstood." *Time*, May 3. http://content.time.com.

Ginsburg, Faye, and Rayna Rapp, eds. 1995. *Conceiving the New World Order: The Global Politics of Reproduction*. Berkeley: University of California Press.

Gleicher, Norbert, Vitaly A. Kushnir, and David H. Barad. 2015. "Prospectively Assessing Risk for Premature Ovarian Senescence in Young Females: A New Paradigm." *Reproductive Biology and Endocrinology* 13 (34). https://doi.org/10.1186/s12958-015-0026-z.

Göçmen, İpek, and Azer Kılıç. 2018. "Egg Freezing Experiences of Women in Turkey: From the Social Context to the Narratives of Reproductive Ageing and Empowerment." *European Journal of Women's Studies* 25 (2): 168–182.

Goldman, Kara N., and Jamie A. Grifo. 2016. "Elective Oocyte Cryopreservation for Deferred Childbearing." *Clinical Obstetrics and Gynecology* 23 (6): 458–464.

Goldman, R. H., C. Racowsky, L. V. Farland, S. Munné, L. Ribustello, and J. H. Fox. 2017. "Predicting the Likelihood of Live Birth for Elective Oocyte Cyropreservation: A Counseling Tool for Physicians and Patients." *Human Reproduction* 32 (4): 853–859.

Goold, Imogen, and Julian Savulescu. 2009. "In Favour of Freezing Eggs for Non-medical Reasons." *Bioethics* 23 (1): 47–58.

Gootman, Elissa. 2012. "So Eager for Grandchildren, They're Paying the Egg-Freezing Clinic." *New York Times*, May 14. www.nytimes.com.

Greenwood, Eleni A., Lauri A. Pasch, Jordan Hastie, Marcelle I. Cedars, and Heather G. Huddleston. 2018. "To Freeze or Not to Freeze: Decision Regret and Satisfaction Following Elective Oocyte Cryopreservation." *Fertility and Sterility* 109 (6): 1097–1104.

Grose, Jessica. 2021. "When It Comes to Fertility, Access Is Everything." *New York Times*, April 17. www.nytimes.com.

Gunnala, Vinay, and Glenn Schattman. 2017. "Oocyte Vitrification for Elective Fertility Preservation: The Past, Present, and Future." *Clinical Obstetrics and Gynecology* 29 (1): 59–63.

Gurr, Barbara. 2015. *Reproductive Justice: The Politics of Health Care for Native American Women.* New. Brunswick, NJ: Rutgers University Press.

Gürtin, Zeynep B. 2021. "Naomi Campbell's Motherhood Is Good News, but Most Women Don't Have Her Reproductive Choices." *Guardian*, May 22. www.theguardian.com.

Gürtin, Zeynep B., Trina Shah, Jinjun Wang, and Kamal Ahuja. 2019. "Reconceiving Egg Freezing: Insights from an Analysis of 5 Years of Data from a UK Clinic." *Reproductive BioMedicine Online* 38 (2): 272–282.

Gürtin, Zeynep B., and Emily Tiemann. 2021. "The Marketing of Elective Egg Freezing: A Content, Cost and Quality Analysis of UK Fertility Clinic Websites." *Reproductive BioMedicine & Society Online* 12:56–68.

Gutmann, Matthew. 2019. *Are Men Animals? How Modern Masculinity Sells Men Short.* New York: Basic Books.

Guzman, Zack. 2020. "Egg Freezing Up 41% in June–Sept 2020 versus Last Year: NYU Langone." *Yahoo!Finance*, October 27. https://finance.yahoo.com.

Haimes, Erica, Ken Taylor, and Ilke Turkmendag. 2012. "Eggs, Ethics and Exploitation: Investigating Women's Experiences of an Egg Sharing Scheme." *Sociology of Health and Illness* 34 (8): 1199–1214.

Hammarberg, Karin, Veronica Collins, Carol Holden, Kate Young, and Robert McLachlan. 2017. "Men's Knowledge, Attitudes and Behaviours Relating to Fertility." *Human Reproduction Update* 23 (4): 458–480.

Hammarberg, Karin, Maggie Kirkman, Natasha Pritchard, Martha Hickey, Michelle Peate, John C. McBain, Franca Agresta, Chris Bayly, and Jane Fisher. 2017. "Reproductive Experiences of Women Who Cryopreserved Oocytes for Non-medical Reasons." *Human Reproduction* 32 (3): 575–581.

Hartman, Harriet, and Moshe Hartman. 2009. *Gender and American Jews: Patterns in Work, Education, and Family in Contemporary Life.* Waltham, MA: Brandeis University Press.

Harwood, Karey A. 2018. "Decentering Whiteness in Feminist Bioethics: Assisted Reproductive Technologies as an Illustrative Case." In *Reproductive Ethics II*, edited by Lisa Campo-Engelstein and Paul Burcher, 99–112. New York: Springer.

Heilman, Uriel. 2013. "Pew Survey of U.S. Jews: Soaring Intermarriage, Assimilation Rates." Jewish Telegraphic Agency, October 1. www.jta.org.

Heinemann, Laura. 2016. *Transplanting Care: Shifting Commitments in Health and Care in the United States.* New Brunswick, NJ: Rutgers University Press.

Hertz, Rosanna. 2008. *Single by Chance, Mothers by Choice: How Women Are Choosing Parenthood without Marriage and Creating the New American Family.* Oxford: Oxford University Press.

Hewlett, Sylvia Ann. 2002. *Creating a Life: Professional Women and the Quest for Children.* New York: Miramax.

Hodes-Wertz, Brooke, Sara Druckenmiller, Meghan Smith, and Nicole Noyes. 2013. "What Do Reproductive-Age Women Who Undergo Oocyte Cryopreservation Think about the Process as a Means to Preserve Fertility?" *Fertility and Sterility* 100 (5): 1343–1349.

Honey, Minda. 2022. "Single Black Women and the Lies about Our Love Lives." *Andscape*, February 14. https://andscape.com.

Hughes, Virginia. 2012. "Freezing the Fertility Clock." *New Scientist* 214 (2860): 40–43.

IFFS. 2019. "International Federation of Fertility Societies' Surveillance (IFFS) 2019: Global Trends in Reproductive Policy and Practice, 8th Edition." *Global Reproductive Health* 4 (1): e29. https://journals.lww.com.

Ikemoto, Lisa. 2015. "Egg Freezing, Stratified Reproduction, and the Logic of Not." *Journal of Law and the Biosciences* 2 (1): 112–117.

Inhorn, Marcia C. 1994. *Quest for Conception: Gender, Infertility, and Egyptian Medical Traditions.* Philadelphia: University of Pennsylvania Press.

———. 1996. *Infertility and Patriarchy: The Cultural Politics of Gender and Family Life in Egypt.* Philadelphia: University of Pennsylvania Press.

———. 2003. *Local Babies, Global Science: Gender, Religion, and In Vitro Fertilization in Egypt.* New York: Routledge.

———. 2012. *The New Arab Man: Emergent Masculinities, Technologies, and Islam in the Middle East.* Princeton, NJ: Princeton University Press.

———. 2013. "Opinion: Women, Consider Freezing Your Eggs." *CNN Online*, April 9. www.cnn .com.

———. 2015. *Cosmopolitan Conceptions: IVF Sojourns in Global Dubai.* Durham, NC: Duke University Press.

———. 2017. "The Egg Freezing Revolution? Gender, Technology and Fertility Preservation in the 21st Century." In *Emerging Trends in the Behavioral and Social Sciences*, edited by Robert A. Scott and Marlis Buchmann, 1–14. New York: Wiley.

———. 2018. *America's Arab Refugees: Vulnerability and Health on the Margins.* Stanford, CA: Stanford University Press.

———. 2020. "The Egg Freezing Revolution? Gender, Education, and Reproductive Waithood in the United States." In *Waithood: Gender, Education, and Global Delays in Marriage and Childbearing*, edited by Marcia C. Inhorn and Nancy J. Smith-Hefner, 362–390. New York: Berghahn.

———. 2021. "Egg Freezing Activists: Extending Reproductive Futures to Cancer Patients, Single and Minority Women, and Transgender Men in America." In *Birthing Techno-Sapiens: Human-Technology Co-Evolution and the Future of Reproduction*, edited by Robbie Davis-Floyd, 47–59. New York: Routledge.

Inhorn, Marcia C., Daphna Birenbaum-Carmeli, and Pasquale Patrizio. 2017. "Medical Egg Freezing and Cancer Patients' Hopes: Fertility Preservation at the Intersection of Life and Death." *Social Science & Medicine* 195:25–33.

———. 2020. "Elective Egg Freezing and Male Support: A Qualitative Study of Men's Hidden Roles in Women's Fertility Preservation." *Human Fertility*, January 10. https://doi.org/10.1080 /14647273.2019.1702222.

Inhorn, Marcia C., Daphna Birenbaum-Carmeli, Mira Vale, and Pasquale Patrizio. 2020. "Abrahamic Traditions and Egg Freezing: Religious Women's Experiences in Local Moral Worlds." *Social Science & Medicine* 253. https://doi.org/10.1016/j.socscimed.2020.112976.

Inhorn, Marcia C., Daphna Birenbaum-Carmeli, Lynn M. Westphal, Joseph Doyle, Norbert Gleicher, Dror Meirow, Martha Dirnfeld, Daniel Seidman, Arik Kahane, and Pasquale Patrizio. 2018a. "Elective Egg Freezing and its Underlying Socio-demography: A Binational Analysis with Global Implications." *Reproductive Biology and Endocrinology* 16 (70).

Inhorn, Marcia C., Daphna Birenbaum-Carmeli, Lynn M. Westphal, Joseph Doyle, Norbert Gleicher, Dror Meirow, Hila Raanani, Martha Dirnfeld, and Pasquale Patrizio. 2018b. "Medical Egg Freezing: How Cost and Insurance Coverage Impact Women and Their Families." *Reproductive BioMedicine & Society Online* 5:82–92.

Inhorn, Marcia C., Daphna Birenbaum-Carmeli, Lynn M. Westphal, Joseph Doyle, Norbert Gleicher, Dror Meirow, Martha Dirnfeld, Daniel Seidman, Arik Kahane, and Pasquale

Patrizio. 2019. "Patient-Centered Elective Egg Freezing: A Binational Qualitative Study of Best Practices for Women's Quality of Care." *Journal of Assisted Reproduction and Genetics* 36:1081–1090.

Inhorn, Marcia C., Daphna Birenbaum-Carmeli, Ruoxi Yu, and Pasquale Patrizio. 2022. "Egg Freezing at the End of Romance: A Technology of Hope, Despair, and Repair." *Science, Technology & Human Values* 47 (1): 53–84.

Inhorn, Marcia C., and Pasquale Patrizio. 2015. "Infertility around the Globe: New Thinking on Gender, Reproductive Technologies, and Global Movements in the 21st Century." *Human Reproduction Update* 21 (4): 411–426.

Inhorn, Marcia C., Pasquale Patrizio, and Gamal I. Serour. 2010. "Third-Party Reproductive Assistance around the Mediterranean: Comparing Sunni Egypt, Catholic Italy, and Multisectarian Lebanon." *Reproductive BioMedicine Online* 21 (7): 848–853.

Inhorn, Marcia C., and Nancy Smith-Hefner, eds. 2020. *Waithood: Gender, Education, and Global Delays in Marriage and Childbearing.* New York: Berghahn.

Inhorn, Marcia C., and Soraya Tremayne, eds. 2012. *Islam and Assisted Reproductive Technologies: Sunni and Shia Perspectives.* New York: Berghahn.

Inhorn, Marcia C., Ruoxi Yu, and Pasquale Patrizio. 2020. "Upholding Success: Asian Americans, Egg Freezing, and the Fertility Paradox." *Medical Anthropology* 40 (1): 3–19.

Institute of Medicine. 2001. *Crossing the Quality Chasm: A New Health System for the 21st Century.* Washington, DC: Institute of Medicine.

Kagan, Julia. 2021. "How Much Income Puts You in the Top 1%, 5%, 10%?" *Investopedia*, June 10. www.investopedia.com.

Kahn, Susan Martha. 2000. *Reproducing Jews: A Cultural Account of Assisted Conception in Israel.* Durham, NC: Duke University Press.

Kaplan, Amit, Yael Hashiloni-Dolev, and Charlotte Kroløkke. 2021. "'My Choice, My Responsibility': Views of Danish and Israeli Female Students on Financing Egg-freezing." *Culture, Health & Sexuality*, November 2. https://doi.org/10.1080/13691058.2021.1981454.

Kılıç, Azer, and İpek Göçmen. 2018. "Fate, Morals and Rational Calculations: Freezing Eggs for Non-Medical Reasons in Turkey." *Social Science & Medicine* 203:19–27.

Kim, Ran, Tae Ki Yoon, Inn Soo Kang, Mi Kyoung Koong, Yoo Shin Kim, Myung Joo Kim, Yubin Lee, and Jayeon Kim. 2018. "Decision Making Processes of Women Who Seek Elective Oocyte Cryopreservation." *Journal of Assisted Reproduction and Genetics* 35 (9): 1623–1630.

Kime, Patricia. 2019. "Bill Would Require DoD to Pay for Combat Troops to Freeze Sperm, Eggs." *Military.com*, March 19. www.military.com.

Kuwayama, Masashige, Gábor Vajta, Osamu Kato, Stanley P. Leibo. 2005. "Highly Efficient Vitrification Method for Cryopreservation of Human Oocytes." *Reproductive BioMedicine Online* 11 (3): 300–308.

La Ferla, Ruth. 2018. "These Companies Really, Really, Really Want to Freeze Your Eggs." *New York Times*, August 29. www.nytimes.com.

Lake, Roseann. 2018. *Leftover in China: The Women Shaping the World's Next Superpower.* New York: Norton.

Lampert, Natalie. 2019. "The Unexpected Freedom That Comes with Freezing Your Eggs." *New York Times*, December 11. www.nytimes.com.

Lee, Jennifer, and Min Zhou. 2015. *The Asian American Achievement Paradox.* New York: Russell Sage Foundation.

Lehrer, Evelyn, and Yeon Jeong Son. 2018. "Marital Instability in the United States: Trends, Driving Forces, and Implications for Children." In *The Oxford Handbook of Women and the Economy*, edited by Susan L. Averett, Laura M. Argys, and Saul D. Hoffman, 74–96. Oxford: Oxford University Press.

Levy, Robert I., and Douglas W. Hollan. 2015. "Person-Centered Interviewing and Observation." In *Handbook of Methods in Cultural Anthropology*, edited by H. Russell Bernard and Clarence C. Gravlee, 313–342. Lanham, MD: Rowman and Littlefield.

Lockwood, Gillian M. 2011. "Social Egg Freezing: The Prospect of Reproductive 'Immortality' or a Dangerous Delusion?" *Reproductive BioMedicine Online* 23 (3): 334–340.

London Egg Bank. n.d. "Freeze and Share." Accessed June 6, 2022. https://londoneggbank.com.

Lugo, Luis, Alan Cooperman, Gregory A. Smith, Erin O'Connell, and Sandra Stencel. 2013. *Findings from a Pew Research Center Survey of U.S. Jews.* Washington, DC: Pew Research Center.

Lundberg, Lisbet S., Lubna Pal, Aileen M. Gariepy, Micheline C. Chu, and Jessica L. Illuzzi. 2014. "Knowledge, Attitudes, and Practices Regarding Conception and Fertility: A Population-Based Survey among Reproductive-Age United States Women." *Fertility and Sterility* 101 (3): 767–774.

Luscombe, Belinda. 2021. "Men Are More Likely to Be Single than Women. It's Not a Good Sign." *Time*, October 5. https://time.com.

Martin, Lauren Jade. 2010. "Anticipating Infertility: Egg Freezing, Genetic Preservation, and Risk." *Gender & Society* 24 (4): 526–545.

McDonald, Casey A., Lora Valluzo, Lesley Chuang, Flora Poleschchuk, Alan B. Copperman, and Jason Barritt. 2011. "Nitrogen Vapor Shipment of Vitrified Oocytes: Time for Caution." *Fertility and Sterility* 95 (8): 2628–2630.

McLenon, Jennifer, and Mary A. M. Rogers. 2019. "The Fear of Needles: A Systematic Review and Meta-analysis." *Journal of Advanced Nursing* 75 (1): 30–42.

McMahon, Helena. 2018. "Welcome to the New Spa: Juice Bar and Egg Freezing." *Times* (London), December 12. www.thetimes.co.uk.

Mertes, Heidi. 2013. "The Portrayal of Healthy Women Requesting Oocyte Cryopreservation." *Facts Views & Vision in ObGyn* 5 (2): 141–146.

Mertes, Heidi, and Guido Pennings. 2011. "Social Egg Freezing: For Better, Not for Worse." *Reproductive BioMedicine Online* 23 (7): 824–829.

———. 2012. "Elective Oocyte Cryopreservation: Who Should Pay?" *Human Reproduction* 27 (1): 9–13.

Mertes, Heidi, Guido Pennings, Wybo Dondorp, and Guido de Wert. 2012. "Implications of Oocyte Cryostorage for the Practice of Oocyte Donation." *Human Reproduction* 27 (10): 2886–2893.

Miller, Claire Cain. 2014. "Egg Freezing as Part of Employee Benefits: Some Women See Darker Message." *New York Times*, October 14. www.nytimes.com.

Morgan, Lynn M., and Janelle S. Taylor. 2013. "Op-Ed: Egg Freezing: WTF?" *Feminist Wire*, April 14. https://thefeministwire.com.

Murphy, Caryle. 2016. "The Most and Least Educated US Religious Groups." Pew Research Center, November 3. www.pewresearch.org.

Murphy, Heather. 2018. "Lots of Successful Women Are Freezing Their Eggs. But It May Not Be about Their Careers." *New York Times*, July 3. www.nytimes.com.

Myers, Kit C., and Lauren Jade Martin. 2021. "Freezing Time? The Sociology of Egg Freezing." *Sociology Compass* 15 (4). https://doi.org/10.1111/soc4.12850.

National Center for Education Statistics. 2021. "Degrees Conferred by Race and Sex." https://nces.ed.gov.

National Healthy Marriage Resource Center. 2017. "Frequently Asked Questions About Asian Americans and Marriage." December. www.healthymarriageinfo.org.

North, Anna. 2015. "The Problem with Egg Freezing." *Taking Note* (blog), *New York Times*, April 15. https://takingnote.blogs.nytimes.com.

Notkin, Melanie. 2014. *Otherhood: Modern Women Finding a New Kind of Happiness.* Berkeley, CA: Seal.

O'Brien, Sara Ashley. 2018. "'Fertility Van' Hits Streets of New York City." *CNN Business*, August 3. https://money.cnn.com.

Office of Technology Assessment. 1988. "Appendix F. Religious Perspectives." In *Infertility: Medical and Social Choices*, 364–368. Washington, DC: Office of Technology Assessment.

Oktay, Kutluk, Brittany E. Harvey, and Alison W. Loren. 2018. "Fertility Preservation in Patients with Cancer: ASCO Clinical Practice Guideline Update Summary." *Journal of Oncology Practice* 14 (6): 381–386.

Patrizio, Pasquale, Emanuela Molinari, and Arthur L. Caplan. 2016. "Ethics of Medical and Non-medical Oocyte Cryopreservation." *Current Opinion in Endocrinology, Diabetes and Obesity* 23 (6): 470–475.

Pessin, Léa. 2018. "Changing Gender Norms and Marriage Dynamics in the United States: Gender Norms and Marriage Dynamics in the U.S." *Journal of Marriage and Family* 80 (1): 25–41.

Peterson, Brennan, Catherine Gordon, Julia K. Boehm, Marcia C. Inhorn, and Pasquale Patrizio. 2018. "Initiating Patient Discussions about Oocyte Cryopreservation: Attitudes of Obstetrics and Gynecology Resident Physicians." *Reproductive BioMedicine & Society Online* 6:72–79.

Petropanagos, Angel. 2010. "Reproductive 'Choice' and Egg Freezing." In *Oncofertility: Cancer Treatment and Research*, edited by Theresa Woodruff, Laurie Zoloth, Lisa Campo-Engelstein, and Sarah Rodriguez, 223–235. Boston: Springer.

Pew Research Center. 2014a. "College Graduates Who Are Jewish." Religious Landscape Study. www.pewforum.org.

———. 2014b. "The Religious Landscape Study." www.pewforum.org.

———. 2014c. "The Spiritual but Not Religious." Religious Landscape Study. www.pewforum.org.

Practice Committees of the ASRM and the SART. 2013. "Mature Oocyte Cryopreservation: A Guideline." *Fertility and Sterility* 99 (1): 37–43.

Pritchard, Natasha, Maggie Kirkman, Karin Hammarberg, John C. McBain, Franca Agresta, Christine Bayly, Martha Hickey, Michelle Peate, and Jane Fisher. 2017. "Characteristics and Circumstances of Women in Australia Who Cryopreserved Their Oocytes for Non-medical Indications." *Journal of Reproductive and Infant Psychology* 35 (2): 108–118.

Reeves, Richard V., and Katherine Guyot. 2017. "Black Women Are Earning More College Degrees, but That Alone Won't Close Race Gaps." *Social Mobility Memos* (blog), Brookings, December 4. www.brookings.edu.

Remennick, Larissa. 2000. "Childless in the Land of Imperative Motherhood: Stigma and Coping among Infertile Israeli Women." *Sex Roles* 43:821–841.

Renvoizé, Jean. 1985. *Going Solo: Single Mothers by Choice*. London: Routledge and Kegan Paul.

Richards, Sarah Elizabeth. 2012. "We Need to Talk about Our Eggs." *New York Times*, October 22. www.nytimes.com.

———. 2013. *Motherhood, Rescheduled: The New Frontier of Egg Freezing and the Women Who Tried It*. New York: Simon and Schuster.

Roberts, Dorothy. 2014. *Killing the Black Body: Race, Reproduction, and the Meaning of Liberty*. 20th anniversary ed. New York: Vintage.

Rosemberg, Jasmin. 2019. "Great Eggspectations." *New York Times*, April 5. www.nytimes.com.

Roser, Max. 2016. "Global Population Falling as Human Fertility Rates Decline." Principa Scientific International, July 11. https://principia-scientific.org.

Rosin, Hanna. 2012. *The End of Men and the Rise of Women*. New York: Riverhead Books.

Rottenberg, Catherine. 2017. "Neoliberal Feminism and the Future of Human Capital." *Signs* 42 (2): 329–348.

Sandberg, Sheryl. 2013. *Lean In: Women, Work, and the Will to Lead*. New York: Knopf.

Savulescu, Julian, and Imogen Goold. 2008. "Freezing Eggs for Lifestyle Reasons." *American Journal of Bioethics* 8 (6): 32–35.

Scharff, Christina. 2016. *Repudiating Feminism: Young Women in a Neoliberal World*. London: Routledge.

Setti, Paulo Emanuele Levi, Eleonor Porcu, Pasquale Patrizio, Vincenzo Vigiliano, Roberto De Luca, Paola D'Aloja, Roberto Spoletini, and Giulia Scaravelli. 2014. "Human Oocyte Cryopreservation with Slow Freezing vs. Vitrification: The National Italian Registry Data 2007–2011." *Fertility and Sterility* 102 (1): 90–95.

Shenfield, F., J. de Mouzon, G. Scaravelli, M. Kupka, A. P. Ferraretti, F. J. Prados, and V. Goossens. 2017. "Oocyte and Ovarian Tissue Cryopreservation in European Countries: Statutory Background, Practice, Storage and Use." *Human Reproduction Open* 2017 (1): 1–9. https://doi .org/10.1093/hropen/hox003.

Shiels, Meredith, Anika T. Haque, Emily A. Haozous, Paul S. Albert, Jonas S. Almeida, Montserrat Garcia-Closas, Anna M. Nápoles, Eliseo J. Pérez-Stable, Neal D. Freedman, and Amy Berrington de González. 2021. "Racial and Ethnic Disparities in Excess Deaths during the COVID-19 Pandemic, March to December 2020." *Annals of Internal Medicine*, December. https://doi.org/10.7326/M21-2134.

Shkedi-Rafid, Shiri, and Yael Hashiloni-Dolev. 2011. "Egg Freezing for Age-Related Fertility Decline: Preventive Medicine or a Further Medicalization of Reproduction? Analyzing the New Israeli Policy." *Fertility and Sterility* 96 (2): 291–294.

———. 2012. "Egg Freezing for Non-medical Uses: The Lack of a Relational Approach to Autonomy in the New Israeli Policy and in Academic Discussion." *Journal of Medical Ethics* 38 (3): 154–157.

Shlam, Shosh, and Hilla Medalia. 2020. "Leftover Women." *Independent Lens*, PBS. www.pbs.org.

Singerman, Diane. 2007. "The Economic Imperatives of Marriage: Emerging Practices and Identities among Youth in the Middle East." Working Paper 6, Middle East Youth Initiative, Brookings Institution, Wolfensohn Center for Development, Washington, DC, September.

Slaughter, Anne-Marie. 2012. "Why Women Still Can't Have It All." *Atlantic*, July–August. www .theatlantic.com.

———. 2016. *Unfinished Business: Women Men Work Family*. New York: Random House.

Stinson, Danu Anthony, Jessica J. Cameron, and Lisa B. Hoplock. 2021. "The Friends-to-Lovers Pathway to Romance: Prevalent, Preferred, and Overlooked by Science." *Social Psychological and Personality Science*, July 12. https://doi.org/10.1177%2F19485506211026992.

Stoop, D., E. Maes, N. Polyzos, G. Verheyen, H. Tournaye, and J. Nekkebroeck. 2015. "Does Oocyte Banking for Anticipated Gamete Exhaustion Influence Future Relational and Reproductive Choices? A Follow-Up of Bankers and Non-bankers." *Human Reproduction* 30 (2): 338–344.

Tan, Yvette. 2022. "What Singapore's Move to Legalise Egg Freezing Says about Its Society." *BBC News*, April 27. www.bbc.com.

Theobald, Brianna. 2019. *Reproduction on the Reservation: Pregnancy, Childbirth, and Colonialism in the Long Twentieth Century*. Chapel Hill: University of North Carolina Press.

Thompson, Charis, 2002. "Fertile Ground: Feminists Theorize Infertility." In *Infertility around the Globe: New Thinking on Childlessness, Gender, and Reproductive Technologies*, edited by Marcia C. Inhorn and Frank Van Balen, 52–78. Berkeley: University of California Press.

Tober, Diane. 2018. *Romancing the Sperm: Shifting Biopolitics and the Making of Modern Families*. New Brunswick, NJ: Rutgers University Press.

Traina, Cristina, Eugenia Georges, Marcia C. Inhorn, Susan Kahn, and Maura A. Ryan. 2008. "Compatible Contradictions: Religion and the Naturalization of Assisted Reproduction." In *Altering Nature*, vol. 2, *Religion, Biotechnology, and Public Policy*, edited by B. Andrew Lustig, Baruch A. Brody, and Gerald P. McKenny, 15–85. New York: Ford Foundation.

Traister, Rebecca. 2016. *All the Single Ladies: Unmarried Women and the Rise of an Independent Nation*. New York: Simon and Schuster.

Tsafrir, A., H. Holzer, T. Miron-Shatz, T. Eldar-Geva, M. Gal, I. Ben-ami, N. Dekel, A. Weintraub, D. Goldberg, O. Schonberger, N. Srebnik, and J. Hyman. 2021. "'Why Have Women Not Returned to Use Their Frozen Oocytes?': A 5-Year Follow-Up of Women after Planned Oocyte Cryopreservation. *Reproductive BioMedicine Online* 43 (6): 1137–1145.

Twenge, Jean M. 2013. "How Long Can You Wait to Have a Baby?" *Atlantic*, July–August. www .theatlantic.com.

US Census Bureau. 2020. "US Census Bureau Releases New Educational Attainment Data." Press release. www.census.gov.

Valdez, Natali, and Daisy Deomampo, eds. 2019. "Centering Race and Racism in Reproduction." Special issue. *Medical Anthropology* 38 (7).

Van de Wiel, Lucy. 2020a. *Freezing Fertility: Oocyte Cryopreservation and the Gender Politics of Aging.* New York: New York University Press.

———. 2020b. "The Speculative Turn in IVF: Egg Freezing and the Financialization of Fertility." *New Genetics and Society* 39 (3): 306–326.

Van Empel, Inge W. H., Eline A. F. Dancet, Xander H. E. Koolman, Willianne L. D. M. Nelen, Elly A. Stolk, Walter Sermeus, Thomas M. D'Hooghe, and Jan A. M. Kremer. 2011. "Physicians Underestimate the Importance of Patient-Centeredness to Patients: A Discrete Choice Experiment in Fertility Care." *Human Reproduction* 26 (3): 584–593.

Varlas, Valentin Nicolae, Roxana Georgiana Bors, Dragos Albu, Ovidiu Nicolae Penes, Bogdana Adriana Nasui, Claudia Mehedintu, and Anca Lucia Pop. 2021. "Social Freezing: Pressing Pause on Fertility." *International Journal of Environmental Research and Public Health* 18 (15): 8088.

Waldby, Catherine. 2015. "'Banking Time': Egg Freezing and the Negotiation of Future Fertility." *Culture, Health & Sexuality* 17 (4): 470–482.

———. 2019. *The Oocyte Economy: The Changing Meaning of Human Eggs.* Durham, NC: Duke University Press.

Ward, Jane. 2020. *The Tragedy of Heterosexuality.* New York: New York University Press.

Wee, Sui-Lee, and Elsie Chen. 2019. "China Blocked Her from Freezing Her Eggs. So She Sued." *New York Times,* December 23. www.nytimes.com.

Wentzell, Emily A., and Marcia C. Inhorn. 2014. "Reconceiving Masculinity and 'Men as Partners' for ICPD Beyond 2014: Insights from a Mexican HPV Study." *Global Public Health* 9 (6): 651–675.

Woodruff, Teresa K. 2010. "The Oncofertility Consortium—Addressing Fertility in Young People with Cancer." *Nature Reviews Clinical Oncology* 7:466–475.

World Bank. 2021. "School Enrollment, Tertiary (Gross), Gender Parity Index (GPI)." https://data.worldbank.org.

Wu, Ellen D. 2015. *The Color of Success: Asian Americans and the Origins of the Model Minority.* Princeton, NJ: Princeton University Press.

Wyndham, Nichole, Paula Gabriela Marin Figueira, and Pasquale Patrizio. 2012. "A Persistent Misperception: Assisted Reproductive Technology Can Reverse the 'Aged Biological Clock.'" *Fertility and Sterility* 97 (5): 1044–1047.

Yu, Lissa, Brennan Peterson, Marcia C. Inhorn, Julie K. Boehm, and Pasquale Patrizio. 2016. "Knowledge, Attitudes, and Intentions toward Fertility Awareness and Oocyte Cryopreservation among Obstetricians and Gynecology Resident Physicians." *Human Reproduction* 31 (2): 403–411.

INDEX

ABOUT THE AUTHOR

MARCIA C. INHORN is the William K. Lanman, Jr. Professor of Anthropology and International Affairs at Yale University, where she directs the Council on Middle East Studies. A medical anthropologist focusing on gender and reproductive health, Inhorn has written seven award-winning books on men's and women's fertility issues and the use of assisted reproductive technologies around the globe.